NORTHEASTERN
INDIAN LIVES

- MAINE
- VERMONT
- Rawandagon
- Molly Ockett
- NEW YORK
  - Molly Brant
  - Theyanoguin
- NEW HAMPSHIRE
- MASSACHUSETTS
  - Thomas Waban
- CONNECTICUT
  - Robin Cassacinamon
  - Uncas
- Awashunkes
- Daniel Spotso
- RHODE ISLAND
  - Miantonomi
  - Wyandanch
- OHIO
  - Pisquetomen
  - Tamaqua
- PENNSYLVANIA
  - Shickellamy
- Moses Tunda Tatamy
- Suscaneman
- NEW JERSEY
- MARYLAND
- WEST VIRGINIA
- DELAWARE

NORTHEASTERN INDIAN LIVES, 1632–1816

EDITED BY

Robert S. Grumet

FOREWORD BY

Anthony F. C. Wallace

Native Americans of the Northeast:
Culture, History, and the Contemporary
Colin G. Calloway and Barry O'Connell
Series Editors

UNIVERSITY OF MASSACHUSETTS PRESS
Amherst

55.00

A VOLUME IN THE SERIES:

Native Americans of the Northeast:
Culture, History, and the Contemporary

EDITED BY Colin G. Calloway
and Barry O'Connell

Copyright © 1996 by
The University of Massachusetts Press
All rights reserved
Printed in the United States of America

LC 95–33144

ISBN 1-55849-000-0 (cloth); 001-9 (pbk.)
Designed by David C. denBoer
Set in 10/14 Linotype Walbaum
Printed and bound by Thomson-Shore, Inc.

Library of Congress Cataloging-in-Publication Data
Northeastern Indian lives, 1632–1816 / edited by Robert S. Grumet ;
foreword by Anthony F. C. Wallace.
p.   cm. — (Native Americans of the Northeast)
Includes bibliographical references (p.   ) and index.
ISBN 1–55849–000–0 (cloth : alk. paper).
—ISBN 1–55849–001–9 (paper : alk. paper)
1. Indians of North America—Northeastern States—Biography.
I. Grumet, Robert Steven.   II. Series.
E78.E2N67   1996
974'.00497'00922—dc20   95–33144
                                                        CIP

British Library Cataloguing in Publication data are available.

CONTENTS

FOREWORD

INDIAN BIOGRAPHY, as Robert Grumet points out in his introduction, was a popular genre in nineteenth-century American literature. Much of it was inspired, however, by a hagiographical urge to "praise famous men"— from the Northeast, men like Pontiac, Logan the Great Mingo, Joseph Brant, and Tecumseh. Lesser figures were not totally ignored; witness Samuel Draper's compilation of biographical sketches of Indians active during and after the Revolution, including the autobiography of Governor Blacksnake (now happily edited and published by Thomas Abler). But most of Draper's biographical materials were left in manuscript. The first *Handbook of the American Indian* (the old "Bulletin 30") contains short notices on half a dozen of the persons memorialized in this volume. By and large, however, attention was directed to the allegedly most "important" Indians, those who qualified for the historians' honor roll because of their military exploits.

Anthropologists' attention to individuals began, of course, with an interest in informants, those native persons (like Morgan's Ely S. Parker) willing and able to provide the fieldworker with information, translations, introductions, and physical access. In the 1930s and 1940s, however, the life history became a concern of those cultural anthropologists who studied acculturation and the relations between culture and personality. These life histories, represented by such well-known works as *Sun Chief* (Hopi), *Smoke from Their Fires* (Kwakiutl), and *Crashing Thunder* (Winnebago), were usually autobiographical accounts by contemporaries who were guided by their anthropological amanuenses to reveal information about intimate aspects of their cultures. Several social types involved in processes of culture change were identified, such as the "marginal man," caught between two worlds; the "culture broker," mediating between those worlds as a conduit of culture content; the "prophet," leader of a revitalization movement in an effort to resolve the contradictions of culture contact; and

ix

the members of "progressive" and "conservative" factions, embracing or resisting culture change. My own biographical studies of Teedyuscung and Handsome Lake were prompted by such analytical interests, although the data had to be documentary because, as Margaret Mead once wrote (disparaging historical sources), "Handsome Lake is dead."

Ethnohistory, however, is not about dead people; it is about life. And there are real advantages to working with historical documents in doing biography. Written sources can reveal facts, actions, and opinions, particularly on political issues sensitive at the time that probably would have been kept secret from a fieldworker. It is possible to assemble and compare the accounts and actions (and writing letters and keeping ledgers are actions) of different participants in the same event. One has access to a longer time period in which to observe processes of social change than is possible for a single fieldworker who has to complete his or her dissertation in a timely fashion.

The papers in this volume represent a flowering of a dynamic approach to historiography that sees in the careers of less famous leaders—but leaders well known in their time and place—the opportunity to explore in detail the processes of historical change. The authors, the reader may note, are about evenly divided between professional historians and anthropologists, a fact signifying the entry into ethnohistory of a new generation of historians, trained both in historiography and ethnology and interested in the social history of what have often been regarded as the unimportant people of the world.

I have been greatly impressed by the high technical quality of the research presented here; I know full well the enormous amount of time required to find, copy, collate, and analyze the scattered bits and pieces of primary data that make up such studies. This book is an admirable work, revealing in detail how leaders of Native American communities in the Northeast coped with and creatively adapted to the presence of the colonists from Europe.

Anthony F. C. Wallace
Aston, Pennsylvania

ACKNOWLEDGMENTS

I'VE OFTEN HEARD that edited books do not count for much in academic tenure decisions. After working on this project, I think that preparation of an edited volume should be a tenure requirement. There is no experience quite like it. All scholars should have the opportunity to forge the contributions of a diverse and talented group of colleagues together into a single, coherent framework. Such work is both challenging and rewarding.

I happily discharge a special debt of gratitude to series editors Colin G. Calloway and Barry O'Connell. Both have done more than series editors must or should do. I am grateful, too, for the help given by James Merrell and Ray Fogelson. Thanks also go to the many readers whose comments strengthened the volume, and to Janet Benton of the University of Massachusetts Press for her able copyediting.

It has been a privilege to work with the historians, cultural anthropologists, and archaeologists whose papers appear in this volume. Collectively and individually, their articles expand the horizons of interdisciplinary ethnohistoric research. Each has endured the editorial process with grace and good will. Their contributions have not ended with the publication of this volume. All have donated their royalties to a fund administered by the University of Massachusetts Press to support books by and about Northeastern Indian people.

Thanks also to Laurie Weinstein, whose efforts allowed several of the contributors to present early drafts of their papers at a symposium at the 1993 Northeastern Anthropological Association Meeting at Western Connecticut College in Danbury, Connecticut.

National Park Service regulations require that I, as a federal employee, formally affirm that this is not a government publication and that government resources were not used in its preparation. The opinions expressed herein, moreover, neither reflect nor represent the policies or programs of the National Park Service.

NORTHEASTERN
INDIAN LIVES

INTRODUCTION

Robert S. Grumet

BIOGRAPHICAL ACCOUNTS OF individual Indian lives have long commanded considerable interest. First appearing during the initial flowering
of American historical writing, Indian biography emerged as a distinct
genre by the second quarter of the nineteenth century. Since that time, it
has grown into an extensive and highly varied body of literature.

The emphases and points of view of authors interested in Indian biography have shifted significantly over the past 150 years. Initially, most writers
focused attention upon such well-known figures as Sequoyah, Sitting Bull,
and Geronimo. Although such figures continue to be the subject of considerable scholarly scrutiny (see Edmunds 1980 and Josephy 1961 for two
examples), accounts of less prominent figures are increasingly finding
print in sourcebooks edited by scholars such as Clifton (1989), Moses and
Wilson (1993), and Szasz (1994a).

The history of Indian biography in the Northeast reflects these developments. Many of the earliest biographies of Northeastern Indians were
written about people documented in colonial records from the first centuries of the Historic Contact period. Full-length studies described the
careers of such prominent figures as Pontiac (Parkman 1851), Joseph
Brant (Stone 1838), and Tecumseh (B. Drake 1841). Briefer sketches
of less well-known personalities appeared in Samuel G. Drake's much-
reprinted *Book of the Indians* (1833) and other compilations.

A substantial number of these early works were hagiographic in nature.
Writers like Parkman, Stone, and the Drakes used their biographies primarily as vehicles to celebrate the victory of American civilization over
savagery—Indians, European adversaries, and other enemies of what they
regarded as progress. Often passionate partisans of local history, many of
these writers were also avid genealogists. In their search for ancestors

1

capable of adding lustre to reputations of lineages and localities, they often linked themselves symbolically to what they regarded as the tragically noble subjects of these biographies. Asserting that the Indians of their area were somehow nobler and more worthy of emulation than others, such writers basked in the reflected glory of ancestors who had befriended, converted, or subdued such objects of emulation.

Although the hagiographic tradition of Indian biography has endured into this century (see, for example, Bonfanti 1971–72; Sipe 1927), most recent studies have been written by academic anthropologists and historians. Scholars using new perspectives to interpret data unavailable to their predecessors have reexamined Pontiac (Peckham 1947), Brant (Kelsay 1984), and Tecumseh (Edmunds 1984), and produced new biographies on such figures as Squanto (Salisbury 1981) and King Philip (Leach 1958; Bourne 1990).

Attention remained focused primarily on famous males until recently. Anthony F. C. Wallace began using the biographical form to tell the story of Northeastern native societies through analyses of documented careers of lesser-known men during the 1940s. His studies of the Delaware leader Teedyuscung (first published in 1949 and reprinted in 1990) and the Seneca prophet Handsome Lake (1969) remain benchmarks in the field.

Studies devoted to Northeastern Indian women have only begun to appear in some numbers in recent years. Jean Johnston's essay, "Molly Brant: Mohawk Matron" (1964) was one of the first modern studies to shed light on the career of an influential but almost forgotten female frontier diplomat and leader. Other studies have chronicled aspects of the lives of figures such as the Mohawk medicine woman Coocoochee (Tanner 1979), Cockacoeske, the Queen of the Pamunkeys (McCartney 1989), and Montauk sunksquaw Quashawam (Strong and Karabag 1991). Ann Marie Plane's work on the Saconet squaw sachem Awashunkes, Lois M. Feister and Bonnie Pulis's updated account of the life of Molly Brant, and Bunny McBride and Harald E. L. Prins's essay on Molly Ockett, all in this volume, together represent a considerable contribution to this still small but growing literature.

The stories of most other less well-known Indian personalities documented during the Historic Contact period in the Northeast largely continue to languish in obscurity. New editions of earlier biographies of figures such as William Apess (O'Connell 1992), Crashing Thunder (Radin 1983), Governor Blacksnake (Abler 1989), and Mary Jemison (Namias

1992) are beginning to appear. Scholarly articles on such figures as the Mahican leader Hendrik Aupaumut (Ronda and Ronda 1979), the Niantic sachem Ninigret (Sehr 1977), and, most recently, Delaware diplomat Andrew Montour (Hagedorn 1994) and the Mohegan divine Samson Occom (Szasz 1994b; Weinstein 1994) are scattered in journals and sourcebooks surveying far broader topics, time periods, or areas. The lives of most of the hundreds of less famous native Northeastern people chronicled in records dating to the Historic Contact period are today almost entirely ignored or forgotten.

The authors of the papers in this volume redirect attention to some of these all-but-forgotten lives. Each has gathered together and analyzed bodies of documentary evidence chronicling the careers of some of these people. Placing these data within their social and historical contexts, they reveal something of the range and diversity of Indian life in the region during the seventeenth and eighteenth centuries.

The papers in this volume tell the stories of sixteen men and women documented in colonial records in what is today the northeastern quarter of the United States. The area covered by these authors stretches from Maine to Pennsylvania and west to Ohio. Other areas of the Northeast were not deliberately excluded.

The biographies in this volume describe the lives of Indian people chronicled in European records during the first two centuries of sustained contact in the region. Each is presented in chronological order. They begin in the 1630s, when Indian people first began to be identified by name with some regularity in Dutch and English documents. Continuing through the turbulent era widely known as the Historic Contact period, coverage extends to the first decades of the nineteenth century.

Paul A. Robinson begins the volume with an analysis of the documented career of Narragansett sachem Miantonomi (fl. 1632–43). Miantonomi's life history exemplifies the dilemma faced by many Indian leaders who confronted European colonists during the early years of sustained contact in the region. Robinson shows how Miantonomi dealt with the possibilities and problems of contact as he worked to serve his people's interests in the formidably complex arena of regional intercultural politics and diplomacy. Miantonomi is revealed as an innovative and resourceful leader who struggled to take advantage of opportunities presented by the movement of English settlers to the frontiers of Narragansett Country in today's western Rhode Island during the early 1630s.

Robinson shows how Miantonomi pursued his people's interests by establishing close political and economic relationships with Rhode Island merchants and settlers. Robinson's recognition of Samuel Gorton's importance in intercultural relations in the area represents an important corrective to accounts almost entirely focusing upon the far better-known Roger Williams. Descriptions of similar intercultural relationships in many other papers in this volume demonstrate that such connections were both widespread and often vital to the success and survival of Indian and European communities.

Robinson also shows how Miantonomi dealt with problems of intercultural conflict, which were also confronted by others described in this volume. Initially coming to the aid of colonists against the Pequots in 1636, Miantonomi was disgusted by the English massacre of the occupants of the Mystic Fort the following year. Relations worsened after English victory over the Pequots in 1637 suddenly shifted the region's balance of power in favor of the colonists. Charting the decline in these relations, Robinson shows how Miantonomi's efforts to forge an Indian confederacy capable of opposing English expansion ended when Mohegan sachem Uncas assassinated him, with English approval, in 1643.

Uncas (fl. 1636–83) is the subject of the following biography. Eric S. Johnson uses a wide range of archival sources to trace the turbulent career of this controversial figure. Unlike established leaders of powerful, populous communities, such as Miantonomi, Uncas struggled to lead a small group of family and followers surrounded by powerful and predatory neighbors, Indian as well as European. Departing from previous studies depicting him as a noble hero or a self-serving parvenu, Johnson presents a far more complex picture of the man. He shows how Uncas established and exploited ties with the English to free the Mohegan people from Pequot domination and legitimate his authority as the Mohegan sachem. He further describes the tactics Uncas used to extend authority over other Indians in Connecticut and to provide for the safety and survival of his followers during the particularly trying years between the Pequot War and King Philip's War (1675–76).

Viewing Uncas's career as one of resistance, Johnson constructs an elegant case study, showing how leaders of small, threatened groups with limited resources at their disposal used subtlety, skill, and craft to combat colonialism. By playing off political rivals both English and Indian, Uncas managed to safeguard Mohegan lands and lives during the most difficult years of his people's history. Federal recognition of the Mohegan community as an Indian tribe in 1993 testifies to the success of his efforts.

John A. Strong examines the life of the Montauk sachem Wyandanch (fl. 1637–59). Like Uncas, Wyandanch rose to prominence in English records in the years immediately following the end of the Pequot War. Extant documentation indicates that he became the key intermediary between the Indians of eastern Long Island and European settlers moving onto their lands. Like Uncas and Miantonomi, Wyandanch found himself caught in a web of diplomatic intrigue and ruthless power politics. Unwilling to submit to the rule of one or another of the powerful Indian nations on the far banks of Long Island Sound, Wyandanch instead chose to subordinate his people nominally to the then-faraway English on the New England mainland. In so doing, he hoped to secure a maximal amount of protection at a minimal cost in autonomy.

Wyandanch's strategy worked for a while. English officials defended Montauk interests against the claims of Niantic leader Ninigret and other sachems trying to reduce Wyandanch's people to submission. Taking advantage of these same connections, Wyandanch attempted to extend authority over the Indians of western Long Island. Strong shows how the Montauk sachem became a key broker in a series of Long Island land disputes. He further shows how Wyandanch used English courts to gain control over Shinnecock lands and otherwise further his people's interests.

Wyandanch died at the height of his power in 1659. Some say he was poisoned. Although his unprecedented influence died with him, the legacy of skillful diplomatic accommodation he left behind helped the Montauks to endure English colonization of their land and to survive to the present day.

Kevin A. McBride next reviews documentation chronicling the life of Robin Cassacinamon (fl. 1638–92), the founder of the Mashantucket Pequot community. Like Wyandanch and Uncas, Cassacinamon struggled to lead a community surrounded by powerful contending Indian and European interest groups. Unlike these figures, he was a leader of a people defeated, dispersed, and subjugated by English colonists.

Cassacinamon first appeared in Connecticut records as the leader of Nameag Pequots compelled to live under the supervision of John Winthrop, Jr. at Pequot Plantation (today's New London area) in the years following the Pequot defeat in 1637. McBride shows how Cassacinamon cultivated his relationship with Winthrop to rise to prominence as a key regional cultural intermediary. Winning Winthrop's confidence, he drew exiled Pequots to his community as he skillfully played contending Indians and colonists against one another.

Cassacinamon's efforts gradually paid off. In 1650, he secured a 500-acre reservation for his people at Noank (present-day Mystic, Connecticut), far from Nameag and in the heart of their traditional homeland. Four years later, he successfully petitioned Connecticut authorities to release his people from Mohegan domination. Seeking a more secure land base, he was granted a 2,000-acre reservation at Mashantucket in 1666. Today, Mashantucket Pequot people honor Cassacinamon as the founder of their community.

Harald E. L. Prins recounts the career of another skillful Indian diplomat, the Abenaki leader Rawandagon (fl. 1639–75). Known among Maine settlers as Robin Hood, English authorities regarded him as chief sachem of the area between Casco Bay and Pemaquid. Like Wyandanch, he acted as the key intermediary between the people of his district and the English. Unlike the Montauk sachem, who allegedly hired a shaman to kill some of Uncas's followers, Rawandagon himself was reputed to possess shamanic powers.

Tracing the etymology of the English sobriquet shared by Rawandagon, Cassacinamon, and other Indians documented in colonial records, Prins shows that it was one of several names of picaresque figures from popular culture used to nickname Indians. Referring to the coarse, comedic, sharp-dealing "Lord of Misrule" instead of the romantic, noble bandit-hero of more recent romantic literature, the nickname speaks volumes about English attitudes towards Indians.

In my essay, I piece together the scattered and fragmentary documentation chronicling the career of the Matinecock go-between Suscaneman (fl. 1653–1703). Suscaneman fixed his mark upon eighty-four deeds to lands within the 160-square-mile town of Oyster Bay between 1667 and 1700. Few other Indian leaders are known to have placed their marks on so many deeds to so small an area over so long a period. Analysis of the contents of these and other documents mentioning Suscaneman or one of his aliases reveals his rise to prominence in western Long Island, sheds light on his role as the designated Matinecock representative in land sales to English families settling in the town of Oyster Bay, and suggests that the particular pattern of selling numerous small plots over a long period of time represented a delaying strategy rather than a wholesale capitulation to English demands.

Ann Marie Plane surveys archival records that describe aspects of the career of Saconet squaw sachem Awashunkes (fl. 1671–83). Like other women known to have led coastal Algonquian communities during the Historic Contact period, Awashunkes's life is documented fragmentarily. Plane weaves previously known facts of her life together with heretofore unpublished records to provide what is the most complete extant account of a seventeenth-century female leader. Her analysis shows how the politics of power and gender eroded the authority of a prominent and resourceful squaw sachem at a critical point in her people's history.

Plane begins by charting Awashunkes's role as an independent-minded leader involved in the highly charged intercultural diplomatic arena during the years preceding the military conflagration known most widely as King Philip's War, which embroiled all people in southern New England from 1675 to 1676. Subsequently, she shows how English ideas about women, Indians, and savagery were reflected in Benjamin Church's account of his wartime relations with the influential squaw sachem. Plane then shows how English magistrates struggled to impose their own views about the subordination of Indians in general and Indian women in particular in a 1683 court case involving assault, fornication, and infanticide. In so doing, she reveals how colonists used courts to subjugate Indian people and diminish the authority of female leaders.

Daniel Mandell tells the story of another leader of an Indian community engulfed by English expansion in the years after King Philip's War. Thomas Waban (fl. 1647–1722) was eldest son of Waban, the first Indian convert of Puritan missionary John Eliot and a leader of Natick, the first Massachusetts Bay Indian praying town. Educated by Puritan teachers, Thomas and other Natick people supported the English against their Indian enemies during the war. Afterwards, they did their best to maintain the integrity of their community as it became an isolated enclave surrounded by English settlements.

Thomas, whose Indian name was Weegramomenit, came to prominence in Massachusetts records as a leader of the Natick community following his father's death in 1684. Fluent and literate in English as well as in Massachusett, he maintained the town's records, taught school, became a town selectman, and served as one of the community's three judges. Mandell shows how Thomas worked with other Natick leaders to accommodate demands for troops to serve in English armies fighting against the French, while mediating increasingly acrimonious disputes with encroaching English neighbors intent upon taking control of their town. He further shows how the community's decision to put an end to communal landholding and adopt land ownership in severalty ultimately hastened Natick's dissolution. Gradually taken over by English settlers, the Natick Indian community dissolved fifty years after Thomas's death.

Elizabeth A. Little describes the documented career of Nantucket sachem Daniel Spotso (fl. 1687–1741). Spotso became a key land broker for his people. Like Suscaneman, he conveyed Indian title to substantial quantities of his people's land to English colonists. Unlike Suscaneman, Spotso played a major role in carrying on a novel and innovative form of transferring usufruct rights first pioneered by his predecessor Nickanoose in 1675. Known as horse commons, such agreements conveyed grazing rights to one horse on common lands. Developed as a way to apportion rights equitably to a critical, limited resource, horse common agreements averted what Hardin (1968) has called a "Tragedy of the Commons."

Little shows how Daniel Spotso sold, purchased, rented, and gave away horse common rights to Indians and colonists alike. She further shows how he convinced English land purchasers to recognize formally the Indian land tenure principle of periodic land-right renewal in a deed signed in 1715. Surveying other archival records in English and Massachusett documenting Spotso's life, she provides additional insights into Nantucket Indian kinship, women's roles, and intercultural diplomacy.

The life of the Mohawk sachem Theyanoguin (fl. 1690–1755) is examined by Dean R. Snow. Known to the British as King Hendrick, he was a noted warrior who became one of the most prominent Indian diplomats of his day. Extant records indicate that he devoted much of his life to intercultural affairs. Extraordinarily well-travelled, Theyanoguin moved throughout the Northeast and journeyed twice to England (first in 1710 as one of four "Indian Kings" presented at Queen Anne's court; then around 1740). Close friend to Conrad Weiser and Sir William Johnson, two of the most influential frontier power-brokers of their era, he played a pivotal role in preserving his people's alliance with the British at a time when the Iroquois Confederacy as a whole maintained an official position of neutrality in conflicts between colonial powers.

Analyzing the large corpus of archival data documenting the career of this cosmopolitan figure, Snow shows clearly that Theyanoguin never lost sight of his primary loyalties to the Mohawk people or his identity as a Mohawk man. Throughout his career, he consistently represented the interests of his people. He was not always successful. Reports alluding to the removal and reinstatement of antlers symbolizing his chiefly office represent some of the few documented examples chronicling the role of Iroquois matrons in appointing and deposing League sachems.

Portraits of and stories about Theyanoguin testify to the fascination he inspired among the British. Snow describes several portraits portraying the man at different times of his life and analyzes stories and quotations associated with the Mohawk leader, several of which can be attributed directly to Theyanoguin; others are most probably apocryphal. Retold in various ways up to the present time, their widespread and persistent appeal attests to the enduring influence of this personable and powerful eighteenth-century Mohawk leader.

James H. Merrell analyzes evidence documenting the life of the Susquehanna Valley diplomat Shickellamy (fl. 1727–48). Drawing on a wide range of archival records, Merrell shows how Shickellamy, an Oneida by birth, rose to become the principal go-between for Indians and colonists along the strategic stretch of borderland separating Iroquoia from Pennsylvania and the southern colonies.

Like Theyanoguin and other diplomats examined here, Shickellamy established close relationships with particularly influential colonial figures. He used his friendships with powerful Pennsylvanian provincial secretary James Logan, the ubiquitous Conrad Weiser, and other influential frontier figures to forge what Merrell terms "an axis of interest that ran from Philadelphia to Onondaga."

Like other frontier diplomats, Shickellamy almost always conducted his affairs with secrecy and discretion. Carefully sifting through records documenting a notorious murder case that threatened the peace of the region in 1744, Merrell has analyzed a rare body of documentation that describes in detail the diplomatic methods Shickellamy used to defuse a particularly dangerous frontier incident. These documents reveal the complex interplay of move and counter-move that characterized intercultural diplomacy of the period. They also reveal something of the skill that enabled go-betweens like Shickellamy to emerge as important actors on the contested frontiers of northeastern North America.

Next, the late William A. Hunter tells the story of another Indian go-between, Moses Tunda Tatamy (fl. 1733–60) a singular and still poorly understood frontier diplomat. Tatamy was born in New Jersey to a community in the process of being engulfed by English settlers. One of the first Delawares to accept Christianity, he was also among the few Indian people known to have patented land in fee simple as a private landowner in Pennsylvania.

Tatamy rose to prominence as a guide, messenger, interpreter, and intermediary during the 1740s. His people gave him power of attorney to represent them in litigations settling outstanding land claims in New Jersey. Unlike most Delawares, he remained friendly with the British after many of his people went to war against them following Braddock's defeat in 1755. Refusing to break with either adversary, Tatamy found his skills in high demand throughout the Seven Years War. Hunter charts Tatamy's travels between British and Indian settlements in search of peace for his people. Chronicling his participation in the series of treaties at Easton that reestablished peaceful relations between the Delawares and the British, Hunter shows how Tatamy worked to expand the framework of peace up to the time of his death in 1760.

Michael N. McConnell analyzes documentation chronicling the lives of two of Tatamy's contemporaries, the Delaware leaders Pisquetomen (fl. 1731–62) and Tamaqua, also known as the Beaver (fl. 1750–69). Like Tatamy, both men figured prominently in the frontier diplomacy of their era. Unlike Tatamy, who lived and died on the margins of frontier society, Pisquetomen and Tamaqua stood at the very center of Delaware culture. Brothers, they belonged to the prominent lineage from which Delawares living in exile in Pennsylvania and Ohio chose brokers to negotiate with colonial authorities. Known among the British as "Kings," such leaders achieved particular prominence during the violent decades of the mid-eighteenth century.

Pisquetomen first appeared in European documents as the protégé of his uncle, the Delaware King Alumapees. Fluent in English, he served as interpreter, guide, and messenger. Disliked and distrusted by James Logan for reasons that remain unclear, he did not succeed to the Delaware Kingship when Alumapees died in 1747. Instead, he joined his younger brother, Tamaqua, and his other brothers, Shingas and Delaware George, in their move west to Ohio Country far from the reach of Pennsylvania authorities. It was in Ohio that Tamaqua attained the status of Delaware King during the early 1750s.

McConnell shows how the two men embodied a complementary op-position that characterized Delaware society of the 1750s. Pisquetomen went to war against the enemies of his people; Tamaqua dedicated himself to the role of peacemaker. Similar binary role oppositions were common in

Northeastern Woodland Indian society. McConnell's careful documentation of this unusually well-recorded dyadic relationship represents a rare and significant contribution to the literature.

Lois M. Feister and Bonnie Pulis pull together and analyze the large body of data documenting the life of the influential Mohawk woman Molly Brant. Brant is known most widely as the sister of the Mohawk leader Joseph Brant and the consort of British Superintendent of Indian Affairs Sir William Johnson. She rose to prominence thereafter as a key intermediary between her people and the British.

Expanding upon this view of her life, Feister and Pulis present a more fully realized portrait of this important frontier diplomat. They describe her roles as daughter, mother, and Mohawk matron, and show how she drew upon her cultural background and connections with powerful men to forge a strong identity of her own. Moving skillfully between her own culture and British society, Brant played a major role in maintaining Mohawk loyalty to the British cause as she worked to preserve Mohawk traditions during and after the American War of Independence.

The final essay of the volume, written by Bunny McBride and Harald E. L. Prins, tells the story of Pigwacket medicine woman Molly Ockett (fl. 1749–1816). Throughout a lifetime spanning more than half a century of conflict, Ockett travelled across the northern New England frontier as an itinerant healer and herbalist. Using a wide range of primary and secondary sources, McBride and Prins place their data within the context of events that shaped intercultural relations in Maine during her lifetime. They examine the names of places named after Ockett and assess stories about her life and deeds.

McBride and Prins follow Ockett and her people from their homeland in Maine's upper Saco River Valley to the Canadian mission town of St. Francis, where she and her family survived Robert Rogers's raid in 1759. She and a small number of other dispossessed Pigwacket people returned to their Maine homeland as wandering itinerants. Resuming their migratory round, they made their living by hunting, fishing, and trading furs and homemade crafts and cures to English settlers.

Ockett established close relations with several settlers. One of these, a somewhat shady character named Henry Tufts who went to Ockett to cure a knife wound in his thigh, wrote an account of his stay with her. His account represents a rare extant intimate glimpse into the private life of an Indian healer during the late eighteenth century.

Few other biographies in this or any volume reveal much about the inner lives of their subjects. It is not that Dutch or English colonists ignored or disparaged the innermost thoughts of Indian people; a look at their own writings shows that few expressed deeply personal thoughts or feelings in even the most private journals. Although some writers, such as the Anglo-Irishmen William Johnson and George Croghan, often expressed themselves freely on paper, most of their English contemporaries were evidently reluctant to do so. This reticence may be more indicative of a somewhat taciturn literary style than of a deliberate and complete indifference to the views and sensibilities of native people.

The paucity of other kinds of information is harder to explain. Comparatively little is known about the domestic or spiritual lives of most Indian people appearing in the pages of European chronicles. Information bearing upon the lives of women, children, younger men and women, and elders is particularly scant. Some of these lacunae almost certainly must be attributed to a lack of interest on the part of European chroniclers. Others, however, almost as surely must arise from Indian desires to shield their private lives from the penetrating gaze of foreign observers.

If a reading of the biographies in this book reveals one thing, it is that there was nothing simple about the lives and times of these Indian men and women. None were simply heroic defenders of tradition; neither did any merely capitulate to foreign hegemony. Their lives and situations were complex and challenging. The authors in this volume show how these figures struggled to rise to the challenges posed by these complexities, responding in a range of ways to problems and opportunities presented by contact with European colonists and other Indians. Collectively, this group of prominent Indians reveals how all Indian people struggled to adapt to changing circumstances at a time when defeat, destruction, and dispossession were still unthinkable possibilities.

CHAPTER ONE

⸎

Lost Opportunities: Miantonomi and the English in Seventeenth-Century Narragansett Country

Paul A. Robinson

Introduction

TODAY, SOME NARRAGANSETT people speak of the differences between Indian and non-Indian society and the need to understand those differences in order to sustain Narragansett culture. Tribal Medicineman Lloyd Wilcox (Running Wolf) is one of those most responsible for continuing Narragansett traditions. At the same time, Wilcox is deeply involved in efforts to attain economic self-sufficiency. Summarizing the difficulties his people face in participating in the non-Indian world, Wilcox has stated, "The problem we have is that we're trying to bring the best advantages of the twentieth century to our Tribe without turning our backs on our heritage" (Mendels 1982:A12).

Like other leaders throughout Narragansett history, Wilcox believes that mutually beneficial relations based on need and opportunity can be established. For the Narragansetts and other Indian communities in southern New England, the need to establish and define such relationships with non-Indians began when English and Dutch colonists founded their first settlements in the region during the early decades of the 1600s. Although the earliest documented contact between Europeans and native people occurred when Giovanni da Verrazzano visited Narragansett Bay in 1524, it was not until the Dutch began regular trading voyages and English towns were established that local Indians were confronted with the need to deal politically and socially with Europeans on a sustained basis.

Between 1620 and 1640, the number of European colonists in southern New England increased from a few to more than twenty thousand, while disease and warfare caused the indigenous population to decline precipitously. Miantonomi came of age in this rapidly changing and uncertain world. With his uncle Canonicus, Miantonomi represented the Narragansetts in dealings with the newcomers. The two men shared the responsibilities of leadership in what some scholars have termed a "dual sachemship" (Simmons 1989). Between 1632 and 1643, Miantonomi represented the Narragansetts in diplomatic matters with the Europeans and in political and military relations with other Indian communities. However, according to Roger Williams (1988 [1]:76n.), he could not act without his uncle's consent.

Miantonomi was one of the first Narragansett leaders known to work at understanding and dealing with the differences between European and Indian society. Seeing opportunity in the new European presence, he recognized that Narragansett interests might be pursued advantageously. Miantonomi's diplomatic and political tasks grew more difficult, however, as English and Indian interests became entangled. When the dangers of this relationship outweighed its advantages, he began to work against English interests. Commissioners of the newly formed United Colonies, alarmed by Miantonomi's resistance, approved and encouraged his assassination by the Mohegan leader, Uncas, in 1643.

Analysis of records chronicling the documented eleven-year portion of Miantonomi's life between 1632 and 1643 shows that the choices available to him and other indigenous leaders narrowed considerably. At the beginning of Miantonomi's sachemship, the Narragansetts shared regional domination with the Pequots, Dutch, and English. At its end, the Pequots had been slaughtered at Mystic, and Narragansett power was greatly reduced. Ironically, Miantonomi played a key role in solidifying the English position; having done that, he found that his homeland and his place in it had come apart.

Sources

> A life-view by the living can only be provisional. Perspectives are altered by the fact of being drawn; description solidifies the past and creates a gravitational body that wasn't there before. A background of dark matter—all that is not said—remains, buzzing.
> —John Updike, "Self-Consciousness"

Almost everything we know of Miantonomi's life and times is based on the observations and experiences of a small number of European men, each of whom pursued his own interest. Some worked with Miantonomi and the Narragansetts; others worked against them. Miantonomi's diplomatic and political responsibilities required periodic visits to English towns and houses as well as meetings with European visitors at his house in Narragansett. Some of these meetings and conversations were described by Puritan officials in letters, journals, and official colonial records.

Outside of Narragansett Country, writers like John Winthrop, Jr., of Connecticut, John Winthrop, Sr., and Edward Johnson of Massachusetts Bay, and William Bradford of Plymouth contended with one another for Narragansett land and resources. These men often described Miantonomi and his actions in unfavorable terms. Bradford, for example, characterized the Narragansett leader as "ambitious and politic," undesirable qualities that in Bradford's puritanical view described a man who could not be trusted (Bradford 1962:211–12). Edward Johnson, a devoted follower of Winthrop, described Miantonomi as "a very stern man, and of great stature, of a cruel nature, causing all his nobility and such as were his attendance [*sic*] to tremble at his speech" (Jameson 1910:162).

English people living in Narragansett Country such as Roger Williams and Samuel Gorton apparently held more favorable opinions of the man. Both depended on Narragansett hospitality and protection to maintain their territorial and economic positions against threats from Connecticut, Massachusetts, and Plymouth competitors. Samuel Gorton, for example, had been expelled from Massachusetts Bay. Settling on Shawomet lands in what is now Warwick, Rhode Island, he worked to further Narragansett interests as he pursued his own. Miantonomi and the Shawomet sachem, Pumham, sold land use rights to Gorton and his followers in 1643 (RIC [1]:130). This action angered Massachusetts Bay officials attempting to expand their own influence into Narragansett Country.

Conflicting reports purporting to represent the Narragansett response to Miantonomi's death in 1643 reflect the range of European views depicting this influential Indian leader. Emphasizing the extent of the grief displayed by Miantonomi's people, Gorton reported that the Narragansetts mourned "continually" for a year and a half (Force 1846 [4]:99). Edward Johnson of Massachusetts Bay, who had participated in the 1642 Massachusetts attack on Warwick that resulted in Gorton's capture and deportation, noted with evident satisfaction that some of the "lesser princes were joyful" when Miantonomi was assassinated (Johnson 1910:222). Both characterizations were accurate to a point. Like most powerful leaders, Miantonomi was beloved and mourned by his friends, disliked and feared by his enemies.

The letters of Roger Williams (1988), founder of Providence and proprietor of a trading post in Narragansett Country between 1637 and 1651, are a major source of information about Miantonomi. Williams, like Gorton, had been banished from Massachusetts Bay. Establishing the capital of his new province of Rhode Island in Providence in 1637, the expatriate Williams nevertheless continued to supply John Winthrop, Sr. and other Puritan officials with information about Narragansett people and their leaders.

Williams (1988 [1]:99) also identified prominent Indian figures and sent advice on how to flatter and influence them. Williams further served as a valuable sounding board, verifying the truth of the many rumors of Narragansett and other Indian conspiracies to attack English settlements (R. Williams 1988 [1]:102).

Some of Williams's reports are probably as close to the thinking of Miantonomi and other Narragansetts as we will ever get. Williams (1988 [1]:72, 131) sometimes described the dispositions of his Narragansett acquaintances (e.g., Canonicus "was very sour"; Miantonomi "rests well persuaded"). He also attempted often to evaluate their actions in terms of Narragansett needs and values, a task he performed so well that some questioned the extent of his attachment to English ways. Responding to an accusation lodged by the senior Winthrop alleging that he was overzealous in his defense of the Narragansetts, Williams (1988 [1]:163) felt compelled to reply, "I am not yet turned Indian."

The biases of Edward Johnson, the Winthrops, and other writers openly hostile to Miantonomi and the Narragansetts do not necessarily invalidate their observations. Neither should we uncritically accept the views of chroniclers writing favorably about Miantonomi or his people. Both detractors and supporters shaded what they chose to record and left out what they regarded as uninteresting or threatening. The records are incomplete and sometimes unreliable, yet they reveal nevertheless a great deal about how he came to terms with the novel and ultimately devastating prospect of European settlement in his homeland. Taken together, these records describe an articulate, intelligent leader considered charismatic by friends and treacherous by enemies. They construct the portrait of a man who toiled to make comprehensible a world that was increasingly complex and uncertain.

Miantonomi left nothing of his own in the written record. His silence both exemplifies the many difficulties encountered by investigators studying nonliterate peoples and underscores the possibilities of potential harm that such scholarship can cause. Responding to the prospect of someone writing his biography, John Updike (1989:xv) writes, "The idea seemed so repulsive that I was stimulated to put down, always with some natural hesitation and distaste, these elements of an autobiography. They record what seems to me important about my own life."

We may never know what Miantonomi thought most important about his own life, yet we can find, in his actions and in what the various colonial officials chose to record (or not to record), some understanding of his attempts to understand and control the new world being made by Indians and Europeans. We might also imagine that, like Updike, this essay or the extant work of other scholars would have provoked him to set down or speak about what he thought important in his own life.

The Relationship Begins

> Canonicus's son, the great sachem of Narragansett, came to the governor's house with John Sagamore. After they had dined, he gave the governor a skin, and the governor requited him a fair pewter pot, which he took very thankfully, and stayed the night.
>
> —John Winthrop, Journal entry, July 13, 1631

Though Miantonomi's birth date was not recorded, he was one of the first Narragansett leaders to come of age in a world shaped by Europeans as well as Indians. His protector, teacher, and uncle, Chief Sachem Canonicus, was reportedly in his fifties when Plymouth was settled in 1620 and close to seventy when he granted Roger Williams permission to settle in Narragansett Country in 1637. Miantonomi was perhaps thirty years younger than his uncle, in his late teens in 1616, when the first of several deadly epidemics ravaged Indian communities from the Penobscot River in Maine to southeastern Massachusetts. These epidemics left much of the area depopulated and open for English settlement by 1620. Plymouth, for example, was founded near the site of a village decimated by disease and abandoned by survivors.

English accounts indicate that the epidemics left the Narragansetts and other Indian communities on the western side of Narragansett Bay untouched. William Bradford, the governor of Plymouth Colony, was one of many English to contrast the carnage on the Bay's east side with the lack of pestilence farther west. Writing in 1621, he reported that east of Narragansett Bay the "soil was good and the people not many, being dead and abundantly wasted . . . the Narragansetts had not been at all touched by this wasting plague" (Bradford 1962:87).

The epidemics were a turning point in the Indian history of the region. Large areas of coastal New England were depopulated, enabling the English to land unopposed and establish permanent villages. Epidemic contagion also changed the way surviving Indians thought about themselves and other Indian groups. The deadly effects of the epidemics caused some to doubt the power of local medicine people; others blamed themselves for the diseases and examined their behavior to discover what had caused the spirits to harm their people so terribly (Morrison 1984).

Some Indians believed that powerful Narragansett medicine people had halted the sickness at the borders of Narragansett Country. A Narragansett burning ritual was credited particularly with keeping the sickness and death away from Narragansett families (Young 1841). Unlike most people to the east, who were shaken and confused by the epidemics, the Narragansetts may have felt reassured by their escape. Such feelings may have been heightened when some survivors urged their leaders to emulate the Narragansett burning ritual. With the Indian population decimated to the east, the epidemics left the Narragansetts and several allied communities west of Narragansett Bay positioned to play a dominant role in English-Indian relations in southern New England.

In early winter of 1621–22, Canonicus announced the Narragansett claim to dominance in the region by sending a gift of several arrows wrapped in the skin of a rattlesnake to Governor Bradford of the newly established Plymouth Colony. Advised by Tisquantum (Squanto), Bradford viewed the act as a Narragansett attempt to "domineer and lord" over Indian communities in the region by openly challenging the power of the newcomers. He responded in kind by filling the snake skin with bullets and returning it to Canonicus. Canonicus, however, refused to accept the snake skin and returned it to Plymouth (Bradford 1962:82; Young 1841:284).

Through this mutual act of rejection, each party signalled its refusal to submit to the other. Gifts or presents were used by Indian people to establish and represent symbolically social and political obligations. Acceptance of gifts inferred acceptance of obligations to givers. Gift rejection symbolized denial of an obligation. Colonial officials quickly became quite adept in using gift exchange to establish and maintain relations of mutual obligation with Indian people.[1]

The English were not the only Europeans the Narragansetts were dealing with at the time of the snakeskin incident. Dutch traders from New Amsterdam, for example, sailed regularly to Narragansett Bay to obtain purple and white shell beads known as wampum (Ceci 1990; Salisbury 1982:148–49; L. Williams and Flinn 1990:7). Highly valued by interior fur-producing tribes, these beads served as currency with which Dutch and English traders obtained pelts for export back to Europe. It is thus possible that Dutch merchants concerned with protecting their wampum market in the Narragansett Bay and Long Island Sound region encouraged the Narragansett hostility toward Plymouth.

The shells used for making beads were particularly plentiful in this area. Responding to European demand, Pequot, Narragansett, and Long Island Indian communities became involved in the production and distribution of the beads. The extent of this involvement can be seen in the itinerary of Dutch West India Company trader Pieter Barentsen on a trip in 1626: Barentsen visited the Narragansett Bay communities, the Sequins, the Shinnecocks, the Mohawks, the Wappingers, and the Mahicans (Ceci 1977:193; Wassenaer in Jameson 1909:87).

Plymouth became involved in the wampum trade in 1628, when Dutch merchants, operating with the understanding that the English would stay out of Narragansett Bay, provided Governor Bradford with wampum worth fifty pounds sterling to trade with Indians at Kennebec (Ceci 1977:196–97; Salisbury 1982:151). The Indians at Kennebec first refused attempts by Plymouth traders to engage in wampum exchange. Two years later, however, Bradford reported that the Indians "could scarce ever get enough" of the shell beads (Bradford 1962:139).

Bradford's account of the beginning of the wampum trade is important because it described what the governor called the "Great Alteration." More recently, historian Neal Salisbury (1982:147–52) has called it the "wampum revolution." Bradford noted that Plymouth colonists trading wampum possessed an overwhelming advantage over other traders not having shell beads in their inventories. He wrote,

> And strange it was to see the great alteration it made in a few years among the Indians themselves; for all the Indians of these parts, and the Massachusetts, had none or very little of it, but the sachems and some special persons that wore a little of it for ornament. Only it was made and kept among the Narragansetts and Pequots, which grew rich and potent by it . . . But after it grew to be a commodity in these parts, these Indians fell into it also, and to learn how to make it; for the Narragansetts do gather the shells of which they make it from their shores. (Bradford (1962:139)

Puritan officials noted that the wampum trade was an important factor in the growing strength and political importance of the Narragansetts: Bradford observed that the trade had made the Narragansetts "rich and potent," and in 1634 William Wood of Massachusetts Bay described the Narragansetts as "curious minters" of wampum, "the most rich also; and the most industrious; being the storehouse of all such kind of wild merchandise as is among them" (Wood 1977:61).

Seemingly satisfied with their relations with the Dutch, the Narragansetts initially showed little interest in trading with Plymouth; in 1623, they rejected the offers of a trading party from Plymouth, and Bradford's accounts of the years immediately following mention little of the Narragansetts. It was not until 1631 that they established regular relations with the English, and interestingly, they chose to establish relations with the newly arrived Massachusetts Bay colonists rather than with their more entrenched, closer Plymouth neighbors. Visited by one of Canonicus's sons, the Massachusetts Bay settlers formalized the new arrangement with mutual exchanges of gifts, dinner, and hospitality (Winthrop 1908 [1]:65).

Miantonomi followed his cousin's 1631 visit to Boston with one of his own the following year. According to Governor Winthrop, Miantonomi and his party were treated well: they were feted at a formal dinner and "made much of" (Winthrop 1908 [1]:89). But, in what may be the first recorded instance of cultural misunderstanding between the English and the Narragansetts, three of Miantonomi's men created a stir among the Puritans when they attempted "to break into a neighbor's house" during sermon hour (Winthrop 1908 [1]:89).

Although it is possible that larceny was on the minds of these men, it is more likely that they were simply behaving as they might have done had they been visiting an Indian house. Roger Williams, in *A Key into the Language of America*, first published in 1643, gave the impression that Narragansett doors were rarely closed; friends and strangers alike could come and go at will. "In this respect," Williams wrote, "they are remarkably free and courteous, to invite all strangers in; and if any come to them upon any occasion they request them to come in, if they come not in of themselves" (R. Williams 1866:36).

If the "housebreak" attempt was, in fact, a cultural misunderstanding, it was one of the first of many misunderstandings, large and small, intentional and unintentional, that in time caused Miantonomi to rethink his relationship with the English. And as the relationship deteriorated, Roger Williams, once full of good fellowship for Miantonomi, began to see him instead as "proud and angry and covetous and filthy, hating, and hateful" (R. Williams 1988 [1]:163).

The Relationship Thickens

> The Narragansetts are at present doubtful of reality in all our promises.
>
> —Roger Williams to Governor Henry Vane,
> Massachusetts Bay Colony, May, 1637

By the end of the decade, Narragansett fortunes and those of most other southern New England Indian communities were in decline. A second major epidemic hit southern New England in 1633 and 1634. This time, the sickness (smallpox) penetrated Narragansett Country and swept west through Connecticut (Salisbury 1982:191). As numbers of native people decreased, more English towns were established.

Indian people initially saw advantages in having English neighbors living nearby. Traders were especially welcome. In 1634, Narragansett sachems unsuccessfully tried to persuade John Oldham to establish a trading post in Narragansett Bay on Dutch Island. Three years later, Roger Williams became the first European allowed to set up a permanent post in the heart of Narragansett Country when he moved from Providence to Cocumscussoc (Salisbury 1982:212; R. Williams 1988).

Relations between the new neighbors did not proceed without incident. Narragansetts, led by Canonicus and Miantonomi, soon found themselves embroiled in English politics. These interests came to affect internal Narragansett policies as English influence and power increased.

Although direct documentation is lacking, records describing Pequot policy indicate that the Pequots came to a clear understanding of the dangers of European settlement before their neighbors. In the summer of 1636, the Pequots were at war with the Dutch, fighting the Narragansetts, and under tribute demands from the English. They approached the Narragansetts, appealing for unity against the colonists (Salisbury 1982:210–12). Informed of the overture by Narragansett sachems, Bradford was told that the Pequot envoys declared to the Narragansetts that "the English were strangers and began to overspread their country, and would deprive them thereof in time, if they were suffered to grow and increase; and if the Narragansetts did assist the English to subdue [the Pequots], [the Narragansetts] did but make way for their own overthrow, for if [the Pequots] were rooted out, the English would soon take occasion to subjugate them" (Bradford 1962:182).

Six years later, Miantonomi would say essentially the same thing at Montauk. In 1636, however, Canonicus and Miantonomi decided that there was more to be gained in siding with the English. In October, Miantonomi traveled to Massachusetts Bay and promised Narragansett support to the English against the Pequots. In return, he hoped to increase his people's power by gaining control over some of the Pequots' wampum trade. In May 1637, Narragansett warriors joined Mohegan and Niantic men in the English attack on the Pequot fortified village at Mystic. When English soldiers turned the attack into a slaughter, the Narragansetts complained bitterly that what the Puritans had done was "naught," that it was evil and had killed too many people (Jennings 1975:223; Underhill 1897:62).

Less than a month before the massacre, Miantonomi had visited Roger Williams at his house in Providence and sought reassurance that the English would not harm Pequot women and children. In a May 1 letter to officials at Massachusetts Bay, Williams passed along Miantonomi's counsel concerning the planned attack. Williams wrote that "it would be pleasing to all natives, that women and children be spared" (R. Williams 1988 [1]:73). That the English not only did not spare women and children but went out of their way to kill them was, to Miantonomi and many other Indian participants, an egregious and fearful act that made it clear that these Puritans could not be trusted.

The Relationship Sours

[Miantonomi] replied in these words, Chenock eiuse wetompatimucks? that is, Did ever friends deal so with friends?
—Roger Williams to Governor John Winthrop at
Massachusetts Bay, August 20, 1637

Narragansett power eroded in the years following the end of the Pequot War. Nearby Indian communities that accepted Narragansett hegemony prior to the Mystic massacre first questioned and later defied Narragansett domination. The political power of the Narragansetts over adjacent communities such as Shawomet, Coweset, and Pawtuxet had been based, in part, on Narragansett ability to influence English policy. The massacre dispelled that notion. Abandoned by former allies and tributaries, the Narragansetts found themselves increasingly unable to resist Puritan demands or obtain justice in Puritan councils (Robinson 1990).

Problems with the English centered on what Miantonomi and Canonicus considered Puritan violations of their October 22, 1636 agreement to assist the English in the war against the Pequots. Copies of this agreement have not survived and Winthrop's recollection of its terms was partial and perhaps fallacious (Jennings 1975:214; R. Williams 1988 [1]:115n.; Winthrop 1908 [1]:237–38). From Miantonomi's point of view, the slaughter of women and children at Mystic was a serious infraction, and Williams's letters after the massacre suggest that other problems were also on Miantonomi's mind. In one letter, Williams conveyed Miantonomi's claim that he had not received a promised musket (R. Williams 1988 [1]:96).

More serious disagreements arose over the disposition of the Pequot survivors. Williams met with Canonicus and Miantonomi during the summer of 1637 to let the sachems know of Winthrop's displeasure over the protection of Pequot war refugees by Narragansetts and Niantics. According to Winthrop, the Narragansetts had agreed not to do this without the consent of Massachusetts (Sainsbury 1975:114–15). Miantonomi denied holding Pequots, claimed to have been "faithful and honest," and confronted Williams with ten instances of English dishonesty "since these [Pequot] wars." Miantonomi remarked to Williams, "Did ever friends deal so with friends?" Canonicus complained as well that "although he and Miantonomi had paid many hundred fathom [of wampum] to their soldiers, as Mr. Governor did, yet he had not received one yard of bead nor a Pequot" (R. Williams 1988 [1]:113–14).

Although frustrated at the failure of the English to make good on promises, the Narragansett leaders still worked to advance and protect English interests. These were now represented by Roger Williams at Providence and, in the heart of Narragansett Country, by his and other English trading posts at Cocumscussoc. In working to further the interests of Williams and other English people, Miantonomi and Canonicus ultimately undermined the interests of their former Indian allies. Two incidents occurring shortly after the Mystic massacre illustrate how the Narragansett leaders subordinated basic Indian social and political values to English interests.

In May of 1638, Williams described an incident involving a Pequot man named Weqashcook who had helped the English at Mystic and a Coweset man named Weeokamin, who blamed Wequashcook for the loss of two of his sons in the "Pequot Wars." Assaulted by Weeokamin while visiting a friend at Coweset, Wequashcook lost his coat "and other small things." Wequashcook complained to Williams, who asked the Narragansett leaders to intervene. According to Williams, Canonicus and Miantonomi responded quickly: "Canonicus sent his son and Miantonomi his brother (Yotash) who went to Coweset and demanded the reason of such usage and the goods and so came to my house causing the goods to be restored, professing the sachem's ignorance and sorrow for such passages and giving charge to all natives for their safe travel" (R. Williams 1988 [1]:153).

Three months later a Nipmuc man was robbed and killed by four English colonists after visiting Narragansett. The murderers made off with five fathoms of wampum and three coats (R. Williams 1988 [1]:170–73). Responding quickly, Miantonomi managed to prevent friends of the murdered man from avenging the killing. Williams reported the incident: "The natives, friends of the slain Penowanyanquis, had consultation to kill an English man in revenge. Miantonomi heard of it and desired that the English would be careful on the highways and sent himself express threatenings to them etc. and informed them that Mr. Govr would see justice done" (R. Williams 1988 [1]:176).

These incidents reveal a contradiction between an essential structural principle, that the sachem's power and authority was based in persuasion and consensus-building, and acts of officially sanctioned coercion against individuals and families. Unlike the English, who considered killings of individuals as crimes against the state, traditional Indian beliefs viewed murder as an act against the family of the victim. Just as it was the obligation of the European state to deal with the killer, it was the obligation of the Indian family to seek retribution from relatives of the killer (Gookin 1806:149; Jennings 1975:148–49).

The maintenance of the Narragansett social order now seemed to rest not on what Roger Williams termed the "gentle persuasion" of the sachems, but on mollification of English officials and acquiescence to English demands (R. Williams 1866:164). In the cases of Weeokamin and Penowanyanquis, Miantonomi indicated his willingness to use threats of violence to prevent Indians within his sphere of influence from carrying out actions considered natural and necessary, thus advancing English aims. Acting like an English leader, he placed himself and those associated with him within the English system of rules and government.

Perhaps Miantonomi and Canonicus hoped Williams would help them in their relations with Massachusetts Bay. In November 1637, the sachems conveyed Prudence Island to Winthrop and Williams for twenty fathoms of wampum and two coats. The exchange, Williams observed, was a gift, not a sale. Williams (1988 [1]:165) wrote, "truth is, not a penny was demanded . . . and what was paid was only a gratuity." In the context of native gift exchange and the social obligation it imposed on Winthrop and Williams, the gift of land was difficult, perhaps impossible, to match. It appears likely that Miantonomi was trying to control the English by gifting them into debt (Robinson 1990).

Dependent on Narragansett goodwill for security, Williams might have honored such an obligation. Living far from Narragansett Country, Winthrop had no intention of doing so and considered the transaction a sale with no strings attached. The English from Massachusetts Bay neither lived up to Miantonomi's idea of exchange nor honored the pledges they had made to secure Narragansett assistance against the Pequots. Allowed to incorporate captured Pequot people, Wequashcook and Uncas gained power and influence at Narragansett expense. At the same time, English authorities insisted that Narragansett sachems continue to be responsible for the acts of these now independent communities. In 1638, for example, Massachusetts Bay levied a 100 pound fine on the Narragansetts for injuries sustained by a cow and some horses caught in Coweset traps. In 1640, Rhode Island held the Narragansetts responsible for damage caused by fires set by their neighbors (RIC [1]:107–8, 125; R. Williams 1988 [1]:192–96).

The years 1640 to 1642 were filled with rumors of a region-wide Indian conspiracy against the English. Narragansetts were thought to be at the center of these plans. Records document constant maneuvering by the Indians and the English to maintain advantage in an increasingly hostile environment. These same records chronicle the slow but relentless erosion of Narragansett influence with the English. In nearly every encounter, the English offended, insulted, or threatened Narragansett people. Responding as best they could, the Narragansetts were forced ultimately to appease their English neighbors. Angered and alienated, Miantonomi began to try to undermine the strong position that he had helped the English atttain.

In September 1640, Winthrop wrote that "there was some rumor of the Indians plotting mischief against the English." Earlier that year, Bradford wrote to Winthrop that Miantonomi had sent "a great present of wampum to the Mohawks, to aid him against the English and that it was accepted, and aid promised" (Winthrop 1908 [2]:6). Similar news coming from colonial authorities in Connecticut prompted the Bay Colony to strengthen its defenses and confiscate the powder and shot of local Indians (R. Williams 1988 [1]:204n.; Winthrop 1908 [2]:6–7). Miantonomi was summoned to Boston. Arriving in October, he was compelled to answer questions about the alleged conspiracy.

Miantonomi asked Roger Williams, a man he apparently trusted, to act as his translator during these interrogations. But, banished from Boston five years earlier, Williams could not accompany Miantonomi. Unable to proceed without an interpreter, the English offered him a "Pequot maid" to translate. The English had made a similar offer earlier that summer and knew that Miantonomi might find the offer insulting. Winthrop's description of the meeting conveyed how dramatically the English style in dealing with the Narragansetts had changed since the visits in 1631 and 1632:

> [Miantonomi] refused to treat with us by our Pequot interpreter . . . and the governor [Thomas Dudley] being as resolute as he, refused to use

any other interpreter, thinking it a dishonor to us to give so much way to them. [Miantonomi then acted in a "rude manner"] whereof the governor informed the general court, and would show him no countenance, nor admit him to dine at our table, as formerly he had done, till he had acknowledged his failing, etc., which he readily did . . . and did speak to our committees and us by a Pequot maid who could speak English perfectly. (Winthrop 1908 [2]:15)

The English then read the provisions of the 1636 agreement to Miantonomi. This time, however, they added that he would be responsible for damage to English livestock caused by Indian traps (Winthrop 1908 [2]:15) set by Indian people from communities that no longer recognized Miantonomi as their leader. Miantonomi had come to Boston to answer questions about an alleged conspiracy, was treated roughly, and departed with an extra "English" responsibility that he could not carry out.

The year before, in May 1639, Miantonomi had brought gifts to Winthrop: wampum from Canonicus and himself and a basket for Mrs. Winthrop from Miantonomi's wife, Wawaloam. With these gifts, Miantonomi asked that he be given both Pequot survivors and free use of Pequot land. Accepting the gifts, Winthrop gave Miantonomi neither Pequots nor guarantees of hunting rights (R. Williams 1988 [1]:196). To make matters worse, a year earlier, Uncas had visited Boston bearing a gift of wampum and had left with a red coat, corn for the journey home, and a letter of protection. According to Winthrop, Uncas "departed very joyful" [Winthrop 1908 [1]:271]. So when Miantonomi returned home from Boston in 1640 with (in Winthrop's words) "an injury in his breast," the vise had tightened from the east and the west.

Given the circumstances, it is understandable why rumors of a Narragansett-led conspiracy became common. Confirmation of these rumors finally emerged when reports of Miantonomi's visit to Montauk reached Massachusetts in August 1641.

Unlike his previous visits to Montauk, on this visit Miantonomi brought rather than took gifts. Distributing them to the Montauks, he appealed to them to join him and others against the English: "for so are we all Indians, as the English are, and say brother to one another; so must we be one as they are, otherwise we shall be all gone shortly" (Gardiner 1859: 26). Miantonomi's call for unity was not heeded. The Montauks instead reported Miantonomi's speech to officials of the newly formed United Colonies of New England. As their first official act, they arranged to allow Uncas to assassinate Miantonomi (Sainsbury 1975:118–19).

Avenging Miantonomi's death became an unfulfilled Narragansett obsession. His death, moreover, ended any hope of unification against the English (Salisbury 1982:235), a hope that had already become slim. Miantonomi's influence and his ability to pull together communities in the region had been lost since the summer of 1637, when the Narragansetts and their then-allies participated with the English in an English war. For Miantonomi and other Narragansetts, the opportunities presented by English settlement had instead become a disaster. The Pequot warning about the dangers of the "English strangers" was heard too late.

Notes

I have run up many debts in my search for materials documenting this important Narragansett leader. I want to especially thank members of the Narragansett Indian Tribe, particularly John Brown III, Dr. Ella Sekatau, and Lloyd Wilcox, for teaching me (among other things) that what the Europeans started with Miantonomi continues to the present day. I also want to acknowledge the importance of the work of Glenn LaFantasie and Neal Salisbury in studies of the Narragansett documentary record. Volume editor Robert Grumet provided useful review comments and valuable criticism.

I have substituted modern spellings and capitalizations for all archaic usages in quotations cited in this article. Original wording and sentence structure, however, have been retained throughout.

1. See Robinson (1990) for a more detailed discussion of gift exchange between the English and the Narragansetts. An excellent theoretical discussion of the social context of gift exchange may be found in Bourdieu (1978).

Chapter Two

꒓

Uncas and the
Politics of Contact

Eric S. Johnson

Introduction

Most people know Uncas as one of the heroes of James Fenimore Cooper's *The Last of the Mohicans*. The real Uncas was actually far more
interesting than Cooper's rather wooden character. He was the political
leader, or sachem, of the Mohegan community of southeastern Connecticut from at least the 1630s (when he first appears in documentary records)
until his death in 1683. Over this fifty-year period, Uncas acquired considerable political power in the face of strong challenges to his legitimacy. A
study of his career can provide insight, therefore, into both the variety of
strategies used to gain, legitimize, and retain political power within Native
society and the ways these strategies varied under different circumstances.
An examination of his career also makes plain that Native motivations
were grounded in the complex workings of internal Native politics. Finally, Uncas's somewhat unique historical position provides a fascinating
example of our own contradictory and confusing attempts to come to terms
with what Francis Jennings (1975) called "The Invasion of America."

To understand Uncas's career requires first a brief description of the
Mohegans and Pequots—the polities within which he operated. The Mo-
hegans and Pequots occupied and still live in parts of what is now eastern
Connecticut. The Mohegan homeland is the Thames River Valley. The
Pequot homeland comprises the lower Mystic River Valley and adjacent

29

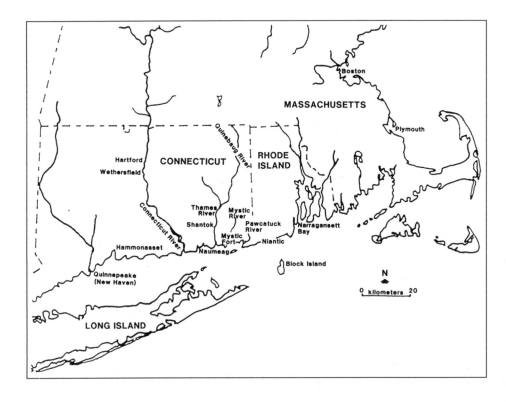

parts of the Connecticut coast. Both groups also exercised their political
influence and power beyond the river valleys, estuaries, and shorelines of
their homelands, allying with or subordinating communities to the west as
far as the Connecticut River Valley and Quinipeake (the New Haven area),
to the north into the southern parts of Nipmuck Country (the Quinebaug
Valley), and to the south into parts of Long Island.

To the east lay an area of shifting alliances. Here, the Pawcatuck River
(the present Connecticut-Rhode Island border) marked the eastern extent
of Pequot political power and the western extent of Narragansett influence
(De Forest 1851:72–73; O'Callaghan 1855 [1]:149–51; Gookin 1806:8;
Salisbury 1982:210). Mohegan territory might be envisioned best as a
stable homeland consisting of the Thames Valley and surrounded by a
region of shifting political alliances.

Although the Mohegans and Pequots were closely allied up to the
Pequot War of 1636, and although their subsequent histories are also
closely linked, they were separate communities, albeit closely tied through
kinship and political alliance. As early as 1614 the two groups were

described as distinct entities by their first Dutch chroniclers. Early land deeds also suggest that the two groups held distinct territories.[1]

The Early Career of Uncas

Uncas was born in the late sixteenth or early seventeenth century to a family of high status. His father, Owaneco, was the sachem of the Mohegan community, which at the time of Uncas's young adulthood was part of the larger Pequot confederation. Uncas also claimed descent from Pequot sachems in "The Genealogy of Uncas," a document whose reliability has been questioned.[2] By 1627 Uncas had married the daughter of the Pequot principal sachem, Tatobem. When Tatobem was killed by the Dutch in 1634, his son Sassacus (Uncas's brother-in-law) became the principal Pequot sachem until he was killed in the Pequot War in 1637.[3]

In the years before that war, Uncas had attempted on five separate occasions either to usurp or threaten Sassacus's authority or to overcome the constraints on his own power. Each attempt failed, and he was forced to take refuge among Narragansett allies. Each time he was subsequently reinstated as a Mohegan sachem, but only after "he humbled himself to the Pequot Sachem" and had his power reduced by loss of lands and followers (CPR [3]:478–80). These several restorations may indicate Uncas's persistent power among his Mohegan brethren, his maintaining of some legitimacy as a sachem, or the possibility that Pequot sachems commonly forgave such transgressions after some punishment. Uncas's kinship with Sassacus was almost certainly a factor in the Pequot sachem's somewhat lenient treatment of his brother-in-law. Because of one or more of these considerations, sterner measures could not command a consensus among the Pequots (E. Johnson 1993:192).

Although his life had been spared, Uncas's authority had been so reduced by 1636 that, according to Native informants, he had little land and did not even have enough men to hold a deer hunt (CPR [3]:479). In 1637, Roger Williams estimated Uncas's Mohegan followers at fewer than fifty adult men, which when adjusted to reflect their families gives a total of under 400 people.[4] A higher estimate of 600 is given by Mooney (1928:4). Native estimates are less quantitative but give a similar impression; Miantonomi declared that "these [Mohegans] are but as a twig[,] we [Narragansetts] are as a great tree" (R. Williams 1988 [1]:119).

Alliance with the English

Despite or because of his reduced status, Uncas turned to the English, who had begun settling Connecticut in the mid-1630s, and began to cultivate alliance with them. By June of 1636, Jonathan Brewster of Plymouth Colony called Uncas "faithfull to the English" in a letter to John Winthrop, Jr. At the same time, Uncas did his best to instigate and nurture the growing enmity between the English and the Pequots. In the same letter in which he praised Uncas, Brewster repeated a story that Uncas had told him in which the Pequots, led by Sassacus and his brother, had planned to attack a Plymouth ship, only to be foiled when, "as soone as those bloody executioners arose out of Ambush with their canoes, the[y] deserned her under sayle with a fayre wind returning Home." Uncas went on to claim that the Pequots were so certain of an English attack that they would soon strike first "out of desperate madnesse." He further falsely accused Sassacus and his brother of direct involvement in the death of Captain Stone, whose murder provided one of the pretexts for English aggression in the Pequot War (Winthrop 1929–47 [3]:270–71).

This incident marks the first appearance of Uncas in the historical record. He was already pursuing a strategy that was to characterize his relationships with the English: ingratiating himself with an English interest group and feeding them false stories about his Native opponents in order to encourage hostility between the two, in the hope of triggering an English attack. Uncas was not the first or only one to do this. In 1621 Tisquantum (also known as Squanto) had used misinformation in an unsuccessful attempt to incite the Plymouth colonists to attack the Pokanoket sachem, Massasoit (Bradford 1901:136–37; Humins 1987; Salisbury 1981; Winslow 1841:287–90). Misinformation was so widespread that in 1647, Roger Williams wrote to John Winthrop, Jr. that "concerning Indian affaires, Reports are various: Lyes are frequent. Private interests, both with Indians and English, are many" (R. Williams 1988 [1]:234).

When the English attacked Pequot and Block Island Native settlements in the fall of 1636, war seemed imminent; yet events proceeded relatively slowly for the next nine months. During this time, Uncas appears to have continued to encourage English aggression. After the Pequots attacked Wethersfield in April 1637, Uncas turned up the pressure. Thomas Hooker wrote John Winthrop that "the Indians here our friends [probably meaning

Uncas] were so importunate with us to make warr presently that unlesse we had attempted some thing we had delivered our persons unto contempt of base feare and cowardise, and caused them to turne enemyes agaynst us" (Winthrop 1929–47 (3):407–8). Uncas was not alone in arguing for a decisive English offensive; Hooker and John Higginson were especially instrumental in securing military assistance from Massachusetts Bay (Salisbury 1982:220).

Uncas's motive for allying with the English and inciting them against the Pequots is consistent with Native political practices. Subordinate groups such as the Mohegans could use war to change their status; by forming new alliances and then proving their strength in battle, former subordinates could create and legitimize a new position of equality with their erstwhile superiors (E. Johnson 1993:200–7). Thus, the story of Uncas reminds us that the variety of ways in which Natives interacted with English interest groups was dependent on objectives, circumstances, and traditional expectations that existed within a complex and often volatile Native political arena, an arena often perceived poorly by the English.[5]

The Pequot War

Uncas and a small group of Mohegan warriors joined the English when the Connecticut Colony sent an expedition commanded by John Mason to attack the Pequots in May 1637. His assistance was welcome; Edward Winslow advised Winthrop to encourage the Mohegan-Pequot enmity and to use the Mohegans as tools against the Pequots, even as the Mohegans were using the English as tools against the Pequots (Mason in Orr 1897; Winthrop 1929–47 [3]:391–92). When the expedition, joined by a small force from Massachusetts Bay led by John Underhill, sailed to Narragansett Bay, they were joined by the Narragansetts and set out overland to the west to attack the Pequots.

By then the English and Indian force included as many as 500 Indians, mostly Narragansetts and Niantics. As they penetrated deeper into Pequot territory, Mason reported, "I then enquired of Onkos, what he thought the Indians would do? Who said, The Narragansetts would all leave us, but as for himself He would never leave us: and so it proved: For which Expressions and some other Speeches of his, I shall never forget him. Indeed he was a great Friend, and did great Service" (Mason in Orr 1897:25). No other principal chronicle of the Pequot War reported this conversation or painted Uncas in such a favorable light. Underhill (in Orr 1897:47–86), one of the leaders of the English contingent, made no mention of Narragansett desertions and didn't even mention Uncas by name. Gardiner (in Orr 1897:113–49), who was not present at the Mystic massacre, painted no such positive portrait of Uncas. In Vincent's narrative (in Orr 1897:102–6), although not mentioning Uncas by name, he noted that the Mohegans "behaved themselves stoutly" and did mention the desertion of about half of the Narragansetts and Niantics, still leaving between two and three hundred for the battle.

Only Mason's account presented Uncas as an heroic figure, or even as a major actor in the war, and only Mason so emphasized Uncas's loyalty. Mason's account was written long after the war was over, after he had made land transactions with Uncas, argued on Uncas's behalf to English authorities, and held a personal stake in Uncas's welfare. Is it any wonder that he chose to depict his friend and ally in such glowing terms?

Uncas and his Mohegan warriors participated in the massacre of the Pequot fort at Mystic (May 26, 1637) and in the battles and skirmishes that ensued. Sassacus and several other Pequot sachems fled to the Mohawks seeking safety, but instead were executed. By the summer of 1637, in Mason's words, "the Pequots now become a prey to all Indians. Happy were they that could bring in their heads to the English: Of which there came in almost daily to Win[d]sir or Hartford" (Mason in Orr 1897:39–40). The Pequot War was an important experience for both the English and Indians in learning how to make and use alliances with one another. Of the alliances forged in the war, that between Uncas and John Mason (and to a lesser extent between Uncas and the Connecticut Colony in general) proved enduring and mutually beneficial. The English had chosen their allies and enemy well in this, their first major military action. By siding against the Pequots they aligned themselves with a powerful network of Indian allies already in the process of isolating and breaking up the Pequot confederation. The ease with which the once-extensive network of Pequot allies and tributaries disintegrated testifies to its inherent instability and to the fact that it was already crumbling under pressure from the Narragansetts, other Indian groups, and the Dutch (Salisbury 1982:208–10). By the terms of the final treaty, the Treaty of Hartford (1638), the English had become a dominant power in southern New England, exacting tribute from almost all Native groups there.

To the Indians, the value of English military assistance had been proved conclusively. With English military help, the Mohegans were able to break out of the Pequot confederation and eventually to replace them as the core of a Mohegan confederation that included or aspired to include Pequots as well as former Pequot tributaries and allies on Long Island, in southern and eastern Connecticut, and in the Connecticut Valley (Salisbury 1982:226). The Narragansetts were able to defeat their long-time enemies with a finality they might never have thought possible.

But the Indians also learned, or would soon realize, that alliance with the English had its costs. The English were domineering allies, requiring large payments in wampum and showing less respect to their allies than was customary among Natives. The English were also dangerous; the Pequot War had revealed their military tactics as brutal and even genocidal. Finally, the English were unpredictable compared to Native allies, since their political decisions were grounded in a different culture. Despite these drawbacks, the English were now a significant force in southern New England because of their victory in the Pequot War, their guns and growing numbers, and the decimation of Native communities by disease. Native groups and leaders had to deal somehow with their new neighbors. The skill and success with which Native groups and individuals tried to manipulate, resist, or avoid the English was a critical factor shaping the events of the middle and late seventeenth century.

The victors (the Connecticut and Massachusetts Colonies, the Narragansetts, and the Mohegans) began competing almost immediately to fill the power vacuum left by Sassacus's death and the Pequot defeat. Pequot survivors and lands had to be dealt with, and their former allies and tributaries, or subordinate allies, had to realign. Opportunities abounded for great shifts in political power. Uncas quickly took advantage of those opportunities. He began gathering Pequot refugees before the war was over. The Treaty of Hartford lent English approval to this strategy; it awarded many Pequots to Uncas as part of the English plan to erase the Pequots permanently. Uncas's success in attracting his former enemies is suggested by population estimates, which show Mohegan numbers jumping from 400 to 600 pre-war to 2,500 six years later (Mooney 1907:926–27; 1928:4; Salisbury 1982:26; R. Williams 1988 [1]:117–21). This change both enhanced and endangered Uncas's leadership. His community had many new members, yet many had fought against Uncas in the Pequot War. He was now obliged to legitimize his authority as sachem among many former enemies. He also faced new challenges from former Narragansett allies who opposed his growing prominence. The ways in which Uncas faced these challenges gives us insights into the variety of political strategies available to leaders, the ways different strategies were employed, and the circumstances under which different options were chosen.

Uncas chose a number of strategies to legitimize himself as sachem to the new members of the Mohegan community, as well as to his English allies and to competing Native groups. He cultivated his relationship with the Connecticut Colony, especially with Mason, by offering continued military assistance, by selling land (some of which was Mohegan land), and by providing information, some of which was true. He signed an agreement in 1640 that has been variously interpreted but that at least gave the English exclusive rights to purchase Mohegan land. One year later he sold a large tract around Guilford that had belonged to the Hammonasset community, and in 1659 he deeded all his lands to his ally and staunchest defender, John Mason.[6]

Shortly after the Pequot War, Uncas attempted to broaden his base of English allies and to answer Narragansett charges that he was harboring Pequots, slandering Miantonomi, and "carrying away the [Pequot] people and their treasure which belong to yourselves [the English]" (R. Williams 1988 [1]:150, 157–59). On June 5, 1638, he arrived in Boston with thirty-seven of his men and his English ally John Haynes, and presented Governor Winthrop with twenty fathoms of wampum. The Massachusetts Bay Council refused to accept his gift at first, citing problems with reports that Uncas was harboring Pequots. But two days later the English had "received good satisfaction of his innocence" and the two parties reached an agreement. By this agreement Uncas "promised to submit to the order of the English touching the Pequods he had, and the differences [conflicts] between the Narragansett and him" (Winthrop 1908:271).

Upon taking his leave, Uncas made a speech to Governor Winthrop expressing his loyalty with what seems like considerable hyperbole but which may have been conventional Native oratory (Bragdon 1987):

> This heart (laying his hand upon his breast) is not mine but yours; I have no men; they are all yours; command me in any difficult thing; I will do it; I will not believe any Indian's words against the English; if any man shall kill an Englishman, I will put him to death, were he never [sic] so dear to me. So the governor gave him a fair, red coat, and defrayed his and his men's diet, and gave them corn to relieve them homeward and a

letter of protection to all men, etc., and he departed very joyful. (Winthrop 1908 [1]:271)

Uncas had reason to be joyful. By establishing friendly relations with the Bay Colony, he now had allies to the west and north of the Narragansetts, although the strength and utility of his most recent alliance had yet to be tested. He was now in direct competition with the Narragansetts for English allies. Uncas was now better positioned to take advantage of any strain in the Massachusetts Bay–Narragansett relationship.

Uncas used this alliance to attack and to defend himself from his Native enemies. The English were often quite willing to assist him, especially when doing so coincided with their own interests. It was English intervention that rescued Uncas from Narragansett-led attacks in 1645 and 1657 (De Forest 1851:211–18, 253; Winthrop 1908 [2]:157; 1929–47 [5]:19–20). The English even assisted Uncas in forcing Pequots to accept his authority. Shortly after the Pequot War, the Connecticut militia was retrieving Pequots who had failed, according to Uncas, to go to or remain with the Mohegans (Mason in Orr 1897:40–41).

Their ignorance of Native languages, their limited contacts among more remote Native groups, and the difficulty in verifying information made the English more susceptible to false rumors than were Native allies (Burton 1976:77). Uncas took advantage of this vulnerability by conducting an effective smear campaign against the Narragansetts, whom he accused constantly of conspiring with other groups, notably the Mohawks, against the English (R. Williams 1988 [1]:241–43; Winthrop 1908 [2]:6; 1929–47 [4]:418–19). Eventually some of the English, like John Winthrop, realized that "all this might come out of the enmity . . . between Miantonomo and Uncas, who continually sought to discredit each other with the English" (Winthrop 1908 [2]:75–76). Still, Uncas's repeated accusations did foster mutual suspicion and fear between the English and Narragansetts, which helped to unravel the English–Narragansett alliance and assisted Uncas in involving the United Colonies in the murder of the Narragansett sachem, Miantonomi, in 1643.[7]

The Politics of Religion

Despite their cooperation with the English in military matters, the Mohegans did not accede to all English designs. Led by Uncas, they effectively resisted English missionary efforts. Their success is evident in a complaint by Cotton Mather, who wrote to the Connecticut General Assembly in 1718 that "it has appeared a matter of no little grief and shame unto many considerate minds, among us as well as among yourselves, that in the very heart of a colony reknowned for the profession of Christianity, there should for fourscore years together be a body of the aboriginals persisting in the darkest and most horrid paganism" (Mather 1971:265).

James Fitch, pastor of the English church in Norwich, attempted to Christianize the Mohegans from 1660 to the end of the seventeenth century with little success. Foremost among the obstacles facing Fitch was Uncas. In 1674 Gookin wrote, "I am apt to fear, that a great obstruction unto his [Fitch's] labours is the sachem of those Indians, whose name is Unkas, an old and wicked, willful man. . . . who hath always been an opposer and underminer of praying to God" (Gookin 1970:108). Fitch's letter to Gookin of November 20, 1674 describes an incident in a previous year in which Uncas opposed the missionary very actively.

> These [Uncas and other Mohegan leaders] at first carried it [preaching] teachably and tractably; until at length the sachems did discern that religion would not consist with a mere receiving of the word; and that practical religion will throw down their heathenish idols, and the sachems' tyrannical monarchy and then the sachems, discerning this, did not only go away, but drew off their people, some by flatteries and others by threatenings, and they would not suffer them to give so much as an outward attendance to the ministry of the word of God. (Gookin 1970:109)

The scene described is interesting in two respects: It shows that Uncas had various tools of persuasion at his command, among them peaceful persuasion and threats; and it reveals that Uncas and the other sachems apparently did not object to the preaching until it threatened their "heathenish idols" and "tyrranical monarchy." The mention of "heathenish idols" may simply reflect the values of the missionary, or may in fact refer to real materials used in religious contexts. In any case, once a threat to traditional authority was perceived, the sachems acted quickly through "flatteries" and "threatenings" to prevent the mission's success.

It should be no surprise that missionaries were resisted by powerful sachems such as Uncas, Massasoit, and the Narragansett leadership. It is also no surprise that missionaries were most successful among groups that had already been subject to epidemics, loss of their land base, and political subjugation, such as the Massachusetts after their submission to the Massachusetts Bay Colony (Salisbury 1974:30). As Brenner (1980:139) summarizes, Native groups that were able to maintain their lands, resources, and sociopolitical organization resisted conversion. In return for conversion, Natives were promised land, housing, subsistence, medical services, and trade items. I would add that some conversions were undertaken for political motives within Native society (see Jennings 1975:239–41, 243–44).

Conversion did not necessarily entail the destruction of Native political roles. Brenner has shown that leaders of the Christian Indian communities were either sachems or their close relatives and that these leaders engaged in external political activities, including the continuation of traditional alliances and enmities (Brenner 1980:142–45). However, the leaders of Christian Indian communities were obliged to share power and tribute with English authorities, to whom they were clearly subordinate. In contrast, Uncas dealt with the English on a more equal footing and with much greater autonomy. Although community leaders might retain much of their authority under the missionary system, the authority of principal sachems of large confederations with extensive interests would be undermined by the missions.

The Politics of Marriage

One of the strategies Uncas used to consolidate his authority both within the Mohegan community and among its new allies and tributaries was to create marriage and kinship ties. This strategy was based on a belief that marriage and kinship were equated with alliance and amicability, and that groups allied by marriage could share privileges and responsibilities. Thus, marriage could be used to acquire political office, to validate status, to inspire allegiance, or to claim new privileges (E. Johnson 1993:164–87).

Relationships based on marriage or kinship were not always amicable, as the relationship of the brothers-in-law Uncas and Sassacus shows.[8] Yet when Uncas began to compete with other Native groups for Pequot survivors and for alliances with their former tributaries, his efforts were probably helped by his marriage to the late sachem's sister. To further strengthen his claim, Uncas made another marriage only months after the Pequot War to one of the wives of his late father-in-law, the former Pequot sachem. As a political strategy, this marriage succeeded; Roger Williams (1988 [1]:146) wrote that it was "one reason . . . that [Uncas] hath drawn all the scattered Pequots to himself."

Uncas continued to marry high-ranking Pequot women. In the spring of 1638, he sent a delegation to Boston to buy or ransom a Pequot woman whom he intended to marry. His offer of ten fathoms of wampum was equivalent to the maximum bride-price for a sachem's daughter, according to Roger Williams (1973:206). By 1640 Uncas reportedly had an unprecedented six or seven wives and had just married a daughter of the Pawtucket squaw sachem (R. Williams 1988 [1]:168–69, 202). This extraordinary series of marriages to some of the highest-ranking women from the Pequots and other communities was an important part of Uncas's effort to legitimize his claim to leadership of former Pequots and their former allies and tributaries.

The Politics of Coercion

War, violence, or the threat of violence were another set of political strategies available to communities and their leaders. Since violence was only legitimized by community consent, it was used cautiously and judiciously. The successful use of force (for example, the execution of a murderer or an attack on a rival community) demonstrated the sachem's ability to mold group consensus, the cohesiveness of his or her group, and the relative strengths of the sachem's group and the opposition.

Just as subordinate groups could use war to change their status, as the Mohegans did in the Pequot War, a war or raid could also reinforce a dominant group's position. The purpose of such a war was to make a statement; usually few people were killed. An example of such a raid is the Mohegans' attack on the Pequot community at Nameag, the ancestors of the Mashantucket Pequots. Uncas claimed authority over this group; they resisted that claim and brought in their own English ally—John Winthrop, Jr., who had founded a settlement there in 1646. The following year Uncas sent 300 warriors to attack the Pequots.

Several accounts show that the intent was to rob, vandalize, insult, and humiliate rather than to exterminate. A petition written by New London settlers noted:

And soe [the 300 Mohegans] fell upon the [Nameag] indians presentlye tearing up there wigwoms cutinge And sloshinge and beatinge in a sore maner which was A sad sighte to the beholders takinge there wompum there skins there baskets tearing there breaches there hose from there legs there showes from there feete forcinge them in the water and there shootinge at them allsoe forcinge into English mens houses also carding away A great deal of mr. Winthrops wompum. (Winthrop 1929–47 [5]:111–12)

Another document written by New London colonists stated:

We the Inhabitants of Nameag do solemnely protest the late inrode by Uncas and his Crue upon the indians in this place in Robbing all their wigwams and depriving them of their necessaries for their very life in this very depth of winter as their coats shoes stockins corne beanes hatchets whereby they should provide firing also their kettles and breaking their pots they should boyle all their meate in beside all their traies dishes matts baggs sacks baskets they lye upon, and all their wampam, wounding divers men and women and stripping old, and yong. (Winthrop 1929–47 [5]:124)

The attack was met with virtually no opposition and the Mohegans could have slaughtered many. Yet none of the accounts, despite their tone of outrage and lengthy lists of offenses, mentions the killing of even one person. Clearly, the goal of this attack was to make a statement of political dominance. The stated motive for this attack was to punish Pequot trespass into Mohegan hunting territories (Winthrop 1908 [2]:287). But Uncas, perhaps more than anyone, knew the potential value of English allies, and rightly saw the new relationship between his erstwhile tributaries and the new English settlement as a threat to the tributary relationship between the Mohegans and the Nameag Pequots. In this regard it should be noted that Uncas's closest English ally, John Mason, was a political and economic competitor of John Winthrop, Jr. Perhaps the interests of both the Mohegans and the English faction that most strongly supported them were in convenient coincidence in this matter.

When the commissioners of the United Colonies, who were meeting in New Haven, were told of this incident, they sent for Uncas and scolded him. Apparently the commissioners were most concerned over the destruction and theft of English property and the danger of such activities to the English, for in dragging Pequots out of the English houses, the

Mohegan warriors frightened the English women and children (Winthrop 1929–47 [5]:111–12). Admitting, in turn, that he had done wrong, Uncas "promised to go to the *English* [emphasis added] there, and acknowledge his offence and make full satisfaction, and for time to come, would live peaceably with them" (Winthrop 1908 [2]:287).

Moreover, the English, especially the Winthrops, were also concerned for their new Indian allies. John Winthrop, Sr. (1929–47 [5]:82–83) wrote directly to Uncas, telling him quite frankly that he (Uncas) was indebted to the English for protection from the Narragansetts and that if he threatened other Indians helpful to the English (namely, Cassacinamon and the Nameag Pequots), the English would not defend him against the Narragansetts.

Shortly after this incident (July 1647), the Pequots petitioned the United Colonies, requesting that they be assigned a place to live under the protection of the English where they might be free of the tyrannies of Uncas (which they enumerated at length). The commissioners denied this request; however, John Winthrop, Jr. and John Mason negotiated an agreement between Uncas and Cassacinamon whereby the Pequots agreed to pay Uncas tribute (the amount to be agreed upon by the English and Uncas), and Uncas agreed not to molest the Pequots. The following year the commissioners considered the matter again and determined that the Pequots should remain in "subjection to" Uncas, that "Uncas shall have order and liberty by constraint to enforce them," and that the English of Nameag should not oppose, interfere, or hide Indians or their goods in their houses. Later that year, commissioner Edward Hopkins wrote to John Mason reiterating the commissioners' decision and affirming that Uncas had "leave by violence" to enforce his authority on the Pequots of Nameag, but at the same time charging that "Uncas doe not rule over them with rigor, or in a tiranicall manner but so as they may have noe just occasion to complaine" (NPNER [1]:97–103, 111–12; Winthrop 1929–47 [5]:131, 281–82).

The next Pequot petition to the commissioners met with more but still only partial success. This was brought by John Winthrop, Jr. in July of 1649. In the petition, Winthrop asked that the Indians around his area be allowed to live free from Uncas's rule (or the rule of Ninigret or the Narragansetts) and that "they may live under the shadow of English Justice free from tyrany and oppression." The commissioners decided that Connecticut could set aside a place for the Nameag Pequots to live, but stopped short of detaching them from Uncas. Instead, they instructed

Uncas to "carry himself towards them in a loving way and doe not tiranise over them" (De Forest 1851:242; NPNER [1]:145–46; Winthrop 1929–47 [5]:354).

In many of these negotiations among the Mohegans, Pequots, and the colonies of Massachusetts Bay and Connecticut, and in many other meetings with English representatives, Uncas declined to participate directly, preferring to be represented by a Mohegan named Foxon. For example, it was through "Foxon who wayted all this meeting on the behalfe of Uncas" that Uncas was advised to carry himself towards the Pequots in a loving way (NPNER [1]:146). Foxon appears to have been an individual skilled in language and diplomacy, not a sachem, who had nevertheless attained a high position based on his ability to serve his community.

With the assistance of Foxon, Uncas and the Mohegans kept the Pequots under their authority until 1655. It was only then, after the Pequots had assisted the United Colonies in a brief war against Ninigret and the Niantics and after many of the Pequots living among the Niantics had moved in with the Nameag and Paucatuck communities, that the Pequots were given their reservation and their independence from Uncas. In order to assuage Uncas, the commissioners further enacted that any Pequots wishing to go back among the Mohegans should be forgiven any debts of wampum, that Cassacinamon must not attempt to lure away those Pequots who chose to remain with Uncas, and that the Pequots must not trespass on Mohegan hunting or fishing grounds (De Forest 1851:244–48).

The Politics of Trade and Tribute

An important reason for these political struggles among Native communities and confederations was competition for the fur and wampum trades. In the course of the seventeenth-century, the native exchange system was transformed in ways that had profound political consequences. New goods entered the system, coming from European sources who represented potential allies. In many cases it was the prospect of new alliances more than the utility of the goods themselves that made trade so desirable. Another important reason to trade for European goods was that redistribution within the community was one of the most important ways for sachems to legitimate their positions. Sachems were thus under pressure to maintain or increase the flow of trade goods, and the key to obtaining such goods was furs. When local fur supplies were depleted, the Natives of southern

New England sustained trade by making or acquiring wampum, which could then be traded for furs.

Wampum, a traditional item of exchange, was transformed in both its significance and its abundance. The growing political tensions and conflicts of the seventeenth century demanded intensified alliance building, and this required larger supplies of wampum, which served as traditional gifts to allies. In addition, the English, who were using wampum as currency, exacted large payments of wampum from their Indian allies. Because of these demands, wampum production soared, and various groups, both Native and European, struggled for control of wampum production and distribution.

The flood of wampum and European goods into the traditional redistribution system, the demands made by allies both Native and European, and the increasing competition for wampum strained and in some cases transformed traditional values and behaviors in both exchange and politics. In particular, the relationship changed between powerful communities or confederations and their tributaries. Once predicated on reciprocal obligations that benefited both recipient and tributary, the relationship became more exploitative. Eventually many sachems, Uncas included, began to use coercion and extortion to acquire wampum from their subordinate allies.

The Nameag Pequots complained of such treatment in 1646, protesting that they had given Uncas wampum forty times over a period of less than ten years, and had sent wampum to the English through him twenty-five times, without knowing whether it had been delivered. They further complained that "when Uncus had a child dyed, he made an offering and gave his wife a gift, and commanded the Pequats to doe the like. They being afraid collected 100 fathome of wampan and gave it as a present, which pleased Uncus, and he promised thence forward to esteeme them as Mohegens" (NPNER [1]:98). This and similar complaints brought against Uncas during the 1640s and 1650s suggest that outside of the core Mohegan communities, Uncas used coercion to extort goods that were then redistributed among his supporters (De Forest 1851:231).

Conclusion: The Politics of History

Such actions were controversial, as were many actions Uncas took, including marrying seven high-ranking women, participating in the murder of

Miantonomi, and allying with the English. Uncas was a controversial figure in his own time, and contradictory portraits of him emerged immediately in the writings of his contemporaries. To his friend and ally John Mason, Uncas was a man of exceptional bravery and "a great Friend" (Mason in Orr 1897:25). To the missionary Daniel Gookin, to whom Uncas represented an obstacle to Christianity, he was a "wicked, willful man, a drunkard and otherwise very vitious" (Gookin 1806:108).

Nineteenth-century historians, captivated by Uncas's role as a consistent ally of the English, presented a more favorable picture of the man. William Stone (1842) described Uncas as "brave and fearless, the white man's friend," and "the great Indian benefactor." The establishment of the Uncas memorial in Norwich, Connecticut, in 1842 by its white, middle-class women citizens culminated in ceremonies in which he was described as generous, of good faith, and of a lofty and chivalrous character (Handsman 1990:2). Frances Caulkins (1874:117) noted Uncas's talent, wisdom, and "persevering activity in securing the independence of his tribe." John De Forest was one exception: acknowledging Uncas's courage and intelligence, he wrote, "He favored his own men and was therefore popular with them; but all others who fell under his power he tormented with continual exactions and annoyances. His nature was selfish, jealous, and tyrannical; his ambition was grasping, and unrelieved by a single trait of magnanimity" (De Forest 1851:86).

Today, Uncas is viewed widely as a self-serving collaborator. John Sainsbury (1971:122) describes his career as one of "extortion and petty crime," and goes on to say, "He stands as one of the first and most successful real-estate agents on the North American frontier." Francis Jennings (1975:268) writes of Uncas "grovelling" to the English. However, Burton (1976:232) disagrees, noting that Uncas was often contemptuous of his allies.

To the Mohegans, Uncas is a hero. Their view is best understood in the light of Native political organization. Uncas, like all sachems, was a servant of his people. He cooperated with the English for the most part on his own terms, in the interests of the Mohegan community, and with its consent and support. With Uncas's guidance, the Mohegans went from a small, subordinate community to a dominant regional power within a span of twenty years. If he acted selfishly, it was towards subordinate communities at a time when relationships between dominant and subordinate communities were changing, and when sachems other than Uncas also violated traditional rules of behavior in this area.

The story of Uncas is perhaps surprisingly one of resistance, but of resistance of a different form than the more easily recognized resistance of Miantonomi or Metacom. If we look past the military cooperation with the English, which benefited the Mohegans as much if not more than the English, we find that Uncas effectively resisted English encroachment on Mohegan lands and successfully defied Puritan missionary efforts (Burton 1976:139–46). By the end of King Philip's War, the Mohegans were one of very few Native communities in the region that had avoided invasion by English troops and had retained their guns, much of their land, their religion, and their political autonomy. By these measures, the Mohegans, through their sachem Uncas, resisted the forces of colonialism. That the Mohegan community survives today is a testament to four centuries of struggle by many Mohegan men and women, not the last or least of whom was Uncas.

Notes

I would like to thank Bob Grumet, Arthur Keene, Dena Dincauze, Neal Salisbury, Barry O'Connell, and Rita Reinke for their helpful comments and encouragement.

1. De Laet in Jameson 1909:42–43. A map attributed to Adrian Block shows "Morhicans" on the west side of the Thames River and "Pequats" on the west bank of the Mystic River. See Salisbury 1982: 82, 263 and Weinstein 1991.

2. "The Genealogy of Uncas" is found in Trumbull (1885:101–4). This document was created by Uncas in 1679, with English legal assistance, in order to justify his claims to Pequot territory long after his rivals were dead. For these reasons, Salisbury (1982:289) cautions against uncritical use of the genealogy.

3. Tatobem (sometimes known as Wopeqworrit) is the first Pequot principal sachem about whom much is known. The Dutch purchased land around Hartford, Connecticut from him in 1632. The Dutch commander at Fort New Hope, which was built on the present site of Hartford, ordered him killed while holding him as a hostage in 1634. See De Forest 1851:72–73; O'Callaghan 1855 (1):149–51; Salisbury 1982:210.

4. See R. Williams 1988 (1):117. The adjustment uses the formula in Salisbury 1982:26.

5. The most successful recent attempts to understand Native actions in their cultural and political contexts include Brenner 1984; Burton 1976; Burton and Lowenthal 1974; E. Johnson 1993; Metcalf 1974; Robinson 1990; Salisbury 1982; Thomas 1979.

6. See De Forest 1851:182–84, 292. For a more detailed account of Mohegan land sales, see Weinstein 1991.

7. On the death of Miantonomi, see NPNER (1):10 and Winthrop 1908 (2):134–35. Secondary sources include E. Johnson 1993:193 and Sainsbury 1971.

8. John Mason (in Orr 1897:24) noted that "they [have] many times some of their near Relations among their greatest Foes."

CHAPTER THREE

♒

Wyandanch:
Sachem of the Montauks

John A. Strong

Introduction

WYANDANCH, WHO WAS BORN at Montauk on eastern Long Island at about
the time of the Pilgrims' arrival, became an important intermediary between the Algonquian communities and the English. From his first meeting with Lion Gardiner, the English commander at Fort Saybrook, immediately after the devastating defeat of the Pequots in 1637 and until his
death in 1659, Wyandanch played a major role in Indian affairs on Long
Island. The evolution of his role as broker between the two cultures, each
with its distinct values and systems of social organization, provides some
important insights into developing institutions on the colonial frontier.

Before the arrival of the Europeans, the Algonquian peoples on Long
Island lived in scattered village communities along the banks of freshwater
streams near tidal estuaries and saltwater bays (Salwen 1978:164; Strong
1983:7–45). These communities were linked in an intricate web of kinship
relations which was continuously reinforced through exogamous marriage
customs. This network, which extended across the sound to the Mohegan-
Pequot, Narragansett, and Niantic peoples of southern New England,
served as a basis for social, political, and economic interaction (Goddard
1978a:72; Smith 1950:110–16; L. Williams 1972:5).

These villages would, on occasion, form temporary associations beyond
the village level. An influential sachem would negotiate a temporary alli-

48

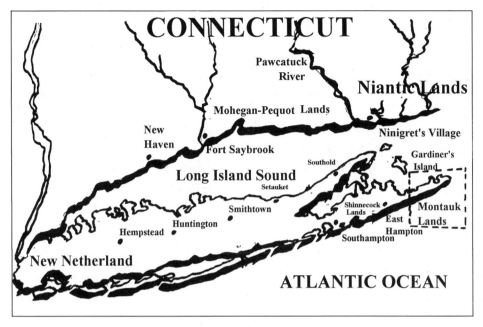

Southern New England and Long Island, 1650. Drawn by David Bunn Martine, Shinnecock Reservation

ance with several neighboring villages to join in a great hunt or form a war party. These alliances generally dissolved once the goal was either accomplished or hopelessly frustrated. Military alliances appear to have been more common after the Dutch and English settlements were established. Tribal systems did emerge, as we shall see, as a response to European presence in the seventeenth century, and Wyandanch was to play a significant role in this development.

As the English and Dutch settlements expanded, they came into direct conflict with one another, first in the Connecticut Valley and later on Long Island.[1] The English challenged the Dutch attempts to develop a trade route along the Connecticut River and later sent Lion Gardiner, a professional soldier and military architect, to build a fort at Saybrook on the mouth of the Connecticut River. The intrusion of the two contending European powers into the Native American political arena upset the existing alliances and forced many tribes to establish new external relationships for security and trade. In these increasingly unstable times, local sachems had to keep a wary eye on a complex and continually shifting political scene.

When the English crushed the Pequot resistance in the spring of 1637,

New England sachems had to seek some form of accommodation with the victors. The dramatic and devastating massacre of the Pequot village near Mystic had demonstrated vividly the potentials of English technology and military organization. The Montauks, close relatives and tributaries of the Pequots who had depended on them for protection, also looked to the English for security. The New England Algonquians had given tacit submission to whichever English colony claimed their territory. Uncas, the Mohegan sachem, had already committed himself to the English in Connecticut; Miantonomi, the Narragansett sachem, had allied himself with Massachusetts Bay; and Ninigret, the Niantic leader, formed an alliance with Roger Williams in Rhode Island.

These alliances between the English and the Algonquian peoples brought together two sharply contrasting systems. The sachems, unlike their English counterparts, governed by persuasion and had limited control over their followers. As Richard White (1991:36–40) has pointed out, the Europeans had to create a new political office among the Algonquians, which he called the "alliance chief." To establish this position, Europeans gave friendly sachems goods to redistribute and military support when necessary. The role of the alliance chiefs was to mediate disputes between their own followers, to keep in fairly close touch with the English, to prevent any of their group from harming the English or their property, and to negotiate land sales.

"To Augment their owne Kingdom": Alliances and Intrigue on the Middle Ground

When Wyandanch first learned of the Pequot massacre on May 26, 1637, he went to Lion Gardiner at Fort Saybrook to assure the English that, in spite of their kinship and historic ties with the Pequots, the Montauks wanted friendly relations with the victors (Gardiner in Orr 1897:137–38). Gardiner told the Montauk sachem that he had to show good faith by helping the English troops hunt down all of the Pequots on Long Island who had killed Englishmen. According to rumor, Sassacus and a large number of Pequots had fled to Long Island.

Gardiner's charge to Wyandanch put him in a difficult position, because Pequots and close relatives of Pequots could be found in nearly every village on eastern Long Island. A purge of these people could result in near chaos. One of the Long Island sachems who protected Pequots was Youghco (later called Poggatacut), an influential elder sachem closely related to Wyandanch who lived on Shelter Island (Munhausett) in Peconic Bay, a short distance from the Montauk villages. Youghco did not oppose an alliance with the English, but he was unwilling to cooperate in the killing of Pequots.

When Gardiner asked Wyandanch to kill an influential sachem who had allegedly slain two Englishmen, the Montauk sachem replied that Youghco would not allow the execution (Gardiner in Orr 1897:146). Wyandanch may have faced similar opposition to the killing of Pequot refugees who had fled to Long Island. He apparently resolved the dilemma by joining with the English troops in pursuit of the fleeing Pequots in southern New England. Wyandanch presented Gardiner with twelve trophy heads, which he may have taken when he was serving under English command.[2] In so doing he avoided any direct conflict with Long Island sachems such as Youghco.

During the next two months, as English troops pursued remnants of the Pequot across southern Connecticut, more Long Island sachems made overtures to the English. One sunksquaw from Long Island apparently tried to establish alliances with the Narragansetts and the English by sending them both wampum tribute.[3] Two other Long Island sachems went directly to the English and worked out an agreement, apparently that summer. The sachems agreed to become tributaries to both the Connecticut and Massachusetts Bay Colonies in exchange for military protection. The treaty is mentioned in a letter from John Winthrop, Sr. to William Bradford, but unfortunately no copy has survived. Although no sachems were named in the letter, it is very likely that one of them was Wyandanch (Ales 1979:31; Winthrop 1908 [1]:231; 1929–47 [3]:457). The other sachem was probably Youghco, who may have been willing to accept tributary status with the English as long as he did not have to antagonize Miantonomi or Ninigret unnecessarily or shed Pequot blood. The sachems would pay wampum to both colonies, but Massachusetts Bay was to receive twice as much as Connecticut.

The Long Island sachems believed that they would receive the same protection that they had received as tributaries to the Pequots. The English colonies, however, were very reluctant to become involved in disputes between Native American sachems unless some clear interest of a particular colony was at stake. The protection anticipated by Wyandanch and his allies, therefore, was unlikely to come unless it would also serve the policy interests of one or more of the English colonies.

It is important to note that the complex political affairs in southern New England and Long Island can not be simplified into "English" and "Algonquian" interests because both groups were divided into sharply contentious factions. The colonies were constantly feuding among themselves over boundary lines, and the Algonquian sachems engaged in intricate schemes to strengthen their power and influence at the expense of their rivals. Israel Stoughton wrote to John Winthrop, Sr. in July, 1637 warning that the sachems were "so eagerly sett upon their own ends, to gett booty etc. and to augment their owne Kingdom etc., that upon the matter they use us as their stalking horse . . . " (Winthrop 1929–47 [3]:442).

The tangle of conflicting interests became evident in the late spring of 1638 when Ninigret, leading a war party of eighty men, came across the sound to convince Wyandanch that he should ally his people with the Niantics instead of with Connecticut and Massachusetts Bay.[4] Ninigret was attempting to take advantage of what he believed was a power vacuum on Long Island. He hoped to break the newly formed alliance between the two English colonies and the Montauks and to draw the former Pequot tributaries into an alliance with his Niantics. It was a daring plan that would strengthen his position against his rivals, Uncas and Miantonomi. It was also one way sachems had expanded their power and influence in the past.

Shortly after he landed on Long Island, Ninigret sent a delegation to Wyandanch urging him to abandon the English alliance and accept a tributary status with the Niantic (Ales 1979:32; Winthrop 1929–47 [4]:43–44). Wyandanch refused and went into hiding to avoid capture. Ninigret caught him and pressed the Montauk sachem to reconsider, arguing that the Connecticut and Massachusetts Bay Colonies would take their wampum but would not protect them as well as he would. The Englishmen, he said, "are liars they doe it but only to gett your wampum." The English of Connecticut, said Ninigret, "will speak much but doe little," and the Massachusetts Bay English could be paid off with wampum (Ales 1979:32; Winthrop 1929–47 [4]:43–44).

When Wyandanch refused again to abrogate his alliance with the English, Ninigret humiliated him by stripping him in front of his people, seizing thirty fathoms of wampum and other goods, and burning several wigwams. The Niantics then attacked several neighboring villages, finally convincing some Montauk elders to accept his terms. Ninigret demanded future payments in corn and wampum as the terms of the alliance.

Wyandanch immediately went to Windsor, where he told his story to Roger Ludlow and demanded that the wampum be recovered. According to Ludlow, the Montauk sachem made a compelling argument. How can I pay tribute to the English, asked Wyandanch, if they allow the Niantics or others to steal it from me at will? Ludlow agreed and ordered John Mason, the commander who had led the troops against the Pequots, to take an armed guard of eight men to confront Ninigret. The Niantic sachem, acting upon the advice of Roger Williams, reached a peaceful accommodation with Mason and paid back the wampum.

The following spring two English settlements, Southampton and Southold, were established on the eastern end of Long Island, several miles west of the Montauk lands. The Southampton settlers negotiated a treaty with Mandush, the sachem from Shinnecock, and several others who apparently represented neighboring villages. Mandush and his colleagues, probably thinking about Ninigret's raid, made sure that the treaty included a clause which read, "the above named English shall defend us the said Indians from the unjust violence of whatever Indians shall illegally assaile us" (Pelletreau 1874–1910 [1]:12–14). The second group of settlers established Southold near the Corchaug village on the north fork of the island. Wyandanch, who had close family ties with the sachems in both villages, undoubtedly was pleased because the expanded English presence meant better protection and more trade.

Two years later, according to an account by Lion Gardiner in his brief history of the Pequot War, Wyandanch foiled a dangerous plot against these new English settlements (Gardiner in Orr 1897:140–43). Miantonomi, reported Gardiner, had visited Wyandanch and his elder counselors and told them to stop sending wampum to Connecticut. Wyandanch replied that he did not want his people to suffer the same fate as had befallen the Pequots at Mystic. The Pequots were destroyed because they killed an Englishman, said Miantonomi, but since the Montauks had not done so, they need not fear them.

Wyandanch reported this to Gardiner, who told him to tell the Narragansetts that he needed a month to discuss their proposal with the other Long Island sachems. As soon as Miantonomi left, Gardiner sent Wyandanch with a letter to John Haynes, a wealthy Connecticut settler who was to be elected governor of Connecticut in 1643. Haynes told Wyandanch not to pay any tribute to Miantonomi and informed Gardiner of this in a letter. When a Narragansett delegation returned to Montauk, Gardiner met them and sent them away with a copy of Haynes's letter, telling them to have Roger Williams read it to Miantonomi. Haynes and Gardiner apparently felt that if Williams was informed, he would dissuade Miantonomi.

There is very little documentation about these events other than Gardiner's account. If Williams attempted to intervene, he was not successful; according to Gardiner, Miantonomi came back to Montauk when Wyandanch was away and delivered an address in secret to the Montauk elders, telling them that the Mohawks had joined in an alliance with the Narragansetts to destroy all English settlements. Miantonomi laid out a very specific plan calling for the Montauk to raise 100 men from Shinnecock and another 100 of their own warriors and to prepare for an attack forty days later. The signal for the attack would be three fires, apparently on Block Island, on the given night. The elders, according to Gardiner, endorsed the plan enthusiastically.

When Wyandanch returned, the elders would not reveal the contents of Miantonomi's message. He questioned them several times for three days but was told nothing. Wyandanch then came to Gardiner for advice. It was inappropriate, said Gardiner, for the Narragansett sachem to address the elders when Wyandanch was absent. Clearly Wyandanch did not have the full support of the Montauk elders. An alliance chief was expected to have more control over relations with other Native American communities. Gardiner concluded that Wyandanch's influence over his elders had to be strengthened by English economic and military support.

Gardiner sent Wyandanch back with a strategy to deceive the elders into revealing Miantonomi's plan. Gardiner did not record what the strategy was, but Wyandanch was successful and brought back a full report. Gardiner then wrote to New Haven and Hartford about the conspiracy. Unfortunately, related Gardiner, his boat was not available for several days, and the letter did not arrive until two weeks later. In the meantime, said Gardiner, the Montauk elders discovered that the conspiracy had been reported and sent a canoe over by night to warn Miantonomi to call off the attack.

Shortly after Gardiner's letter arrived in New Haven, Governor Eaton received another conspiracy account from Roger Ludlow, who came from Fairfield, Connecticut, to New Haven with the news (Anonymous 1833

[3]:161–64; Sainsbury 1971:116–17). Ludlow said that a sachem near Fairfield had come to him and told him in confidence about the conspiracy. The sachem said that he would be killed by Miantonomi or his allies if Ludlow revealed his identity. The two accounts were similar in general outline, but Ludlow's account was more detailed.

Connecticut responded to the reports of Miantonomi's conspiracy with an immediate call to arms, but John Winthrop, Sr. wanted to talk directly with Miantonomi before he took any precipitous action. He called the Narragansett sachem to Boston, where he could question him face to face. Miantonomi came and denied that he was involved in any plot against the English. When the Narragansett sachem asked to confront his accusers, Winthrop said that he didn't know who they were. Winthrop probably knew who the informants were but did not call them forward because he did not want a confrontation that might provoke bloodshed. Winthrop was apparently satisfied that Miantonomi had yielded to his authority by coming to Boston at his request and submitting to the interrogation. If Miantonomi had ever entertained any notion of attacking the English, the glare of publicity would force him to abandon the scheme. Winthrop announced that he believed Miantonomi, and the matter was put to rest (Sainsbury 1971:117; Winthrop 1929–47 [2]:76).

The following spring, Miantonomi and Uncas were at war. Uncas defeated the Narragansetts, took Miantonomi prisoner, and reported to the Connecticut authorities for instructions. The English told Uncas they would not object to the execution of Miantonomi as long as it was not done in the English settlements (Sainsbury 1971:119). The Mohegans took the Narragansett sachem away and executed him. Thus Uncas increased his power and influence, but he also reaffirmed his acceptance of Connecticut jurisdiction.

The defeat of Miantonomi must have seriously weakened opposition to Wyandanch among the Long Island sachems. The Montauk sachem took this opportunity to strengthen his alliance with the English by paying the annual tribute in wampum, which had apparently been done irregularly since the agreement in 1638 (NPNER [10]:171). From then on he continued to pay it regularly until Ninigret's raids disrupted the Montauk economy in 1653.

The death of Miantonomi may have prompted four Long Island sachems—Youghco, Wiantause (Wyandanch), Moughmaitow, and Weenagamin—to appear before the September 1644 meeting of the United

Colonies, a confederation formed by Connecticut, Massachusetts Bay, Plymouth, and New Haven, where they negotiated a treaty of friendship.[5] Although the document does not give the location of the groups represented by Moughmaitow and Weenagamin, later documents indicate that the former probably came from Corchaugs on the north fork of Long Island and that the latter may have been from Shinnecock. The commissioners granted the sachems a "certification" that acknowledged the sachems as "tributaries to the English." They pledged not to harm English or Dutch people or their property, and to turn over to the English any of their own people who did so. The United Colonies, however, made no promise to protect the Indians from their enemies.

That same year, according to Gardiner, Ninigret again attempted to interfere in Montauk affairs (Ales 1979:38–39; Drake 1857:74; Gardiner in Orr 1897:143–44). His agent was captured by Wyandanch, who came to Gardiner for instructions. Gardiner advised Wyandanch to send the man to Governor Eaton of New Haven for questioning. Gardiner says that he wrote a letter to Eaton warning him of Ninigret's conspiracy. Bad weather forced Wyandanch's party ashore on Shelter Island, where Youghco's village was located. Youghco made Wyandanch release Ninigret's agent, but allowed the letter to go on to Eaton. There is no mention of the letter in the New Haven records, and the incident is not mentioned by Rhode Island historians.[6] If it is true, the conflict between Wyandanch and Youghco suggests that Ninigret had support among the Long Island sachems and that Youghco was again playing a cautious role by staying neutral.

In 1648, East Hampton, a third settlement, was established on eastern Long Island. The English officials met with Wyandanch and the sachems from neighboring villages to negotiate the purchase of a 31,000 acre tract of Montauk land on the eastern boundary of Southampton.[7] The Shelter Island sachem was the first to sign, suggesting that he held the highest status and led the delegation. He was also the first one mentioned in the 1644 agreement at Hartford. Wyandanch was clearly a minor sachem at the time.

Two other men who played an important role in the negotiations signed the deed. Thomas Stanton, one of the first English colonists to become fluent in the local Algonquian languages, served as interpreter for the English. The Algonquian sachems brought their own interpreter, Cockenoe, who may have been trained by the Massachusetts Bay Colony missionary Reverend John Eliot (Tooker 1896). Cockenoe soon became one of Wyandanch's chief advisors in his dealings with the English.

Soon after the East Hampton deed was signed, nine families arrived and put up the first buildings in East Hampton. According to a local legend recorded in the East Hampton Trustee's Journal, a Montauk hunting party discovered them and the settlers invited them into the houses for a meal. The hunters, apparently unaware of the agreement signed by Wyandanch, returned to their village and made plans to drive the English out. The men went to their sachem, presumably Wyandanch, to approve the attack. The sachem asked them, "Did they invite you into their houses?— They did.—Did they give you [food] to eat?—They did.—Did you experience any harm from what you ate; did it poison you?—It did not." The reply of the sachem, turning to his warriors was, "You shall not cut them off."[8] The account may be apocryphal, but later events indicate clearly that Wyandanch was eager to establish good relations with the English. Any attempts to harm the English would certainly have been opposed by Wyandanch.

In the spring of 1649, Wyandanch demonstrated his diplomatic and political skills as he resolved an ugly conflict between the English in Southampton and the Shinnecocks and used the opportunity to expand his own power base. A white woman was murdered in Southampton, apparently in retaliation for the Shinnecock killed by the English six years earlier (Gardiner in Orr 1897:144; Pelletreau 1874–1910 [1]:158). Mandush, the Shinnecock sachem, apparently felt that the woman's death restored Shinnecock honor and that the matter should not be pursued further.

The Shinnecocks' refusal to respond to the demands from Southampton led to an armed stand-off between the two communities. John Gosmer and Edward Howell, the Southampton magistrates, attempted to resolve the crisis by calling on Wyandanch to honor the clause in the 1644 treaty requiring that Indians accused of injury to English people be turned over to the English authorities. Wyandanch consulted Gardiner, who urged him to go to Southampton and capture those responsible for the murder. Gardiner gave the sachem a paper that asked English settlers to grant Wyandanch safe conduct and to provide him and his men with food while he was on a mission for the English.

One man had already been taken by the English, and Wyandanch captured two more. The town officials met with Wyandanch and Mandush, the Shinnecock sachem (Pelletreau 1874–1910 [1]:158). Mandush, who had signed the 1640 deed for Southampton, was apparently convinced by Wyandanch and, undoubtedly, by the presence of so many armed men from Southampton to turn over the accused men and accept Montauk sovereignty. This proved to be a mixed blessing for Wyandanch because, although he now held the right to sell Shinnecock land for his own profit, he was also responsible for Shinnecock behavior. The three accused men were taken to Hartford, where they were tried and hanged by the colonial authorities (Gardiner in Orr 1897:145).

Wyandanch strengthened his political position with his success in resolving a potentially dangerous impasse between the Shinnecocks and the English. The Montauk sachem demonstrated to his people that he had material and military support from the English, which increased his power well beyond that of other sachems. Viewed from the context of Algonquian culture, Wyandanch had exacted blood revenge on those who opposed him. The English were pleased because Wyandanch forced the Shinnecocks to comply with the colonial legal system and assumed responsibility for the sale of Shinnecock land.

Wyandanch and Mandush were called upon again several months later to help settle a dispute between the Town of Southampton and Indians living at Sebonac, a short distance north of the Shinnecock village. The English complained that the Sebonac villagers had continued to plant corn on land that the whites believed they had purchased in 1640, and that their cattle were often injured when they fell into food-storage pits abandoned when wigwams were relocated. The Indians complained that English livestock destroyed their crops. A compromise was reached that called for fences to be constructed, abandoned pits to be filled, and restrictions to be placed on livestock grazing (Strong 1983:69).

At the same time as Wyandanch was increasing his ties with the English, his Algonquian rivals, Uncas and Ninigret, were working to improve their own power bases. The Long Island sachems accused Ninigret of sending an agent to kill Mandush, perhaps because the Shinnecock sachem had formed an alliance with Wyandanch (Ales 1979:50; NPNER [10]:96–97). The Niantic sachem was also accused by John Mason of plotting to assassinate Uncas in the spring of 1649 (Sehr 1977:49). Both plots failed. Mandush captured his assailant when his gun misfired and took him to Wyandanch. The two Long Island sachems brought the Niantic agent to Hartford, where he was tried and found guilty by the colonial court. Connecticut did not execute the man, probably because they did not wish to strain their ties with Ninigret. Instead, they turned the agent over to Wyandanch and Mandush, who killed him and burned the body in a calculated affront to Ninigret (NPNER [10]:98).

By 1650, the Algonquian sachems were engaged in complex and intricate diplomacy that involved shamanism as well as European forms of statecraft. Uncas, perhaps seeking to undermine Wyandanch's growing influence with the Connecticut officials, accused Wyandanch of hiring a shaman to kill some of his men and to bewitch others. Uncas demanded that the United Colonies take action against Wyandanch. The commissioners investigated, but there is no record of any action against the Montauk sachem (NPNER [9]:167). Uncas also accused Ninigret of hiring a shaman to poison him and complained to the United Colonies.

The stakes and tensions increased in 1652, when England and Holland went to war. Although the fighting did not spread to the Atlantic colonies, the two European powers there watched each other warily. Uncas, in an attempt to undermine Ninigret's ties with the English, reported that the Niantic sachem was plotting with the Dutch to attack English settlements. Ninigret and Peter Stuyvesant, the Dutch governor, denied that they had any such intention, but the Long Island towns were not convinced. The English in East Hampton were even more concerned about rumors of Dutch intervention in Montauk affairs. They were alarmed about a rumor that the Dutch, who had been trading guns and powder to the Algonquians, had urged the Montauk to reject Wyandanch and follow a sachem allied with them (Osborne 1887:31).

The East Hampton officials took defensive precautions. In April, 1653 they passed a resolution requiring all Indians to have a permit before entering the town. Guards were set with orders to shoot any Indian who did not identify himself when he approached the village (Osborne 1887:31). The East Hampton settlers were also concerned about protecting Wyandanch from internal and external threats to his status as a sachem. They supported Wyandanch against any attempt by rivals on Long Island to gain influence over the Montauk, but they did not take adequate precautions against the threat from his Niantic rival across Long Island Sound.

Ninigret may have made overtures to the Dutch, but it is unlikely that he would ever have joined in a war against the English. The Niantic sachem was much more interested in seeking some opportunity in the Dutch-English conflict to strengthen his position within the Algonquian communities in southern New England. As later events demonstrate, his primary interest was in eclipsing Wyandanch's influence over the eastern Long Island Indians. According to Roger Williams, Ninigret came to Governor Endicott of Massachusetts Bay early in the spring and asked if he could retaliate against the Montauks for the execution of his agent who had attempted to kill Mandush (NPNER [10]:442). Williams reported that Endicott gave "implicit" approval for Ninigret to "right himself." Endicott probably told Ninigret only that Massachusetts Bay would not interfere in Algonquian matters. The governor apparently had concluded, after the exhaustive inquiry that spring, that the alleged Niantic-Dutch alliance, if it existed, was directed against Uncas, not the English.

Later in the spring, perhaps during the green corn powwow, Ninigret attacked the Montauk village, killing thirty men and capturing fourteen prisoners, including two male sachems and Wyandanch's daughter.[9] One captive was killed and his body burned in revenge for the similar treatment suffered by Ninigret's agent. The United Colonies investigated the incident and discussed an appropriate response at their September 1653 meeting. Connecticut, New Haven, and Plymouth voted to send troops against Ninigret, but Massachusetts Bay vetoed the declaration of war, stating that the English had no obligation to protect Wyandanch and that it was bad policy to get involved in a dispute between the Algonquian sachems (NPNER [10]:99).

Apparently Massachusetts Bay felt that Ninigret's gesture of submission in seeking permission for the attack had satisfied the crucial aspect of their relations with the Niantics. The proper policy now was to let the two sachems resolve the issue. Another attack followed in which several more Montauks were killed and a few captives were taken, but soon after this incident, Ninigret sent a woman to deliver a peace proposal to Wyandanch.

According to Ninigret, Wyandanch sent representatives to the village of a Narragansett sachem named Pessacus, where an agreement was negotiated in front of two English witnesses (NPNER [10]:170). The captives were released, said Ninigret in a later testimony, and Wyandanch acknowledged Ninigret as his chief sachem, with control over all Montauk land. It was the same arrangement that Mandush had made with Wyandanch in 1649. If these were the terms, they held serious implications for the towns of East Hampton and Southampton, because all of the unpurchased Shinnecock and Montauk lands would be under the control of Ninigret. The Niantic sachem might sell the property to purchasers in Rhode Island and Massachusetts Bay.

Wyandanch later repudiated Ninigret's account, stating that he had rejected Ninigret's terms and had, instead, sent him a ransom for the release of the captives. The ransom was paid, said Wyandanch, by Lion Gardiner, who "as a father . . . giving us money and goods . . . ransomed my daughter and friends."[10] Given the clear implications of Ninigret's demands, Gardiner's "generosity" is easy to understand. According to an account by Roger Williams, the captives were restored "upon the mediation and desire of the English," but no other details are mentioned (NPNER [10]:442). The uncertainty about the agreement may have been a factor in a surprise attack launched by the Montauk against a party of Niantics visiting Block Island in September 1654. Ninigret's nephew, two Niantic sachems, and over thirty others were killed by Wyandanch's men.[11] The raid may have been encouraged by the English towns on Long Island because it would dramatically demonstrate Wyandanch's independence from Ninigret.

Wyandanch: The Chief Sachem of "English" Long Island

In the spring of 1655, Wyandanch had problems closer to home. A dispute arose between the Montauk and the settlers in East Hampton over the grazing habits of the English livestock. Cattle frequently invaded Montauk corn fields and destroyed food supplies needed to sustain the people through the winter. Wyandanch and two of his advisors, Sassakata and Pauquatoun, met with Gardiner and several representatives from East Hampton to discuss this issue and to further clarify the larger questions of the unpurchased Montauk lands and Wyandanch's role as an alliance chief (Montauk Indian Deeds: Folder 3).

The conflict over grazing rights was resolved by requiring the English to build and maintain a fence to protect the Montauk fields. The English also promised to pay for damages caused by any livestock that got through the fence during the late spring and summer, when crops were in the ground. In return the Montauks allowed the English cattle and horses to graze at will after the fall harvest and until the time came for the spring planting. In addition, the English were granted access to the salt hay near the wetlands.

As for the threat that Ninigret posed to their rights to the unpurchased lands adjacent to the town, the settlers included a clause in the treaty prohibiting Wyandanch and his successors from selling their land to anyone other than the proprietors of East Hampton. And in addition to having supported Wyandanch's attack on Ninigret, the East Hampton officials gave the Montauk sachem a monopoly on the distribution of alcohol to his

Wyandanch's "stick figure" signature (May 29, 1659) appears on several documents. The figures probably represent Wyandanch's close relationship with the English. From New York Secretary of State, Record of Deeds [2]:152 (New York State Archives series A0453).

people. East Hampton ruled that no Indian may purchase liquor without a "writine ticket" from Wyandanch (Osborne 1887:81). The English also made sure that Ninigret could not regain a military advantage over Wyandanch: they commissioned an armed sloop, under the command of Southold settler John Youngs, to patrol the route across the sound. Youngs was empowered to block any attempt by Ninigret to bring his men across the sound "by taking, sinking, and destroying so many of his canoes . . . as shall come within your power" (Ales 1979:57; NPNER [10]:151). Youngs maintained the blockade for a year and a half and was paid 153 pounds by the United Colonies. In contrast, the missionary John Eliot was paid a yearly stipend of only fifty pounds that same session for his "Indian work" (NPNER [10]:167). The English also sent Wyandanch some lead, presumably to cast into musket balls (NPNER [10]:175). Few Long Island sachems would challenge openly any leader who could draw upon this level of support from the English.

Ninigret, prevented from using traditional means to expand his influence, turned to the English institutions. He sent his agent, Newcom, to the United Colonies meeting in 1656 with several complaints against Wyandanch (NPNER [10]:169). Ninigret had carefully selected charges that he believed would impress the English. Newcom began by accusing Wyandanch of murdering an Englishman named Drake in what must have been an unsolved crime. He next charged that, when Wyandanch attacked Ninigret on Block Island after the settlement, he broke the peace treaty that had resulted in the release of the Montauk prisoners. The third complaint concerned witchcraft, a matter that both cultures took very seriously. Wyandanch was said to have hired a witch to kill Uncas. This latter charge may have been related to the one Uncas himself brought against Wyandanch in 1650.

The United Colonies required Wyandanch to come to Plymouth for questioning. Ninigret and Uncas did not appear at the hearing. The witnesses for the witchcraft charge had either changed their account or did not appear, for no further action was taken. Newcom brought some witnesses who said that they heard an Indian named Wampeague confess that Wyandanch had hired him to kill Drake and steal his goods; one witness confirmed Newcom's charges, but Wampeague did not appear at the hearing. The commissioners dismissed the charge. Newcom then turned to the terms of the settlement between Wyandanch and Ninigret, stating that an Englishman named Robert Wescott had witnessed Wyandanch's surrender on Ninigret's terms, but Wescott did not appear to testify. That charge was also dismissed.

Ninigret's attempt at using the English court system did not work for him in this instance, but the incident provides insight into the developing patterns of accommodation taking place on the New England frontier. Alliance chiefs were becoming more adept at using European institutions to advance their own political agendas, and Newcom showed a great deal of ingenuity and understanding of English court procedures in his use of witnesses and presentation of the charges.

Newcom lost the case against Wyandanch, in part because the English on Long Island testified that the Montauk sachem was both innocent and a good and loyal friend of the settlers. Wyandanch, too, deserves some credit for the decision: his testimony, although not recorded, was so effective that, in addition to winning his case, he was given a respite from his tribute payments, which were four years overdue (NPNER [10]:171).

In the spring of 1657, a serious conflict between settlers and Shinnecocks erupted in Southampton. Several houses were burned, apparently by rebellious Native American and African American servants. The town officials, in a panic, appealed to the Connecticut court at Hartford for aid. They were distressed, they said, "by reason of the insolent and insufferable outrage of some heathen upon that land and near that plantation" (Records of the Connecticut Particular Court 1928 [22]:175–76). On May 11, 1657, the Connecticut court heard their complaints and listened to the testimony of Wigwagub, a Shinnecock, who said that he had been hired to burn down Mrs. Howell's house by two men whom he identified as Awabag and Agagoneagu. Wigwagub said he was promised a gun and seven shillings, six pence. Another man, Auwegenum, had been present when Wigwagub was hired, but his role was not clear. The sparse report in the Connecticut Particular Court records makes no mention of the motive or extent of the conspiracy. One possible cause may have been the destruction of Shinnecock planting fields by English livestock; the Shinnecocks had made this complaint to Wyandanch for several years prior to 1657.

Four days later, the court approved a carefully worded commission sending nineteen men armed with twenty-five pounds of powder and fifty pounds of shot to investigate the incident, under the command of Major John Mason. Mason was told to go with "all convenient speed" to Southampton and meet first with the town magistrates, then with Wyandanch. He was instructed to find out what was done, when, and by whom (CPR [1]:295).

These general orders were followed by detailed instructions about the procedures Mason was to follow. Perhaps fearing that too heavy a hand would provoke more violence, the court told Mason that he must explain his mission to Wyandanch and make certain the Montauk sachem fully understood why the Connecticut troops were there and what their orders were.

Mason, veteran of the Pequot War of twenty years earlier, was told that he must not act independently in an attempt to settle the conflict. If Wyandanch was unwilling to help, Mason was to report back immediately (CPR [1]:295). If the Montauk sachem was willing to help but faced local opposition from his own community, Mason was to assist him with arms. The people responsible for the fire were to be sent to Hartford for trial. Once again, Mason was reminded not to take any independent action and "make after any Indians in the woods" (CPR [1]:295). Clearly, colonial officials wanted the matter settled through the offices of the alliance chief, if possible.

Mason arrived to find that forty townsmen had been issued gunpowder in preparation for a conflict (Pelletreau 1874–1910 [1]:154–55). There is no record of Mason's activities in Southampton, but neither Wigwagub nor anyone else was brought to trial for the arson. The Shinnecocks agreed, undoubtedly with considerable reluctance, to accept an exorbitant fine of 700 pounds sterling to be paid over a seven-year period (NPNER [10]:180). Perhaps the evidence against the men accused by Wigwagub had proved inconclusive, or perhaps they were prominent men whom the community did not wish to surrender. For whatever reason, the issue was resolved by a determination of collective guilt. The sentence is an example of the cultural innovations that took shape during the early contact period; English trial procedures, intended to establish individual guilt and punishment, were often frustrated by cultural differences, as the Algonquians usually protected members by refusing to give them up or by providing alibis.

Ironically the concept of collective guilt, so alien to the English legal system, was more in harmony with the Algonquian value system, where retribution was often exacted against an enemy people for the acts of individual members. The Southampton settlers wanted both punishment and some assurance that the acts of rebellion would cease. The fine was a convenient solution, as it allowed the Shinnecocks to protect the individuals responsible while forcing them into a debt servitude that could be used as both a method of social control and a mechanism to force the sale of Shinnecock land in the future. The seven-year installment plan may have been viewed by the Shinnecocks as a form of yearly tribute.

Wyandanch was responsible for collecting the tribute and paying the Connecticut court because he had accepted control over the Shinnecocks after the murder of the English woman in 1649. The Montauk sachem demonstrated that the role of the alliance chief could be more than that of a passive conduit for English governance when he sent a representative with a written petition to the United Colonies session in Boston the following September to appeal the Connecticut court's sentence (NPNER [10]:180). His decision to go over the head of the Connecticut court and the articulation of his arguments indicated a growing familiarity with English legal institutions.

Wyandanch began by reporting that the Shinnecocks had sustained losses from English horses. Wyandanch was careful not to suggest that the arson was justified because he knew that this would offend the English and weaken his chances of winning the appeal.

Next, he discussed the facts of the arson case, and again was careful not to directly criticize Mason, who had just been elected as a commissioner from Connecticut. Wyandanch reported that Mason had not been fully informed. The houses were burned, said Wyandanch, by "a wicked Indian who wee heare desperately killed himselfe to prevent just execution; and partly by a mischievous Negar woman servant; far deeper in that capitall miscarriage then any or all of the Indians" (NPNER [10]:180). This account is most intriguing, whether true or false. If true, it raises some interesting questions about the African woman who was able to plan and carry out a conspiracy involving Shinnecock Indians. If false, it indicates that Wyandanch may have played astutely on English prejudices against Africans.

There are no records to verify either account of the arson. If Wyandanch's report was an invention, it was well-suited to win support and gain a successful appeal. If the guilty Shinnecock was dead, and the plot had been planned and directed by an African servant, there was no justification for fining the Shinnecock community. The commissioners accepted Wyandanch's explanation, and with Mason's approval they acknowledged that the fine was excessive. The matter was returned to the Connecticut court with a recommendation that the sentence be reviewed.

When he submitted the petition, Wyandanch also sent seventy-eight fathoms of wampum to the United Colonies' treasurer at New Haven to influence the commissioners (NPNER [10]:194). While the matter was pending before the Connecticut court, the town of Southampton paid twenty shillings to Mrs. Howell for damages suffered to her house and ten pounds to Major Mason for his part in protecting the town (Pelletreau 1874–1910 [1]:119). It seems clear that all of the damages done to the town could have been repaired with a small fraction of the fine; the fine was obviously intended to serve as a mechanism for social control.

The Connecticut court took no action until a year later, when they agreed to reduce the fine to 500 pounds over seven years (CPR [1]:316–17). It was still an amount well beyond the means of the Shinnecocks to pay and left them in debt bondage to the English. Although the success of the appeal did little to change the actual impact of the fine on the Shinnecocks, it indicates that Wyandanch was becoming more involved in English political institutions.

Wyandanch's reputation and influence as an alliance chief was now recognized by all of the English settlers on Long Island. In 1657 Wyandanch negotiated land sales in Huntington (Street 1887:10–11) and Mastic (Hutchinson 1887:2–3). His role as a certifying agent for the deeds sets an important precedent that the English hoped would bring some order to the process of land dispossession.

For their part, the English were beginning to realize just how useful a grand sachem could be. In the summer of 1657, according to testimony taken twenty years later, a dispute arose between the English settlers at Hempstead and the sachem Tackapousha about payments due under the 1643 deed. Wyandanch served as an arbitrator in an attempt to resolve the conflict, showing independence from the English by requiring additional payments to Tackapousha and to Mangobe, a sachem from Rockaway (Hicks 1896–1904 [1]:312–13). This indicates a growing sense that Wyandanch, in his role as chief sachem, could provide a mechanism to avoid unnecessary conflict and endless litigation. The endorsement of the "chief sachem" was becoming accepted by the English settlers as a requirement for the purchase of Algonquian land. Near the end of March, 1658 Wyandanch sent his trusted adviser, Cockenoe, to Hempstead with his authorization to mark out the town boundary (Town of North Hempstead Court Proceedings 1657–60:91).

In one instance Wyandanch overreached his authority: he prohibited the Pequots from coming to Long Island to gather shells for wampum. The Pequots, realizing that traditional means of resolving such grievances were no longer possible, brought their case to the United Colonies and asked that their ancient privileges be restored. The commissioners gave notice to Wyandanch that "the Pequots . . . bee permitted to freely fetch shells there . . . as formerly they had done" (NPNER [10]:199–200). They took the opportunity to humble Wyandanch further by reminding him that he was four years behind in tribute payments.

In spite of these minor setbacks, Wyandanch knew that local sachems had to acknowledge his authority when English interests were in harmony with his. This was demonstrated in January 1659, when Wyandanch was called in to settle a dispute over land claims between the Indians at Corchaug and the English at Southold, on the north fork of Long Island. The record of the meeting was kept by the Southold Town clerk, who does not mention the names of the Corchaug Indians or their specific complaint. All we know is that Wyandanch stood forth and proclaimed in a loud voice that the land on the north fork had always been his and that he and his brothers had sold it to the English. Wyandanch was referring to the deed made with Eaton and Goodyear in 1649. According to the clerk, the Corchaug delegation stood silently and accepted Wyandanch's statement.

That same month, Wyandanch brought suit against Jeremy Daily for damage done to his "Great Cannow" (Osborne 1887:152). The vessel, probably used for trips across the sound, may have been thirty to forty feet long; canoes this large were observed by John Smith and John Winthrop. This must have been one of the earliest trials involving an Indian plaintiff and an English defendant in colonial history.

Lion Gardiner testified for Wyandanch against Daily, who was charged with negligence. Daily and Anthony Waters, another East Hampton man, had repaired the canoe, and Daily was given permission to take some goods over to Gardiner's Island with Gardiner's son, David. The two men apparently met with bad weather and did not take the time to secure the canoe when they came ashore on the island. Gardiner met the men, and when he asked them if they had pulled up the canoe, they replied that there was time for that later. According to Gardiner, he took them back to take proper care of the canoe, but the weather was so bad that they could do nothing. When they were finally able to reach the vessel, it had sustained considerable damage and was full of water. The court ruled for the plaintiff and awarded Wyandanch ten shillings for damages. Daily also had to pay one pound and one shilling in court costs.

The last seven months of Wyandanch's life were unusually busy. In addition to this trial, he was involved in eight land transactions and two sales of the rights to beached whales.[12] Prior to that he had negotiated five deeds in 1658, three in 1657, and two with the East Hampton settlers in 1655 and 1648. The sharp increase in land sales, of course, reflects the growth in English population on Long Island. A related factor may have been the devastating epidemic, which according to Lion Gardiner took the lives of nearly two-thirds of the Algonquian population on Long Island (Gardiner in Orr 1897:146).

The last three documents were signed jointly by Wyandanch and his son, suggesting concern about the sachem's longevity. The last deed bearing the marks of Wyandanch, his wife, and his son, Wyancombone, was signed on July 14, 1659. Executed shortly before his death, this document reads more like a will than a deed. Wyandanch granted a tract of land in what is now Smithtown to Lion Gardiner to repay "much kindness of him, not only by counsell and advise in our propertie, but in our great extremytie, when wee were almost swallowed upp by our enemies, then wee say he appeared to us not only as a friend, but as a father, in giving us his monie and goods, whereby wee defended ourselves, and ransomed my daughter and friends, and wee say and know that by his meanes we had great comfort and relief from the most honorable of the English nation heare about us." The land, said Wyandanch, was the only thing of value that he had left to reward Gardiner for his "fatherly love, care and charge" for the past twenty-four years (Paltstits 1910 [2]:408–9).

Wyandanch died later that year. According to Gardiner, the sachem was poisoned, but he gives no further information about the suspected assassin, nor does he suggest a possible motive (Gardiner in Orr 1897:46). The office of grand sachem collapsed with the death of Wyandanch. The sachem's wife and son died shortly afterwards, and his daughter, Quasha-wam, was named sunksquaw over the Montauks and Shinnecocks by the towns of East Hampton and Southampton in 1663, but no attempt was made to assert her authority over the other Long Island sachems. The following year the English conquered New Netherland and established a centralized colonial administration over the towns of Long Island.

The new English governor, Richard Nicolls, saw no need for a chief sachem in the new system. Nicolls assumed the responsibility for supervising all Indian land purchases, and ruled that the title of grand sachem was no longer valid. He issued a resolution stating that "every sachem shall keep his particular property over his people as formerly" (Albany Deed Book 2:127).

Conclusion

Wyandanch spent the last twenty-two years of his life moving adroitly between two cultures. Having witnessed the destruction of the Pequots in 1637, he concluded that military resistance was futile and proceeded to pursue his own interests within the English sphere. In order to expand his influence in the Algonquian communities, Wyandanch obtained the necessary access to English trade goods by agreeing not to harm English persons or property and by accepting English jurisdiction over all Montauks accused of such acts.

Wyandanch gave up a measure of his sovereignty, but he rapidly increased his stature in Algonquian society on eastern Long Island. He served the English by resolving two major disputes between the Shinnecocks and the town of Southampton, but in the process Wyandanch gained control over Shinnecock lands. Although the English were initially reluctant to provide Wyandanch with military protection, they finally agreed to finance an armed patrol blocking Ninigret's route across the sound to Montauk. This show of English support enabled Wyandanch to expand his influence over Algonquian villages throughout eastern Long Island. During the last two years of his life he supervised nearly all of the major land sales as far west as Hempstead and enriched himself in the process.

Another important aspect of Wyandanch's success was his growing familiarity with English legal institutions, which he used to advance his own interests. His rivals, Uncas and Ninigret, became equally adept at operating within the English system. The modern descendants of the eastern Algonquians continue to press their interests in federal, state, and local courts. Contemporary Shinnecocks, Pequots, and Narragansetts have all developed extensive contractual relations with outside public and private agencies, enabling them to maintain and strengthen their Native American identities.

Notes

I am indebted to many colleagues, library archivists, and family members for their support in completing this essay. Gaynell Stone, founder of the Suffolk County

Archaeological Association, first encouraged me to explore the rich seventeenth-century archival sources on eastern Long Island over a decade ago. Dorothy King, archivist for the East Hampton Library, patiently guided me through the relevant primary documents. My wife, Jane, and my daughters, Lisa and Lara, read the rough drafts and provided me with equal measures of criticism and comforting support.

1. The English never recognized the legitimacy of the Dutch enterprise. Soon after the Dutch built a small trading facility on Manhattan in 1613, an English vessel commanded by Captain Samuel Argall stopped and demanded that the Dutch submit to the jurisdiction of the Governor of Virginia and pay a token tax to him (O'Callaghan 1855 [1]:69). The Dutch responded by sending out more ships to explore and map the coastal waters from Manhattan to Narragansett Bay. When the United Netherlands issued a charter to the Dutch West India Company in 1621, Argall, who was then governor of Virginia, joined others in appealing to King James I to stop the Dutch colonization plans. King James protested the Dutch action and asserted English possession of the area in question. The Dutch ignored the King's protest and proceeded to develop the trading post on Manhattan into a colony. The eastern end of Long Island was a primary area of contention until 1650, when the Dutch accepted an eastern boundary line just east of Hempstead.

2. Gardiner said that Wyandanch went away and sent him "five heads, three, and four heads for which I paid them that brought them as I had promised" (Gardiner in Orr 1897:138). There are several references indicating that Wyandanch participated in a "search and destroy" campaign following the massacre at Mystic. According to Gardiner, Wyandanch took part in the "Swamp Fight," the last stand of the Pequots (Gardiner in Orr 1897:136). Richard Davenport, an Englishman on the trail of Pequots, sailed to Long Island, where he reported picking up a sachem, who may have been Wyandanch. The sachem was eager to help the Englishmen track down Pequots. Davenport's men killed nine Pequots, seven men and two women, near Quinnipiac, and later took part in the Swamp Fight (Winthrop 1929–47 [3]:452).

3. Cf. Winthrop (1929–47 [3]:442) and Ales (1979:30). In a letter from Israel Stoughton to John Winthrop, Sr. dated July 6, 1637, the sunksquaw was reported to have 200 warriors under her command. She sent ten fathoms to Miantonomi, ten to Canonicus, and ten to the English. Her gifts to the sachems may have been related to her coming marriage to another Narragansett sachem. Miantonomi opposed the marriage because it would strengthen a rival. He tried to turn the English against her, but she sent an agent to the English to establish an alliance in spite of Miantonomi. Unfortunately, neither she nor the man she married are named.

4. Cf. Winthrop (1929–47 [4]:43–45). The account of the raid is found in a letter from Roger Ludlow to John Winthrop, Sr. dated July 3, 1638. Ludlow's account is clearly biased against Ninigret. The Long Island sachem is not named, but the context of the raid and the events that followed strongly indicate that the raid was the beginning of a conflict between the two sachems that lasted until

Wyandanch's death in 1659 (Ales 1979:32–33; Bradner 1925:15; Sehr 1977:44–45). The role of such raids in the context of Algonquian culture is discussed in Eric Johnson's chapter on Uncas in this volume.

5. Cf. NPNER (9):18–19. Also see Ward (1961:118–35) for a discussion of the United Colonies' Indian policy.

6. Sehr (1977:44) and Bradner (1925:16) state that, after the 1638 raid, Ninigret did not interfere in Long Island affairs for fifteen years. Samuel Drake (1857:74) does describe the incident, but he either misread Gardiner's account or got his information from another source. Drake says that Wyandanch delivered his prisoner to Gardiner at Fort Saybrook. Gardiner, however, had been living on his island just offshore from Wyandanch's village for at least four years. Drake also has Gardiner sending Wyandanch to New Haven in stormy weather, which blows him off course and forces him aground on Shelter Island in Peconic Bay. Reference to a map of the area suggests that Drake's account is most improbable. Travel by canoe from Fort Saybrook west to New Haven would have been done close to the shore, particularly in bad weather. It is most unlikely that a canoe heading west would be blown to the south all the way across the sound, east around Orient Point on the north fork of Long Island, and back west into Peconic Bay past Gardiner's Island to Shelter Island. Was there a second primary source documenting the incident? Drake gives no citation for his version.

7. Cf. Osborne (1887:2–4). The names of the sachems from Shelter Island and Shinnecock are different from the ones recorded on the earlier documents. They were probably the same people, but we have no corroboration.

8. Cf. Sleight (1926 [1]:158–59). The account is in a footnote by the editor. Sleight says that fifty years earlier (Sleight began work on the journal in 1897), a Montauk man, who was 100 years old at the time, told people in East Hampton that he heard the story as a child from his elders.

9. The report citing the numbers is in NPNER (10):88. The identification of one of the female captives as Wyandanch's daughter is in Winthrop 1865:482–83.

10. This reference is in a land grant to Gardiner from Wyandanch in 1659. The original is in the Montauk Indian Deeds Collection, on file in the Brooklyn Historical Society. An endorsed copy, entered in the Albany Deed Book 2:118–19, has been published in Gardiner (1890:64).

11. Cf. NPNER (10):170. Ninigret reported to the commissioners of the United Colonies on September 15, 1654, that Wyandanch had killed sixty of his men, one of whom was a sachem's son (NPNER [10]:125). Williams reported in his October, 1654 letter (NPNER [10]:442) that thirty men were killed, two of whom were of great note. One of these men was the son of Wepiteammock, who was Ninigret's brother.

12. The surviving records documenting these actions are listed below in chronological order: January 30, 1659 confirmation of the Corchaug deed, with Cockenoe present (Case 1882–84 [1]:193–94); April 27, 1659 sale by Wyandanch of Plumb Island (Albany Deed Book 1:15); May 12, 1659 sale by Wyandanch of land west of Southampton to John Ogden (Pelletreau 1874–1910[1]:162); May 12,

1659 confirmation by Wyandanch of a deed to Horse Neck negotiated on July 23, 1657 (Street 1887:21–22); May 25, 1659 confirmation of Wyandanch of Oyster Bay deed negotiated by Tackapousha (Cox 1916–40 [1]:347–49); June 8, 1659 grant by Wyandanch and his son, Wyancombone, of whale rights to Gardiner for a stretch of beach running from the western bounds of Southampton to Kitchaminchoke in the present-day town of Mastic (Albany Deed Book 2:85–86; Pelletreau 1874–1910 [2]:34; W. Tooker 1911:83–84); July 14, 1659 grant by Wyandanch, wife, and son of land between Huntington and Setauket to Gardiner (Albany Deed Book 2:118–19; Gardiner 1890:64); July 28, 1659, Wyandanch and his son extend whale rights granted on May 8, above, from Mastic to Enoughquamuck (present-day Moriches Inlet) (Pelletreau 1874–1910 [2]:38; W. Tooker 1911:61–62). There are also two undated documents in the Brookhaven Town records that William Tooker believes were written in 1659. Wyandanch and Cockenoe negotiated the sale of a tract of land near the village of Setauket known as "Old Field" (Albany Deed Book 2:185; Hutchinson 1880:13, 16; W. Tooker 1911:184–85). The entry in the Albany Deed Book suggests that the Brookhaven documents may be variants of the same deed.

CHAPTER FOUR

✿

The Legacy of Robin Cassacinamon: Mashantucket Pequot Leadership in the Historic Period

Kevin A. McBride

THE PEQUOTS LOST almost half of their pre-war population of four thousand by the time the Pequot War ended in the fall of 1637 (K. McBride 1990:104). Approximately fifteen hundred Pequot people had been killed in the fighting, and hundreds more were given as indentured servants to colonists or sold into slavery after the fighting stopped. Remnant communities and villages of Pequots were scattered throughout southern New England, and Pequot sachems and leaders were pursued and killed by the English and their Mohegan and Narragansett allies. The goal of both the colonies (Connecticut, Massachusetts Bay, and Plymouth) and their native Mohegan and Narragansett allies was to eliminate the Pequots as a viable political entity.

This goal had been all but achieved when the Connecticut government concluded the 1638 Treaty of Hartford with the Mohegan and Narragansett. The treaty stipulated among other conditions that surviving Pequots were to be divided equally among the Mohegan and Narragansett and "shall no more be called Pequots but Narragansetts and Mohegans . . . and shall not suffer them for to live in the country that was formerly theirs" (Rhode Island Historical Society Collections [3]:177–78). Over the next thirty-five to forty years, the Mohegans, Narragansetts, and Eastern Niantics engaged in a struggle to replace the Pequots as the dominant native political, social, and economic force in the region. The surviving Pequots were to play an important role in this struggle, and in the process regain a degree of autonomy. Led by Robin Cassacinamon, the Mashantucket Pequots managed to reestablish themselves as a self-governing people in their old territory only twelve years after the Treaty of Hartford. These events took place contrary to the Treaty of Hartford and in spite of strong opposition from colonial governments and the Mohegan and Narragansett tribes.

Most of the Pequot tribe fled their territory, seeking safety with relatives and allies throughout southern New England, following the Mystic Fort massacre in the spring of 1637. These groups of Pequot represented remnants of lineages or villages under the leadership of family heads known as sachems. The social structure of the tribe appears to have remained relatively intact after the Pequot War in spite of losses during the war and the forced dispersal that followed, yet the magnitude of war losses suffered by the Pequots resulted in reductions in both the number of families and lineages and the proportion of adult males. This latter development resulted from deliberate policies pursued during the war: Both colonists and their native allies tended to kill all known belligerent sachems and warriors captured. As Roger Williams reported, "these [sachems], with the [alleged] murderers [of John Stone, the pretext for the declaration of war], the magistrates desired to cut off" (R. Williams 1988 [1]:184). The policy proved effective; of the twenty-six Pequot sachems mentioned at the beginning of the war, no more than six survived. The families of many of these murdered sachems and warriors were singled out and sold into slavery or given as indentured servants to colonists.

The war aims of the English were evident and direct. They wished never to see the Pequots reemerge as a viable political force in the region. The Mohegans, Eastern Niantics, and Narragansetts, for their part, wanted not only to ensure the destruction of the Pequots as a political entity, but also to use the ensuing social fragmentation for their own political ends. They achieved these goals by eliminating Pequot leadership while keeping the basic social structure intact in order to incorporate survivors into other political and social entities. The wives and children of deceased Pequot sachems, as well as their kin groups and communities, were sought after by Native leaders, such as the Mohegan sachem Uncas and the Eastern Niantic chiefs Wequashcook and Ninigret, to expand their power base and influence. In the years immediately following the Pequot War, Native (primarily Narragansett) and colonial leaders complained constantly that Uncas, Wequashcook, and Ninigret were furthering their own political ends by hiding Pequots and marrying or arranging marriages with surviving wives and children of Pequot sachems.

The activities of these men in the years immediately following the Pequot War reveal much about the role of women in native societies. Women clearly had significant nondomestic roles to play in native society. Pequot women of higher status, for example, were considered desirable marriage partners for individuals anxious to achieve some social or political end; a marriage between Uncas's elder brother and the daughter of Tattobam, the chief sachem of the Pequots killed by the Dutch in 1634, had been arranged so that "they [the Mohegans and the Pequots] should keep their lands entire from any violation either from neighboring or foreign Indians" (Trumbull 1885:103).

Uncas's brother died prior to the marriage, and "by determination of the Indian Council, both of the Pequots and Mohegans, it was concluded and jointly agreed that Uncas, the next brother to the deceased, should proceed in the said match" (Trumbull 1885:103, from The Genealogy and Lineage of Uncas, Sachem of Moheag, March 1679). Although this document is riddled with self-serving exaggerations and falsehoods, this particular passage suggests the significance of some marriages among Mohegan and Pequot people. In the ten-year period following the Pequot War, other Pequot women played a significant role in the efforts by native leaders such as Uncas to construct new political entities out of the remnants of the Pequot tribe.

Wequashcook married the mother of Sassacus (the chief Pequot sachem during the Pequot War) within a year of the end of the fighting (R. Williams 1988 [1]:119). On more than five occasions within three years after the war, Uncas was noted as marrying or desiring to marry seven Pequot women. On February 28, 1638, for example, Roger Williams reported that Uncas "hath Sassacous his sister to wife and one of the wives of Sassacous his father Tattaopame" (R. Williams 1988 [1]:146). Williams noted on the following June 7 that Uncas sent to Wequashcook for "a Pequot Queen" (R. Williams 1988 [1]:161). On July 23, Williams reported that Uncas had dispatched nine Mohegans and Robin Cassacinamon to John Winthrop, Jr., in Massachusetts Bay to buy a Pequot woman (presumably a war captive), whom Uncas "intended for his wife" (R. Williams 1988 [1]:168), and in the same report, Williams noted that Uncas "hath taken 2 daughters Marie and Jane both to wife." Two years later, Williams reported that "the Squa sachims daughter is married to the sachim Onkas" (R. Williams 1988 [1]:202).

Uncas and Wequashcook apparently tried to strengthen their standing and influence in the region's native communities through marriage to these women. Although the precise mechanisms of their strategies are not fully known, surviving documents show how both men used these women to attract and control a significant number of refugee Pequots. This strategy did not pass unnoticed among the colonists.

Colonial governments did not approve of all of these marriages. The Commissioners of the United Colonies, for example, expressed grave concern over a marriage "shortly intended" between Ninigret's eldest daughter and "a brother or brothers sone of Sassaquas the mallignant furious Pequot" named Tausaquonawhut. Suspecting the worst, they wrote that the natives would use the marriage "to gather together and reunite the scattered conquered Pequots into one body and sett them upp againe as a distinct nation" (Acts of the Commissioners of the United Colonies July 1649:145). Tausaquonawhut, a son of Tattobam, was also "sought to by Uncas to marrie his daughter but not affecting her (because of her sore eyes) came to [Ninigret's] daughter (R. Williams 1988 [1]:230).

These documents show that the implications of such marriages were not lost on colonial authorities. Anxious to prevent the reestablishment of the Pequot tribe, they also worried that leaders from the other tribes would grow too powerful and replace the Pequots as the dominant political and military force in the region.

It is not clear if the status of these women was based on their previous marriages to Pequot sachems or on their position in their natal communities and lineages. In all likelihood, they derived status from both sources. The "wealth" they brought to their marriages almost certainly came in the form of the labor provided by people obligated by ties of kinship and politics to these women and their lineages. Service provided by warriors and wampum makers constituted much of this labor value.

Strategic marriages also could give husbands and wives access to lands of their spouses. Although several sources indicate "yt according to theire custome ye title of lands goes by ye man and not by ye woman" (New London Records, Declaration of Uncas the great Sachem of the Mohegans, June 11, 1683), women also evidently possessed land rights.

Uncas, for example, repeatedly invoked rights conferred by kinship connections to both men and women in land disputes with other tribes. Uncas claimed "a right on the east side of Pequot [i.e., the New London–Nameag area] from his father, from his mother, and from his wife [the daughter of Tattobam]" (Connecticut Records, Series 1, Document 101). Other claims to "considerable tracts of land" were claimed by Uncas in his own right, and "in right of a certain Pequot squaw he married" [Tattobam's daughter]. On another occasion, Uncas maintained specifically that his marriage to Tattobam's daughter made his right to Pequot country "good and unquestionable" (Winthrop Papers 1908 [2]:310).

Some native women evidently played an active political role beyond the confines of marriage. Colonists recognizing the mercy shown to two white captives by the wife of Mononadtuck, a prominent Pequot sachem killed in the war, spared her and her children from death and slavery after their capture in the Fairfield Swamp Fight. She lived at Nameag after the war, and it was reported that she "informs all Pequots and Narragansetts that Mr. Govrs [Governor's] mind is, that no Pequot man should die, that her 2 sons shall ere long be sachims there etc." (R. Williams 1988 [1]:200). Such reports show that influential women could and did exert influence in political affairs in the region during these years.

Both Uncas and Wequashcook had great success in using marriages to influential women to attain wealth and power. On September 9, 1637, Roger Williams (1988 [1]:117) reported that Uncas "had about 300 men with him on Pequot [Thames] River some 16 miles from the house, wch I believe are most of them Pequots and their confederates . . . and with whom he [Uncas] hath made himself great." Writing on February 28, 1638, Williams (1988 [1]:146) observed, "and thats one reason beside his ambition and neerenes that he hath drawn all the scattered Pequots to himself and drawn much wealth from them." Noting that both Uncas and Wequash [Wequashcook's father] "carry[ied] away the people and their treasure" through these marriages, Williams also reported that Wequash-cook had "grown rich and a sachem with the Pequots . . . and hath filled many baskets with beans from Pequot sachems and 120 Pequots wch he sheltreth now at Niantic" (126–27).

These reports provide considerable insight into native social and political dynamics in the seventeenth century. All clearly indicate the importance of kinship in the creation and maintenance of political entities in the region. Through marriage and the subsequent incorporation of surviving Pequots into the Mohegan tribe, Uncas succeeded in greatly expanding his influence. It is within this context that the two principal surviving Pequot communities sought to attain political independence from their colonial, Mohegan, and Narragansett and Eastern Niantic overlords.

Both Pequot communities emerged shortly after the signing of the Treaty of Hartford. The group eventually known as the Pawcatuck Pequots originally resided in the Misquamicut area of southwestern Rhode Island under the control of the Narragansett and Eastern Niantic sachems. Early records note that this community contained 120 adult warriors (approximately four to seven hundred people). This community was led initially by the Eastern Niantic leader Wequashcook, a Pequot/Niantic sachem whose father had guided the English to the Mystic Fort during the Pequot War. Descendants of this community reside presently in North Stonington, Connecticut, on a 250-acre state reservation that was granted in 1683.

The second community, successively known as the Nameag, Noank, and Mashantucket Pequots, originally consisted of approximately eighty adult men (ca. three to five hundred people). People belonging to this community resided first in the Nameag area, in and around present-day New London, between 1638 and 1650. Compelled to acknowledge Uncas's authority, the community was led by Robin Cassacinamon. Under Cassacinamon's leadership, Pequot people living at Nameag managed to move back to the Mystic River in their traditional homeland, despite colonial and native opposition in 1650. By 1666, most of these people had moved north, from Noank on the Mystic River to Mashantucket. Possessing neither substantial land nor a large population and lacking great political influence, the Mashantucket Pequots managed nevertheless to maintain their independence and identity into the twentieth century.

This achievement was largely the result of effective leadership by sachems such as Robin Cassacinamon. Throughout his career, Cassacinamon demonstrated an astute understanding of native and colonial politics, managing to emerge from the Pequot War as one of the few Pequot leaders not identified by colonists with the banned traditional Pequot power structure. Quietly assuming authority over the Nameag community, he worked to gain independence from Uncas and colonial supervision. Adept at using the power of persuasion, Cassacinamon forged a close relationship with John Winthrop, Jr., the governor of Connecticut and the founder of the Pequot Plantation at Nameag.

Robin Cassacinamon first appears in colonial records documenting events at Nameag shortly after the Pequot War ended in 1638. The fact of his survival indicates that he was neither a sachem nor a combatant during the fighting. He is mentioned in a 1662 document as having hunted for a

Kevin A. McBride

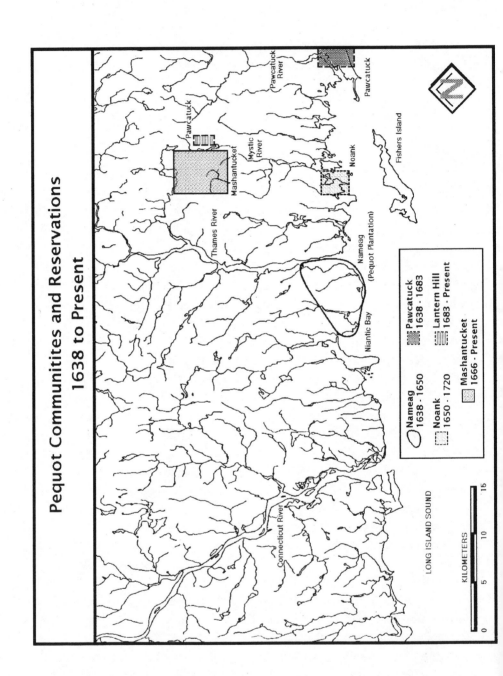

sachem on the east side of the Pawcatuck River when he was a boy (Potter 1835:267). His acceptance as a sachem, first by the Nameag Pequot community and later by native leaders throughout the region, indicates that he possessed the requisite social credentials for such a position of authority, although he did not assume full leadership immediately; extant records show that it took many years for Cassacinamon to be recognized as a peer by Uncas, Ninigret, and other native leaders. Cultivating his connection with Winthrop carefully, he consolidated his position by cooperating with the English in wartime and by serving as a mediator between English and native peoples during peacetime.

It was in this latter context that Cassacinamon made his first appearance in colonial records. Writing on July 23, 1638, Roger Williams noted that Uncas had sent a party of nine Mohegan men and "the Pequot Robin" to Boston to secure the freedom of a Pequot woman residing in Winthrop's household at Nameag (R. Williams 1988 [1]:168). Noting that Uncas "intended that maide for his wife," Williams noted that Uncas had instructed Cassacinamon to remain at the Winthrop house to help the woman escape in case they could not buy her. Extant records show that the woman later moved to Mohegan, and Cassacinamon received ten fathoms of wampum as a reward.

Robin Cassacinamon was next mentioned eight years later, in 1646. He lived as a servant in the Winthrop household during these years, and it is not known whether this was voluntary or involuntary. He became known to and trusted by the Winthrops. His particularly close relationship with John Winthrop, Jr., seems to have played an important role in Winthrop's selection of Nameag as the site of Pequot Plantation at New London in 1646.

Winthrop evidently acknowledged Cassacinamon as the main leader of the Nameag Pequot community in 1646. Drawn to the locale by the presence of a deepwater port and access to interior areas where he was prospecting for minerals, Winthrop regarded the Nameag Pequots as "a people which live very near the English, and do wholly adhere to them, and are apt to fall into English employment" (Trumbull 1885 [9]:45). His establishment of an English settlement at Nameag was an important strategic move; anxious to curb Uncas's political ambitions, Winthrop wrote that "it was of great concernment to have [Pequot Plantation] planted, to be a curb to the [Mohegan] Indians" (Winthrop 1908 [2]:274).

At least twenty years passed between Winthrop's establishment of the

Pequot Plantation at Nameag and the wider recognition of Cassacinamon's leadership abilities in the region. The first indication of this increase
in status appears in a treaty document establishing friendship between the
Esopus Indians and the governor of New York in 1665 (NYCD [13]:399–
401). Identified as a witness to the proceedings, his participation in events
occurring more than one hundred and fifty miles beyond the borders of his
homeland indicates that he had earned the trust of both colonists and
native people in the region.

Documents recording events associated with an "Indian Conspiracy" in
1669 affirm Cassacinamon's status as a prominent cultural intermediary.
Rumors of an alleged widespread Indian plot threatening settlements
throughout New England were brought to the attention of colonial authorities. Although the existence of the plot was never proven, several documents implicated Cassacinamon as a conspirator. Thomas Stanton, a
trader, interpreter, and militia commander, transmitted "credabell Indian
reportes heare yt Daniel Robin Sanananes partner hath bin with the
Mowakes [Mohawks] this spring with a great sum of wampum and since
his return hath uttered discontent and yt hee would live no longer under
the English." John Mason, a local official who had earlier commanded the
force that destroyed the Mystic Fort in 1637, reported that Cassacinamon
hosted a dance at Noank in which "the Indians did speedily intend to cut of
the English" (Stonington Town Records, July 8, 1669).

Mason's report of Uncas's and Ninigret's attendance at this dance
sparked intense interests among colonial authorities. Mason wrote that
"Ninegrats and Unckas beeing togeather at the dans at Robins town is and
was a matter of wonderment to mee yt thaye who durst not looke each
uppon other this 20 years but at the missell of a gun or at the pile of an
arrow" (Connecticut Records, Indian Papers, 1st Series [1]:10). Stanton
soon arrived with a force of militiamen to break up the dance and seize
Ninigret. Confronting each other with weapons drawn, Ninigret's and
Stanton's men prepared to fight. Cassacinamon stepped in to defuse the
situation. Afraid that "Ninegret's men [would] have fyred Inglishmans
houses and that a great deal of hurt might A com of it, and it may be the
Pequot Indians and other Indians might A bein blamd that had noe hand
in it but for the prevention of any danger," Cassacinamon promised to pay
Stanton "a great deal of wampum" as "wampum was like the grass when it
was gon it would com againe but if men be once kild they will live noe
more" (Connecticut Records, Indian Papers, 1st Series [1]:9). Cassacina-

mon's presence of mind and his guarantee that he would personally ensure maintenance of the peace diffused a potentially volatile situation. Whatever the actual circumstances surrounding the incident and the conspiracy, the outcome of the standoff at his town attests to his standing among both the English and his native neighbors. For Uncas and Ninigret to gather at Noank after twenty years as enemies was a testament to Cassacinamon's newly won status and respect among native leaders. Although suspicious of his possible role in the plot, the English decided to trust him.

While Mason continued to support Uncas, the Mohegan's reputation for friendship with the English did not emerge untarnished from this incident. Native and colonial leaders throughout the region worried about Uncas and his political ambitions. Speaking for many, John Winthrop, Jr., wrote that "Uncas plotteth universal monarchy between his Indians and Long Island and laies strong foundations for the future greatness of his family (ICRC [1]:181).

Recognizing the importance of cultivating and maintaining a good relationship with Cassacinamon and his followers, Winthrop reported that "I look at the quiet of our plantation principally, and conceive a greate security to have a party of the [Nameag Pequot] Indians here, to have their chiefe dependance upon the English. They will easily discover any Indian plotts" (Winthrop 1908 [2]:520). The desire of the United Colonies to maintain the status quo among the Narragansett and Mohegan as well as the recognition of the importance of the surviving Pequots in the power struggle then developing between the Mohegan, the Eastern Niantic, and the Narragansett provided Cassacinamon with opportunities to pry his people loose from Uncas's authority. The strategy he used took full advantage of the political, social, and economic divisions among Indian and colonial societies in the region.

Cassacinamon had begun housing colonists and hunting for them during their first winter at Pequot Plantation in 1646. Working to cement relations with his new neighbors, he soon looked for ways to use them as levers against Uncas. Designated in the Hartford Treaty as overlord over the Nameag Pequots, Uncas repeatedly extorted wampum payments from his charges as he forced them to support him in his wars against other Indians. Growing restive, Pequots living under Uncas's control at Mohegan began moving to Nameag after 1646. Growing in numbers and emboldened by proximity to their new English neighbors, Cassacinamon's followers soon defied Uncas's authority. They began during the winter of

1646 by extending a hunt for the Pequot Plantation colonists into conquered Pequot lands that were claimed by Uncas, by virtue of his marriage to a Pequot woman. Retaliating against what he regarded as an unauthorized trespass of his domain, Uncas raided the Pequot villages at Nameag.

Winthrop and the colonists responded much as Cassacinamon had hoped. Complaining of "the late inrode by Uncas and his crue upon the indians of this place in robbing all their wigwams and depriving them of their neccessaries for their very life," they felt that "it was an unexpected disturbance to our families, frightening and amassing our wives and children" (ICRC [1]:124). Uncas evidently hoped that his demonstration at Pequot Plantation would intimidate both the Pequots and their new English neighbors, but instead his raid only succeeded in angering colonists, who immediately protested his actions to the Commissioners of the United Colonies.

Presenting himself before the Commissioners in New Haven, Uncas acknowledged that his attack was a "miscarriage" of his authority. He went on, however, to explain that "divers of the Pequots formerly granted to him were drawn from him under colors of submitting to the English plantation at Pequot," and that the Pequots at Nameag "hunted within his proper limits without his leave" (ICRC [1]:72). The Commissioners were unsympathetic. They issued a strong rebuke to Uncas and demanded that he not attack the Pequots at Nameag without the Commissioners' permission. Yet they did not rescind his authority over Pequots living there or at Mohegan.

The Nameag Pequots also refused to acquiesce to Uncas's demands for military support. On one occasion, Uncas wanted to mount an expedition to Long Island to avenge one of his men, who had been wounded there. He "required Robin alias Cassmon with other Pequots to goe with him . . . The rest not knowing any cause why Uncas should take so many men with him, excused themselves, yet promised if any should shoote an arrow against him upon notice they would come over and assist him" (ICRC [1]:98).

Eager to be free of Uncas's domination, Cassacinamon petitioned the Commissioners "to take us under the subjection of the English and appoint us some place where wee may live peaceably under the Government of the English" (Connecticut Records, Indian Papers, 1st Series [1]:1). Although only ten years had passed since the end of the war, Cassacinamon believed that it was an opportune time to act. His belief was justified. Supporting Cassacinamon's petition, Winthrop warned the Commissioners that "if the Pequot's be not taken under the English, if these Indians that we must live neere be still under Uncas command, there will no living for English there; we must not expect to be quiet" (Winthrop 1908 [2]:520).

Assured of Winthrop's support, Cassacinamon and his people began to intensify their efforts. Growing numbers of Pequot people living at Mohegan began accepting Cassacinamon's invitations to resettle at Nameag. They also began refusing to make wampum tribute payments to Uncas. But Cassacinamon's petition brought a quick response from Uncas. Delivering a message from Uncas, his councilor Foxon told the Commissioners that "some of the petitioners were in Misticke fort in the fight against the English and fled away in the smoake. That others of them were in other places to fight . . . so that the grounds of their petition proved false and deceitful" (ICRC [1]:97). This was a powerful argument to settlers still fearful of Pequot resurgence.

Rejecting Cassacinamon's petition, the Commissioners affirmed provisions of the 1638 Hartford Treaty stating that "the remnant of [Pequot] nation should not be suffered (if the English could help it) either to be a distinct people, or to retayne the name of Pequots, or to settle in the Pequatt country, but that they should all be devided betwixt the Narragansett and Mohegan Indians, and that under a tribute to the English . . . to return to Uncas" (ICRC [1]:100).

The Nameag Pequots did not immediately obey the Commissioner's directive. Writing to Winthrop in 1648, the Commissioners reminded him of the "continued mindes and resolutions of the Commissioners for the [Nameag Pequots] return" to Uncas's authority. Giving Uncas permission "by constrainte to Inforce them," they advised that he "Hee bee not opposed by any English, Nor the Pequots, or that any of these Indians should be harbored or sheltered in any of their [English] houses" (Connecticut Records, Indian Papers, 1st Series [1]:11). The tone of the letter indicates that it was intended as a rebuke to Winthrop.

The Commissioners were not the only people concerned by Winthrop's support of Cassacinamon and his people. Other native leaders writing to Winthrop advised him to treat Cassacinamon and the Nameag Pequots "as youre little dogs, but not as your confederates" (Winthrop 1908 [2]:273).

Pressed by both native leaders and fellow colonists, Winthrop continued to support Pequot attempts to place themselves under the direct authority of the English. Maneuvering to counter opposition from Connecticut governor John Haynes, John Mason, and Uncas, Winthrop helped Cassacinamon gain a degree of independence from Uncas in 1649 by forging a compromise. Winthrop talked both Uncas and the Commissioners into giving the Nameag Pequots "libertie for the present to settle and plant [outside of the bounds of Pequot Plantation] thay owneing Uncas as theire Sachem and in all things carrying themselves as his other subjects" (Massachusetts Archives, Acts of the Commissioners of the United Colonies 1649:146).

Having won the right to live in their own settlement, Cassacinamon and his people prevailed upon Winthrop in 1650 to grant them a small, five-hundred-acre reservation at Noank, in the heart of their traditional territory, which he did. Four years later, Winthrop helped Cassacinamon submit another petition to the Commissioners. Eager to secure their support in a projected attack against Ninigret and his people, they formally freed Cassacinamon's Pequots from Uncas's subjection and released them from tribute payments (ICRC [2]:134). Cassacinamon immediately placed his people under direct English authority.

But freedom from Uncas's control did not end Pequot troubles. The Noank reservation soon proved small and inadequate for its inhabitants. As early as 1658, Cassacinamon complained to the United Colonies that the soils were exhausted and that there was no firewood. The Commissioners granted Cassacinamon an additional two thousand acres at Mashantucket in 1666. Although the Noank reservation was lost in 1720, the addition of the Mashantucket tract represented one of the few net increases in Indian lands in southern New England during the colonial era.

Pequot reluctance to aid Uncas's military adventure did not extend to the English. Both the Mashantucket and Pawcatuck peoples supported their English neighbors in every major conflict during the colonial era. Never able to field collectively more than two hundred men at any one time, the Pequots nevertheless provided important service. The Pequot warriors fighting alongside Connecticut soldiers helped ensure that the Connecticut militias suffered the lowest casualty rate of any New England force in King Philip's War (1675–76).

The importance given to and trust placed in the Mashantucket community by Connecticut colonists during this conflict and subsequent wars with the French is reflected in the recent discovery of a fortified village on the Mashantucket Pequot Reservation (McBride 1994). Although primary

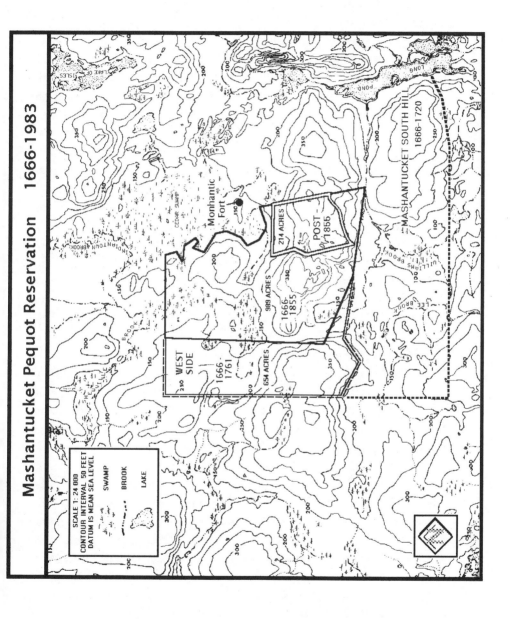

Mashantucket Pequot Reservation 1666-1983

documents identifying the fort specifically have yet to be found, material culture recovered from site deposits date it to the last quarter of the seventeenth century (ca. 1675–1700). This period roughly coincides with King Philip's War.

Serving as a protective bastion for the Mashantucket community, the fort was situated along what was the eastern frontier of Connecticut Colony during the period of King Phillip's War. This strategic location would have served to protect the colonial settlements of New London, Norwich, and Stonington as well against attacks from Narragansett and Wampanoag warriors during that War. Discoveries of a wide range of military artifacts—gun parts, lead shot, lead bar, molten lead sprue, iron spear and projectile points, and native-made gunflints—affirm the military function of the fort. Recoveries of carbonized corn; stone pestles; native and European ceramics; glass, brass, and shell beads; and iron kettles and knives, by contrast, document the post's function as a domestic site.

The plan of the fort, a square-shaped enclosure with bastions at each corner, plainly reflects the influence of European military design. The overlapping narrow entranceway uncovered at the front of the fort, by contrast, perpetuates native architectural ideas documented at the Mystic Fort and other aboriginal fortifications.

Although no records associate Robin Cassacinamon or any other Pequot leader with the fort, he remained the sole leader of the Mashantucket Pequot community to the time of his death in 1692. Several documents reveal that problems of succession caused the Pequot community to split into rival political groups afterwards (McBride 1994). One group, consisting of the "Old men and Councilors," supported Cassacinamon's designated successor, a boy named Kutchamaquan who was considered too young to succeed to the sachemship at the time of Cassacinamon's death. Writing to the Commissioners in Hartford, this group asked "in the name and with the knowledge and consent of the rest of the council and in the name of the greatest part of the Pequots ancient men and young men that the Great sachem that we honored and loved declared at his death that Kutchamaquan, Mamohos son, should succeed as sachem as his will and desire" (Connecticut Records, Indian Papers, 1st Series [1]:44). The Commissioners responded by appointing Daniel as "governor" of the Mashantucket community until Kutchamaquan came of age (CPR [4]:86).

Daniel died two years later. He was soon succeeded by a man named Scattup (CPR [4]:122). Petitioning the Commissioners in 1701, the old

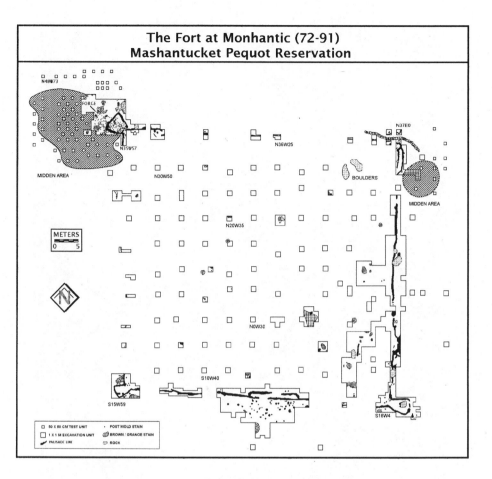

men and councilors noted that their choice of sachem was not being recognized and asked that Kutchamaquan "be not denegrated and made inferior to Scattup." What followed was a bitter controversy within the tribe over leadership and the nature of succession.

The split caused by Scattup's refusal to step down from his position of leadership affected every aspect of Mashantucket life throughout the 1700s (McBride 1994). Contesting political groups invoked Cassacinamon's name and other symbols of his leadership in their struggles for power. Scattup, for example, used Cassacinamon's distinctive mark when signing documents as the community's leader. Other documents indicate that Kutshamaquan or his successor adopted Robin Cassacinamon's name.

Over the next two hundred years, the Mashantucket Pequot tribe expe-

rienced the loss of most of their reservation lands and a significant portion
of their population. The emigration of over half of the reservation population at the end of the eighteenth century in the Brothertown Indian Movement was a direct result of continued encroachment on reservation lands
by Euro-Americans. By 1855, the Mashantucket Pequot reservation con-

sisted of only two hundred and fourteen acres, with a population estimated at fifty (K. McBride 1990). In 1935, forty-two tribal members were reported, with nine residing on the reservation and the remainder living in nearby towns. By the early 1970s only two elderly women resided on the reservation.

Nearly two hundred and fifty years passed before Cassacinamon's name and mark were again used by the Mashantucket Pequot as symbols of tribal identity and sovereignty. Following his election as Tribal Chairman in 1975, Richard Hayward embarked on a program to obtain federal recognition, reunite the tribe, and provide housing and economic opportunities for returning tribal members. What makes these achievements all the more remarkable was that Hayward was faced with a situation in many ways analogous to what Cassacinamon faced in 1650. In 1975 the Mashantucket reservation consisted of only two hundred and fourteen acres of rocky land. The remaining tribal members were widely dispersed throughout the Northeast as a result of Connecticut policies on reservation lands, resulting in the lack of adequate housing and jobs and the prospect of the loss of remaining reservation lands. Hayward and the tribal council pursued a strategy of accommodation, building lasting relationships with a number of state and federal officials. This strategy continued after federal recognition, and has allowed the Mashantucket Pequot tribe to become one of the most successful Native American tribes in the United States. When the Mashantucket Pequot tribal logo was designed in the mid-1970s by Richard Hayward, Cassacinamon's distinctive signature was featured prominently. The tribe's logo was adopted just as the Mashantucket Pequot tribe was beginning the process of seeking federal recognition and of developing a strategy to deal with the federal and state governments. Cassacinamon's relationship with John Winthrop, Jr., and other Connecticut officials greatly influenced the Mashantucket leadership in the recognition process. The use of Cassacinamon's signature in this context is a testament to his continued influence and importance to the Mashantucket Pequot tribe.

Notes

This research was made possible by funding from the Mashantucket Pequot Tribe. Skip Hayward, Mashantucket Pequot Tribal Chairman, assisted me in developing many of the ideas presented in this paper. Robert Grumet commented on earlier drafts and provided me with additional primary source materials. Tara Prindle produced all graphics. I gratefully acknowledge the contributions of the aforementioned individuals. I alone, however, take responsibility for any errors in the presentation and interpretation of the data.

CHAPTER FIVE

⁂

Chief Rawandagon, Alias Robin Hood: Native "Lord of Misrule" in the Maine Wilderness

Harald E. L. Prins

Introduction

NICKNAMED ROBIN HOOD by the English, Rawandagon achieved prominence among natives and newcomers on Maine's central coast in the mid-
seventeenth century. Yet today, very little is known about this Abenaki
frontier chieftain. Almost completely ignored by anthropologists and historians alike, he comes to mind only through place names in the lower
Kennebec River area. A Georgetown Island village is called Robinhood
and is located at the entrance of Robinhood Cove; Merrymeeting Bay,
situated nearby, is another symbolic reference—although its connection to
our subject has apparently gone unnoticed.[1] Formed by the confluence of
the Kennebec, Androscoggin, Muddy, Cathance, and Abagadusset Rivers,
this bay was once known by its Abenaki name, *chisapeak*—"at the big part
of the river" (C. Allen 1931:281). Here, Rawandagon, alias Robin Hood,
and his Abenaki cohorts ("merry men") held their periodic festive gatherings, which in seventeenth-century English were known as "merry meetings" (OED 1985:1776).

Rawandagon lived during the antebellum period, stretching from the
1616–18 pandemic that scourged the native population to the 1675 outbreak of King Philip's War. During his lifetime, northern New England

93

was sparsely populated. Abenaki remnant groups and their native neighbors dwelled in tenuous company with small clusters of European settlers and a changing cast of merchants and fishermen. While the local tribespeople maintained aboriginal title to their ancestral lands, rival French and English powers each asserted sovereignty over the region— the French claim reaching south from Nova Scotia (Acadia), the English stretching north from Massachusetts. In this ill-defined transition area and contested middle ground, uneasy accommodation could turn quickly into violence. Political and commercial alliances were volatile; ambiguity reigned supreme.

Residing at a strategic locale near the mouth of the Kennebec River, Rawandagon and his close kinsfolk lived along a cultural divide. The English, who traded, fished, and farmed on the coast, especially between the Saco River and Pemaquid Point, were his immediate neighbors. The French were active only some fifty miles downeast at Penobscot Bay. Other Abenaki bands ranged through their hunting and trapping territories in the vast upriver woodlands. Beyond them, less than 250 miles to the northwest (about seven days of fast canoe-travel), stood Quebec, center of the fledgling colony of New France.

From his geographic vantage point, Rawandagon had ample opportunity to develop into a coastal power broker. Enjoying direct access to European commodities and developing a cross-cultural information network, he became a widely recognized political figure. Rival upriver chieftains envied his political connections and feared his shamanic powers. By the 1660s, English colonial authorities officially acknowledged his political position, appointing him "chief sachem" (Grand Chief) of the district from Casco Bay to Pemaquid. As such, he assumed responsibility for the actions of his native compatriots in the region, and mediated in negotiations and conflicts between them and the English. His final public act took place in 1675, when he intervened in a smoldering conflict between his cohorts and settlers.

A Contextual Approach—Some Theoretical Considerations

"Insofar as a life is the locus of experience" (Marcus and Fischer 1986: 183), Rawandagon's history is highly significant. In contrast to that of European individuals, very little is known about Abenaki personhood on the colonial frontier. Few surviving manuscripts reveal anything more than the mere surface of seventeenth-century Abenaki life. And even then, all that we can extract meaningfully are shreds of information—a name, a reference, an act, a fact—only vaguely hinting at what was a very complex cultural universe. Of necessity, we depend almost exclusively on documents produced by European outsiders. These documents, selectively reflecting the social categories of the observers rather than the observed, do not convey in-depth knowledge about the Abenakis as cultural "others."

Because written records represent our major source of information, our reconstructions concern primarily the European side of the cultural divide. Accordingly, except on the level of interethnic aggression and commodity exchange, our understanding of frontier cultural dynamics is still very limited. Barring the unlikely discovery of more revealing information about Rawandagon as an individual, we must concede that much about him will remain shrouded in the mist of time. However unfortunate, this does not mean that we cannot gain insight into the particular conditions of his life. A broadly defined contextual approach to Rawandagon's life history promises to yield some meaningful insights into the nature of cross-cultural interaction on the colonial frontier.

My contextual approach takes its cues from what we know about his natural environment, his cultural embedment, and his social encounters. Circumnavigating this elusive character, I outline his personal contours by retrieving fragments of historical information. These reveal the constructive elements that made Rawandagon potent as an Indian political broker straddling the Anglo-Abenaki cultural divide.

In the following pages, I describe Abenaki culture and Rawandagon's structural position in a wider field of social force. Following a summary of the European invasion that shook the world of his youth, I recount the basic political and economic transformations on Maine's coast born of the burgeoning fur trade and the fisheries. An inquiry into the cultural symbolism of Rawandagon's English nickname follows, offering insights into English folk attitudes toward Native Americans in the early colonial period. Not only *reflecting* popular cultural categories, but also reflecting *on* them, this remarkable naming practice represents a unique window into the complexities of Anglo-Abenaki frontier interaction (cf. Blok and Buckser 1990:1–3). Within this contextual framework we can distinguish Rawandagon's rise and reign as a frontier chieftain, or *sagamore*.

Rawandagon: Description of a Seventeenth-Century Sagamore

As just noted, few details about Rawandagon's personal life have survived. Known facts include the following: Born around 1600 A.D., he was the son of a local sagamore named Manawormet, whose personal domain lay in the Sheepscot area (Sewall 1847:190; 1859:121; Levett 1847:92; Purchas 1905–1907:405). His immediate network of kinfolk and friends probably stretched from Saco Bay to Pemaquid, and included the lower Kennebec, Merrymeeting Bay, and Androscoggin Rivers (York Deeds [2]:32, [9]:188; [10]:261; JR [38]:35–39; Wheeler 1878:11; cf. Baker 1989:249). Rawandagon had children, including two sons. One, in contrast to his father, became notorious as an inveterate enemy of the English (W. Hubbard 1865 [2]:38; Mather 1704; MDH [23]:204–7). Although no documents chronicle his demise, he probably died shortly after his final appearance in English records during the summer of 1675.[2]

How should we imagine Rawandagon and his fellow Abenaki tribesmen? While existing European records do not describe him personally, a comparative ethnographic composite allows us to reconstruct his resemblance. As a young man, he was probably lean and strong, about six feet tall. He likely greased his reddish-brown skin with seal oil or bear lard and shaved his raven-black hair well back from his forehead, leaving a long shank at the back, which he wove into a braid intertwined with feathers. From his pierced ears, no doubt, hung shell pendants. On occasion, he may have painted designs on his face and body with red, black, blue, or white pigments. In addition, he was probably tattooed.

If he followed a custom widespread through the Northeast, he would have blackened his face when mourning. And, like other Abenaki men of the time, he very likely wore a soft leather breechclout and leggings with a white moosehide coat or tanned deerskin mantle decorated in painted patterns or embroidered with colored moose hair and flattened, red and white porcupine quills. When bitter cold, he may have covered himself with a thick fur robe made of beaver or otter skins and walked in moosehide or sealskin moccasins, no doubt also with a quill edging. Adding to his splendor as a young chieftain, he could have worn white and blue wampum bracelets and necklaces, and had small red copper ornaments stitched on his clothing. Indeed, he may have worn a leather belt such as the one found in his former domains at Merriconeag Sound, which bore about 400 red copper tubes of varying sizes attached with soft leather thongs (MDH [10]:462; Denys 1908:370, 407, 411, 413–14; Josselyn 1988; Lescarbot 1907–14 [3]:135, 157–58; Morton 1883:201, 207–10; Porter 1979:270–71; Wood 1977:69, 73–74, 108; JR [3]:75; Hist. Mag. 1869:247; cf. Prins 1994).

Early Conflicts in the Gulf of Maine

Traditionally, native subsistence activities in this region were based on hunting, fowling, and fishing. In contrast to migratory bands living east of the Kennebec, tribal villagers from this river westward also planted gardens of corn, beans, squash, and tobacco (Champlain 1922–38 [1]:327–28). When Rawandagon was born, Abenaki traditional life was about to be upset and radically transformed.

During the later 1500s, European commodities had begun trickling down to coastal Maine from the nearby Gulf of St. Lawrence (where French Breton, Norman, and Basque, as well as Spanish, Portuguese, and English fishing vessels had plied the waters since the early part of the century), but the region remained mostly unaffected by European contact until the seventeenth century. The handful of sixteenth-century transatlantic ventures into the Gulf of Maine (beginning with Verrazzano's 1524 exploring voyage for the French Crown) left the local Abenaki peoples more or less untouched. Neighboring Mi'kmaqs, Montagnais, and other Gulf of St. Lawrence coastal peoples were swept up in a whirlwind of culture change. From the 1530s onward, fishing fleets returning annually from ports across the ocean carried iron hatchets, skinning knives, awls, copper kettles, cloth, and other commodities, which the sailors traded for thick beaver skins and other precious furs (Innis 1930:5–19; Prins 1989a, 1993, 1996).

Some Mi'kmaq entrepreneurs turned into fur-trade middlemen. Engaging in long-distance trading voyages, they learned to sail small, open boats called shallops (sloops), taking valuable European trade goods to remote villages in order to get high-quality furs. By 1600, at about the time of Rawandagon's birth, native mariners from the Gulf of St. Lawrence area had begun to venture to Maine's shores and probably beyond (Archer 1906:73–74; Brereton 1906:137–38; Bourque and Whitehead 1987; Prins 1994). Soon, coastal Maine turned into hotly contested territory. In addition to the Mi'kmaqs, who not only traded but also raided the corn-and-fur-producing Abenakis and their neighbors, some English, French, and Basque explorers, traders, and fishers began venturing into the region (De Costa 1878:76–80). In 1604, a French colony was founded at Passamaquoddy Bay, from where Samuel de Champlain launched his coastal explorations, going initially as far south as the Kennebec (Champlain 1922–38 [1]:234, 269–73, [3]:358–59). All too soon, Rawandagon's people found out that the strangers landing on their shores brought trouble. In 1605, five tribesmen were kidnapped on an English vessel at Pemaquid. One, a sagamore named Natahanada, returned from England the following year. Recounting his adventures in the land of the strangers, no doubt he raised alarm among his kinsfolk and their allies (Thayer 1892:57–82; Prins 1993).

In 1607, the English returned to the mouth of the Kennebec, guided by another captive named Skidwarres (Thayer 1892:57–66). Planning to establish a permanent colony less than fifteen miles from Rawandagon's village on the nearby Sheepscot River, the settlers (many of whom were convicted felons) erected Fort St. George (Thayer 1892:205–6). Soon, Rawandagon's people were getting European manufactures such as copper kettles, steel knives, swords, cloth, and woollen blankets directly from the Europeans.

Cut from the profitable trade loop, the Mi'kmaq middlemen quickly turned to violence. Newly equipped with French muskets, Mi'kmaq marines swept over the coastal Abenaki region, killing several local chieftains of Saco River in battle before retreating (Champlain 1922–38 [1]:451; Lescarbot 1907–14 [3]:497–508; Thayer 1892:68). Within a year of its founding, the English colony at Kennebec collapsed. Internal problems, compounded by deteriorating relations with the region's tribespeople, had overwhelmed the settlement (JR [2]:75; Gorges 1890:17–18; Prins 1993).

Still, knowledge of the region's rich fishing grounds, plentiful furs, and enormous stands of valuable timber excited the imaginations of growing numbers of the English and French who frequented Maine's coastal waters in search of wealth. Meanwhile, on the heels of yet another punishing raid by Mi'kmaqs that swept through the Penobscot valley in 1615, an apocalyptic event struck Rawandagon's world: a two-year pandemic of bubonic plague, coupled with what has been suggested was hepatitis (Spiess and Spiess 1987), scourged the area from Penobscot to Cape Cod. Although precise figures are lacking, this pandemic may have killed over ninety percent of the coastal population. In 1619, small and beleaguered remnant bands of kinsfolk and associated families regrouped, joining surviving sagamores such as Rawandagon's father, Chief Manawormet, at Sheepscot (Sewall 1847:190; 1859:121; Levett 1847:92).

Codfish and Soft Gold for Guns and Alcohol

English commercial activities in the Gulf continued to expand, and soon the time was ripe for a renewed colonization effort. In 1620, the English Crown granted the territory from the Kennebec to Piscataqua to Sir Ferdinando Gorges, who later styled himself Lord Proprietor of Maine (Abbott 1875:106). By 1622 some thirty English fishing vessels were anchored offshore, close to Rawandagon's home range (Levett 1906:89–101; cf. Churchill 1978:26–27). Typically making three voyages per year, the vessels hailed from ports in southwest England such as Barnstable and Bristol. Many first arrived in February, anchoring in island or mainland coves where stages were constructed to dry the salted fish (Josselyn 1988; New Hampshire Provincial Papers [1]:81).

Soon, year-round fishing stations were established within Rawandagon's immediate neighborhood, each manned by up to sixty workmen—the first at nearby Damariscove, directly followed by Cape Newagen, Piscataqua, Monhegan, and Pemaquid (Churchill 1978:27). At about the same time, land-hungry yeomen began building small farms on the islands and coastal mainland, growing crops and rearing cattle, hogs, sheep, and goats. In addition to the English, there were French, Basque, and Dutch rivals operating from their fishing or merchant vessels that coasted Maine, eager to cash in on the lucrative fur trade. Anxious to obtain a monopoly on the trade, English merchants petitioned the Council of New England in London for special patents guaranteeing them the exclusive trading rights in certain areas. Thus, from 1628 onwards, special truck houses (trading posts) for the Indian trade were built at strategic coastal locations and at riverine sites at their heads of navigation, first at Richmond Island between Saco and Casco Bay, at Cushnoc on the Kennebec (some forty-five miles upriver at the head of the tide), and at Pejepscot Falls on the lower Androscoggin. But these by no means stopped the fishermen and freebooting merchants from trading activities (cf. Abbott 1875:89; Baker 1985:4; Churchill 1978:39–40; Holmes 1912:154).

After the 1620s, the English greatly outnumbered natives in the coastal area from Penobscot Bay to Cape Cod. Excluding the hundreds of seasonal fishermen, the Maine coast soon counted well over 1,500 permanent settlers, most concentrated in the area from the Kennebec to Pemaquid (Abbott 1875:89; Holmes 1912:154). By this time, having reached manhood during the century's turbulent first decades, Rawandagon must have realized fully that his people were powerless to resist the encroachment of foreigners. Indeed, the Abenakis did not—could not—pose a significant threat. As one English record notes: "The natiues of the Countrie . . . liue nere and amone the English but are beneficiall to them onely in the trade of Beauer wch they exchange for our Commodities. Their want of people makes them not feared by us as not beinge able to doe much mischeife . . . " (Anonymous 1886).

Sharply reduced in number, many of their cornfields deserted because of Mi'kmaq raids, their spirits shaken by strange diseases, coastal Abenakis were essentially cornered into becoming pawns in the burgeoning fur trade (Champlain 1922–38 [1]:320–21). Beaver, otter, marten, and other furs had become greatly valued as profitable export (Bradford 1901). Beaver, in particular, had become so precious that it served English trading post agents and settlers as a currency in their dealings with each other and with fishing captains from Europe, who supplied them with merchandise and services (New Hampshire Provincial Papers [1]:68–69; MeHS Coll. II, 3:54).

In order to get this "soft gold," merchants and fishermen, operating from hundreds of islands, coves, and inlets on Maine's jagged coast, offered local Abenaki trappers almost anything they wanted for their furs, including firearms and alcohol. Given their hunting way of life and their pressing need to defend themselves against enemy attacks, the Abenakis eagerly purchased European weapons, guns in particular. In 1623, Chief Manawormet and other local sagamores, including Squidrayset, traded with English merchant and would-be colonist Christopher Levett at Casco Bay. Speaking broken English, they complained about Tarratines (Mi'kmaqs) "being enemies to them," and requested protection (Levett 1847:92).

Soon, Rawandagon's band was fully armed with muskets, pistols, steel hatchets, knives, and swords. But such hardware rarely came cheap. Regaled with English rum (sometimes identified in documents as "killdevil"), French brandy, or some other strong alcohol, the Indians all too often fell victim to the swindling schemes of unscrupulous merchants. Such repeated abuse caused great resentment among the Abenakis, who repeatedly protested the "hard dealing of the English" (W. Hubbard 1865 [1]:97–98).

In 1627, complaining about "base fellows" who "begin to leave fishing, and fall wholly to trading [furs]," Pilgrim Governor William Bradford of New Plymouth Colony called attention to "the wrongs they did [the Indians on the Kennebec], both the last year and this; and besides they still continue to truck pieces [sell firearms], powder and shot with them" (MD [6]:143). Four years later, in a largely unsuccessful effort to put a stop to the proliferation of firearms among the Abenakis and their neighbors, English authorities decreed "that noe person whatsoever . . . imploy, or cause to be imployed, or to their power permit, any Indian to use any peece [firearm] upon any occacion or pretence whatsoever" (MBR [1]:76; W. Sainsbury 1860–1912 [6]:140). Soon afterwards, trying to monopolize the fur trade, the Council for New England ruled in 1632 that "no fishermen [are] allowed to trade with the savages, nor with the servants of the planters" (W. Sainsbury 1860–1912 [6]:156).

Venting their anger, some frustrated Abenakis took up arms in protest. In 1631, Casco Bay sagamore Squidrayset and other warriors, perhaps including Rawandagon, killed two English traders at Richmond Island, burned "the house over them, and carried away their guns and what else they liked" (New Hampshire Provincial Papers [1]:104). Two years later, an English crew visiting the island took revenge, hanging Manatahqua, alias Black Will, an innocent sagamore from Massachusetts Bay who happened to visit the newly built trading post (Drake 1854: 112; Winthrop 1908). In the winter of 1636, angry Indians once again raided Richmond Island, killing 200 hogs and some goats (Trelawney Papers in MDH [3]:34–43, 52–53, 102).

Meanwhile, settlers at nearby Saco Bay accused local Abenakis of stealing their hogs, and authorized a local ship master "to execut any Indians that are proved to have killed any swyne of the Inglishe" (Libby 1928–31 [1]:2). Several years later, a hungry band of Abenakis on the Kennebec planned to rob the Pilgrim trading post at Cushnoc (Augusta), "there being store in the Plimouth trading house," but bolted at the last minute (Winthrop 1853 [1]:387–88). Soon afterwards, some Abenakis broke into several English homesteads at Saco, stealing their firearms and ammunition (Winthrop 1853 [2]:98).

A Seaside Theater of the Absurd

What did the Europeans think of Rawandagon and his Abenaki cohorts on
the Maine coast? No doubt many viewed them as benighted brutes inhabiting a godforsaken wilderness (Bradford 1901:33–34; Purchas 1905–
1907 [4]:33–34, 231). Others regarded them as hideous, yet somewhat
ridiculous, "wild men." Not unlike their Mi'kmaq neighbors, who spoke
Basque, Spanish, or French trade jargon (Prins and Whitehead 1985), the
coastal Abenakis used "broken English," sometimes swearing crudely like
sailors and fishermen (Levett 1847:92, 97; JR [2]:9). Clearly amused by
their pidgin speech and fragmentary European dress, one visitor commented: "Since they have had intercourse with our Europeans, they are
more motley than the Swiss. . . . One has a red hood, another a green one,
and another a gray, all made . . . best suited to their convenience. Another
will wear a hat with the brim cut off, if it happens to be broad. . . . You will
see Savages dressed in [our] attire, with worsted stockins and a cloak, but
without any breeches; while before and behind are seen two large shirt-
flaps hanging down below the cloak" (JR [44]:289, 295; cf. JR [2]:9; A.
Bailey 1969:59–62; Prins 1996:92–95).

Typical of the derogatory attitude toward Indians are William Wood's
observations (1977:70, 72, 76, 84, 96) in 1634: "when they frolick in their
antique deportments and Indian postures . . . they are more amiable to
behold . . . than many a compounded Phantasticke in the newest fashion
[so that] their carriage and behaviour hath afforded more matter of mirth,
and laughter, than gravity and wisedome." Showing general contempt for
native folk in their neighborhood, the English generally referred to them
as "rogues" or as "black rogues" (cf. MDH [9]:456–57; W. Hubbard 1865
[2]:174; Rowlandson 1913:118–67). They belittled well-known tribesmen
by giving them nicknames, some of which were gleaned from burlesques,
ballads, legends, and other elements of the rich repertoire of seventeenth-
century English popular culture.[3]

In this context, it is important to recall that, in contrast to the Pilgrims
and Puritans of Massachusetts Bay, the Maine coast was settled primarily
by non-Calvinist Protestants from southwest England (Josselyn 1988:61).
Falling into disrepute as "the receptacle of vicious men," the Maine coast
attracted not only rowdy English fishermen, but also a host of other
characters, including social renegades, religious dissidents, runaway felons, freebooters, and sea pirates such as Dixie Bull, who "with fifteen

fellow English" plundered the Maine coast (New Hampshire Provincial Papers [1]:105; cf. Young 1846:362; Churchill 1978:40). No doubt enjoying a "looser" lifestyle than their righteous Puritan neighbors, they let their more ribald language flow freely in the makeshift taverns in seaside Maine. There, whiling away some of their time with merry ballads, they may have amused themselves by staging comical burlesques.

And what about Rawandagon, nicknamed Robin Hood by the English? His sobriquet first shows up in a 1639 document stating that he was by then "commonly called Robinhood" (Sewall 1847:190; 1859:121). What did the English intend when they gave him this odd name? A compliment? A malicious put-down? A vulgar joke?[+] Careful investigation reveals that they were not simply identifying Rawandagon with Sherwood Forest's noble bandit, but linking him to the Robin Hood featured in popular English ballads of the time. These songs "showed a zest for lawlessness which was bound to appeal to the truculent, unbuttoned element in any class"—as evidenced in William Shakespeare's decision to have "Justice Silence trying to sing of 'Robin Hood, Scarlet and John' after a drunken feast with the fat knight" (Holt 1976:248–49, 251).

Beyond ballads, the English cast a man as Robin Hood in their ribald May Fair festivities. At these annual spring fairs, people danced around the maypole and played games. All tenets of common decency were typically overturned and for the duration of the revels, vulgarity reigned. Reflecting an arresting instance of symbolic inversion in English popular culture, a 1597 text fragment offers: "sundry loose persons . . . become Robin Hoods" (OED 1985:2562). From the late sixteenth century onwards, "a king or lord of the May" was elected to holding sway over these rabble-rousing revelries. In due time, this "Lord of Misrule" assumed the character of Robin Hood. In addition, a game known as Robin Hood, originally instituted for the encouragement of archery and later blended with the morris dances, was counted among the fair's favorite events (Douce, in Gutch 1847 [1]:313, 316–17; Billington 1984:37).

Condemned as "light, lewde, and lascivious dauncing" by Calvinists (Fetherston 1582, in Douce 1847:336–37), "Robin Hood with his Morris Dance" provoked sharp disapproval in a 1583 tract titled *Anatomie of Abuses:*

> First, all the wilde heads of the parish, flocking together, chuse them a graund captaine (of mischiefe) whome they innoble with the title of "my Lord of misrule," and him they crowne with great solemnitie, and adopt

for their king. [Then this] heathen company [marches to the church] to strike up the Devils Daunce. [After the celebrations,] they goe againe and againe, and soe foorth into the church yard, where they have commonly their sommer haules, their bowers, arbours, and banquetting houses set up. [Dancing all day long,] these terrestial furies spend the Sabboth day. (Stubbes 1583, in Douce 1847:335–36)

Throughout the seventeenth century, English Protestants in their preachings and invectives tried to banish "insolent plays" such as Robin Hood and the May-games. In a 1661 tract titled *Funebria Florae*, Thomas Hall wrote "that these sensual sports and carnal-flesh-pleasing wayes of wine, women, dancing, revelling, &c., [the Pope] hath gained more souls, than by all the tortures and cruel persecutions that he could invent" (Douce 1847:351).

Also popular at these fairs were the fools, traditionally associated with the devil. These grotesque, costumed characters with blackened face, "belled cap and particolored hose," represented "the nadir of human behaviour" (according to Geoffrey Chaucer) and made the people laugh (Billington 1984:9, 12, 115, 118). Rarely absent at the festivities was the fool named Jack Pudding—a name associated not only with the word sausage, but, more significantly, with penis. Other fools, including buffoons and "incredible oatfish rustics," bore such names as Toby, Simpkin, John Swabber, and Daniel Swash: "These Merry Wags . . . always appear in a Fool's Coat and commit such blunders and Mistakes . . . as those who listen to them would be ashamed of" (Billington 1984:54; see also 39, 42, 46, 71–72; Hughes 1956:21–23, 171, 191, 204–17, 220). An announcement for London's annual Bartholomew Fair sums up the scene: "A comic Droll here ev'ry Hour is shewn; Here Robin Hood and Little John are known: A City Rake, a noble King appeares; His Tinsel Dress each gazing Clown reveres" (Rosenfeld: 22).

Thus, drawing on popular farce, featuring favorite folk heroes and comical drolls, the English on the Maine coast came up with a medley of bizarre nicknames for local Abenaki tribesmen. Jack Pudding, Diogenes, Captain Sunday, Erle Duglas, King Harry, Old Robin, Dick Swash, and Little John are among the "foolish" names given to Maine Indians in the mid-seventeenth century.

No doubt, while these monikers sounded hilarious to the English, their exact significance went undetected by the victims of their mockery. And who would guess today that some of these names belonged to well-known English fools, buffoons, or other farcical characters? (cf. Wood 1977:65)[5]

In light of these considerations, it seems clear that Rawandagon did not earn his peculiar sobriquet because the English somehow associated him with their own heroic outlaw of tradition, the noble bandit of medieval Sherwood Forest, who stole from the rich and gave to the poor. On the contrary, the English made a mockery of this Abenaki sagamore and his fellow hunters of the Maine woods. Imagine how the hard-boiled and hard-drinking Englishmen on the coast viewed Rawandagon and his companions when these tribesmen approached them in birchbark canoes loaded with furs to be bartered away. Here was a motley crew of men carrying bows and arrows (as well as newly purchased muskets). Due to the ceremonial importance of the visit, they would have been colorfully dressed in special costumes bedecked with tinkling copper and wampum beads. In addition to feathers in their long hair, they would have painted their tattooed faces. Most were probably blackened, mourning deceased kinsfolk (Purchas 1614, in Thayer 1892:89).

In English eyes, the Abenaki tribesmen were funny-looking, funny-talking "wild men"—reminiscent of the fools, mummers, or strollers of the May fair. Words used by Wood (1977:65) in 1634 to describe New England's natives are revealing: "Bare Skinned Morris Dancers, who presented their Antiques before [a captive] . . . When they had sported enough about this walking Maypole, a rough hewne Satyre cutteth a gobbit of flesh from his brawnie arme, eating it in his view, searing it with a firebrand" (Wood 1977:65). Given this mindset, it is easy to imagine how Rawandagon, as an Indian headman, came to be identified with the fair's Lord of Misrule—Robin Hood.[6]

Accommodation as Strategy—They Robin-Hood bargains Are Call'd

Not surprisingly, the English also associated the name Robin Hood with deception by trickery, as in the saying, "When . . . a Purchase you reap, that is wondrous cheap, they Robin-Hood bargains are call'd" (Child 1858 [3]:45; OED 1985:2562). Indeed, viewing Rawandagon and his co-horts as credulous fools, the English duped them into signing documents that served as proof that the Indians no longer owned parts of their

Robin Hood's mark on a deed signed in 1650 concerning the selling of Rasthegon Island (York Deeds [10]:252)

traditional territories. Typically, they were paid a mere pittance for their land. Consider Rawandagon's first deed, a 1639 contract first identifying him as Robin Hood. In exchange for a considerable piece of land located on the east bank of the lower Kennebec (at Nequaseg, now Woolwich), which had "one wigwam, or Indian house" on it, he received the sum total of "one hogshead of corn and thirty sound pumpkins" (Sewall 1847:190; 1859:121). Given the buyer's deal, not unusual among seventeenth-century "Indian deeds" in coastal Maine, this surely qualifies as a typical "Robin-Hood bargain" (MDH [9]:358–59; cf. Baker 1989).

While Rawandagon and his fellow Abenakis may have known that they were being cheated out of their coastal and riverine property, they were also aware that they were outnumbered and outgunned by their English neighbors. Increasingly suffering from the deleterious effects of alcohol abuse and addiction in their communities, Abenakis, now dependent on European imports, probably felt they had no choice but to maintain good relations with the colonists. With the English population ever-growing, the "deed-game" soon turned into a familiar ritual for the man nicknamed Robin Hood. For instance, he sold two islands in the lower Kennebec in 1649 and 1650, and was mentioned again two years later when he and two other sagamores (alias Dick Swash and Jack Pudding) signed a deed for the sale of a Sheepscot river tract (CMHS 4:219).

For the next twenty-five years, Rawandagon continued selling numerous small tracts of land for a mere token. Alcohol probably played a role in most of these transactions. Some early deeds specifically note that the Indian selling his land is entitled to, for instance, "two gallons of wine and a bottle of strong waters to him in hand paid" (in Leger 1929:69–70). By way of example, the earlier noted Casco Bay sagamore, Squidrayset, sold a large stretch of land to an English fisherman in the summer of 1657, who agreed in exchange to "yearly pay unto the sd Scittergussett, Sagamore, during his life one Trading Coate for [land along the] Capussicke & one Gallone of Lyquor for Ammo[c]ingan" (York Deeds [1]:83).

There may have been other reasons why Rawandagon pursued a strategy of accommodation, no matter how detestable he may have found the
English. In addition to supplying him with weapons, they provided him
with a measure of security against his enemies. Having earlier been raided
by seafaring Mi'kmaqs, the Abenakis were now threatened by Iroquois
aggression from the opposite direction. Made up of five nations, including
the formidable Mohawks, these Iroquois could field about 2,200 warriors.
From the late 1630s onwards, they began spreading mayhem, soon reaching all of the Algonquian-speaking peoples from the Great Lakes to the
Gulf of St. Lawrence (JR [45]:203–5; Jennings 1984:35–36, 206). In the
winter of 1642–43, a party of ten Mohawk raiders captured an Abenaki
hunting band on the upper Kennebec. They reportedly tortured six men to
death and adopted the women and children into their stronghold at Osser-
nenon on the Mohawk River (Talbot 1935:273–74).

Black Robe and Robin Hood—A Struggle for Spiritual Power

These Iroquois threats spurred the Abenaki villages upriver to seek closer
ties with the French and their Algonquian allies. Perhaps viewing baptism
as an alliance-building ritual, some Abenakis traveled to Canada, where
they converted to Catholicism (JR [25]:117–21; Morrison 1984:26, 78). In
the spring of 1646, following yet another epidemic, two sagamores from
Norridgewock led a delegation to the Jesuit mission at Sillery, requesting
a French priest to return with them to the Kennebec (JR [28]:203). After
one year of successful proselytizing among the Abenakis, Father Gabriel
Dreuillettes was forced to leave the area. His native converts on the river,
however, "published everywhere that prayer was good, and that it had
cured their children" (JR [28]:215; [31]:199).

Coupled with the deadly horror of diseases such as smallpox and the
cruel terror of Iroquois incursions, the Abenakis found themselves confronted with the risk of game depletion in their hunting districts, in particular of beaver. When a party of thirty armed Abenakis ventured to
Quebec in the summer of 1649, they tried to buy beaver from their Algonquin and Montagnais allies, planning to take these valuable furs back to
the Kennebec to sell to the English (JR [36]:53).

Like the Abenakis, the French colonists in Canada were greatly distressed about the increasingly brazen Iroquois attacks on the Algonquian-

speaking nations on its frontiers. In the summer of 1651, Dreuillettes was again dispatched to the Kennebec to secure Abenaki support against the Iroquois. After the missionary was welcomed with "a salvo of arquebus shots," Norridgewock's headman, Oumamanradok, asked the Jesuit to come with him downriver to the English trading post at Cushnoc, in present-day Augusta, to protest against the ruinous English policy of selling alcohol to his people (JR [37]:249). Due to his strategic position between the French in Canada and the English on the Maine coast, Chief Oumamanradok emerged as a new political broker on the Anglo-French colonial frontier.

Apparently, these shifts in power relations stirred up tensions between Rawandagon and his upriver rivals at Norridgewock. According to Dreuillettes, Rawandagon was the "most noted and most feared" of all shamanchiefs.[7] The death of one of Norridgewock's sagamores was blamed on his evil witchcraft. Referring to Rawandagon by his English nickname, rendered as "Aranbineau," the French priest reported what he had heard upriver:

> The sudden death of one of our Captains, following upon a quarrel that he had with the Captain of the People living at the mouth of our river, made us believe that man [Rawandagon, alias Robin Hood], who is regarded as a great sorcerer, had killed him secretly by means of his sorcery. Our hearts were already arousing old-time hatred that we had for those peoples, and we were on the point of cutting one another's throats and making war on one another. (JR [38]:35–39)[8]

Impressed by the "black robe" and regarding him as a powerful shaman-chief, Rawandagon appears to have realized that the Jesuit's return to the Kennebec represented a new turn in the dynamics of political power in the region. As such, he probably thought it to his advantage to show the missionary his respect. As reported by Dreuillettes, a converted chieftain at Norridgewock issued the following statement: "It is time that all the sorcerers [shamans] now acknowledge their weakness, and the power of Jesus, some even inviting the [Jesuit] Father into their cabins, and treating him with high honor. [Robin Hood] has shown himself so docile to the Father's words that he now makes profession of having him as an intimate friend" (JR [38]:35–39).

In 1652, after one year among the Abenakis at Kennebec, Dreuillettes was again called back to Canada. By then, a new trading post had been built at Taconnet almost seventy miles upriver from the coast and well above Cushnoc, which saw its profit base further undermined. The fur trade was also damaged by the ongoing "beaver wars," pitting the Iroquois against the Abenakis and their Algonquian-speaking allies. These hostilities were triggered by the fierce competition over diminishing stocks of fur-bearing animals in the traditional hunting territories, some of which had become depleted by the mid-seventeenth century. Because of the fighting, it was dangerous for small parties to venture into the woods. Moreover, the demands of war left little time for trapping or trading (NYCD [13]:355, 356; cf. Prins 1996:105–15).

Finally, after more than thirty years on the river, the Plymouth merchants were forced out of the Kennebec fur trade in 1661 (cf. Baker 1985:9–10). Two years later, following a devastating Mohawk raid against an Indian encampment near an English trading post in the Penobscot River Valley, an allied force of Abenaki, Sokoki, and other Algonquian warriors waged a bloody campaign in the Connecticut River Valley, finally defeating the Mohawks (NYCD [13]:297–98; 308–9; cf. Calloway 1990:55–75; Day 1965:243). Obviously, this turmoil also affected Rawandagon and his cohorts, all of whom depended on the flow of furs to provide them with the means of exchange to purchase European commodities.

Double Bind—Robin Hood as Indian Sachem

Rawandagon's life was conditioned not only by the complexities of New England's colonial frontier, but also by political changes in Western Europe. Soon after the restoration of the English Crown to Charles II, the Puritan Commonwealth of Massachusetts Bay was forced to relinquish its control over the Province of Maine in 1664. The Puritan Commonwealth had annexed this vast feudal domain west of the Kennebec (to Piscataqua River) during the interregnum more than a decade earlier (and renamed it Yorkshire; coincidentally, this British county is associated with the Robin Hood legends). The King returned the province (which at that time was smaller than the state of Maine) to the grandson of Maine's original proprietor, Sir Ferdinando Gorges. A year later, in 1665, he granted the region east of the Kennebec (to Penobscot River) to his own brother James, the Duke of York. Officially renamed Cornwall, this region fell under the same jurisdiction as New York, the newly captured Dutch colony that had been granted to the Duke a year earlier.

Formally quashing the notion that Abenaki chieftains such as Rawandagon actually possessed legal title to their ancestral territories, English authorities issued official instructions to the settlers on the Maine coast that expressly disallowed them "to make Purchase of the pretended Tytle of any of the Sagamores or Indians which is derogatory to the grant [made by the King] but after contract made with you then if they be willing it is very acceptable . . . that they give somewhat to the adjacent sagamore or native for their consent so as it to be no considerable sum" (Libby 1928–31 [1]:205). While the ordinance reflected a less equitable political philosophy with respect to Abenaki land rights, given the trifling terms of the earlier "Indian deeds," this new regulation made little practical difference for Rawandagon and his cohorts.

A subsequent decree had a more profound effect on Rawandagon's position, as it introduced a policy of indirect rule over regional tribespeople. In 1665, the Duke of York's Commissioners concluded a treaty with Indian chieftains between the Kennebec and Penobscot that required "[t]hat if any Mischief should happen to be done by the English or Indians one against another, though it were to the killing any Person, neither Side should right themselves, but Complaint should be made to the Sagamores, if the Indians did the Wrong, and to the Court it were done by the English. Both which did promise Satisfaction should be made for the preventing any Quarrel" (W. Hubbard 1865 [2]:91–92).

Pursuing this policy, the Massachusetts Court ruled two years later that:

> some principall Indian be appointed & declared to be the *sachem,* or cheife, or head of them, to whom the English may have recourse upon all occasions of wrong donne them by the Indians, expecting from such Cheife Indian or Indians, so appointed by this Court, the discovery & delivery into the hands of our Justice any of their Indians as shall be any ways injurious to the English; and upon neglect or refusall thereof, it being apparent that the Indians have donne the wrong, that then such Sachem or Sachems be proceeded against in a course of lawe, as being guilty for such injuries, liable to answer for ye delinquency. (MBR [2]:359, my emphasis)[9]

No stranger to the English, familiar with their language and acquainted with their customs, Rawandagon was picked as the Abenaki candidate for "Indian Sachem." While this newly minted title recognized him as the region's Grand Chief, his new status came with a price: the English authorities now held him personally responsible for the actions of native troublemakers in the area. Although Rawandagon must have been called upon to answer to numerous conflicts of varying significance, only a few were recorded in surviving documents.

One noteworthy instance occurred in the wake of a French punitive expedition against the Mohawks in 1666. Their villages burned to the ground and their gardens destroyed, the Mohawks finally agreed to make peace with their former enemies and their allies, including Abenakis from as far east as the Kennebec. That summer, perhaps celebrating this newly concluded peace with the Iroquois, Abenaki warriors were reported to be in the Connecticut River Valley feasting on English livestock. Some farmers complained to the authorities, blaming visiting tribesmen from the Kennebec area for "shooting, wounding, & killing sundry of their swyne and cattle, and in cutting the flesh of the bones, & carrying away the flesh of the catle so killed . . . " Pointing the accusing finger at "Robin Hood, Cheife Sachem of the Indians at Kennybeke," the Massachusetts Court deemed Rawandagon responsible (MBR [2]:361; Gookin 1806:167–69).[10] Obliged to make reparations, probably in the form of a considerable number of beaver skins and other furs, he was threatened "with the utmost severity, if the like should be repeated" (Drake 1854:284). Furthermore, some of Rawandagon's people may have been demanded "as hostages or pledges for . . . fidelity and true performance," a common practice at the time (MDH [10]:7–11). The chief's own son Wohawa, alias Hope Hood, who was "once a servant of a Christian master in Boston," may have been one of these Abenaki hostages (Mather 1702:598).

As sachem, Rawandagon was also expected to ratify and confirm deeds signed by fellow tribesmen in the region. In addition to confirming earlier deeds, such as one involving land near Wiscasset Bay signed by two local sagamores (one of whom was Obias, alias Dick Swash), he also ratified a 1670 deed signed by sagamore Derumkin and two other Indians involving a tract near Muddy River "unto Amoscoggon," which was "sold" for "one peck of Corn on every five & twentieth Day of December . . . for ever" (York Deeds [9]:188; [10]:82).

Rawandagon's Final Act—Brokering for Peace on the Eve of War

In 1669, after a bloody battle near a major Mohawk stronghold, the Algonquian-speaking nations, including the Abenakis of Kennebec, agreed to yet another peace with their Iroquois enemies (Gookin 1806:

167–69). An all-too-brief period of comparative calm followed, during which Rawandagon continued to put his personal mark on Indian deeds. In June 1675, he cosigned a contract "for a certain Sum of good & sufficient pay" for the sale of a tract of land near the mouth of the Androscoggin River to an English fur trader and settler, Thomas Purchase (York Colonial Records [9]:254). It proved to be the last document he signed (York Deeds [9]:228, 229; cf. York Colonial Records [9]:254; York Deeds [2]:191; Wheeler 1878:11; Baker 1989).

That same month, already tense Anglo-Indian relations in New England suddenly turned to slaughter. Wampanoag warriors killed several English settlers at Swansea, signalling the beginning of a ruthless Anglo-Indian war known as King Philip's War. Within a year, fighting claimed the lives of some 6,000 natives and about 600 colonists (Drake 1857; Jennings 1975:309; Vaughan and Clark 1981:9). In an effort to cut off the Indians from their supplies, the Massachusetts Court ruled soon after the outbreak of hostilities that all trading posts "shall wholly cease, and none to presume to make any sale [to the Indians], except in open shops and tounes where goods are sold unto the English" (Massachusetts Archives, Indian Records [5]:63).

In reaction to these troubles, English troops from their garrison at Arrowsick on the lower Kennebec were dispatched to the upriver trading post at Taconnet, where they removed all valuable goods, including gunpowder and shot. This occurred in July, when the Abenaki were given an ultimatum stating that "in Case they would not come down and deliver up their Arms, the English would kill them" (MDH [6]:92–93). Protesting that they would starve without their weapons, only a dozen tribesmen from the Kennebec and Androscoggin came downriver and surrendered "an inconsiderable Part of their Ammunition, as a few Guns, a little Powder and Shot, with a few Knives" (W. Hubbard 1865 [2]:98–100).

Clearly frustrated by what many must have felt was unreasonable intimidation, one Androscoggin warrior, "having an Axe in his hand, struck at one Hosea Mallet, a French-man, but was prevented from doing him Mischief." Immediately, the English jumped on him, tied him up with ropes, and locked the hothead up in a cellar. Recounting the events, Puritan minister William Hubbard (1865 [2]:99–100) noted later, "The ancient Indians being asked what they thought was meet to be done in the said Case? said, he was worthy to die for such an Affront, yet they would be glad if his life might be spared, offering to be jointly bound in his behalf, to pay forty beaver-skins at the next fall voyage. . . . And also leaving their arms in the hands of the English as a pledg of their faithful keeping those articles of peace . . . " The English promised to return these, if "they proved themselves to be honest Men."

Outnumbered by well-armed Englishmen surrounding them and with some of their leading men held hostage, local Abenakis had good reason to be alarmed. Feeling threatened and hoping to avoid further escalation of the conflict, they turned to Rawandagon, at the time described as "an Indian of great note amongst them." Now in his seventies, the Grand Chief acted as an intermediary, deflecting a conflict that could have turned into a battle. The following day, on July 19, 1675, Rawandagon, alias Robin Hood, "with great applause of the rest, made a [peace] dance, and sung a song to declare their intent in what was transacted. And so they parted, setting the Indians at liberty, that had engaged thus for their friend Sowen, the Indian." Retreating upriver, the Abenakis were forced to leave some of their fellow tribesmen behind as English hostages. Among them may have been Rawandagon. Some time afterwards, however, "how civilly soever they were treated, [they] ran all away at the last, trusting more the celerity of their own feet than to the civility of their English friends" (W. Hubbard 1865 [2]:98–100).

Meanwhile, the revolt initiated by the Wampanoag continued to spread and quickly engulfed the entire region from the Hudson to the Piscataqua Rivers, reaching Maine by summer's end (W. Hubbard 1865 [2]:91–92). Seeking to escape the carnage in New England, groups of Indian refugees migrated into Abenaki country and beyond (Abbott 1875:177; W. Hubbard 1865 [2]:113; cf. Prins and Bourque 1987; Prins 1992). Clearly, the time for mediation was over, and Rawandagon's once-significant role as power broker had been played out. Frontier relations quickly took a turn for the worse, and a three-year-long Anglo-Abenaki war devastated English settlements on the Maine coast (MDH [6]:90–93, 118–19; MHS [6]:94; Morrison 1984:106–11). One of the most prominent Abenakis in this war was Rawandagon's son Wohawa, the man also identified as Hope Hood, who quickly earned an odious reputation among Englishmen, who claimed that he "excelled all other savages in acts of cruelty" (Drake 1854:302; Mather 1702:598).

After 1675, there is no longer mention of Rawandagon. His exit from the stage represents the end of the colonial antebellum on the New England coast. Was he killed? Did the sachem die of old age in the Maine woods? At any rate, without his presence as a power broker straddling the culture divide, the Abenaki no longer pursued a strategy of accommodation but opted for armed resistance against the English invaders in their increasingly desperate struggle for survival.

Notes

As usual, I thank my wife, Bunny McBride, for her help in editing this article. Earlier versions were presented at the 1986 symposium, "Peoples in Contact: Indians and Europeans in the Seventeenth Century," hosted by Brown University's Haffenreffer Museum of Anthropology, and at the "Native Northeastern Culture Brokers" session at the Annual Meeting of the Northeastern Anthropological Association held in Danbury, Connecticut, in 1993. The spelling of Mi'kmaq throughout this chapter reflects current orthographic practice among the Mi'kmaqs. See Harald Prins, *The Mi'kmaq: Resistance, Accommodation, and Cultural Survival* (Fort Worth: Harcourt Brace, 1996), 5 n. 2.

1. I first proposed this linkage between the English legendary bandit Robin Hood and his "Merry Men" and the Abenaki on the lower Kennebec (including Merrymeeting Bay) in Prins (1986). In this paper, I suggested that the toponym "Merrymeeting Bay," first documented about 1637 (C. Allen 1931:94), forms part of this same early folkloric complex. As such, I disagree with alternative explanations made by Eckstorm (1941:138–39) and others.

2. Records suggest that Rawandagon's various other (inherited?) names included Damarine, Rawmegin, Rogemock, and Mahotiwormet. The issue of who is who among the Abenaki in the colonial period is complex. In addition to changing personal names, or being known under different names simultaneously, tribespeople also inherited names from deceased kin. These and other factors make any reconstruction a hazardous undertaking. Rawandagon, the name used in this article, is first mentioned in a 1660 document (York Deeds [10]:261). Other documents drafted that same year identify him as Rawmeagon (York Deeds [2]:32) and Rogemocken (MDH [23]:204). He is identified as Mahotiwormet, alias Damarine, in a document written in 1639 (Sewall 1849:190, 1859:121).

3. In New England, sobriquets also applied to fellow settlers. For instance, as relayed by Cotton Mather (1702:596), one Robert Rogers, because of "his corpulency . . . was usually nicknamed, Robin Pork."

4. Compare the European tradition of insulting native African chieftains in the same period. For instance, English traders nicknamed a Pokoso "big man" at Ashanta "Johnny Konny" (as in "no money, no coney"—i.e., cunt). The Dutch called a powerful leader on the Guinea Coast "Jan Claessen"—a squeaky-voiced, coarse, and boastful puppet (Wolf 1982:209).

5. No doubt, not unlike the Penobscot Indians of Maine today, as described by Speck (1940:248–49), these early Abenakis also used nicknames among them-

selves. It stands to reason that they had their own cultural repertoire of funny nicknames for English people with whom they came in regular contact.

6. In this hermeneutic exercise, I obviously disagree with Drake (1854:284 n.), who concluded that "This name [Robin Hood] was adopted, I have no doubt, as it came something near his Indian name."

7. It was not unusual for powerful chieftains in the region to be credited with great supernatural powers. Several are known to have been important shamans (cf. Hoffman 1955:428–76, 570–72). Cotton Mather, who was well-known himself for encounters with spiritual beings, wrote that "the Indians, whose chief sagamores are well known unto some of our captives to have been horrid sorcerers, and hellish conjurers, and such as conversed with daemons" (Mather 1702:620).

8. In his influential book, *Histoire des Abenakis*, Abbé Joseph A. Maurault, resident priest in the Western Abenaki village of Saint Francis (Odanak, Quebec), offers an interesting folk etymology for the name Aranbinau. Spelling it as Aran-bino, he fails to recognize it as a French orthographic rendering of Robin Hood. As such, he erroneously traced the etymological origins of the English name to the Western Abenaki word *Arag8inno*, meaning "he is of iron" (Maurault 1866:143n.). Maurault evidently attributed Western Abenaki origins to several other French and English names (cf. Day 1981:12, 32, 66, 73–75, 96; Eckstorm 1941:251).

9. In seventeenth-century New England, colonists typically referred to grand chiefs or paramount chieftains as Kings or Sachems, in contrast to local chieftains, who were called Petty Lords or Sagamores (cf. Lechford 1642:115).

10. Since 1636, English colonists in the Connecticut Valley decreed "where any Company of Indians doe sett downe neere any English plantacions, that they shall declare whoe is their Sachem or Cheife," and declared "that the saide Cheife or Sachem Shall paye to the saide English such trespasses as shal be committed by any Indian in the said plantacion adjoyninge, either by spoilinge or killinge of Cattle or Swine either with Trappes, dogges or arrowes & they are not to pleade that it was done by Strangers unlesse they cann prduce the prty, and deliver him or his goods into the custody of the English" (CPR [1]:19).

≈≈≈

CHAPTER SIX

Suscaneman and the
Matinecock Lands, 1653–1703

Robert S. Grumet

Introduction

THE NAME OF a man variously identified as Suscaneman, Chascaneman, Shoskene, Runasuck, Rompsicka, Rumasackromen, Captain Ramerock, and Captain Lambert appears in 113 documents recording dated events involving Indian people and colonists in central and western Long Island and central New Jersey from 1655 to 1703.[1] One hundred and one of these documents chronicle events occurring in and around the 160-square-mile area originally comprising the Long Island town of Oyster Bay in present-day Nassau County, New York.[2] Oyster Bay is located in what was the easternmost part of Munsee Country during Historic Contact period times.[3]

Virtually all documents mentioning Suscaneman by name are deeds. The 91 deeds to central and western Long Island lands bearing his mark (Suscaneman was almost surely illiterate) were signed over a period of nearly fifty years. Most of these deeds represent conveyances or conveyance confirmations, through which Suscaneman and other Indian people transferred title and sovereignty to almost all of their unsold lands within the town of Oyster Bay to English purchasers between 1667 and 1700. The particular pattern of land alienation chronicled in these records appears to represent an intriguing body of documentation; few other Indian people in the Northeast are known to have negotiated so many deeds to so small an area of land over so long a period of time.[4]

This paper surveys written records documenting these events in order to discern Suscaneman's identity, delineate his social and political affiliations and status, determine the extent of his power and authority, and inquire into the causes and consequences of his actions. The nature of extant documentation requires consideration of several questions. Do documents mentioning people identified as Suscaneman, Runasuck, or Captain Lambert, for example, refer to the same individual? Was this person the man repeatedly identified in colonial records as the chief Indian proprietor of Matinecock? Was Matinecock itself a locality, a village, a region, or a tribe? If Suscaneman was the chief Matinecock proprietor, what was the extent of his authority? Was he a leader of his people, a representative of the Matinecock leadership, or a colonial puppet? Most importantly for our purposes here, did he have the right to sell 91 deeds worth of his people's homeland in Oyster Bay?

Verification of Suscaneman's identity and status permits examination of other questions. Why, for example, did this man place his mark on so many deeds to lands in so small an area? Did he sign them freely or was he duped or forced into putting his mark on these documents? Was the extent and intensity of these activities unique? Does the pattern observed in this documentation reflect historical reality or is it an accidental result of differential preservation of a portion of the manuscript record? Such verification will permit the framing of a larger question: did the Indian and European people mentioned in these documents completely misunderstand one another, or did they arrive at creative misunderstandings in which people viewing events from different cultural perspectives nevertheless manage to arrive at some form of accommodation?[5]

This paper begins by reviewing the written record of Suscaneman's documented career. These data are then used to shed new light onto the identity of the Matinecock locale and people. Findings are then used to address questions bearing upon Suscaneman's identity, status, and role in intercultural relations on central Long Island.

Suscaneman

Inexplicably, Suscaneman has been ignored by scholars. Local historians such as Benjamin F. Thompson (1918) and William W. Tooker (1911) do little more than mention his name. More recent studies by such students of Long Island Indian culture and history as anthropologist Theodore J. C.

Brasser (1966) and historian Allen W. Trelease (1960) have focused attention almost entirely upon more prominent personalities, such as the Montauk chief Wyandanch (see Strong in this volume) and Tackapousha (fl.
1643–97), the Massapequa sachem who became the most influential Indian leader in seventeenth-century western Long Island. Most people
tracing descent from Matinecock ancestors barely remember more than
Suscaneman's name.

Suscaneman's obscurity is surprising. Few Indian individuals are so
frequently mentioned by name in Long Island colonial records. Fully 92 of
the 113 documents known to chronicle his life identify him by some
variant of this name. It first appears as "Susakatucan" in a confirmation of
a deed to Lloyd's Neck (in the present bounds of the Suffolk county town of
Huntington), signed on May 14, 1658 (Street 1887–99 [1]:16).[6] The name
next appears as Sasaketawuh, Chawescome, and Chascaneman in deeds
to other tracts in what was then Queens County (a large area that today
also includes the county of Nassau), signed between 1659 and 1668.[7]
Documents listing an individual variously identified as Shoskene, Shoskcock, and Shoskeene in Oyster Bay records produced between 1667 and
1669 almost certainly refer to Suscaneman as well.[8]

Suscaneman's name first appears in its most extensively reproduced
form as "suskaneman of longisland in ye Bounds of Matenecoke" in a
November 16, 1677, deed conveying approximately ten acres of land near
"doytons swomp" in Oyster Bay (Cox 1916–40 [1]:148–49). The name
appears in substantially the same form in another 78 documents produced
between 1678 and 1700.[9]

A deed to land in Oyster Bay executed on December 20, 1678, is the
earliest known document explicitly linking Suscaneman's name with the
name Runasuck (Cox 1916–40 [1]:355). All told, 39 documents mentioning Suscaneman list Runasuck as his other name.[10] Yet the 1678 deed is
not the first document to mention Suscaneman by this alias. It first appears
in the forms Ronessock and Ronnessoke in statements made to English
settlers at Flushing, Queens, dated May 14 and 16, 1653, in the midst of
the First Anglo-English Naval War (1652–54). These documents reported
an alleged Dutch conspiracy between the Dutch and the Narragansett
sachem Ninigret to destroy all English settlements in and around New
Netherland.[11] The name appears in other documents as Runnasuk, Runisuk, Runasark, Ramoreck, Capt. Ramerock, and Rompsicka.[12] This latter
document also identifies Rompsicka as a man named Captain Lambert
(NYCD [14]:540).

Runasuck and its variants appear to be short forms of another name variously rendered as Rumashekah, Rumasackromen, Romasickamon, Romosowe, Lumasowie, Lummusooron, Lumoseecon, Lourkamsaman, and Wallamassekaman in documents written between 1657 and 1703. Several of these names appear on documents chronicling events on central and western Long Island.[13] Others are listed in documents recording land sales in the Navesink and Raritan sections of central New Jersey transacted between 1676 and 1703.[14] All of these names were documented at times when the name Suscaneman did not appear in Long Island records.

Neither the number of names associated with Suscaneman nor their range of orthographic variation is unusual. Collaborative research conducted by historian Clinton A. Weslager (1971, 1974) and Eastern Oklahoma Delaware traditionalist Nora Thompson Dean indicates that Munsees and other Delaware-speaking people have always possessed several names. Most are unique names closely associated with particular owners. Many are causal nicknames. Others are spiritually charged personal names rarely shared with strangers.

Whatever their emotional, social, or spiritual content, Delaware names have always been specifically associated with particular individuals. And as the following passage penned by Long Island colonist Daniel Denton (1670:9–10) shows, most died with their owners:

> Any Indian being dead, his name dies with him, no person daring ever after to mention his name, it being not only a breach of their law, but an abuse to his friends and relations present, as if it were done on purpose to renew their grief: and any other person whatsoever that is named after that name does incontinently change his name, and [10] takes a new one, their names are not proper set names as among Christians, but every one invents a name for himself, which he likes best. Some calling themselves *Rattle-Snake, Skunk, Bucks-horn,* or the like: And if a person dies, that his name is some word which is used in speech, they likewise change that word, and invent a new one, which makes a great change and alteration in language. [spelling modernized][15]

Several factors probably account for the patterns observed in the documentation containing Suscaneman's name and aliases. The comparatively wide variety of spellings used during early decades of his career may almost certainly be attributed to his relative obscurity and suggest his lack of importance among settlers. The remarkable regularity exhibited in spellings of his name in Oyster Bay records during the final thirty years of his documented career, by contrast, may reflect his higher status as a respected elder familiar to colonial scribes.

Appearances of large numbers of similar or identical spellings may also arise from more mechanical factors. Increased governmental land-sale regulation during the later seventeenth century was reflected in a trend towards greater uniformity in the form and wording of deeds. Although all deeds bearing Suscaneman's mark were handwritten documents executed without the benefit of legal aid (more than one hundred years would pass before printed deeds and lawyers appeared in ever-growing numbers), many were form documents that differed from one another only in the names of the buyers and sellers, location of the land to be sold, and the price. Suscaneman put his mark upon as many as seven such form deeds in one day on March 1, 1682 (Cox 1916–40 [1]:183–87, 197–98, 277–78, 401).

Orthographic uniformity was almost assured in such documents. The overall regularity in spellings of Suscaneman's name in so many documents written by different scribes during the last thirty years of his recorded career was all the more notable in that it occurred in an era not noted for standardized spelling. Other factors may account for the unique orthographic felicity of the spellings of Suscaneman's name in colonial documents. Although no document informs us of the extent of Suscaneman's linguistic abilities, he may well have either spoken English or the trade jargon combining English, Dutch, and Delaware words that emerged in the region during the 1600s. At the very least, he was probably able to pronounce his name in such a way that it was clearly discernable to English scribes unfamiliar with his language. Since he became the best known western Long Island Indian leader after the Massapequa sachem Tackapousha, scribes had many opportunities to hear and read his name and its aliases.

The mark entered next to Suscaneman's name on most of the deeds mentioning him on file in the Oyster Bay town records is an open curled circle resembling an open-ended figure six. The similarities displayed by these marks, however, may not reflect a regularity in the way Suscaneman signed deeds. None of these deeds is an original document signed by Suscaneman. All, instead, are transcribed copies of original records entered into town record books by the town scribe. Since no unequivocally original specimens of Suscaneman's mark are currently known to exist, it is presently impossible to determine if the figure used to depict Suscaneman's mark in the town record books is his actual signature or a conventional representation used by town scribes.

Most documents mentioning Suscaneman in town records and other papers do little more than list his name and an alias. Few note his status or identify his kinsfolk. None directly reveal anything about his thoughts or feelings. Investigators using this kind of documentation thus must work like archaeologists, piecing together small bits of fragmentary and often disjointed data. Unable to draw upon ethnographic data gathered from contemporary informants, scholars must rely upon analogies drawn from other societies to make sense of emerging patterns.

Review of this documentation indicates that Suscaneman's rise to documentary prominence was neither meteoric nor, evidently, assured by particularly high birth. The earliest known reference to the man identifies him as "a little Sachem [who] hath few men under him" (NPNER [2]: 44). Although many subsequent documents refer to Suscaneman as chief proprietor of Matinecock, none disclose a kinship relationship between Suscaneman and Asharoken (fl. 1648–69), the preceding Matinecock sachem.

Both Asharoken and Suscaneman placed their marks on eleven deeds to lands at Matinecock between 1655 and 1669. Following a subsequent nine year hiatus, during which no deeds for lands in and around Oyster Bay were signed, Asharoken's name did not appear on a deed dated November 16, 1677, bearing the mark of "Suskaneman of longisland in ye Bounds of matenecoke" (Cox 1916–40 [1]:148–49). Little more than a year later, Suscaneman signed a deed to another piece of land as "ye Chiefe proprietor of ye Lands of Matenacock and Successor unto Asiopum alias Mahams deceased" (355). The absence of this or any other orthography of Asharoken's name in subsequent documents affirms that the senior chief fell from power, moved away, or died sometime between 1669 and 1677.[16]

Another document, dated October 29, 1683, suggests that Suscaneman's rise to prominence at Matinecock Bay may be traced to a different source of authority (Cox 1916–40[1]:267). This document notes that Georgacuran (Quarapin fl. 1683–92), his sister's eldest son, was also Chepouse's eldest son. Most properly known as Chopeyconnaws (fl. 1658–99), Chepouse was the eldest known brother of the powerful Massapequa sachem Tackapousha.[17] Quarapin's status as the eldest son of Chopeyconnaws and Suscaneman's sister suggests that Chopeyconnaws was married to Suscaneman's sister, providing Suscaneman with an affinal link to the family of central and western Long Island's most influential Indian leader. Acting with the support of such a powerful kinsman, Suscaneman could have secured his authority among Indians living in and around Matine-cock following Asharoken's documentary disappearance.

No matter how Suscaneman achieved his position, the 81 documents that include his name on Long Island between 1678 and 1700 show that he continued to place his mark on deeds conveying title to Indian lands in and around Oyster Bay for nearly a quarter of a century. Whatever Indian people living in this area thought of his conduct, they evidently accepted his eldest son, Surrukunga (fl. 1683–1711), as their leader after Suscane-man's final appearance in Long Island records in 1700.[18]

Matinecock

The greater bulk of the above mentioned documentation links Suscane-man to the Matinecock people and locale. The nature of the evidence documenting Matinecock is both scanty and equivocal. The archaeologi-cal evidence is particularly skimpy. Little more than a few fragmentary remains indicative of seventeenth-century Indian occupation have been found in highly disturbed deposits at the north-shore sites at Motts Point, Muskeeta Cove, and Soundview. More extensive deposits are preserved at the Fort Massapeag National Historic Landmark along the southern shore.[19] Although findings of small amounts of Shantok-like wares sug-gest some contacts with Indian people living farther north and east, discov-eries of much larger amounts of stone tools made from argillaceous shales from Delaware Valley outcrops and pottery types most frequently encoun-tered in Hudson and upper Delaware Valley archaeological locales suggest that the occupants of these sites maintained closest connections with Indian people living farther west.[20]

The linguistic evidence is equally scant. The last speakers of Matine-cock and other central and western Long Island Indian languages died before scholars began working among people tracing descent from the area's original inhabitants. The extant evidence is thus limited to some personal and place names, a couple of brief word lists, and a few words and phrases either recorded by colonial chroniclers or remembered by modern descendants. Although all scholars agree that these words come from an

Eastern Algonquian language, most continue to debate their dialectical relationships.[21]

Few oral traditions can be directly attributed to seventeenth-century sources. Colonial chroniclers preoccupied by pecuniary and political concerns generally showed little interest in recording Indian views of events. Even Daniel Denton, one of the few colonists to write a general account of Long Island Indian life, failed to do more than sketchily describe customs in his promotional brochure encouraging English settlement. As a result, Indian voices and viewpoints are almost entirely unrepresented in Long Island colonial records.

Twentieth-century scholars interested in recording modern traditions of earlier central and western Long Island Indian life have encountered other obstacles. Those working with Delaware and Munsee people living in Ontario, Wisconsin, and Oklahoma have found few people who remember anything about ancestors from Long Island. Investigators such as William Hawk (1984), who work with present-day Long Islanders who trace descent to Matinecock forebears, have been able to elicit little information on earlier Indian language or culture. Postcolonial oral traditions largely focus upon symbolically significant events. Foremost among these is Dutch devastation of Indian communities in 1643 and 1644 during the bloodiest years of Governor Kieft's War (1640–45). Others recount provincial orders requiring Indians to kill their dogs, and the almost certainly apocryphal account of an Indian deed whose stipulations limited the buyer, Richard Smith, to those lands at present-day Smithtown around which he could ride atop a bull in one day (Hawk 1984:35; cf. J. L. Smith in Munsell 1882:1–5).

Written records comprise the preponderant body of evidence directly documenting Matinecock places and people. The earliest of these were written by Europeans moving to the Dutch colony of New Netherland, established on Indian lands between the Connecticut and Delaware River Valleys during the early 1600s. After erecting the colony's capital at New Amsterdam at the southern tip of Manhattan in 1626, Dutch authorities soon allowed English immigrants from New England to settle on central and western Long Island.

A consortium of ten English settlers obtained their first deed to lands within the boundaries of the newly chartered town of Oyster Bay from Indian people in 1653. The town of Oyster Bay grew quickly; its English population grew from nothing to more than fifty landholders (perhaps as many as two hundred to two hundred and fifty people, if each landholder moved his or her family into the town) by the time their countryfolk conquered New Netherland and named it New York in 1664 (Prime 1845:264). Over five hundred settlers had probably made their homes in Oyster Bay by 1700.

Few documents written by colonists do more than briefly mention particular Matinecock people or places. A brief passage penned by New Netherland colonial secretary Cornelis van Tienhoven on March 4, 1650, provides the most extensive known description of the locality. In a promotional brochure touting the attractions of various uncolonized parts of the province, he noted:

> *Martin Gerritsen's bay* or *Martinnehouck,* is much deeper and wider than Oyster Bay, and runs westward in, divides into three rivers, two of which are navigable; the smallest stream runs up in front of the Indian village, called Martinne houck, where they have their plantations. This tribe is not strong, and consists of about 30 families. They were formerly in and about this bay, great numbers of Indian Plantations, which now lie waste and vacant. (NYCD [1]:366)

Affirming van Tienhoven's documentation of Indian cultivation, writers such as Denton, Isaack de Rasiere (in Jameson 1909:102–15), and others described the Indians living in and around western Long Island as a hunting, fishing, and foraging people who lived in bark- or grass-covered, sapling-framed wigwams and longhouses. Writing about the effects of war and disease on Indian population, Denton and others also corroborated van Tienhoven's assertion of Indian demographic decline at Matinecock.[22]

It is difficult to estimate Matinecock population on the basis of existing information. The thirty families mentioned at Matinecock in 1650 may represent a population of two hundred people.[23] As mentioned earlier, Suscaneman was noted as having few men under him in 1653 (NPNER [2]:44). Whatever their numbers, extant documentation indicates indirectly that probably fewer than five families remained in Oyster Bay by 1700.[24]

Colonial records provide better coverage of the range and extent of Matinecock external associations. As John A. Strong points out in this volume, the Montauk sachem Wyandanch claimed hegemony over lands in and around Matinecock. Other documents record the participation of Suscaneman and other central and western Long Island Indian leaders such as Mattano and Nappamoe in land sales and other events in New Jersey and lower New York (Grumet 1979:117, 119–20, 126–27, 148–49). These findings corroborate earlier-mentioned archaeological evidence suggesting similar connections and indicate that connections like these allowed most central and western Long Island Indian people to move west among Munsee friends and kinsfolk after losing most of their lands by 1700.

Various orthographic forms of the term Matinecock appear as place and community names in contemporary records.[25] It was first noted when "Gauwarowe, sachem of Matinnekonck" sued for the Dutch for peace on behalf of his village and the "Marospinc [Massapequa] and Siketeuhacky [Setauket]" communities at the height of Governor Kieft's War, on April 15, 1644.[26]

Philologists have proposed several translations of the term. William W. Tooker (1911:115–16) translated *Matinnecock* as an Algonquian word meaning "at the place of observation." Edward M. Ruttenber (1906:95) suggested that it was a Delaware word meaning "along the edge of an island."

Oyster Bay settlers adopted the term as the name of a point, bay, and island in the present-day Matinecock Point area. Few colonial documents limit the term to this locale. And just as Wiechquaesgeck, the Indian name for Dobbs Ferry, New York, came to be used as a general term identifying all Indians in Westchester County, Matinecock became the term used to refer to all north shore Indian people living between Flushing Bay in Queens County and Nissequogue Bay at the western end of Suffolk County (Grumet 1981:31–33, 59–62). Yet colonists dealing with Indian people in this area also frequently identified them as proprietors or residents of the Matinecock locale.

Analysis of the Evidence

Suscaneman rose to prominence as the chief proprietor of Matinecock as one of Tackapousha's retainers.[27] The successor of Penhawitz (fl. 1636–43), the first sachem known to exercise widespread influence in central and western Long Island (MacLeod 1941), Tackapousha maintained his own authority by appointing kinsfolk as sachems of particular communities. One of his brothers, Chopeyconnaws, became the chief of Secataugue. Other sons evidently inherited the sachemships of Canarsee (Waumitompack, fl. 1655–84), Rockaway (Monguamy, fl. 1655–81 and Waumitompack), and Merrick (Pomwaukon, fl. 1643–81).[28]

Documents chronicling Tackapousha's career show that he did not maintain influence by kinship ties alone. A skillful and savvy diplomat, he allied himself closely first with the Dutch and later with their English conquerors. Cooperating with the colonists, he kept the peace, provided warriors for the Dutch and their English successors, and sold food, furs, and land to settlers. Tackapousha did not provide these services for nothing. He claimed, and often received, protection against hostile neighboring Indian nations such as the Montauks of eastern Long Island and the Narragansetts and Niantics of southern New England. But it was his persistent demands for protection against the claims of the Hempstead settlers for the Matinecock lands that presented the greatest challenge to colonial authorities.[29]

Hempstead settlers based their claim upon three documents. Although it was worded as a deed, the first of these, dated January 15, 1639, evidently was understood by the Indians to be little more than a friendship pact extending Dutch protection over their lands (NYCD [14]:15). The second document, a deed signed on November 13, 1643, at the height of Governor Kieft's War, conveyed an unclearly bounded tract of land to the south of Hempstead to the town (NYCD [14]:530). The third document purported to transfer title to a similarly bounded tract of land in the same place to Hempstead on March 17, 1658 (Cox 1916–40 [1]:347–52).

Tackapousha resisted repeated attempts by Hempstead townsfolk to use these documents to take possession of the disputed territory. Many of the earliest records referring to Suscaneman identify him as one of several of Tackapousha's retainers supporting his struggle against the Hempstead colonists. He was among a group of Tackapousha's followers refusing to sell land at Flushing at the western end of the disputed area on January 7, 1664 (NYCD [14]:540). On March 22, 1667, he supported Tackapousha's rejection of Hempstead claims placing the eastern limits of the 1643 deed to lands east of Hempstead Harbor (New York Colonial Manuscripts Endorsed Land Papers [1]:30).[30]

At the same as he was assisting Tackapousha against the Hempstead claims, Suscaneman seems to have embarked upon a new strategy calculated to divide the settlers and slow their rate of expansion. On June 22, 1667, Suscaneman sold four small parcels of land containing from four to sixty acres in the disputed zone to four settlers from the neighboring (and competing) town of Oyster Bay.[31] Dangling the promise of further sales in front of other Oyster Bay settlers, he secured their support against increasingly intransigent Hempstead town fathers. This strategy of playing off contending European interest groups while buying them off with relatively small land concessions characterized Matinecock diplomacy for the next twenty-five years. As an architect of this strategy, Suscaneman worked to employ it effectively in efforts to protect his people's interests during the most challenging years of their history.

Like his counterparts elsewhere, Suscaneman searched constantly for opportunities to play contending colonial interest groups against one another. Not surprisingly, the most contentious colonial disputes involved land issues. Suscaneman accordingly looked for ways to exploit this situation. Like other Northeastern Indian leaders, he encouraged his people to sell adjoining tracts of land possessing unclear boundaries to competing colonists or colonial interest groups in an Indian version of the "Deed Game."

As described by Francis Jennings (1975:128–45), colonists playing the Deed Game used Indian deeds to support land claims against all European and Indian rivals. By selling unclearly bounded adjacent tracts to contending colonists, Indian people too encouraged land disputes among the Europeans while clouding claimant titles. Although Indians and Europeans had different land tenure systems and beliefs, both knew that disputed lands could not be occupied with complete assurance.

The more acrimonious of these disputes took decades to resolve. Leaders such as Suscaneman who were able to exploit disputes could stave off and in some cases completely stop occupation of their people's lands for many years. By exploiting the litigation process, such leaders often managed as well to get formal colonial recognition of the validity of the title or affirm the boundaries of their people's remaining lands.

Sale of small portions of land to competing land purchasers helped forestall more devastating demands. Issues such as price also figured into native strategic thinking. It is difficult to know how Indian people regarded prices offered for their lands. The fact that purchasers rarely turned around and sold the same land to colonists further makes it difficult to directly contrast contemporary land values. Yet early deeds clearly show that Indians often received a small fraction of the relative value of the land on European markets. Purchasers buying Lloyd's Neck in 1654, for example, paid the Indians "three coats, three shirts, two cutlasses, three hatchets, three hoes, two fathoms [six feet] of wampum, six knives, and two pairs of shoes and stockings" [spelling modernized] (Barck 1927 [1]:1–4). Four years later, they sold the same tract of land to an English settler for one hundred pounds sterling (Barck 1927 [1]:4–9).

This situation soon changed. Suscaneman, for example, often bargained for cash payments ranging from one-fifth to one-half the English market value. While such prices did not approach parity, they nevertheless represented what the market would bear. More importantly, people like Suscaneman, who lived in close contact with English neighbors and participated in over eighty deed transactions over a period of more than thirty years in a single town, almost surely came to know that they were receiving less than purchasers were getting. It is difficult to imagine that Suscaneman neglected opportunities to cultivate and take advantage of a sense of obligation among the English.[32]

Although the records are silent on the subject, bargaining over price and other considerations probably played a part in every deed negotiated by Suscaneman. The position of the negotiating parties also affected deed transactions. Long Island records show that colonists always solicited sales from Indians and that colonial buyers often competed with one another for the chance to acquire particular tracts. Documentation recording Indian attempts to take advantage of divisions created by the Hempstead-Oyster Bay controversy and other land disputes shows that Indians were aware of this. It is therefore unlikely that native people accepted willingly the first offers of colonists trying to buy cheap and sell dear. Presenting opportunities to raise prices, cost and boundary negotiations also provided venues tailor-made for dramatic symbolic demonstrations of power and ability. Further, these exchanges furnished opportunities to gather information and obtain insight into the minds and motives of negotiating partners.

Both Indian and non-Indian deeds utilized the same formulaic documentary framework. Each identified the parties to the transaction, set out the boundaries of the land in question, specified the transfer price, listed the rights and authorities transferred, and contained the date of the deed. Both types of deeds, moreover, generally used simple and direct language. While it is impossible to know if colonists represented the contents of these deeds fully and accurately to Indian sellers, the regularities observed in form and substance suggest that an effort was made to minimize misunderstanding.

All deeds were signed by individuals identified as native proprietors or leaders. Marks of Indian and non-Indian witnesses affirmed both the identities and authority of Indian signatories. Affidavits, receipts, and other endorsements appended to deeds further verified identities and rights of signatories, noted claims of other parties, clarified the identification of Indian place names and other boundary markers, noted when payments were made, and recorded the identities of translators and other intermediaries. Signed deeds were then subjected to a rigorous program of survey and registration. The overall aim of this system was to facilitate the orderly transference both of Indian title to individual purchasers and of Indian sovereign rights to the Crown.

Neither Indians nor Europeans fully understood or accepted the other's land tenure systems and beliefs (Grumet 1989). Forced to deal with one another across a wide cultural divide, they arrived at creative misunderstandings permitting a degree of accommodation. Indians did not have to understand English law fully to know that marks placed on pieces of paper called deeds under highly ritualized circumstances almost certainly resulted in the loss of particular pieces of land. Refusing to acknowledge the validity of Indian concepts of inalienability and collective landownership openly, colonists claiming fee simple title on the basis of these deeds nevertheless repeatedly tacitly recognized continuing Indian rights to already sold lands by giving what they called gifts (to symbolically separate such payments from original purchase fees) to Indian claimants.

The several thousand Indian deeds and deed confirmations filed in repositories throughout the Northeast document the range and scope of this creative misunderstanding. One hundred and thirty eight Indian deeds on file in Oyster Bay town records show how vastly the outnumbered native people, refusing to acknowledge colonial law, nevertheless used the provincial legal system in their struggle to hold onto 160 square miles of their homeland at Matinecock for more than half a century.[33]

Such strategies could only succeed when backed by the reality or appearance of force. Overwhelmingly outnumbered by settlers, the Matinecocks presented no direct threat to colonial survival, though panics sparked by the many rumors of Indian conspiracies that circulated through seventeenth-century Long Island towns show that settlers nevertheless continued to fear Indian attack. Long Island Indian leaders played upon colonial apprehensions whenever possible. Tackapousha, for example, quietly but firmly threatened reprisals against Hempstead settlers trying to seize Massapequa lands. Such threats evidently were taken seriously by colonial officials. In 1667, New York Governor Richard Nicolls expressed anger over Hempstead's willingness to compromise the still-equivocal security of his newly conquered colony for the sake of a few acres. His order prohibiting the purchase of additional lands until the settlement of the Hempstead boundary dispute effectively put an end to all English efforts to expand legally into the Matinecock lands for the next eight years (NYCD [14]:595).

Nicolls's successors, Edmund Andros (1678–81), Anthony Brockholls (1681–83), and Thomas Dongan (1683–88) decided to end these and other land controversies by ordering the Long Island towns to buy all remaining Indian lands within their borders. Responding to this threat, Suscaneman used land sales strategically to stall for time. Supported by Maomey (fl. 1654–1707), Syhar (fl. 1653–98), and Werah (fl. 1669–1707), Suscaneman signed 37 deeds to lands in Oyster Bay between March 1, 1681, and February 25, 1685.[34] Most were small conveyances transferring tracts ranging in size from fifteen to one hundred acres in extent to different Oyster Bay landholders. One of these instruments, a deed called the New Purchase, signed on January 9, 1685, conveyed Indian title to all unsold lands in the westernmost part of the town to a consortium of twenty town landholders for sixty pounds sterling.[35]

Oyster Bay town records note that townspeople purchasing many of these tracts soon began questioning the boundaries of their purchases and challenging the authority of the Indians to sell the land. Responding to the latter challenge on October 29, 1683, Suscaneman and Werah ordered Thomas Townsend, the town recorder, to enter in town records an agreement with their sisters affirming their right to sell land at Matinecock (Cox 1916–40[1]:267). Evidently addressing concerns expressed by Tackapousha and others about receiving their shares of the proceeds of these sales, Suscaneman signed a memorandum on January 8, 1684, promising "as he Receives ye pay to Distribute to Tacapowshar a part Yearly and to Every Indian or Squaw Concernd" (Cox 1916–40[1]:182).

Anxious to avoid further disputes, Oyster Bay town fathers invited Tackapousha, nine other prominent central and western Long Island Indian leaders, and a visiting sachem from Westchester County named Patthunk to a meeting on March 6, 1685. Together, they put their marks on a document confirming Suscaneman's right to sell land at Matinecock on their behalf. This document formally empowered Suscaneman "& Samous takapowshoe soon [sic] and quarapin, with ye advise of Capt:

Thomas Hicks & Thomas Townsend" to sell all remaining Indian lands in the town (Cox 1916–1940[1]:283–84). The agreement further stipulated that proceeds from lands sold by Suscaneman and his retainers should be divided equally among all Indians having rights to those lands.

Suscaneman subsequently placed his mark alongside that of Werah on another thirteen deeds to lands in Oyster Bay between March 26, 1685, and February 4, 1686.[36] These deeds, signed in the midst of a malaria epidemic that ravaged Indian communities farther north, resulted in the conveyance of title to most of the last Indian lands remaining within town boundaries that were considered desirable by Europeans.[37]

Worried about the consequences of Indians losing all of their lands, New York governor Thomas Dongan set aside two reservations on the banks of Hempstead Harbor on the north shore of Long Island. The first, established on 150 acres of land at Cow Neck in the town of Hempstead, on the west side of the harbor, was formally assigned to Tackapousha and his followers on June 24, 1687 (New York Colonial Manuscripts Endorsed Land Papers [4]:174). The second, a 200-acre tract south of present-day Glen Cove, on the east side of Hempstead Harbor in the town of Oyster Bay, was granted to the Matinecock people three days later (Cox 1916–40[1]:519). Terms of occupation were simple: Dongan required Indians on each reservation to pay an annual quit rent of one shilling. They were also prohibited from selling reservation land without the permission of provincial authorities.

Suscaneman disappeared from western Long Island records for four years following the establishment of these reservations. During these years, he put his mark next to the names Romasickamon, Rumashekah, Wallamassekaman, and other versions of his alias Runasuck in deeds to Indian lands in central New Jersey, as noted earlier in this paper. Suscaneman's appearance in these documents suggests that he and many of his people chose to move away rather than live in a confined reservation.

Other documents indicate that Suscaneman returned to Long Island sometime between 1691 and 1693. Two deeds to lands at the head of Hempstead Harbor dated March 7, 1693, bear the marks of Suscaneman, Werah, and Syhar. The first of these conveyed lands south and west of the reservation to Moses and Gervis Mudge (Cox 1916–40[1]:527–29). The other evidently transferred their title of their reservation to James Townsend (Cox 1916–40[2]:116–17). Yet the scent of chicanery pervades both documents. Unlike most earlier deeds, in which Indians accepted cash payments or goods for their lands, these deeds conveyed both tracts to the grantees at no cost "in consideration of many favors and kindnesses . . . and for other good causes" [spelling modernized].

It is not known if Suscaneman, Werah, and Syhar actually signed these deeds. If they did, it is not clear whether Townsend or the Mudges truthfully divulged their contents to the signatories. What is known is that Suscaneman subsequently made a personal appearance at a meeting of the New York Provincial Council in Manhattan on December 6, 1694. Identifying himself as "Runasark, an Indian of Nassau" [a contemporary English name for Long Island], he complained that Hempstead settlers were cutting timber on the 200-acre reservation without their permission (New York Council Minutes [7]:109).

This was a bold step. Unlike Tackapousha, who dealt directly with provincial authorities whenever possible, Suscaneman rarely sidestepped town officials to approach the governor and his council. It was also an unusually oblique way to express concern about lands that may have been alienated in contravention of orders expressly prohibiting such unauthorized conveyances. By shifting the charge to trespass (a common crime committed against Indians) and by changing the identity of the trespasser to old Hempstead rivals, Suscaneman may have hoped to avoid direct confrontation with Oyster Bay neighbors.

Whatever his intent, Suscaneman's appeal caused the Council to order a new survey of the lands in question. The Council ordered as well that the new survey should not diminish the size of the reservation. It is not known if the survey was ever undertaken; no record of it or of the reservation appears in subsequent town records.

A deed registered in town records on May 24, 1711, may provide some insight into the fate of the reservation. Under the terms of this deed, Thomas Townsend made a gift of land at the head of Hempstead Harbor to his sons-in-law, Thomas Jones and Abraham Underhill. The boundaries of this tract seem to include the reservation. More importantly, Townsend based his claim to this tract on an unregistered deed signed by "Suscaneman alis Runnasuck" on August 18, 1696 (Cox 1916–40[3]:293–94). This is the only unregistered deed attributed to Suscaneman and may be a fabrication. If not, compensation paid under the terms of the deed may have been sufficient to quiet Indian claims to the tract.

Suscaneman placed his mark on the last ten documents in Oyster Bay known to mention his name between 1694 and 1700. Five of these deeds conveyed tracts of land in the town.[38] Three confirmed earlier purchases, and one, dated October 18, 1695, listed him as a witness to a land sale at Manitoe Hill.[39] Another deed to land in central New Jersey that lay between the South Branch of the Raritan River and the Delaware River, which listed a signatory identified as Lourkamsaman on November 11, 1703, represents Suscaneman's last known appearance in colonial records (New Jersey Deed Books, Liber AAA:434–35).

Suscaneman soon faded from the memories of Long Island settlers. His name gradually became a disembodied icon only invoked in deeds tracing title to original conveyances bearing (or alleged to bear) his mark. By 1731, a deed would list "Suscaneman and RunaSuck" as two Indians (Cox 1916–40[5]:452). Sometime thereafter, virtually all that remained of his memory was the place name Susco's Wigwam, the site of his home in the present Brookville locale, just west of Syosset. Today, only a few specialists and those people tracing descent from Matinecock ancestors remember him.

Conclusion

The man variously identified in colonial records as Suscaneman, Runasuck, and Captain Lambert was the most prominent local mediator between Matinecock people and Oyster Bay settlers for nearly fifty years. These data indicate that if he was not a sachem, he almost certainly represented the Matinecock people. Documents signed by every known native individual claiming interest in Matinecock lands affirmed that they recognized him as their intermediary and representative in all dealings with Oyster Bay town authorities. Other documents listing him among Tackapousha's retinue confirm that he represented Matinecock people at meetings in other towns and in councils with provincial officials.

Patterns revealed by the documents further show that, although Suscaneman probably did not fully comprehend the legal mechanisms of the European land tenure system, he did come to understand and accept the consequences of fixing his mark upon English deeds. He fixed his mark to those deeds, in part, because he had to. English power gave him no choice, and complete refusal would have led to his deposition and the forcible removal of his people. Responding to this hard political reality, Suscaneman acted in much the same way as other Munsee intermediaries responded in similar circumstances in northern New Jersey (Grumet 1979). Both employed deeds tactically as components of an overall strategy of delay. Such tactics allowed numerically weaker Indian people to appear submissive to militarily more powerful colonists while affording the opportunity to play off contending colonial interest groups. Stalling for time, Suscaneman and his colleagues almost certainly hoped for resurgence as they prayed for English decline.

In the end, whatever hopes Suscaneman and his compatriots had for recovery and resurgence in their homeland proved futile. The failure of these hopes was not evident, however, when he put his mark alongside those of Werah, Syhar, and other Matinecock people on papers placed before them by settlers. Their signing was not a wholesale capitulation to foreign hegemony. Instead, their marks are evidence of a strategy that bought fifty years for the beleaguered Matinecocks.

The time they purchased at such cost did not save their homeland. It was, however, enough to permit them to adapt and adjust to the rigors of foreign invasion. And in the final analysis, these adaptations and adjustments enabled the Matinecocks not only to endure the loss of their homeland, but also to survive as a people. Today, people tracing descent from Matinecock ancestors make their homes on Long Island, in reservation communities in Wisconsin and Ontario, and on lands in Oklahoma, Kansas, and elsewhere owe a debt to the efforts of Suscaneman and his kinsfolk.

Notes

An earlier version of this paper was delivered at the 1988 Annual Meeting of the American Society for Ethnohistory in Williamsburg, Virginia. The present version has benefited from review comments from Tad Baker, Bill Bolger, Colin Calloway, Rochelle Lurie, Dennis Montagna, Ann Plane, and Jim Springer. I am particularly indebted to John A. Strong, who both commented on early drafts of this manuscript and brought to my attention the earliest known reference to Suscaneman, the May 14–16, 1653, relations of a man variously identified as Ronessock and Ronnessoke published in the New Plymouth records (NPNER [2]:43–44).

1. Hogden (1974) presents a particularly succinct description of the nature of dated records and the ways anthropologists and historians use dated events to discern patterns of cultural change.

2. The town of Oyster Bay was founded in 1653 by a group of ten English landholders from Massachusetts (Prime 1845:264). Lloyd's Neck, at the eastern

end of the town, was ceded to the town of Huntington in 1684 (Street 1882:18). Other lands on the western side of Oyster Bay were ceded to the newly erected town of North Hempstead in 1784 (Prime 1845:292). Initially one of the original five towns of Queens County, Oyster Bay has been part of Nassau County since the western Queens towns voted to become part of New York City in 1898.

3. The concept of a country as an area where actions and relations between different people occur during particular periods of time is developed in Grumet (1992:19–23). Extending from western Long Island across central and northern New Jersey and lower New York to the upper Delaware River Valley, Munsee Country was home to a number of linguistically and culturally related native communities at the time of initial contact with Europeans (Grumet 1992:96–104).

4. Nantucket Island (see Little, this volume) is the only other area of which I am aware where Indian people signed more deeds to a relatively limited area within a comparable period of time.

5. This idea has been developed from the concept of working disagreements presented in Sahlins (1981:72).

6. The name is spelled Susakatacue in the version of this document published in Barck (1927[1]:2).

7. Sasaketawuh is listed as a witness to the August 17, 1658 sale of three necks of land in Huntington (Street 1887–99[1]:16–18); Chawescome's mark appears on the April 12, 1656, confirmation of a land sale at Maspeth, Queens County (Paltstits 1910[1]:235–37); and Chascaneman was one of the signatories selling one hundred acres of land north of the present municipality of Glen Cove in Oyster Bay on November 7, 1668 (Cox 1916–40[2]:682–83).

8. A deed dated February 20, 1667 (Hicks 1896–1904[1]:681–82), four written on June 22, 1667 (Cox 1916–40[1]:80–81, 89–90, 682–84), and others signed on November 24, 1667 (Cox 1916–40[1]:685–86), November 24, 1668 (Cox 1916–40[1]:686), and May 29, 1669 (Cox 1916–40[1]:686–87) contain variants of Shoskene. The orthography Shoskcock appears on a deposition attesting to the boundaries of Matinecock land dated March 22, 1667 (New York Colonial Manuscripts, Endorsed Land Papers [1]:30).

9. The overwhelming majority of these references list the name as Suscaneman. Other variants include Suskaneman, Susconeman, Suscanemon, Succanemen, Sascenemin, and Susuckoan. The minor range of variation indicates that most scribes of the period were familiar with either the man or the conventional way of rendering his name.

10. Virtually all documents linking Suscaneman with this alias list the name as Runasuck. Its few variations in this context include Runasuk, Runassuck, Runnasuck, and Ranasuck.

11. The May 14, 1653, Relation of Ronessock is in NPNER [2]:44. Also see the statement taken two days later, in which Ronnessoke implicates Ninigret as the leader of a pan-Indian conspiracy against all English settlers (NPNER [2]:43).

12. The first of these, Runnasuk, appears in an unpublished deed dated September 13, 1655, presently on file with a group of documents chronicling land

affairs in Jamaica, Queens County, New York in Record Group 39 M:105 in the Main Branch of the New York Public Library. Runnasuk's name is followed by the marks of Matinecock sachem Asharoken (fl. 1648–69), Monguamy (fl. 1655–81), later the sachem of Rockaway; and Waumetompack (fl. 1655–84), the sachem of Canarsee, who later moved to Matinecock. The latter two figures were sons of the influential Massapequa sachem, Tackapousha. Asharoken put his mark next to the orthography Askasetone, a variation of the spelling Aseton appearing in nine deeds to land at Matinecock signed between 1667 and 1669 (Cox 1916–40[1]:80–81, 89–90, 681–87). Monguamy placed his mark next to the orthography Manguauope. Waumetompack, also known as Bambres, appears in other documents in forms such as Wammattappa (Stiles 1867[1]:77), Womtaxac (New York Colonial Manuscripts Endorsed Land Papers [1]:30), and Waghtummoore (Hicks 1896–1904[1]:43). Adam, another of Tackapousha's associates, also put his mark to this deed as a witness.

The other references to this name include a citation to an individual identified as Ramoreck, who was paid a bounty of a half bushel of corn for killing a wolf by Hempstead town fathers on February 3, 1659 (Hicks 1896–1904[1]:66); a man named Rompsicka, listed among a group of Indians refusing to sell land in the Queens County town of Flushing on January 7, 1664 (NYCD [14]:540); a Capt. Ramerock, who witnessed the sale of Little Neck in Oyster Bay on February 4, 1686 (Cox 1916–40[1]:370–71); a person named Runisuk of Matenicock, given a two-hundred-acre reserve on Hempstead Harbor on June 27, 1687 (Cox 1916–40[1]:519); and an "Indian of Nassau" named Runasark, who complained on December 6, 1694, about Hempstead settlers trespassing upon this reservation to cut timber (New York Council Minutes [7]:109).

13. A document dated July 4, 1657, confirming an earlier purchase of land on western Long Island, lists an individual identified as Rumasackromen (NYCD [14]:416). Another deed to land at Jamaica, Queens dated April 6, 1662, mentions a signatory named Lumasowie (Thompson 1918[2]:588).

14. See New Jersey Deeds, Liber B:181 for Romasickamon (land at the Millstone River sold April 9, 1688), Liber A:263 for Rumashekah (land at South River sold on March 20, 1689), Liber B:179–80 for Lummusooron (land in present-day Mercer County between Princeton and Lawrenceville sold on June 4, 1687), Liber AAA:434–35 for Lourkamsaman (land between the South Branch of the Raritan River and the Delaware River sold on November 11, 1703), and Liber D:147 for Wallamassekaman (land at Waycake Creek in Monmouth County sold on April 6, 1687). This individual appears as a minor signatory in these deeds.

15. Such processes may have played a role in the proliferation of dialect differences noted among speakers of Munsee and other Delaware tongues.

16. Suscaneman's succession was affirmed in a January 1691 deed confirming a 1655 land sale in which Sanakom [Suscaneman] signed for Aseton (Cox 1916–40[2]:350–51). Aseton was one of the many orthographies used by colonial scribes to identify Asharoken (cf. Cox 1916–40[1]:80–81, 89–90, 682–86). Others include "Rasaocume, sachem of motinnacok" (from a May 20, 1648, deed in Cox

1916–40[1]:625–27), Arrazukon (from a November 1, 1650, deed in the Gravesend Town Records 1:15, 43–47), and "Rashaokan sagamore of Matinicock" (in a deposition dated May 4, 1669, in Paltstits 1910[2]:418–19). Only one document, the original September 20, 1654, Lloyd's Neck deed, simultaneously lists sagamores identified as Ratiocan and Asiepam as signatories (Barck 1927[1]:1). Further research is needed to determine whether this was an error or an instance of a single signatory placing marks on a document under two names.

17. A deed to the Massapeage Meadows dated March 17, 1658, lists Chopeyconnaws as "Ye Young Sachem Brother to . . . Tackapoosha" (Cox 1916–40[1]:347–49, 351–52); Siejpekenouw, noted as brother of Tapusagh, chief of Marsepingh, put his mark on the May 15, 1664, treaty ending hostilities between the Esopus Indians of the central Hudson Valley and the Dutch that had flared sporadically since 1658 (NYCD [13]:375–77).

18. Surrukunga was one of several Indian leaders signing several deeds to lands reserved for Indian people at Fort Neck at the southern end of the town of Oyster Bay, along the south shore of Long Island, between 1694 and 1697 (Cox 1916–40[2]:3–5, 260–61, 282–85, 287, 289–90). He later signed deeds conveying or confirming conveyance of small necks of land in Oyster Bay and Hempstead between 1702 and 1711 (Cox 1916–40[2]:255–57, [5]:690–91; Street 1887–99[2]:281–82).

19. These are the only aboriginal sites presently known to contain deposits dating to the seventeenth century in Matinecock country in present-day Nassau County. Other locales identified by Ceci (1980) as historic sites have been found either to date to other time periods or to be places in which Indian toponyms or local traditions comprise the only known indications of native occupation. See Ceci (1982) and Salwen (1962) for Motts Point, Salwen (1968) for Muskeeta Cove, C. Smith (1950) for Soundview, and Solecki (1995) for Fort Massapeag.

20. See C. Smith (1950) for stylistic analyses revealing affinities between pottery found in western Long Island sites and ceramics from others in the Hudson and upper Delaware Valleys. Jacobson's (1980) analysis of Ward's Point National Historic Landmark deposits on Staten Island corroborates Smith's findings and further shows that argillites from the upper Delaware Valley and Hudson Valley cherts comprise the bulk of imported stones found at coastal New York sites.

21. Noting the presence of *r*-sounds in these words, linguist Ives Goddard (1978a) believes that Matinecocks and their neighbors may have spoken an *r*-dialect of Eastern Algonquian similar to that spoken by Quiripi-speaking people across the Long Island Sound in western Connecticut. People speaking the closely related Munsee dialect used *l*-sounds in the place of *r*-sounds. Occurrence of place names like Rockaway in Long Island and New Jersey and the documentation of both *l*- and *r*- sounds in one of Suscaneman's aliases used in both places indicate that words containing these phonemes were used by people throughout Munsee country.

22. See Denton (1670:6–8) for the observation that war, disease, and alcohol abuse killed most Indians living in and around New York. This and other docu-

mentary sources for Munsee depopulation during Historic Contact period times are surveyed in Grumet (1990).

23. Cook (1976:79) based this figure on van Tienhoven's statement and on secondary sources stating that five villages were located at particular locations along the north shore between Flushing and Smithtown.

24. Documents referring to Matinecock Indian people during the last decade of the seventeenth century and the first decade of the eighteenth century (Cox 1916–40[2]:255–57, 287; [5]:690–91) rarely mention more than three or four named individuals. Earlier records, by contrast, list up to fifteen Indian signatories.

25. A compilation of many of these variations may be seen in Grumet (1981:32).

26. This reference appears in NYCD (14):56. Fighting brought on by Governor Kieft's War (1640–45) devastated western Long Island Indian communities. The most complete account of the war appears in Trelease (1960:60–84).

27. Documents dated July 4, 1657 (NYCD[14]:416), May 23, 1659 (Street 1887–99[1]:16–18), January 7, 1664 (NYCD [14]:540), March 19, 1664 (Paltstits 1910 [2]:478–79), and January 8, 1684 (Cox 1916–40[1]:182), are among the several records listing Suscaneman as a retainer of Tackapousha or as a witness to deeds signed by the Massapequa chief.

28. Grumet, in Solecki (1995), traces these identities and connections.

29. Much of Tackapousha's documented career is summarized in MacLeod (1941) and Trelease (1960:passim).

30. As Trelease (1960:195–97) has shown, Tackapousha succeeded in forcing a succession of English governors to intervene on his people's behalf against Hempstead settlers' use of these deeds as a pretext to seize Indian lands at Matinecock.

31. These were four of the documents identifying Suscaneman as Shoskeene or Shoskene (Cox 1916–40[1]:80–81, 89–90, and 682–84).

32. The idea that deeds represented vehicles creating and maintaining reciprocal intercultural relationships between Munsee people and European settlers in northern New Jersey is explored in Grumet (1979:255–63; cf. Grumet 1989).

33. John Cox, Jr., drafted a map showing the approximate boundaries of all registered Indian deeds in Oyster Bay. It appears in a sleeve at the end of volume 8 of Cox (1916–40).

34. These deeds are transcribed in Cox 1916–40(1):126, 129–32, 135–40, 146–56, 172–76, 182–87, 197–98, 248–49, 277–78, 280–84, 292–93, 304–5, 313–14, 328–30, 339–40, 401, 494, 502–3; Thompson 1918(3):27–28. Many of these tracts were sold to a small number of town landholders. In one of these, dated February 16, 1684, Suscaneman and Werah granted fifty acres to a man named Henry Bell and his wife, Jane, "an Indian woman of ye Naragansets one of our own [Matinecock?] Nation" (Cox 1916–40[1]:313–14).

35. A stipulation attached to the deed allowed town residents to purchase equal rights to lands conveyed in this deed within three months of its signing. An appended list shows that 63 landholders subsequently took advantage of this opportunity (Cox 1916–40[1]:331–33, [5]:130–32).

36. Transcribed copies of these deeds are published in Cox 1916–40(1):284–89, 301, 331–32, 359, 370–71, 474–78, 508–9, 545–46, 604.

37. See Grumet (1990:35–37) for evidence indicating that thirteen percent of all prominent Munsee people documented in European records between 1630 and 1801 disappeared from colonial chronicles between 1681 and 1684. Two reported epidemic outbreaks, a malaria epidemic reported in the Saint Lawrence Valley in 1684 (NYCD [9]:242) and an unidentified devastating contagion documented among Indians living farther south in the Hudson River Valley one year later (Leder 1956:95), may account for this observed pattern.

38. Transcribed copies of these deeds appear in Cox 1916–40(1):529–30, (2):25–26, 54–55, 212–14, 514–16.

39. See transcribed copies of deed confirmations in Cox 1916–40(2):11–12, 106–8, 220–22, 244. The October 18, 1695, document appears in Cox 1916–40(2):513–14.

CHAPTER SEVEN

᙭᙭

Putting a Face on Colonization: Factionalism and Gender Politics in the Life History of Awashunkes, the "Squaw Sachem" of Saconet

Ann Marie Plane

Introduction

METACOM'S WAR OF 1675–76 has long been described as a major transition for New England's native peoples.[1] Although a new historical school has explored the ways in which Indian enclave communities retained a distinctive presence in New England society even after their military defeat, there is no question that the war changed the character of native life forever.[2] The life history of one Indian woman, Awashunkes, spans the great historical and historiographical divide of the war, revealing some of these changes and their effects upon indigenous peoples. Awashunkes was not simply any woman, she was a leader—the "squaw sachem" of the Saconet people, who dwelt near what is now Little Compton, Rhode Island. Because of her role, she appears in the official records of New England more often than other native women. Prior to the war, her name shows up in land sales and other colonial business. During the war, Benjamin Church chronicled her exploits and eventual surrender in unusual detail. One final postwar incident, in which English justices investigated her involvement in the possible infanticide of her daughter's new-

140

born, provides a remarkable opportunity to examine the changes in this woman's life. This 1683 investigation marks the only recorded event in which Awashunkes's gender became an issue in her career as a native leader. By forming an alliance with the English at the end of the war, she helped bring about an English cultural dominance that would impose new expectations on native women. Access to powerful, public leadership roles for southern New England's native women decreased with the establishment of English dominion in 1676. The 1683 prosecution may even have diminished Awashunkes's power as a public figure by finally allowing her native opponents to win English censure of her actions.

Awashunkes's political leadership took a form that was typical in many northeastern American Indian societies. Born to a prominent family, she used her charisma to win influence, and then worked with a group of councilors and a co-leader or "chief captain" (her son, Peter) to implement decisions and allocate resources within a small-scale village unit.[3] She maintained power by persuasion, consensus-building, and the regular redistribution of goods. Thus, she played a leadership role that Marshal Sahlins (1962:289–93) labeled (in this case not very aptly) a "big-man." We might better term them persons of influence. As such, Awashunkes and Peter struggled to fend off rivals, including another of her sons, Mammanuah, who led an alternate faction of Saconets.

But Awashunkes lived in a time of great change—a time that brought tremendous alterations to native leadership strategies. Most Europeans found native North American political systems incomprehensible. Colonial authorities sought a single political leader to represent each native community (Edmunds 1980:vii).[4] Awashunkes's ability to manipulate the Saconets' alliance with the English became a critical factor in local native politics. Throughout her career, she coped simultaneously with internal factionalism and external relations, including Saconet relations with other natives (especially Metacom and his followers at Mount Hope/Sowams), individual Europeans (such as Benjamin Church), and the Plymouth and Rhode Island colonial authorities. As a political actor, Awashunkes highlighted certain aspects of her many social identities (including those of mother, Saconet, woman Indian leader, English foe, and English ally) in order to best pursue her goals in the complicated and changing political field of colonial New England (cf. F. Bailey 1960:11–12, 16, 197, and 224).

One aspect of Awashunkes's identity, her gender, would become increasingly important. Her story raises the question of how the multiple political systems of the colonial world interacted with its several gender systems. Awashunkes was marked forever, both for the English colonists and for ourselves, as a "squaw sachem"—a female leader. As such, she could not escape the effects of changes to native gender systems,[5] what one historian has recently termed the "gender frontiers" of colonial America (Brown 1993:313). English dominance would eventually affect Awashunkes's ability to lead, once changing gender expectations had rendered her vulnerable to prosecution for the gendered, English "crime" of infanticide. Over time her position and place in society changed—not simply by chance, but through the workings of colonization itself. Ironically, Awashunkes's own decision, as a sachem, to make peace with the English led to shifts in the balance of power which may ultimately have undermined her ability, as a woman, to remain an effective sachem.

Awashunkes's "career" as a native leader can help us to put an individual "face" on the often monolithic categories of colonization—the clash of "cultures" or "peoples," rather than of people.[6] Her story allows us to reconstruct colonization as experienced and shaped by one individual at a particular moment. But although I will represent Awashunkes as an individual, in each of the vignettes that record her career she also stands inevitably as a symbol of native New England's experience of colonization. The available records reveal little of her personality or views. Given the limited and enigmatic source materials, one needs considerable knowledge of the cultural and historical context in order to glean evidence of Awashunkes the historical actor. Yet by exploring her experience, we can better identify the complex political structures within which a native— and female—leader had to function. Awashunkes's story offers us a rare glimpse of a Native American woman caught within the colonial system.

"Savage Squaw Sachem": Multiple Political Systems in the Colonial World

Awashunkes emerges in the historical record in 1671 as a recognized leader of the Saconets, a group of native people settled in what is today southeastern Rhode Island, then within the bounds claimed by authorities of the New Plymouth Colony.[7] Although the English identified her as a principal leader, they never succeeded in entering into a secure alliance with her. She seems to have headed an anti-English faction (perhaps a majority of her people) in a time when the Saconets were riven by internal power struggles. English records represent her as an exotic, often hostile figure—what the English might have imagined as truly a "savage squaw sachem."

July of 1671 was a moment of rising native-European hostilities. In that month, individuals from several native communities within the boundaries of Plymouth Colony asked to be taken into the figurative English "Household of God." They renounced their "lion-like speritts" in favor of a covenant of mutual aid. They explained that their enemies had "designed our destruction, not for any hurt that wee have done unto them, neither for any propriety that they can challenge to our persons or lands or what wee posess besides, but onely for that wee are seeking after the knowlidg of the true God and his wayes" (NPNER [5]: 71). Awashunkes stood at the forefront of those who plotted against the converts.

The Plymouth Council of War took this for the warning that it was, and three days later sent two messengers "with speed to the Indians att Saconett," demanding that they "bring in all theire English armes within four dayes after notice giuen them." The English also asked that "the chiefe of them, viz, Awashunckes, Tatammanah, Washawam, Wannamuttamett, Mahunnanah, and Wanumunnamin, sachems of Saconett, or any four of them . . . doe psonally come in heer to Plymouth, and acknowlidge theire offence, and vnder theire hands ingage for theire future fidelitie" (NPNER [5]:73–74).[8] If they resisted (and the councilors thought they would), then a force of 100 Englishmen and forty or so "of our trustiest Indians should alsoe be procured to be in a reddines" to march against them (NPNER [5]:73–74).

Rather than face attack, Awashunkes and several other sachems came quickly to Plymouth on the 24th of July and accepted "Articles of Agreement" with the Plymouth court, capitulating to nearly all of the colonists' demands. The conditions of peace included the surrender of the arms and of persons "such as have bine the incendearyes of the trouble and the disturbance of her [Awashunkes's] peace and ours." Within ten days, she was to allow "the disposall of her lands to the authorities of this government," under the pretense "that wee may the better healp her to keep off such from her lands as may heerafter bringe upon her and us the like trouble, and to regulate such as will not be governed by her" (NPNER

[5]:75). Awashunkes also made a verbal promise to pay fifty pounds sterling to reimburse the colony's expenses in securing her submission, "shee
being not able att psent to defray any thinge" (NPNER [5]:75). That
Awashunkes was the "chiefest" of all the anti-English leaders becomes
clear in the title of the submission, "Articles of Agreement made and
concluded between the Court of New Plymouth and Awashunkes, the
Squa Sachem of Saconett" (NPNER [5]:75). While we know almost nothing about those who refused to be "governed" by her, bitter factional
wrangling continued to divide the Saconet community throughout her
recorded career.

Awashunkes's authority as sachem was reaffirmed in her subsequent
dealings with both Plymouth Colony and the neighboring rival English
colony, Rhode Island. In May of 1673, the general assembly of the colony
of Rhode Island and Providence Plantations took action to deal with increasingly frequent "enormities": affronts, assaults, and property damage
resulting from "the extreme excess of the Indians drunkenness." The
governor, deputy governor, and leading men from the towns were formed
into a committee "to treate with the Indian sachems, and with them
seariously to consult," with the hopes that "peace and good order may be
maintained." "Awashunks, of Secunnitt" was one of several invited (RIC
[2]:486–87). Just a few months later, Awashunkes sold land to the proprietors of Little Compton (Church 1975:35).[9]

Despite the Englishmen's tacit recognition of Awashunkes's authority
as sachem, her leadership did not go unchallenged either by English or
native individuals. In July of 1674, the Plymouth court became embroiled
in a power struggle between Awashunkes and a native rival who may have
been another son, Mammanuah.[10] Described as the "Chieffe proprietor of
the lands at Saconett, and places adjacent," Mammanuah complained
against "Awashunkes, pretended Squa Sachem of that place, and We-
wayewitt, her husband, inhabitants there."[11] He asked for five hundred
pounds in damages for the detainment of his lands and an assault upon his
person (NPNER [7]:191). Mammanuah had apparently sold some land to
a few Englishmen, but in mid-March, when he tried to give possession to
the new owners, he found that Awashunkes and her husband had assembled "together with diuers other Indians, . . . upon a psell [parcel] of the
said land." They attacked Mammanuah, "violent[ly] binding [him] . . . ,
insulting over and threatening him, whiles hee lay bound before them,
indeauoring, as they declared, to cause him to relinquish his title to his

said land." While Mammanuah had "fully cleared his title to those land from theire former claime, in his Maties [Majesty's] Court of this collonie," apparently he had neglected to establish his right to alienate lands with Awashunkes and her people. For his effrontery, he was subjected to Saconet retribution, suggesting that the English colonies and their legal institutions had yet to supercede the Saconets' own institutions.

Considering Mammanuah's alliance with the English buyers, perhaps it is no surprise that the jury decided in his favor. It ordered a payment of five pounds in damages (much less than his original request of five hundred pounds, but still a victory), and demanded that the costs of the suit be paid by Awashunkes and her husband. The jury also reaffirmed Mammanuah's "chiefe right" to dispose of the lands in question after having listened to testimonies not included in the record (NPNER [7]:191). This struggle took place in the tense period leading up to Metacom's War, in which sachems and their councilors experienced increasing pressure to sell lands (Salisbury 1987:93–94).[12]

Despite the English court's continuing support of Mammanuah, Awashunkes retained and perhaps even extended her influence as a leader. Benjamin Church opened his popular account of the 1675–76 war (written in 1716, and told in the third person) with a dramatic struggle between evil (Metacom's advisors) and good (Church and the English), in which each side battled to gain Awashunkes's alliance. When Metacom sent six men to Awashunkes in June of 1675 to urge her to join him in opposing the English (Leach 1958:34), she called her people together "to make a great dance, which is the custom of that nation when they advise about momentous affairs." But Awashunkes also sent "two of her men that well understood the English language (Sassamon and George by name) to invite Mr. Church to the dance." Church, a self-aggrandizing military leader and English culture broker, went right away, taking with him "Charles Hazelton, his tenant's son" as an interpreter. They rode down to the appointed spot, "where they found hundreds of Indians gathered together from all parts of her dominion. Awashonks herself in a foaming sweat was leading the dance. But she was no sooner sensible of Mr. Church's arrival but she broke off, sat down, calls her nobles [councilors] round her, orders Mr. Church to be invited into her presence" (Church 1975:69–70).

After careful observation of formalities ("complements being passed"), Awashunkes informed Church that six ambassadors from Metacom were present. He assured her that the English had no plans of war, and that no preparations for an attack on her people were underway in Plymouth. "Then she called for the Mount-hope men [Metacom's emissaries], who made a formidable appearance with their faces painted and their hair trimmed up in comb-fashion, with their powder horns and shot bags at their backs, which, among that nation, is the posture and figure of preparedness for war." After some "warm talk among the Indians," Awashunkes told Church that Metacom meant to compel her to join him by threatening to have some of his men attack the English cattle and houses on her side of the river, "which would provoke the English to fall upon her" (Church 1975:70).

The confrontation grew more ominous when Church, "stepping to the Mount-hopes, . . . felt . . . their bags and finding them filled with bullets, asked them what those bullets were for. They scoffingly replied, to shoot pigeons with." Church suggested to Awashunkes that she should "knock these six Mount-hopes on the head and shelter herself under the protection of the English, upon which the Mount-hopes were for the present dumb. But those two of Awashonk's men who had been at Mount-hope expressed themselves in a furious manner against his advice." Church felt especially threatened by Little Eyes, "one of the Queen's Council." But "with undaunted courage" (according to his own account!) Church "told the Mount-hopes they were bloody wretches and thirsted after the blood of their English neighbors, who had never injured them, but had always abounded in their kindness to them." He then left, after urging Awashunkes to remain loyal to the English; at his suggestion, she "desired him to go on her behalf to the Plymouth government, which he consented to do," and to return with an answer (Church 1975:70). Awashunkes then disappears from the account for a while, during which time we know that she and her people allied with Philip against the English (Leach 1958:208).

Church's account represents Awashunkes as a savage. Despite his depiction of her as having carefully balanced the two opposing councils, his first and most detailed physical description has her leading the dance "in a foaming sweat," using the same language as English contemporaries applied to descriptions of native powwows or of "wizards," who epitomized native "devilry."[13] He recalls that, when he and his men attempted to return to Saconet some time later, "the woods that the track led them through was haunted much with those snakes [rattlesnakes], which the little company seemed more to be afraid of than the black serpents [i.e., the Saconets] they were in quest of" (Church 1975:82). Did the novelty to

Church of a potent "queen" surrounded by male councilors underscore the "savagery" of these "black serpents"?

At the same time, Church manifests some respect for Awashunkes and her people throughout his narrative, perhaps because she finally petitioned the English for peace. Church met with "Honest George," a Saconet whom he trusted, in late May or early June of 1676. George agreed to arrange a meeting between Church and "Awashonks, her son Peter, their chief captain, and one Nompash (an Indian that Mr. Church had formerly a particular respect for)." Against the advice of both the Rhode Island officials and his wife, Church left for the appointed place. He had long thought "that if he could discourse [with] the Sogkonate Indians, he could draw them off from Philip, and employ them against him; but could, till now, never have an opportunity to speak with any of them, and was very loath to lose it" (Church 1975:111–13). He set out with a bottle of rum and a roll of tobacco, the requisite gifts for any negotiations. When he encountered Awashunkes and the others and went to the meeting place, he found himself surrounded by a large group of armed natives, who had hidden in the tall grass until he was seated. He convinced Awashunkes that if she truly desired to treat of peace, that "her men might lay aside their arms and appear more treatable." After distributing the tobacco and passing the rum around (himself first taking a good swig to convince her that it was not poisoned), they began to talk. Awashunkes asked him why he had never returned to Saconet as he had promised, "saying that probably if he had come then according to his promise, they had never joined with Philip against the English" (Church 1975:114–15). He explained the unavoidable delay and then negotiated a peace under which the Saconets would join with the English at Plymouth against Metacom.[14] Church guaranteed that their lives would be spared and that they would not be enslaved and sold out of the colony (Church 1975:116–17). After some delays and difficulties, her son Peter (whom Church called "Peter Awashunks") and others formally surrendered at the Plymouth court (NPNER [5]:75; Church 1975:118), while Awashunkes herself and about ninety Saconets met a detachment of the colonists' army at Punkateese. The Saconets were then ordered to go to Sandwich and "to be there, upon peril, in six days" (Church 1975:120).

A detailed description of Church's arrival in Awashunkes's camp confirms the English commander's image of her as a "savage but honorable" leader. When he located her people a short time later near the Sippican

River, he found a "vast company of Indians, of all ages and sexes, some on horseback running races, some at football, some catching eels and flat fish in the water, some clamming" (Church 1975:125). Church sent word that he intended to dine with Awashunkes. On his arrival in the camp, he was "conducted to a shelter, open on one side, whither Awashonks and her chiefs soon came and paid their respects." A large bonfire was laid near the shelter, and a "supper was brought in, in three dishes; viz., a curious young bass in one dish, eels and flat fish in a second, and shell fish in a third, but *neither bread nor salt to be seen at table* [emphasis added]." Church offers another literary marker of Saconet savagery in noting the lack of amenities.[15] When the dinner was over, the pile of pine knots was lit:

> and all the Indians great and small gathered in a ring around it. Awashonks with the oldest of her people, men and women mixed, kneeling down, made the first ring next to the fire, and all the lusty stout men standing up made the next; and then all the rabble in a confused crew surrounded on the outside. Then the chief Captain stepped in between the rings and the fire, with a spear in one hand and a hatchet in the other, danced round the fire, and began to fight with it, making mention of all the several nations and companies of Indians in the country that were enemies to the English. And, at naming of every particular tribe of Indians, he would draw out and fight a new fire-brand, and at his finishing his fight with each particular fire-brand, would bow to him and thank him. And when he had named all the several nations and tribes, and fought them all, he stuck down his spear and hatchet, and came out. [Each of the "stout" young men did the same in turn.] (Church 1975:126–27)

One gets the impression that Church did not fully understand what was going on. He later learned that "they were making soldiers for him, and what they had been doing was all one swearing of them" (the English rite for creating soldiers). When all was done, "Awashonks and her chiefs came to Mr. Church and told him that now they were engaged to fight for the English, and he might call forth all, or any of them at any time as he saw occasion to fight the enemy." She also presented him "with a very fine firelock." Church accepted the offer, chose "a number of them," and on the next morning they set out for Plymouth (Church 1975:127).

Taken together, Church's experiences reaffirm Awashunkes's great diplomatic skill, not just with the various English colonial officials, but also with different native factions. This last glimpse of her—presiding over the feast of fish and shellfish, the light of the bonfire still flickering—reveals to us the leader of a still vital people, rather than the discouraged "queen" of a defeated remnant. As a political actor, Awashunkes seems to have weathered the dangerous period of anti-English hostilities with her place as a native leader intact, although at the price of a new alliance with the English.

We know almost nothing about Awashunkes's experiences in the seven years after the war. But natives in New England retained a distinctive way of life despite postwar changes. In 1683, when Awashunkes appears once more, it is probable that virtually all Saconets still lived in wigwams made of reed mats, possessed a mixture of English and Indian material goods, and continued their seasonal migrations to exploit natural resources. Because of the increasing interaction between English and Indian towns after the war, a few of Awashunkes's people might have had mixed English, Indian, and African parentage. Like residents of many other Indian towns, by 1683 the Saconets had already lost much of their land base, and were constantly being encroached upon by English cattle, horses, pigs, and "settlers" (cf. Cronon 1983). Nevertheless, the Saconets undoubtedly maintained many indigenous elements of material culture, religious belief, folklore, and economic life for many years (cf. Bragdon 1989:128–29).[16]

We do know that two factions, one led by Mammanuah and the other led, presumably, by Awashunkes, persisted in Saconet, because in 1677, the Plymouth court gave permission to Mammanuah ("Mamanuett"), "an Indian sachem at or about Saconett," along with some kinsfolk and followers "in number about fifteen," to resettle on his lands at Saconet, provided that he would accommodate Englishmen or other Indians when the court so ordered.[17] John Cotton reported going to preach to "Mammanewat, sachem of Sakonett," in 1674 and again in 1677 (although he made no mention of Awashunkes). Thus we can assume that this rival continued both to enjoy a Saconet following and to maintain religious and political alliances with the English (John Cotton Diary, 1666–77; cf. Gookin 1806:200).

We would know nothing more about Awashunkes except for a final court battle that reveals some of the postwar changes in Indian life. In July of 1683, Awashunkes, her son Peter, and her daughter, Betty,[18] were called before the Plymouth court to answer charges of infanticide—aiding and abetting in the willful murder of Betty's newborn child. Because, as with many infanticide cases, evidence was difficult to obtain (Hoffer and Hull 1981:9),[19] the court satisfied itself with the solemn affirmations of Awashunkes and Betty that the child had been born dead, and only punished Betty for fornication (sexual intercourse outside of marriage). But in addition to the murder charges, Awashunkes *the sachem* was called to account for her punishment of one of her own people. The English court chastised her and Peter for "their ill carriage" in ordering Sam's wife "to be whipped for reporting . . . Bettey was with child, when so it afterward appeard to be really so" (NPNER [6]:113).[20]

As I will discuss below, such infanticide prosecutions are extremely rare, and thus this case probably came to court for reasons other than English desires to stamp out infanticide. Although the record is silent, perhaps Sam or his wife approached the English about the unjust whipping in hopes of redress. As in the 1674 dispute between Mammanuah and Awashunkes, the court sided with Awashunkes's opponents, and further undercut her authority by ordering that Saconets should "do what they can to find out any further grounds of suspicion of . . . [the] suspected murder, and if there appear further grounds . . . to secure and send [word] to the English authority, to be dealt with all according to law" (NPNER [6]:113). Like Pohunna and Mammanuah, Sam's wife and her supporters had managed to ally themselves with English "lawful" authority and against Awashunkes's leadership. My hypothesis then is that internal native factionalism could now offer an entrée to colonial intervention, revealing the complex and shifting relationship between native and English political systems.

The 1683 infanticide prosecution signals the effects of a new English influence over postwar Indian politics. No longer would Awashunkes or other Indian leaders be able to wield power separate from and equal to that of English authorities. All natives, not just the leaders, were now subjects of the English government (cf. F. Bailey 1960:114–15), and thus could make appeals for English aid if frustrated by native authorities. In the decades following the war, many native groups petitioned English governing bodies to annul the actions of their sachems (cf. Petition of the Chappaquiddick Indians to William Dummer, 29 November 1726, in Massachusetts Archives, Indian Records [31]:129). Awashunkes's whipping of Sam's wife was just one example in which the local decisions of a native leader had ramifications beyond the native village. Where English leaders found a ruling family that pleased them (for example, the eighteenth-century Ninigret family among the Niantic-Narragansett of Rhode Island), they supported their rule (Campbell and LaFantasie 1978:73; Plane 1993b); but where they found a difficult ruler (like Awashunkes?), they might choose to side with the opposition. This case may also have signalled the end of Awashunkes's career as a sachem; this was her last appearance in the historical record. We cannot take negative evidence as proof of her loss of influence—she could simply have died, taken on a new name, or slipped from active leadership into quiet councillorship, leaving Peter with the more active role of sachem. But whatever the cause of the records' silence, the 1683 case exemplifies important changes in native authority structures, as English leaders undermined the very native rulers they had helped to create.

"Despotic Queen": Changes in the Gender Systems of the Colonial World

I have so far interpreted Awashunkes's career as if her gender made little difference. Yet just as the political autonomy of native groups was affected by English colonization, so too were native gender systems. Native women now faced potential prosecution for such gendered English crimes as infanticide and found it increasingly difficult to rise to positions of public leadership. Although the English had adored their own Queen Bess, and although they encountered women of authority in their own communities (such as a governor's wife), most Europeans were not used to dealing with women who had formal, public, political authority of their own. Hence, the Awashunkes of the English documents was recorded by the English clerk as not just a *sachem*, but as a *squaw sachem*, the marked case. Her opposite, in English thinking, was not the *male sachem* but simply the *sachem*, the normal, unmarked (but not ungendered) leader.

Getting at what Awashunkes's gender might have meant for the pre-colonial Saconet people is a difficult matter. Even the words with which natives described their own gender systems are largely lost.[21] Ethnolinguistic evidence suggests that both political office and tribal identity descended patrilineally (Simmons and Aubin 1975:29). Most sachems were male, although charismatic women from leading families could attract followers as well. The predominance of male leaders is at odds with a current argument that Indian "matriarchies" were only shifted toward "patriarchal" systems by colonization.[22] While we might distrust such an interpretation as a simplistic romanticization of the precontact world (cf. di Leonardo 1991:15), the gender systems of native societies did change under colonial rule. Missionaries attacked native gender roles head-on, arguing that men should farm the land and women should become productive and submissive housewives. At the same time, changes in land use and land tenure forced natives to alter their subsistence activities, lessening mobility. All of this combined to shift economic and political systems, and hence gender roles, toward a more English model.

Yet Awashunkes's gender appears to have had no detrimental impact upon her performance as a leader through Metacom's War, nor does a woman sachem appear to have been particularly remarkable in this period. Awashunkes shared the stage during the war with two other female sachems, Quaiapan and Weetamoo (Grumet 1980:50–51). One might best assume that the English accepted Awashunkes as the appropriate representative of the Saconets because of the balance of power in the prewar period: they were either unable or unwilling to make an issue of Awashunkes's gender, especially during the tense period leading up to Metacom's War.

In contrast, the occasion of her 1683 appearance in court derives entirely from friction along colonial gender frontiers. Awashunkes, her daughter, and other native women faced a new vulnerability to prosecution for the gendered crime of infanticide. In the legal codes of both old and New England, infanticide was a form of murder, punishable by death. Women alone usually faced punishment (Hoffer and Hull 1981:103, 109). Under the English law of 1624, even the concealment of a birth or the secret burial of a bastard infant was considered proof of infanticide (ix–x, 23, 50–51).[23] Proscriptions against both abortion and infanticide were codified in midwives' oaths and in both religious and secular law (154–57).

Although in theory everyone was subject equally to prosecution, in practice most defendants were young, unmarried women. The 1624 statute explicitly linked infanticide to illegitimacy and other forms of sexual misbehavior. We see in the application of English infanticide laws a struggle between the justice administered by elite men and the actions of women with few resources. While English women and men certainly "fornicated," had abortions, and even committed infanticide, most apparently accepted the notion that these actions were criminal (Dayton 1991; Macfarlane 1980:73–78; also cf. Lenemann and Mitchison 1988:483–85). Under the system of "social childbirth" of New England's English communities, neighbors and friends watched over the entire reproductive process, including the birth. From the perspective of neighborhood women, infanticide, although perhaps regarded as a necessary evil, seems not to have been openly accepted as a form of population control (Ulrich 1982; 98–99, 130–32, 198–99).

Indigenous reproductive practice was quite different. Native women tended to give birth alone, away from the watchful eyes of friends and neighbors, in itself sufficient to make them vulnerable to charges of infanticide as defined by the English statute (Plane 1992:15). Like members of many cultures, the indigenous people of New England practiced both abortion and infanticide as methods of population control and perhaps for other cultural reasons as well (Hausfater 1984:501).[24]

Stories of pre–Contact Period "Bastard Rocks" or "Papoose Rocks" where newborn infants had been thrown to their deaths were recorded from the mid-eighteenth to the twentieth centuries. As one eighteenth-century Indian described it (albeit in somewhat prejudicial language), the Indian youths before the coming of the English indulged in "Promiscuous Commerce," and if their "old Women who procured Abortions by profession" were "unable with all their Roots, Powders, & Drinks to procure Abortions. . . . [then] the young Squaws took Care to be delivered alone in the Woods or among Rocks, & instantly to make way with & kill the foetus as soon as born" (Plane 1992:21–22; Stiles 1916:144–45; also cf. Speck 1928:257). When combined with reports of small family size and the prevalence of such practices in other known small-scale societies, we may reasonably conclude that natives practiced infanticide and abortion.[25]

Throughout the colonial period, natives faced increasing pressure to adhere to English practices. This involved accepting new conceptions of legitimate and illegitimate birth and the reinterpretation of abortion or infanticide as murder. The 1683 prosecution of Awashunkes and her children is a prime example of these new pressures, the first in the Plymouth courts. Postwar Saconets occupied an ambiguous position vis-à-vis the English system of laws. Not quite within the English system of courts yet not without, the 1683 case shows a legal system that incorporated English elements. At the time of her suspected pregnancy, Betty's body was examined by two Indian women. The English would have understood these as comparable to their own midwives and middle-aged neighbor-hood women, who have been described as the guardians and watchdogs of youthful female sexuality (Ulrich 1982:98–99). The role of such Indian women was not exactly equivalent to that of the English model (Plane 1993a); nevertheless, the Saconet investigation follows the rough outlines of English practice. This suggests the influence of English fornication laws in the colonial native court system, or at least a native awareness of their new accountability to English authorities.

Awashunkes's final confrontation with the Plymouth court in the post–Metacom's War case reveals a literal *embodiment* of colonization, which was conspicuously absent from her earlier, virtually genderless appear-ances in the colonial record. Native women can be seen, in the case of changing reproductive mores, to embody the effects of colonization, in which women's and infants' bodies themselves become the site of struggle between English and native concepts of right and wrong. Here I intend an embodiment different from that meant by medical anthropologists, who see illnesses, body image, and behaviors as embodiments of social forces—for example, poverty, or oppression (Scheper-Hughes 1992:184–87, 324–26, 474). Of course, New England natives also experienced this type of embodied colonization, especially through disease and alcohol abuse. But a second kind of embodied colonization involves the struggle between English and native systems of law at the level of the individual's body; individual women's reproductive actions resonated intensely within their colonial context (cf. Martin 1987: Chap. 12; see also the argument that culture itself is embodied, in Csordas 1990).

Had Awashunkes not ordered the whipping of Sam's wife (who was, after all, telling the truth), this case might never have come before any magistrate, either Indian or English. Although fornication was theoret-ically in the purview of the separate, colonial Indian magistracy system, the few surviving records of such courts give no hint of the number of fornication prosecutions, if any (Goddard and Bragdon 1988[1]:18–20). Furthermore, the Saconets, who remained outside the network of mis-sionaries' "praying towns," may never have adopted a formalized system of magistrates based on the English system. In June of 1677, Benjamin Church was empowered to "end differences arising among the Indians there, alsoe to see that they demean themselves orderly," but this does not mean that he established a formalized court system (NPNER [5]:234). The only mention of an Indian magistrate comes a few years later, in 1681, when the Plymouth court worked out a solution to the case of Samuel, "a runaway servant," by acting on the "proposal" of "Isacke, Indian magistrate at Saconett and places adjacent" (NPNER [6]:65). Awashunkes's case is a rare instance in which seventeenth-century natives were prosecuted in an English court for a sexual offense.[26]

The justices probably pursued Awashunkes because of some combination of factors: the seriousness of the charge, English fears of a disruptive factional struggle within a pacified native enclave, and the competition between Awashunkes's actions and the alternate, male-run jucidial structures represented by Benjamin Church and Isaac, the Indian magistrate. We can hypothesize that the English used the shifting gender expectations of the postwar world to gain a political advantage over Awashunkes. Like all native women, Awashunkes became vulnerable to prosecution for the previously unproblematic practice of infanticide; unlike most, she was actually prosecuted for this new crime. Like all native sachems, Awashunkes was vulnerable to English encroachments upon her power. But unlike other native sachems (most of them male), Awashunkes the "squaw sachem" was undermined through the vehicle of an infanticide prosecution. I suspect that it is only in the conjuncture of these two strands—her gender and her role as sachem—that we find the underlying reasons for this rare prosecution.[27]

If Awashunkes's authority in postwar New England could be undermined through gendered means, growing English dominance seems also to have made it more difficult for other women to take up positions of formal leadership. Those who have studied native Christianity on Martha's Vineyard note that official religious leaders in the postwar years were virtually all men. Native women developed highly elaborated roles as lay readers and private religious exhorters, and undoubtedly continued to exert considerable sway in their communities. But all of the formal leadership roles (preacher, deacon) went to men (Ronda 1981:372–75, 384–85). Similarly, only a few female sachems would appear in subsequent years. Overall, the ability of native women to exercise political *office* diminished. Yet their participation in politics, like that in religion, may still have been considerable, although well-hidden from English view.[28]

An eighteenth-century Cape Cod dispute over land ownership offers an example of a climate that was increasingly hostile to formal female leadership. The case turned on whether Tinohkanuckom, the granddaughter of a petty sachem, had lawfully willed land to her son, or whether the land had belonged to the regional sachem, Popmonit. The defendants argued successfully that the island in question had belonged "to sd. sachem [Popmonit] . . . & not to *an old Indian woman* yt had no Right" [emphasis added]. After denying that she could even have been a sachem, these eighteenth-century native men then applied English laws of couverture to Tinohkanuckom, the wife of Annawickett. According to their reasoning, she could not have left a valid will, "for a woman cannot dispose of Land by will or deed in her husband's lifetime without his acting with her."[29] Here we see a graphic example of how the changed gender expectations of the eighteenth century precluded women's exercise of public authority.

History and Anthropology in Awashunkes's Life Story

It is nearly impossible to gain any sense of Awashunkes's own perceptions of her life. What we do know of Awashunkes comes through several "ethnographic" filters. The most detailed (and perhaps most distorting) are those of the English culture broker, Benjamin Church, and the English court clerk who recorded her encounter with the English magistrates in 1683. Her story reaches us only after having already passed through many texts and myriad contexts.

This caution should not deter us from trying to learn what we can about that lived experience, from shaping the facts of her life into a life history of our own. In casting Awashunkes's life experiences as a transforming journey in which gender became increasingly important to her role as a leader, we are undoubtedly doing violence to what she herself might have told us (Brumble 1988:13–15; also cf. Bataille and Sands 1984). Yet through this life history, we can see the ways in which one person manipulated both the political and the gender systems in a rapidly changing cultural context. In recognizing the complexity of her life, we can begin to suggest how culture is located not in some distant "social structure," but in the individual, who after all both creates and copes with exterior forces.[30] Each actor holds within himself or herself several different identities, and chooses from a range of possible behaviors associated with each. In this view, each individual, rather than typifying the whole, represents simply a slice of his or her culture (cf. F. Bailey 1960:248–49).[31]

This realization is especially pertinent for women, who are often omitted from the "norm" when cultural models are created. Instead women are

Boulder erected in Wilbur Wood, Little Compton, Rhode Island, in the late nineteenth century, during a period of romantic interest in Awashunkes's story. The engraving reads, "In memory of Awashonks Queen of Sogkonate & friend of the white man." Photograph by James D. Proctor.

marked as perpetually atypical or abnormal—which they are when the norm is defined as the male pole of a bipolar gender ideology. Many feminist historians and ethnographers have explored the life history as a means of correcting the androcentrism of most representations of unified culture (Behar 1990:229; Geiger 1986:335, 337; Watson and Watson-Franke 1985:161–63).[32] Awashunkes's position as a leader allowed her to avoid the ubiquitous "mutedness" of women both in tribal societies and in early modern European society (Ardener 1972:136–37; also cf. Keesing 1985: esp. 31–33). She spoke and acted in ways heard both within and outside of her culture(s), indeed, heard all the way to the present moment. And yet her experiences in 1683 make it clear that this ability to speak was doubly imperiled after Metacom's War, when sachems found their autonomy diminished and women found their opportunities for formal leadership reduced.[33]

Although we have records of only a few individuals like Awashunkes, the study of even these few helps us to particularize the encounter between

Gravestones of Benjamin Church and wife, Alice Southworth, with later memorial in foreground. This display stands in marked contrast to the unknown burial site of Awashunkes. Photograph by James D. Proctor.

Europeans and Native Americans. In her early career, Awashunkes can be described as having been a classic "big-man," or person of influence, with power, prestige, and persuasion within her grasp. From her proud submission to the English in 1671 to the popular assault on the upstart Mammanuah and the conferences and rituals of Metacom's War, she maintained the ability to win followers and inspire loyalty. But how then do we explain the Awashunkes of 1683—as a conquered sachem? As a waning

View of Saconet Point, Little Compton, Rhode Island. Photograph by James D. Proctor.

"big-man"? That is certainly part of the answer. Yet this does not fully explain her decline as a person of influence. The analysis must also account for her position as a gendered person in a world of changing systems of gender. Her position as a woman affected the exercise of her authority as sachem, and her story reveals the interconnectedness of gender and politics in the colonial world. Her life puts a face on the colonial process by bringing cultural clashes to the level of individual choice and individual experience.

Notes

Versions of this essay have been presented to audiences at Purdue University, Michigan State University, the University of South Florida, the 1994 meetings of the American Historical Association, and the Huntington Library in Pasadena, Calif. It has benefited from the reactions of these groups, as well as from the suggestions of Thomas Buckley, Gregory Button, Colin Calloway, Robert Grumet, Ruth Wallis Herndon, David Jacobson, Ann McMullen, James Merrell, Alice Nash, Barry O'Connell, Jenny Hale Pulsipher, Neal Salisbury, and Laurel Thatcher Ulrich. I am also grateful for the assistance of the staff at the public library in Little Compton, R.I. and of Carolyn Travers and Nanepashemet of Plimoth Plantation, Inc., in Plymouth, Mass.

1. Also known as King Philip's War; see the apocalyptic accounts of the war in two classic histories: Leach (1958:250) and Jennings (1975:325).

2. Although it did not erase native identity: see Campbell and LaFantasie (1978), Mandell (1992), O'Brien (1990), Plane and Button (1993), Simmons (1986), and Weinstein (1986).

3. Awashunkes herself was linked by kinship ties (whether by "blood," marriage, or fictive bonds is unclear) to other similar leaders, most notably Ninigret, the sachem of the Niantic-Narragansett (cf. Grumet 1980:48, 50–51).

4. After colonization, the "culture broker" (one who moves between two or more cultures, accruing power and influence by service to both the colonizer and the colonized) became much more important (cf. Richter 1988). Awashunkes rarely functioned as a broker per se.

5. By gender systems I intend the "cultural constructions of male and female, that emerge cross-culturally" (Ortner and Whitehead 1981:25). Different societies construct more or less marked gender categories and sometimes define more than two gender categories (cf. Shapiro 1983).

6. Anthropologists who promote the approach of "action," "praxis," or "practice" have criticized approaches that devalue the individual actor and cast culture as a seamless whole (cf. Keesing 1974:91; Ortner 1984:159). Life histories offer an ideal way to explore the relationship between actors and cultural change. Of course, the whole notion of biography or life history rests upon the assumption that people in the past shared a conception of the self similar to that found in our own modern, individualistic societies (cf. Brumble 1988:3–4 and 18; but also cf. Spiro 1993:116–17 and 144–45).

7. Two earlier mentions may refer to her: Awasha, who was sent by the Narragansett sachems to treat with the commissioners of the United (New England) Colonies during tensions in 1653 (Indian Records [30]:36, in Massachusetts Archives); and Awashaus, who signed on to the 1660 mortgage of the Narragansett lands to the commissioners of the United Colonies. Nowhere is this individual referred to as a woman, and in the second instance is even listed as "Awashaus *his* marke" [emphasis added] (Indian Records [30]:83, in Massachusetts Archives). Although Grumet (1980:52–53) has pointed out that ethnohistorians often erroneously assume that native signatories must have been male when no gender is noted, the case of Awasha(us) is more dubious, and so I have chosen to assume that this is not Awashunkes.

8. The Tatammanna of the 1671 submission is perhaps the same person as Tatacomuncah, who is mentioned in a 1662 complaint against Wamsutta, the brother of Philip, for illegal land sales at Saconet Neck (NPNER [4]:16–17). He is almost surely the same as Takamunna, who offered his submission at the same time as Philip, in September of 1671 (NPNER[5]:80).

9. Her son and eventual co-leader, Peter, also signed the deed.

10. Given the vagaries of pronunciation and spelling, the Mammanuah of the 1674 incident was most probably the same councilor, Mahunnanah, who allied with Awashunkes in opposing the English in 1671. An antiquarian source

reports that Awashunkes had two sons: "the youngest was William Mommynewit, or Maummynuey. Plymouth court ordered the grantees to buy off the oldest [Peter?]. Maummynuey was put to grammar school, and learned latin; designed for college, but was seized with the palsy. He sold some land" (Anonymous 1809a:114). With all this detail, it seems improbable that Mammanuah was only a metaphorical "son," in the sense of a junior leader, rather than her biological son; another possibility, although one I find less likely, is that reported by Milton Travers: that Peter and Mammanuah were the same person (Travers 1957:173–74). The cooperation between Awashunkes and Peter during the war and the Plymouth court records' consistent identification of Mammanuah as a friend to the English while Peter was taken as a hostage suggests that these were at least two individuals.

11. This is the first and only mention of Awashunkes's husband.

12. As scholars have demonstrated, the colonial system transformed the sachem's power to distribute usufruct rights to land into a sachem's power to permanently alienate such lands (Bragdon 1981:108–9; Cronon 1983:55–71; cf. Baker 1989:253). It is not surprising that there were many bitter battles between native factions over the right to sell native lands.

13. Daniel Gookin's 1674 narrative described "powows" who "by their diabolical spells, mutterings, and exorcisms, . . . seem to do wonders. They use extraordinary strange motions of their bodies, insomuch that they will *sweat until they foam;*" [emphasis mine] (Gookin [1674] 1968:154).

14. Awashunkes sent Squattuck, a messenger, to Rhode Island at the same time (June 14, 1676), presumably to treat for peace or to inform this separate group of Englishmen that the Saconets were now allies, not enemies. The Rhode Island colonial records include an order for his safe passage back to his canoe and thence to Awashunkes (RIC [2]:545). Such multilayered diplomacy suggests the complexity of Awashunkes's task, as well as the dangers of using unified colonial categories such as "the English" and "the Indians" to describe all of the various parties.

15. This theme of Indian food as being different and lacking the civilities of salt and bread emerges repeatedly in English descriptions of native life. William Wood (1977:86–88) noted in his 1634 account that the Indians "seldom or never make bread of their Indians corn, but seethe it whole like beans," and that they "keep no set meals," but eat their fill, "it being their fashion to eat all at some times and sometimes nothing at all in two or three days." They insisted on sharing food with the English visitor, which Wood described as a "broth, made thick with fishes, fowls, and beasts boiled all together, some remaining raw, the rest converted by over-much seething to a loathed broth." John Josselyn (1988:93), in his 1674 account of his second voyage to New England (1663–71), described the diet of the Indians, noting "salt they have not the use of, nor bread." Roger Williams (1973:182), characteristically less condemnatory, noted that the natives boiled the liquor of clams and used it to make their broth, *nausaump* (corn broth), and bread "seasonable and savory, in stead of Salt."

16. Early in this century, the anthropologist Frank Speck identified Saconet as one of the few native communities of southern New England to survive into the twentieth century (Speck 1928: Plate 20).

17. The court noted that this group of Saconets had "continued faithfull to the English" during "our late troubles" (NPNER [5]:224–25).

18. Betty appears to have been a "daughter" in the sense that we would mean, and not, as is possible in the English usage of the day, a daughter-in-law, as she was tried for fornication, a crime limited to unmarried women. It is just possible that she conceived this child before marriage to Peter, but this seems unlikely, as English people tried for premarital fornication in Plymouth at this time generally were tried as a couple, or with the man representing both husband and wife.

19. Kawashima (1986:156) argues that juries were reluctant to bring in capital convictions of native defendants in infanticide cases because of the special difficulty of finding evidence.

20. All parties to this cover-up were punished in the end, with Betty and the two women who examined her being ordered to pay total reparations of forty shillings to the wife of Sam.

21. Grumet (1980:49) suggests that Roger Williams, so perceptive an observer in other matters, managed to miss the role played by "saunksquas," the female "Queens," described by Williams as the wives of male leaders. Awashunkes herself was not referred to as a sunksquaw, and thus this essay maintains the English term that was in fact used, the "squaw sachem."

22. For example, see Paula Gunn Allen's (1986:2–3) argument that "traditional tribal lifestyles are more often gynocratic than not, and they are never patriarchal," and "that for millennia American Indians have based their social systems, however diverse, on ritual, spirit-centered, woman-focused worldviews." In her view, "The physical and cultural genocide of American Indian tribes is and was mostly about a patriarchal fear of gynocracy." Yet her argument that "Puritans . . . could not tolerate peoples who allowed women to occupy prominent positions and decision-making capacity at every level of society" contradicts the fact that for long periods of time women like Awashunkes continued to wield legitimate authority, even serving as European allies, and that even after the pressures that discouraged women's formal political authority overcame leaders such as Awashunkes, women often continued to exercise considerable authority within ethnic enclave cultures (cf. Plane and Button 1993:604–5).

23. Thus, in 1712, a different Betty, Bettee Negro, a servant in Marshfield, Massachusetts, was hanged for having "privately buried" her bastard child "so that it could not Come to light whether the sd Child was born alive or not" (Case of Bettee Negro Woman, 25 March 1712, Plymouth County Session, Superior Court of Judicature Records, 1700–14:271, in Massachusetts Archives). The provisions of the Stuart infanticide law were specifically invoked in one 1719 case, in which the grand jury found that an Indian woman could be indicted for concealing the birth of any issue of her body that would have been a bastard under the provisions of an act passed by the General Court of Massachusetts Bay (into which Plymouth

Colony had merged in 1691) in a session begun in May 1696 (Case of Oseth Cognehew, Indian, 28 April 1719, Superior Court of Judicature Records: 8–9, in Massachusetts Archives).

24. Children deemed illegitimate, not of the preferred gender, or deformed in some way are usually most at risk. Some societies killed those infants whom they believed to be dangerous witches (Sargent 1988:83–84). Many peoples do not believe that full personhood or humanity derives from birth alone. In the Japanese past, infants were not considered human until they emitted their first cry, at which time it was believed that an ancestral spirit entered the child. Infanticide was not permitted after this moment (Wagatsuma 1981:131). Children in aboriginal New Guinea were not regarded as truly human until they had survived a few years (cf. Langness 1981:14).

In presenting previous versions of this essay, I have been told that I was being insensitive to the deep emotions that "naturally" accompany infanticide. But as anthropologists have demonstrated over and over, infanticide is widely practiced, through both active murder and passive neglect; often it is regarded with neither horror nor emotional turmoil, but rather is accepted as a form of population control, much as many American women today view abortion (Scheper-Hughes 1985:310–11 and 1992:433; also cf. Hrdy 1992). Nancy Scheper-Hughes (1992:433) notes that it is "indefensible" to argue, as did one anthropologist, that native South Americans "*must* consider all their newborns precious because Western psychobiological theories tell us that all humans *are* this way."

25. These practices also seem to have been continued well into the colonial period. As late as 1732, an elderly Narragansett woman testified that infanticide suspect Sarah Pharaoh came to her "and told her yt She was Not Well and was Much out of Order and Desired . . . Hannah to Get Some Roots for her to Take." Hannah responded that "She Thought She [Sarah] was with Child and if So the Taking sd Roots Would Kill . . . the Child and She [Sarah?] must be Hanged for It." The deposition continued, "She Further Says yt Indians Often Use yt Sort of Roots when they are in Travil Which Soon Cause ym to be Delivered." That Hannah still had access to the dangerous roots, as well as the knowledge to use them, was never in dispute in this incident. So we see that such supposedly intimate activities as pregnancy and childbirth remained a locus of colonization, one that needs exploration (Deposition of Indian Hannah, 8 March 1729, Case of Sarah Pharaoh, in Rhode Island Supreme Court Records, March 1730). For a more complete discussion of infanticide cases in Rhode Island and Plymouth, see Plane (1995: Chapter 5). I do not mean to suggest, however, that individuals continued to practice infanticide in a context unchanged from that of the precontact era. In fact, the depredations of disease alone may well have discouraged infanticide, as they did among other native North American peoples (cf. Helm 1980).

26. By the early eighteenth century, women of color, including Indians, would be tried for infanticide in numbers higher than their proportion of the population (cf. Plane 1995: Chap. 5).

27. As Faye Ginsburg and Rayna Rapp (1991:331) have noted, "the 'politics of

reproduction' cannot and should not be extracted from the examination of politics in general."

28. Among the Narragansett-Niantic group, Weunquesh, the daughter of Ninigret (the Niantic sachem who had been neutral during the war), served as sachem from 1679 until her death in 1686. She was succeeded by a series of male sachems, clients of the English colonial elite, until the ascension of Esther, in 1769, who was the second to last of the Narragansett sachems in the historic period (Simmons 1983:256–257 and 259). Native women retained authority in some areas, and seem to have been respected within their communities (Grumet 1980:59). When the succession to the Narragansett sachemship was in dispute, English authorities turned to elderly women as well as men to determine the "traditional" line of inheritance, and the widows of two successive sachems signed documents and brought action on behalf of their sons (cf. Deposition of Mary, alias Oskoosooduck, 3 Sept. 1746, Ms. File Papers, King's County, Aug. 1755, in Rhode Island Supreme Court Records; Campbell and LaFantasie 1978: 72–73). On Martha's Vineyard in 1707, Judy Caperonend, a sachem's daughter, made a will that left all her land to her daughter and divided her "sachem's right" between her husband and their daughter, in a typical power-sharing arrangement (Caperonend Will, Nov. 1707, in Dukes County Probate Records, Book 1:30). These eighteenth-century arrangements combined elements of traditional authority with innovations such as individual inheritance, leaving the historian to wonder to what extent women retained formal authority in late colonial New England.

29. See Parker, Attorney vs. Simon and Sunkason, 1716: Manuscript Number 12967, p. 109 in Appellee's answer to the reason of appeal: Manuscript on file, Massachusetts Archives).

30. In this context it is nonsensical to ask whether Awashunkes was typical of her times. Rather, like all individuals, and especially like most key informants, she was not at all typical. In the case of life histories of living informants, usually it is a few key personages who are best able to recount their own lives, to be self-reflective, and to see the significance of ordinary events. To borrow from Sidney Mintz's (1989:792) discussion of his own particularly perceptive informant (Taso), Awashunkes is "powerfully representative of [her] culture and [her] time, without being either ordinary or typical."

31. Some anthropologists have argued that there is no such thing as a unitary "culture," but only an "abstracted composite" of the "variant versions of competence among subgroups, roles, and individuals" (Keesing 1974:89).

32. Yet, as Ruth Behar (1990:225) has complained, these life histories sometimes tend to cast one woman's experience as typical of the experience of all women, as when, in Behar's example, Marjorie Shostak's (1981) biography of Nisa becomes less an account of Nisa's life and more an account of the life of a !Kung woman, formed out of the various social roles (wife, mother, economic being, et cetera) that make up the life of any female !Kung individual. Awashunkes cannot be taken as a typical Indian woman, a typical Indian leader, or a typical Indian woman leader.

33. Cf. the "ethnography of the particular," which Lila Abu-Lughod (1991:154 and 158–59) has argued will, "by focusing on particular individuals and their changing relationships, . . . necessarily subvert the most problematic connotations of culture: homogeneity, coherence, and timelessness." Abu-Lughod sees this different sort of ethnography as vital, because, as she argues, ignoring this particularity simply reduces the object of study to a dehumanized, homogenized cultural Other.

CHAPTER EIGHT

᷈

"Standing by His Father": Thomas Waban of Natick, circa 1630–1722

Daniel Mandell

Introduction

THOMAS WABAN REPRESENTS the second generation of southeastern New England natives who worked to maintain their people's power and autonomy within the new world created by the colonial invasion. Born as the "Great Migration" of Puritans reached Massachusetts Bay, Thomas lived nearly a century and experienced many of the events that transformed southern New England. When he was about sixteen years old, his father became the primary intermediary for Puritan missionary John Eliot and for the power of the Bay Colony, gaining authority in the region and establishing the village of Natick with the backing of the colonial and English governments. Waban sent his son, Thomas, to a nearby town to learn to read and write in English; these skills later served him and his community well.

After Waban died in 1684, Thomas became one of Natick's leaders and, although he lacked his father's authority, played a key role in helping the community traverse the treacherous currents of the late seventeenth and early eighteenth centuries. While apparently he tried to follow the path pointed out by his father, the road that Thomas traveled with Natick brought fundamental changes and tore holes in the boundaries that had

166

maintained the Indian enclave. At the close of his life, after the tide of colonial settlements had swept past Natick, the Indian community led by Thomas Waban adopted the Anglo-American manner of landholding and an English minister. Thomas probably saw these actions as necessary adaptations to the changing colonial scene, but the resulting social, economic, political, and demographic problems hurt his descendants and led to the community's destruction.

The hard times suffered by the Waban family following Thomas's death in 1722 foreshadowed the fate of their community. Mary, Thomas's only surviving and apparently childless daughter, died soon after her father— and before her mother, Tasoonque (Elizabeth). The younger of the two Waban sons, Isaac, worked as a laborer, was thrown into debtor's jail, and then fled the province; at his death in 1746 he left an orphaned daughter. Thomas, Jr., died just eleven years after his father, leaving four sons and a daughter. The eldest of these sons, Thomas III, died in 1752, and his widow would follow a year later, leaving an orphaned daughter. Another son, Hezekiah, had three sons (one of whom appears in provincial records) before he joined the army gathered to fight King George's War in 1744 and disappeared in an expedition to Cuba. The last two sons, Moses and Joshua, died without leaving any children (Natick 1910; Natick Church Records; O'Brien 1990:312–17). By mid-century, the Waban family had largely disappeared from town and provincial records, and a census in 1749 showed no Wabans "in or belong[ing] to Natick" (Natick 1749). Twenty-five years later, few Indians remained in the town (Indian Records [32]:131, in Massachusetts Archives).

Natives, Puritans, and Natick

Natick was the product of a unique partnership between Thomas's father and the famous Puritan missionary John Eliot. The native world in the region had been turned upside down in the years between 1616, when Indians along the coast were decimated by a European epidemic, and 1638, when the Puritans destroyed the Pequot tribe and became the primary power in southern New England. Many Indians were ready for a new explanation of the sudden, massive changes in their universe, most notably Thomas's father, Waban, who led the Massachusett village of Nonantum (Newton), fifteen miles west of Boston.

The "Eliot Memorial," located on the border between Allston and Newton, Massachusetts. Photograph by Daniel Mandell.

In October 1646, John Eliot, the Dorchester minister and Puritan missionary who had learned the Massachusett language, brought his message
of Biblical salvation to Waban's village. The Massachusett sachem, Cutshamekin, had spurned the missionary, no doubt because Eliot threatened
his authority. But Waban found the power of the minister and his god
attractive, and gained political influence and material assistance at Cutshamekin's expense. In return, Eliot gained the authority critical for his
missionary work. Waban's influence (and therefore Eliot's) went beyond
Nonantum, for his wife (and Thomas's mother), Tohattawan, was the
daughter of the sachem of Nashoba (Littleton), thirty miles northwest of
Nonantum, and had family connections at Wamesit, the southernmost
Pennacook settlement, along the Merrimack River.

The growing numbers who flocked to Waban's village to hear Eliot soon
agreed to follow the English path of righteousness. In 1651 Waban and
Eliot obtained two thousand acres for the first "Praying Town," named
Natick, and by 1658 the township had expanded threefold. Natick strad-
dled the Charles River, eighteen miles west of Boston and six miles north
of Dedham—and close to the school Thomas Waban attended (Eliot 1647;
Gookin 1806:180–81; Salisbury 1974; Salisbury 1982:101–6, 175–76,
190–92, 209–10).

Within their new village, Waban's people erected a meetinghouse, a
fort, and an arched footbridge across the Charles. House lots were laid
out for nuclear families in the English fashion. The leadership structure
seemed designed to please the English in general and Eliot in particular,
as, on the basis of Exodus, the missionary had the Indians choose first a
"ruler of a hundred," then two "rulers of fifties," and finally ten rulers of
ten. Their legal code overturned many elements of aboriginal culture,
from religious practices to the wearing of long hair by men to the practice
of killing lice with one's teeth. In 1660 a sufficient number of converts,
including Waban, received the blessing of Puritan elites to create a congregational church, and Eliot began training native missionaries to take
the Puritan message to Nipmuc and Wampanoag villages. By 1670 Eliot watched over seven praying towns, including Nashoba and Wamesit.
Some historians have seen this process as the subjugation of dispirited
natives to the Bay Colony's authority, while others see it as the Indians'
wholesale adoption of the Puritan way of life (Axtell 1985:138–46; Jennings 1975:228–53; Salisbury 1974). Yet the most persuasive view sees the
praying towns as places where natives labored to adapt to the rapid trans-

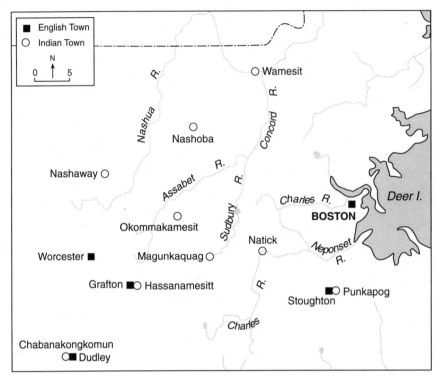

Legend:
- ■ English Town
- ○ Indian Town

N
0 — 5

- ○ Wamesit
- ○ Nashoba
- Nashaway ○
- ○ Okommakamesit
- Worcester ■
- Magunkaquag ○
- Grafton ■○ Hassanamesitt
- Charles R.
- ■ BOSTON
- Deer I.
- Natick ○
- ■○ Punkapog
- Stoughton
- Charles
- Chabanakongkomun
- ○■ Dudley

Rivers: Nashua R., Concord R., Assabet R., Sudbury R., Neponset R., Charles R.

Natick and its environs

formation of their world, on their own ground and at their own pace (Von Lonkhuyzen 1990; O'Brien 1990:39–78).

There is no doubt that the apparently radical changes in Natick and the other towns were moderated by the persistence of aboriginal ideas and customs. On their family house lots Indians built wigwams instead of English clapboard dwellings. Cutshamekin (who became the "top" ruler after he decided to join Natick), Waban (who became Natick's ruler of one hundred by 1655, following the Massachusett sachem's death), and the other native leaders retained their prominence as rulers and maintained a traditional emphasis on concord and consensus. The code that they enforced, while directed by Eliot and made provincial law by the Massachusetts General Court, had originated with the Nonantum council headed by Waban. The public confessions of Indians, recorded when Eliot sought approval for a church in Natick, frequently identified traditional values of kinship and power as motivations for their conversion. Those famous Indian missionaries extended Waban's influence along with the authority of Eliot's Bible—and the Bibles that they carried were printed not in English but in a written form of Massachusett developed by Eliot (Gookin 1806:181–89; Bragdon 1981:134–35; MacCulloch 1966:64–69; O'Brien 1990:60–78). The desire to maintain an Indian community in an English Christian world even extended to the grave: some Natick natives were buried, no doubt after a proper Puritan sermon, with wampum, spoons, beads, and other earthly items (Biglow 1830:15–16).

Waban's son Thomas was involved in this "middle ground" from its inception.[1] He was called Weegramomenit before he became Thomas, and at various occasions throughout his life used that Massachusett name (Middlesex County Deeds [10]:557). Shortly after Eliot's first visit to Non-antum, Waban "voluntarily offered his eldest son, to be educated and trained up in the knowledge of God." While this son was not identified by Eliot, it was almost certainly Thomas.[2] Eliot first met Waban's eldest "standing by his father . . . dressed in English clothes"—which was later considered the mark of a Christian Indian. Thomas was sent to school in Dedham and, in accordance with what became a New England custom, was placed with an English family near the school (Eliot 1647:381–82). While northeastern Indians generally resisted English schooling, Waban obviously thought that such an education, as well as connections to the English that this "adoption" brought, were critical to his people's future.

Thomas was not the only man placed by Waban in colonial homes. At Eliot's third meeting at Nonantum, Waban brought to the missionary two more "young lusty men, who offered themselves voluntary to the service of the English that by dwelling in some of their families, they might come to know Jesus Christ" (Eliot 1647:397, 400). Indian attitudes changed within ten years, however, following the establishment of Natick and its church, when the Christian natives resisted efforts by the Massachusetts General Court to place their children in English homes (Gookin 1806:219; Axtell 1985:159). Waban's son did gain an extra measure of power by learning to read and write not only the written form of Massachusett but also English, as this knowledge would become an important component of Thomas's authority in the community.

By 1674 Thomas Waban was nearly forty-five years old and had doubt-less finished his education in Dedham and returned to his father's side in Natick. Waban's town contained about one hundred and fifty natives and had become a training center for Indian missionaries and teachers, who would be dispatched to Nipmuc villages and other native groups far from Boston (Gookin 1806:189–94). Waban was worried, however, about the increasing tension between the Wampanoags and Massachusetts and Plymouth. One of his people, John Sassamon, who had been trained as a schoolmaster and had served since 1660 as the secretary to the Wampanoag sachems (and as an informer for the Massachusetts), was found dead, apparently murdered. The colonists believed that Metacom (Philip), the Wampanoag sachem, had ordered Sassamon's death.

In April 1675, and again one month later, Waban traveled to an English magistrate to warn that Metacom "intended some mischief shortly to the English and Christian Indians." In July, a party of Metacom's warriors appeared outside Swansea, a town recently established within Wampanoag territory, slaying cattle. An assault seemed imminent. After a boy killed a warrior, the others attacked, killing several colonists, and the war began. The Massachusetts and Plymouth Colonies assembled an army to besiege Metacom in his "capital" at Mount Hope, and a company of fifty-two praying Indians, possibly including Thomas Waban, enlisted in the campaign. Metacom's people escaped, however, and joined forces with Nipmuc allies—including most of those from the newest praying towns— to attack and burn villages west and south of Boston (Gookin 1836:440– 45).

As the situation grew grim, "the clamours and animosity among the common people increased daily, not only against those Indians, but also all such English as were judged to be charitable to them" (Gookin 1836:453). On October 30, after an abandoned shack was burned in nearby Dedham, the "clamors" grew so loud that Waban, his son Thomas, and the other Natick Indians were forced from their homes and interred on Deer Island in Boston Harbor. They were followed by people from Nashoba, Punkapoag, and the other praying towns. Many suffered and some died of disease, starvation, and exposure on the island. After authorizing the release of a few individuals from the island to serve as spies for the colonial militia, the General Court agreed in April 1676 to allow the Indians to form a company of eighty men. While Waban's son is not named in any account of the war, he would have almost certainly joined the Indian company in order to gain glory and maintain his family's prestige. At his death, Thomas was called "Captain Waban," a rank he must have earned in King Philip's War—unless he had insisted on serving in one of the subsequent colonial conflicts despite his age (Middlesex County Probate Records). The Indian company played a key role in the final colonial victory, and men from Natick continued to aid the New England colonies in their many wars against Abenakis and the French (Gookin 1836:472–74, 485, 509–13; Bragdon 1981:153).

Natick Recreated

At the end of the war, Thomas's father led most of the survivors of Deer Island back to Natick, which became the largest Indian community in the Massachusetts Bay Colony—in large part because it brought together natives from nearly all of John Eliot's praying towns. Natick's "mixed multitude" was apparent in its leaders, some of whom had come from Wamesit, Nashoba, various Nipmuc villages, nearby Okommakamesit, and faraway Essex County (Gooking 1806:184–93; Middlesex County Deeds [9]:27–29, 196; [10]:557; Indian Records [30]:488–89, in Massachusetts Archives; Bragdon 1987; O'Brien 1990:112, 116–17).

The community's polity was also quite mixed, for it combined aboriginal, praying town, and colonial elements. In 1679, Natick was represented by Waban and two others, including Piambow, the former deacon of the Nipmuc church in Hassanamisset. While the three were titled "rulers" in documents, they seemed to comprise more of a council or court. Also prominent were three others, whose titles were not given but who doubtless served as councillors (Indian Records [30]:247, in Massachusetts Archives). Later petitions from Natick show that town meetings quickly gained a major role, particularly when the community's land was at issue (Indian Records [30]:276, 277a, in Massachusetts Archives). Waban and other Natick leaders gained their authority in part from their age (as was common in both aboriginal and Puritan societies), in part from personal prestige (one of the councillors was the minister, Daniel Tokkohwompait), and in part from family connections. In addition, some may have derived an extra measure of authority from their mothers or wives. Thomas Waban, for example, held a connection (and land claims) to Nashoba through his mother, and no doubt claimed the support of some families from that town (Middlesex County Deeds [9]:374–75).

The diversity of Natick's population may have led to weak or divided leadership in the community. In 1681, the selectmen from neighboring Dedham asked the General Court to resolve disorder in the Indian town, as they had "received diverse & some complaints about the manners and practices of ye Indians that have come in and dwelt among us or near us since the late wars, something which we have also taken notice of our selves" (Indian Records [30]:261a, in Massachusetts Archives). This was probably a reference to those Nipmucs who had moved to Natick after the war.

The colonists were particularly alarmed at those Indians' "proud & surly behavior." They noted that the Indians "rob us of our corn & other provisions out of our fields, That cattle in ye woods have been torn by their dogs," and that they "have affrighted some women to the great hazard of their lives." But apparently, when the selectmen went to the Indian community to request that their counterparts take care of the problems, the "antient and soberest Indians at Natick complaint [that] their young men are ruined by these Indians [that they] cannot govern or have any command of them" (Indian Records [30]:261a, in Massachusetts Archives). One wonders whether Thomas Waban, about fifty years old but not yet in a position of leadership in Natick, was considered one of the "antient and soberest" or one of the ungovernable "young men."

Natick also established a mixed economy, as its location encouraged the community to combine aboriginal and English traits both within and outside the colonial marketplace. The village had access to regional markets through Dedham, Boston, and other towns, and at the same time lay along the edge of the frontier, which the war had emptied of colonial settlements. As a result, a number of Natick men began trapping beaver once again and also developed a deerskin trade (Job Indian vs. Cyprian Stevens: Folio 96, Group 4 in Middlesex County Court of Common Pleas). When complaining about the "proud and surly" Indians, the Dedham selectmen also charged that their neighbors

> spend almost all their time in hunting, to ye great damage of ye English, wastefully destroying the Deer which might be a great relief to many familys, for [they] take no care to save the flesh, but only get ye skins, & some one of them as they themselves report destroyed & wasted in this manner above an hundred deer in a year, & others of them sixty, fourty, or some such great number apiece. (Indian Records [30]:261a, in Massachusetts Archives)

As late as 1708, the General Court found it necessary during periods of war to control the number of men allowed to go out hunting and to regulate where women and children could gather shellfish (Indian Records [30]:315a, (31):11, 51–51a, in Massachusetts Archives; Acts and Resolves 1705: Chapter 98). During this same period, some Indian men traveled to work for colonial farmers (Indian Records [30]:243, 503, in Massachusetts Archives; O'Brien 1991:175). Yet even farm labor represented a mix of English ways and the aboriginal migratory subsistence economy, for such work was temporary and seasonal, and the men returned to their communities after the harvest. Apparently much of the community resumed aboriginal gender roles following resettlement, for when men went to hunt or worked the white men's farms, women must have been in charge of the community's fields once again.

At the same time, others in Natick sought changes directed towards making the village function more like those of their colonial neighbors. In 1679, the village traded an equal area of land (four thousand acres) with the neighboring English town of Sherburne, and also arranged for a "free school" that English and Indian children would attend together—although the project never materialized (Indian Records [30]:247, in Massachusetts Archives). Seven years later, Natick gave fifty acres to an Englishman for a grain mill to save them the exhausting trip of twenty or more miles to an existing mill, "and sometimes by Reason of flood or great Snows we cannot goe to Either of the mil[l]s round us" (Indian Records [30]:307a, in Massachusetts Archives).

The mill petition points to one of the barriers to intensive agriculture and indicates that some in the village were considering ways to expand production. Thomas Waban may have been among those who sought to live more like their English neighbors: he had lived and learned among the colonists, and helped to arrange the land swap and school with Sherburne and to obtain the grain mill. There is no direct evidence to show how he made a living; the transactions may have been simply to help those who did work the fields—including his wife. Certainly Thomas considered himself a "husbandman" (farmer) when he wrote his will in December 1721, and at that time he owned a house instead of a wigwam, yet no agricultural implements were listed in that will or shown in his estate (Middlesex County Probate Records). As we shall see, other aspects of Thomas Waban's life melded aspects of aboriginal and colonial culture, and he probably tried various methods to help support his family.

In the wake of King Philip's War, colonial leaders considered ways to resettle the "vacant" Nipmuc territory that provided bountiful hunting for many Natick men, particularly as the population of Massachusetts grew rapidly. While the continuing threat of Abenaki and French raids kept whites away from the region, investors were already considering the opportunities of postwar expansion (J. Martin 1991:92–99). Many Indians in Massachusetts, including Waban and his son Thomas, held claims to Nipmuc territory that could not be ignored; the General Court had promised title to Indians who settled in Eliot's praying towns (Gookin 1806:179). Even if the colony's leaders had preferred after the war to ignore that pledge, the threat to all Puritan land grants posed by an increasingly hostile and active English king forced them to acknowledge Christian Indian claims—and many towns sought Indian deeds to cement their own titles (J. Martin 1991:260–68). In May 1681, Waban's name headed a petition from twenty-two men from Natick and two other Indian enclaves that demanded compensation for Nipmuc lands. Over the next two years they would contest bitterly a string of land sales made by a Nipmuc, John Wampus, who apparently had betrayed his position as the Indians' interpreter to sell large chunks of the territory (Indian Records [30]:257–58, 260a, 262a, 265, in Massachusetts Archives; NPNER [5]: 364).

After Waban's death, a very different controversy emerged over the then-empty praying towns, particularly Okommakamesit, which adjoined the English town of Marlborough. In 1682 Waban, along with a few other Natick Indians, had claimed exclusive rights to the reserve, and his son Thomas was to inherit that claim along with his authority. The other Natick leaders apparently planned to see the plantation resettled by some of their people, for rather than selling the town, they arranged for a settler to build a sawmill within its bounds (Indian Records [30]:267–68, in Massachusetts Archives; NPNER [5]:355). Thomas Waban, however, had very different ideas, and his actions would bring temporary disgrace.

Thomas Emerges

Waban died in about 1684, less than ten years after having led his people back to Natick (Indian Records [30]:267–68, in Massachusetts Archives; Middlesex County Deeds [9]:102). Thomas, not only Waban's eldest son but also the grandson of the Nashoba sachem, soon inherited his father's mantle of leadership in the village. Between 1685 and his death in 1722, Thomas Waban served as one of Natick's primary leaders: he maintained the community's records (primarily in the Massachusett language), taught school in the town, and by 1703 was one of three men who ruled on issues of land and law. After 1714, when the enclave adopted the political structure used by its neighbors, Thomas stepped into the top posts in the new government.

Thomas Waban may have inherited his father's authority as Natick's sachem. While none of the petitions or records from the community even hint that the sachemship persisted after the war, an Englishman named John Dunton, who visited the village in the spring of 1686, was "inform'd that the *Sachim*, or the Indian King, and his Queen, were there." This could only have been Thomas and his wife, Elizabeth, especially since Dunton later noted that the eldest son of the sachem would inherit that position. The Indians were all living in wigwams, "no more than so many tents," and the Waban home "tis true, did not look like the Royal Residence; however we cou'd easily believe the Report, and went immediately to visit their King and Queen." Dunton's brief sketch, our only portrait of Thomas, described him as "very tall and well limb'd, but [having] no Beard, and a sort of a Horse Face" (Dunton 1867:217).

The Englishman was clearly more impressed by Elizabeth, who (like all Natick Indian women) was notably absent from provincial and town records. His account is particularly striking for its description of Indian dress during this period:

> The Queen was well shap'd, and her Features might pass pretty well; she had Eyes as black as Jet, and Teeth as white as Ivory; her Hair was very black and long, and she was considerably up in Years; her Dress peculiar, she had sleeves of Moose Skin, very finely dress'd, and drawn with Lines of various Colours, in Asiatick Work, and her Buskins were of the same sort; her Mantle was of fine blew cloath, but very short, and ty'd about her Shoulders, and at the Middle with a Zone, curiously wrought with White and Blew Beads into pretty Figures; her Bracelets and her Necklace were of the same sort of Beads, and she had a little Tablet upon her Breast, very finely deck'd with Jewels and Precious Stones; her Hair was comb'd back and ty'd up with a Border, which was neatly work'd both with Gold and Silver. (Dunton 1867:217–18)

Thomas's succession made sense in both colonial and native worlds. What is less clear, however, is why Thomas Waban waited so long to help lead Natick. Waban's son was about fifty-five years old when he came to the fore, and until a few years before his father's death had never even appeared in a petition or other document from the community. Waban may have been so obsessed with maintaining his influence that he barred his son's ambitions, or perhaps the community only recognized the authority of the head of a nuclear family.

Thomas Waban barely survived the first test of his nascent authority. Two years after Waban's death, Thomas suddenly appeared in the colonial records when he and nine others accepted forty pounds from Marlborough for the six-thousand-acre Okommakamesit reserve. John Eliot and Daniel Gookin protested the deal as contrary to provincial law, and called Thomas and the other sellers "Drunken & debach[ed] indians" who had angered "other more sober indians" (Indian Records [30]:280, in Massachusetts Archives). One month later, on September 10, 1684, twenty-four Indian men, including Natick's minister, Daniel Tokkohwompait, complained that Thomas Waban and "Great James" had sold Okommakamesit without the community's authority and kept the proceeds, and that they were also claiming other reserves, including those at Groton (Nashoba), Concord, and Chelmsford (Wamesit) (Indian Records [30]:287, in Massachusetts Archives).

In May 1685, the General Court supported Eliot and Gookin's case, ruling against the Marlborough purchase (Indian Records [30]:305, in Massachusetts Archives). The Indians' protest against the sale suggested that Thomas Waban had not immediately taken his father's place among the Natick rulers (one of whom was Tokkohwompait), or that he may have been deposed because of his behavior. The budding leader had clearly overstepped the community's perception of his rightful authority. He did not repeat this mistake, was never again described as "drunken" or "debauched," and soon reappeared as one of Natick's rulers.

By mid-1685, Thomas Waban had regained his community's trust. He represented Natick in land deals with colonial authorities, helping to arrange the land trade with Sherburne, to obtain the town's grain mill, and in 1695 to compensate (with land at a low price) the heir of Thomas Eames, a white settler who had been attacked during King Philip's War and blamed several Natick Indians for his misfortune (Indian Records [30]:366–66a, in Massachusetts Archives). By 1700, Thomas served as Natick's clerk, maintaining records of town accounts, meetings, elections, and decisions—including landholding judgments (Mandell 1991:559).

Waban's performance as clerk not only highlights Natick's mixed culture, but also shows how, when Thomas sought to fulfill his father's vision, he helped to move the Indian community in a new direction, perhaps unknowingly. The office of clerk had not existed previously, and the only previous extant records of Natick were accounts by colonists or petitions to provincial authorities. The creation of a town clerk, moving away from a purely oral chronicle, was clearly a significant shift towards the colonial culture. Yet Thomas's new role fulfilled the goal his late father apparently had in mind when he sent his eldest son to learn to read and write in English. Thomas wrote initially in the Massachusett language (even though he was literate in English), and his records "are almost a short-hand in which much relevant information was understood by the clerk and townspeople, and hence not written down" (Bragdon 1981:62). Over time his accounts become more detailed, and then he switched to the English language, representing a cultural evolution that accompanied and perhaps encouraged other changes in Natick.

At the turn of the century, Thomas Waban and the other Natick leaders found their community again subjected to the tides of a war between colonists and natives. This time, however, the conflict was part of two successive international wars involving France and England, the first from 1689–97 (King William's War), and the second from 1702 to 1713 (Queen Anne's War). Indian men found themselves in great demand as both powers mobilized their colonial forces and Indian allies. On August 21, 1689, the General Court ordered the recruitment of ninety Indians from Natick and other Indian villages "to go forth with our Army." Muskets, which had been confiscated by worried whites upon the outbreak of the war, were to be gathered, fixed if necessary at the colony's expense, and returned to the native men (Indian Records [30]:314, 314a, 314b, in Massachusetts Archives).

When war flared anew in 1702, provincial authorities again made a special effort to recruit "several parties" of Indians from Natick and other towns in Massachusetts (Acts and Resolves 1703–4: Ch. 121). One historian estimates that natives formed a seventh of the colonial forces in the 1707 assault on Canada and an eighth in the 1710 campaign—an impressive percentage, given the Indians' shrinking numbers (R. Johnson 1977:628–31).

Since Thomas Waban was nearly sixty years old in 1689, he was an unlikely candidate for the militia. Instead, as a literate elder statesman of the town, he was probably one of the primary mediators between the

Indian community and provincial officials concerned about potential violence with fearful whites. As during King Philip's War, the English colonists found it "very difficult to descern between Friends & Foes," so in
1690 the General Court first confined all Indians to their villages, barring
them from traveling without special permission, and then eight months
later ordered all of those "in amity with us" to live in Natick or another
former praying town, where militia officers were sent to live and "call over
the Names of the Indians men & women every morning and evening"
(Indian Records [30]:313, 315, 358–59, 368, in Massachusetts Archives).

During Queen Anne's War, as Abenaki and French forces raided isolated English towns, the General Court renewed these restrictions, "being
Informed That the friend Indians Do still Presume to Travel into the
Woods, & amongst the Frontier Towns, contrary to the Order of this Court,
whereby her Maj[es]ties Subjects are put in Terror, & the Lives of the sd
Indians Endangered" (Indian Records [31]:51–51a, in Massachusetts Archives). There is little evidence that Natick actually confronted a sudden
influx of refugees forced into this town by the Court's actions. More
significant were the limitations on trips for hunting, gathering, and trading. In 1706 the inhabitants of Natick and the other Indian plantations ran
low on food, forcing the General Court to provide supplies (Indian Records
[30]:451–52, in Massachusetts Archives).

While the renewed frontier war and the renaissance of an aboriginal
economy made Natick a very different place than it had been under John
Eliot's tutelage, the village did not abandon his ideas. Thomas Waban's
records point to a landholding system that mingled native and colonial
customs (Goddard and Bragdon 1988 [1]:272–337). As among the English, heads of households were assigned shares or parcels of common
land by the community's leaders, property was held in perpetuity, sons
inherited from fathers, and men dominated landholding in the town—at
least on paper (15). At the same time, unlike their colonial neighbors,
some women inherited and held property independently, and the community sometimes interfered with land ownership and use (283, 287, 293;
Natick Proprietors Records). In July 1700, Natick's rulers took meadowland away from one man and apparently gave it to another who had
previously owned the area (Goddard and Bragdon 1988[1]:287).

Thomas Waban played a major role in this system, not only as a clerk,
but also as one of the town's three "judges" (no doubt the same as "rulers"),
when in 1703 they clearly departed from English inheritance patterns and

gave some of a man's estate to an unrelated widow who needed land, and the remainder to the deceased man's relatives (Goddard and Bragdon 1988[1]:301). Perhaps most importantly, Thomas and his community did not treat land as a commodity and rarely sold tracts to outsiders. The occasional transactions with surrounding towns and a few white artisans involved outlying areas, leaving the core of the community so intact that in 1703 a provincial official could report that the plantation "hath had but little Incroachment made upon it by the English Neighborhood" (276–77; Indian Records [31]:31, in Massachusetts Archives).

Thomas Waban's church also seemed relatively secluded at the turn of the century. The New England Company paid Daniel Gookin, Jr., minister in neighboring Sherborn and the son of the late Indian superintendent, to preach occasionally in Natick—in a lecture series that brought some visitors from Sherborn. Gookin lacked his father's proficiency in the native language, however, and was forced to use an interpreter (New England Company, Commissioners Minutes: 9 Aug. 1705; Eliot 1794:185). Thus the church's dominant force was Daniel Tokkohwompait, ordained by Eliot before the venerable missionary's death, who apparently preached an unorthodox theology in Massachusett (New England Company, Correspondence: 10 Nov. 1712; Indian Records [30]:503, in Massachusetts Archives).

There are mixed reports on the congregation's condition at that time. In 1686 a New England Company commissioner attended one of Gookin's sermons and noted "about 40 or 50 Men at most and a pretty many Women and Children" at the meeting"—about the number of people in Natick at the time (Sewall 1973[1]:121). Two years later, visiting ministers noted only ten full members, about ten percent of the population and a marked decline from the forty to fifty "visible saints" in 1670 (Gookin 1806:182; Rawson and Danforth 1809:41). In 1704 Cotton Mather mourned that Natick's church was "much diminish'd and dwindl'd away," although only eight years later he proposed an inquiry into the congregation's admission standards to determine whether they had "degenerate[d] into a very lax Procedure" (Mather 1704[2]:439; Axtell 1985:240). While these contradictions indicate that the declension of the Natick church existed primarily in the eyes of worried colonists, the Indians did face problems, due in part to the community's wartime disruptions.

In May 1699, nineteen men headed by Tokkohwompait and Thomas Waban and representing about thirty families described themselves as "the remainder of the church of christ." They told the legislature that their church was "greatly deminished & impoverished" due to "the death of many and removall of others who during the time of the late wars have been sojourning among the English for their support, and are not yet returned." What particularly concerned the Indians, however, was the "impoverished" condition of their meetinghouse, built at the town's founding, which had literally collapsed. They asked permission to give a small plot of outlying land to an English carpenter for a new building (Indian Records [30]:502–4, in Massachusetts Archives).

While Natick got its new meetinghouse, Thomas Waban and the other community leaders were not happy with the response of provincial officials to these reports on the town. In 1706 the commissioners of the New England Company, including Cotton Mather, ordered an inquiry into the state of affairs in the town (New England Company, Commissioners Minutes: 7 Oct. 1706). Three years later they suggested "that an Essay be made of laying out distinct Lots at Natick, in order to Establishing [sic] a more Constant, & Numerous Cohabitation" (New England Company, Commissioners Minutes: 14 Feb. 1709).

The Indians already had "distinct Lots," but refused at this time to adopt landholding in severalty, which was no doubt the New England Company's real goal. In November 1711, the commissioners sent an investigator to report on "what Course may be taken for the Reformation of what is amiss among them" (New England Company, Commissioners Minutes: 6 Nov. 1711). Since the Natick Indians had made no complaints about conditions at this time, no doubt they saw nothing "amiss among them" and resented such interference.

The commissioners' response to their emissary's report probably presented even more of a dilemma for the leaders of Natick. Less than a year later, the commissioners noted "the miserable Condition of the Indians at Natick" and resolved "by suitable Encouragement to endeavour to bring the Indians from Punkapog, and Hassanamisco [the two nearest villages], and such other near adjacent places as may have Scattering Indians in them; unto a Cohabitation at Natick." They no doubt believed that combining the communities would make it easier to reform their manners and religion.

The New England Company's proposal might have offered additional authority to Thomas Waban and the other Natick leaders by swelling the town's population. Yet the prospect of additional pressures on Natick's resources and the disruption of absorbing newcomers was too daunting. When the commissioners came to Natick on July 22 "to see if we can dispose the Inhabitants to a more orderly Cohabitation" and to persuade the Punkapogs and Hassanamiscos to move, Waban and the others must have gently but firmly refused the Company's ideas—for there is no record of the meeting and no changes were made. Natick, which already had cohesive landholding and social systems, was not really interested in being · reformed (New England Company, Commissioners Minutes: 3 July 1712; Correspondence: 12 July 1712; Sewall 1973[2]:694; New England Company, Commissioners Minutes: 10 Feb. 1713; Kellaway 1962:236).

Natick Transformed

As Natick's leaders were dealing with the New England Company commissioners, they were also reshaping their political system in the New England way. Like their fathers half a century earlier, Thomas Waban and the others managed this transformation without significant alterations in the town's leadership. The first extant Natick election results date from 1707, when Thomas Waban and John Wamsquam were chosen selectmen—two of the three men who had "judged" Natick's land and inheritance cases five years earlier (Goddard and Bragdon 1988[1]:301).

When Natick elected new selectmen the following year, along with constables and tithingmen, town clerk Thomas Waban recorded the results—but in English, not Massachusett. Perhaps the increasing tempo of dealings with provincial officials convinced Thomas of the need to keep his records in that language. The elections may have even been held in part to demonstrate the community's sophistication to New England Company investigators (O'Brien 1990:182). The next set of extant election reports (in Massachusett) date from 1712–13, when Thomas Waban again served as selectman. He was not chosen for that or any other town office in 1715—perhaps, at the age of eighty-five, he was ill—but he again served as one of Natick's three selectman in 1716, as well as in 1719, the next documented election (Goddard and Bragdon 1988[1]:335; Natick Town Records).

As selectman, town clerk, and even schoolmaster, Thomas Waban was clearly recognized by his community as one of their most important members and a key asset in their relations with the outside world (New England

Company, Commissioners Minutes: 30 Apr. 1713). Waban's role in Natick at this time was not quite that of the Indian enclave's culture broker—the part his father had played in the mid-seventeenth century—but he represented Natick and acted as one conduit among many for the colonial influences that reshaped the community.

Natick's elections were symbolic of how the Indians' world rapidly changed in the 1710s. After the 1713 Treaty of Utrecht ended Abenaki and French raids in the region, the village lost the isolation that had supported its autonomy as Anglo-Americans now moved into the once-dangerous region between the Charles and Connecticut Rivers. Other Indian villages west and south of Boston were also surrounded and swamped by settlers (Mandell 1992).

This new wave of settlements caused the Indian community to turn inward at the same time as the village developed new connections with the colonial world. Some of its actions were the result of long-term trends, while others were taken to meet new needs. By 1715 the community felt compelled to ban the sale of timber to Englishmen, no doubt because of both the region's rapidly swelling white population and Natick's deepening ties to the market economy and the growing demand for wood in Boston (Goddard and Bragdon 1988[1]:329). A few months later, the Indians decided, despite bitter opposition within the community, to sell Magunkaquog, the last significant piece of land outside Natick (below). Within just four years the Indian community formally instituted landholding in severalty, and two years later, as Thomas Waban neared death, they would adopt an English minister. Despite (or because of) his advanced age, Thomas played a primary role in guiding the community's transformation.

In September 1715 Natick was again faced with the New England Company's "help." The commissioners wanted the Indians to sell to them the abandoned praying town of Magunkaquog, near Natick, along the Sudbury River; the Company would then rent out the land to white settlers and dole out the rent money to Natick families. Magunkaquog meant "a place of giant Trees," and a visitor described in awe the many "great White Oak, and Chestnut Trees here, and much Champion Land very fit for tillage." Perhaps for that reason or perhaps because many in the community still retained deep emotional connections to the place, the Indians "at present shew some Indisposition to part with it" (New England Company, Correspondence: 10 Sept. 1715). Thomas Waban headed the committee that went to Cambridge to negotiate the sale of the plantation. They agreed to sell the land to a four-man committee of white elites, including three chosen by the Indian community, who would lease the land to settlers and administer the rents (Sewall 1973[2]:800–1).

On October 11, the New England Company commissioners traveled to Natick, where "the Indians of the Committee executed the Parchment Deed for the Land at Magunkaquog" (Sewall 1973[2]:800–1). As a token of the deal, the New England Company committee paid the Indians with claims to that reserve three pounds apiece. The bitter feelings within the community had apparently not been satisfied, however, for that night Isaac Nehemiah, a member of the Magunkaquog committee, hung himself with his belt, "3 foot and 4 inches long buckle and all" (Sewall 1973[2]:802). While many probably sympathized with what seemed an act of anger and regret, the rents from that reserve would serve many Natick families for years, including the Wabans.

Natick's church also suffered a turbulent decade. Thomas Waban was an active member of the congregation, as shown by his signature on the 1698 petition, and he served as schoolmaster, receiving an annual stipend from the New England Company (New England Company, Commissioners Minutes: 30 Apr. 1713). When Tokkohwompait died in 1716, the town sent a committee to Samuel Sewall, one of the New England Company commissioners, to request the services of the Rev. John Neesnumun (New England Company, Correspondence: 4 Mar. 1717; Sewall 1973[2]:858). The renowned Wampanoag minister from Cape Cod was, like Thomas, literate in both Massachusett and English, and since 1708 had occasionally preached at Natick (Sewall 1973[2]:586, 589). Neesnumun accepted the post, but tragically followed his predecessor to Paradise only three years later (New England Company, Correspondence: 28 Oct. 1719). After Neesnumun died, Thomas Waban led the congregation (New England Company, Correspondence: 17 Feb. 1720).

By that time the church was again in poor physical (if not spiritual) condition. "[I]t is in danger of falling down; the Boards shattered & falling off, & the Windows broken down, & so open that the Rain & Snow drives all over the House, so that the Seats & Floors are much damnified" (Acts and Resolves, 21 Nov. 1719: Ch. 87). The building was soon repaired, and not long after a new spiritual carpenter arrived to shore up Thomas's congregation. In 1721, Harvard College commissioned Oliver Peabody, one of their students in need of a stipend, to begin preaching in Natick on a regular basis (New England Company, Correspondence: 3 July 1721).

There is no record of how Thomas Waban received the Englishman, but we can guess what he might have thought of this interloper and competitor who did not speak Massachusett and had little knowledge of the Indian community. On the other hand, he (like his father with Eliot) may have seen the newcomer as an important connection to the power and support of the province's elite institution. Peabody's "good Acceptance" indicates that Thomas's optimism won out over any latent hostility or jealousy (New England Company, Correspondence: 22 Feb. 1722).

The transformation of Natick clearly made Thomas Waban and the other leaders of the town increasingly receptive to Anglo-American institutions. His records show that for many years Natick families had claimed, held, and inherited land in the town. And the native egalitarian system was gradually altered as social and political distinctions emerged between older men with long-term ties to the community and higher status and those who were newcomers, younger, or less valuable to the community. Individual ambitions were held in check, however, for the leaders of the town, including Waban, maintained the community's control over the use and disposition of lands, particularly in dealings with outsiders.

But by the late 1710s, Natick was considering an end to communal landholding and the institution of land ownership in severalty through a proprietorship, the standard form of corporate land management in New England. In 1719, a town meeting decided to make the dramatic change, choosing twenty proprietors, apparently the heads of long-established and prestigious families, including Thomas Waban. The twenty then met separately and began dividing the town's land and the Magunkaquog income among themselves (Natick Proprietors' Records; O'Brien 1990:157–66).

The Natick proprietorship severed landholding from the town polity, brought the native community into a closer orbit to the province's legal and economic systems, reduced opportunities for those not granted proprietorship status, and (unwittingly) opened the community to the "invasion" of colonists, who could now purchase land from individual Indians. Waban may have been a major influence in the decision to embrace landholding in severalty. His father had adopted Eliot and Puritanism as a necessary reformation for the problems faced by his people, and the son may have seen the proprietorship, which provided secure land titles and boundaries under colonial law, as a useful institution in the face of outside pressures. Thomas, along with others, would have also been influenced by the belief of their English neighbors that ownership in severalty was essential for economic development. A number of events over the past decade, including the efforts of New England Company commissioners to bring other Indians to Natick and to arrange the Magunkaquog sale, may have also made landholding in severalty seem the best way to stabilize the community.

At the sunset of his life, Thomas Waban must have been sensitive to how his people's world had changed. Born as the Puritans settled at Massachusetts Bay, as a young man he was sent by his father and John Eliot to live and be educated among the English. While much of his life during the subsequent half-century remains a mystery, no doubt he experienced many of the traumas of his compatriots: imprisonment and service in King Philip's War, resettlement in Natick, and re-establishment of many aboriginal ways on the new frontier. Upon Waban's death, Thomas overcame an initial misstep to become one of the community's leaders.

But Thomas held less authority than his father, perhaps because he lacked charisma or political acumen, or (more likely) because postwar conditions had altered the structure and nature of power in Natick. As a growing number of English settlers surrounded Natick, he helped guide the town through the adoption of a New England polity, the Magunkaquog sale, landholding in severalty, and the traumatic loss of two outstanding native ministers—all the time maintaining the community's essential autonomy. He recorded most of these changes, usually in Massachusett, which seemed to remain the dominant language in the community, and sometimes in English. The arrival of the English minister may have seemed a disturbing alteration, but Thomas had little time left to contemplate this threat.

Thomas Waban died in 1722, leaving a will—an unusual document for an Indian, and one that highlights how far Thomas had moved from his illiterate, "propertyless" father, although this was a change that Waban had set in motion. Most of Thomas's real estate went to his younger son, Isaac, including his thirty-five acre house lot, the use of the house on the lot, his orchards, and two acres of meadowland. Thomas's proprietary rights were divided between Isaac and his older son, Thomas Jr. Fifteen acres went to help two other young relatives. His widow, Elizabeth, about whom little is known, was to inherit forty pounds, to be raised by selling some of his land, along with Waban's "household Goods, debts, and moveable Effects." Despite being the town's leading citizen, Thomas Waban had owned very few consumer goods: a few books in the Massachusett language, a brass kettle, an iron pot and pot hooks, wooden dishes and spoons, and an old barrel. His estate was administered by Nathaniel Coochuck, who had married Waban's third child, Mary. Waban's debts were quite large, and unfortunately these grew soon after his death when his widow (who challenged the will) and three other relatives died, probably in one of the many epidemics that scourged the Indian town. Their funeral expenses, including four coffins, were charged to Waban's estate (Middlesex County Probate Records).

Consequences

In the wake of Thomas's death, the changes that he had helped bring to Natick multiplied and led to new problems for the community. In 1723 the Indians accepted Peabody as their minister and, lacking capital, offered him their most valuable resource by making him a proprietor—the only Englishman given that status (Natick Proprietors' Records). Natick was, in fact, the only Indian town in eighteenth-century Massachusetts to adopt a minister who did not speak the native language. While Peabody used an interpreter, he bent much of his energy to spreading Anglo-American culture among the Indians, particularly the English language. Peabody began keeping vital records, the first in Natick and the only such records kept for an Indian community in New England. One of the first events recorded by Peabody was Thomas Waban's death (Baldwin 1910).

Peabody also worked to bring English families into the Natick church to help "civilize" his congregation, and later supported the sale of Indian lands to white settlers in order to soothe his loneliness and isolation. By the end of the decade, many Natick Indians were disillusioned with Peabody. When a delegation from Harvard in 1729 came to visit the church and ordain Peabody, nearly as many whites (most from nearby towns) as Indians attended the church. The visitors noted that many Indians rarely attended public worship, and that some of those present during a service became angry when the minister asked a white man to read a Psalm (Anonymous 1925). Indian membership in Peabody's church never approached that of whites, and none of Thomas Waban's descendants joined that congregation (Natick Church Records).

Natick's proprietorship was the other primary agent transforming the town after 1720. The system allowed individuals to sell their property to outsiders, providing openings for a growing number of English settlers.

Even from the grave Thomas Waban was involved in this change, as his children sold much of his estate in 1728 to pay colonial creditors in nearby towns (O'Brien 1990:214). The need to finance the economic changes sought by many Natick Indian families—changes initiated at least in part by Waban—brought about land sales to outsiders in the 1730s. A number of extant land sale petitions and deeds attest to land sold to pay debts, build houses and barns, buy livestock and tools, and purchase English-made consumer goods (Mandell 1991:566–67, 572).

As the region's economy slid into recession, an increasing number of Indian men with large debts absconded rather than face jail or sell family land. With Natick's proprietorship, however, county courts simply sold land owned by such fugitives (O'Brien 1990:342). Not atypical was the experience of Thomas's youngest son. In 1739 Isaac was imprisoned in the Cambridge jail for debts. A white settler in Natick, Isaac Coolidge, paid the bond in exchange for Waban's indenture. The Indian fled the province, however, so the county court gave Coolidge some of Isaac's land to fulfill the Indian's obligation (Indian Records [31]:336–38, in Massachusetts Archives; Acts and Resolves 1741–42: Ch. 87). Natick was unique among Indian towns in embracing the Anglo-American landholding system, and in the end the proprietorship proved to be the principal element in the community's destruction.

Toward mid-century the Natick Indian enclave was reshaped by increasing demographic problems, including epidemics, low birth rates, and the economic travails that forced many men to seek their fortunes elsewhere. A growing number of widows and helpless men, many of whom owed debts to Englishmen, sold land to meet their medical needs and pay for food and clothing (Mandell 1991:572–74, 577). In 1742, for example, Thomas Waban's grandsons, Moses and Joshua, sold family land to build a house for their aged and infirmed mother and to pay debts from Moses's illness; one year later they sold another twenty acres (Indian Records [31]:440, 442, in Massachusetts Archives). These transactions brought in a flood of white settlers. By 1744, nearly twice as many whites as Indians lived in the town. Two years later, at the request of Anglo-American settlers in Natick, the General Court gave the Indian community the status of a parish instead of that of an Indian plantation. This change allowed the English inhabitants to gain political control of the town (Mandell 1991:564, 576).

In the wake of the two major colonial conflicts at mid-century, King

George's War (1744–48) and the French and Indian War (1754–60), the Indian population of Natick shrank dramatically. Many men went to serve in the colonial militia and perished; those who survived brought new epidemics back to the Indian community. Some returned crippled and were forced to sell land to support their families (Mandell 1991:573). A census taken by the Indian leaders in 1749 reported 167 natives in fifty-five households—but not one Waban. There were fifty-one women, the same number as in 1698, but the number of men—who had become the economic backbone of the community—had dropped from fifty-nine to only thirty-four, and nearly one-fifth of the women (eleven) were widows (Anonymous 1809b:134–36; Rawson and Danforth 1809:134).

The lives of Thomas Waban's grandson Hezekiah and great-grandson Jabez illustrate the fates of many Natick Indian men and boys. Hezekiah Waban, a son of Thomas's eldest son, Thomas, Jr., entered the provincial military service at the onset of King George's War and soon disappeared in an expedition to Cuba. Hezekiah's son Jabez was given to an Englishman, Benjamin Muzzy of Sherborn, but ran away to Boston at the age of seventeen and enlisted in an English man-of-war. Captured by Muzzy before the ship sailed, he fled again two months later. Jabez fell ill during his final flight, returning after five months, and died in March 1751 (O'Brien 1990:315–16; Middlesex County Probate Records).

With few men remaining in the community, widows and young women increasingly married African Americans—slaves and servants who shared their low socioeconomic status (Mandell 1992:304–6; O'Brien 1990:402–4). As the Indian population ebbed, the town became increasingly inhospitable to the natives, causing many to seek better opportunities and conditions elsewhere. In 1754 there were about 160 Indians in Natick; ten years later, only thirty-seven remained. By the time the American Revolution had erupted, only a half-century after Thomas Waban's death, the Natick Indian community had dissolved (Mandell 1991:564, 576–79).

Conclusion

Despite his best intentions, Thomas Waban apparently led Natick in the wrong direction after 1710, opening the door to white domination of the town as well as to much of the ill fortune suffered by his descendants. His efforts could perhaps best be seen as an effort to continue Waban's policies.

His father had gained power for himself, his family, and his village by building bridges through John Eliot to Puritan authorities. After Waban's death, Thomas worked to maintain those bridges as the best means to preserve his people's virtual autonomy.

As conditions changed at the sunset of his life, he almost certainly believed that the province's expanding colonial population would over-whelm Natick unless his community widened their connections to the dominant culture. Instituting an English-style proprietorship in severalty appeared the best way to ensure the strongest legal standing for Indian landholdings. Accepting the minister urged on Natick by Harvard College no doubt seemed sensible, particularly since the town apparently had no other qualified candidates. Thomas may have even seen Peabody as an-other Eliot. But the new minister was no Eliot, and the proprietorship only aided the transfer of land to English colonists. After Thomas's death, these alterations led to the enclave's destruction. While Natick was not the only Indian group in Massachusetts to dissolve during the eighteenth century, it was by far the largest native enclave to suffer that fate. Thomas Waban tried to guide his community down the path that his father had put him on; unfortunately, changing circumstances caused that road to lead past Natick's crucial boundaries.

Notes

I wish to thank Ann Plane for her comments on a draft of this article, and Constance Crosby for her transcripts of New England Company records.

1. White (1991:x) identifies that space as "the place in between: in between cultures, peoples, and in between empires and the nonstate world of villages." He explains the workings of the middle ground as "a process of creation" that "de-pended on the inability of both sides to gain their ends through force," and in which both colonial and native representatives "arrive at some common concep-tion of suitable ways of acting" (51–52). While Puritan colonists clearly held the balance of power in southern New England by 1640, they were also clearly unwilling—probably for political if not military reasons—to actually force their will or religion (despite passing numerous laws) on friendly native groups. Thus the strange dance of Eliot and Waban, involving the ruling of nearly autonomous Indian towns by the native elite who administered a few Puritan rules in the native fashion, the construction of wigwams on house lots, and the training of Indian missionaries to carry Bibles written in the native language; this was about as close to a middle ground as Puritans and natives reached in southern New England.

2. While it is conceivable that Waban had a first son who died after 1647 without this being recorded by Eliot or Gookin, and that the younger son Thomas also received an English education—since he kept the Natick records in both Massachusett and English—the evidence points to Thomas as Waban's eldest. Yet there are certain elements of confusion in the records concerning Thomas Waban. Natick church records show the death of three different Thomas Wabans between 1722 and 1752 (Baldwin 1910:245). Fortunately, Jean O'Brien (1990:312–17) has done an excellent job of dissecting the Waban family genealogy, and I have relied heavily on her work when describing the fate of Thomas Waban's descendants. But some questions remain. The subject of this biography, the Thomas Waban who died in 1722 and left behind a will (Middlesex County Probate Records), is identified as a captain in the Natick records. Yet none of the many petitions that Thomas signed between 1682 and 1716 mention his military rank; this appears only in the Natick vital records and the administration of his will. Normally people in colonial America carefully noted such social distinctions in order to establish their authority. This mystery deepens in light of a complaint made in 1684 against Thomas Waban by a number of Natick men—including a "Capt. Tom" (Indian Records [30]:287, in Massachusetts Archives).

CHAPTER NINE

⚞

Daniel Spotso: A Sachem
at Nantucket Island, Massachusetts,
circa 1691–1741

Elizabeth A. Little

Introduction

STUDIES OF SPECIFIC social changes in historical contexts have shown the
richness of the ethnohistorical data available in the Northeast (Jennings
1975; Salisbury 1982). Using historical sources for the Indians of Massachusetts, Bragdon (1981), Brenner (1980), Simmons (1986), and Thomas
(1985) have demonstrated the persistence of ancient ways and the adoption of new ones in coping with the changes that occurred following
European settlement. At Nantucket Island, off the coast of Massachusetts,
a study of county deeds, wills, court records, and other documents has
revealed an Indian sachem, Daniel Spotso, who was a major land and land
use grantor. Here I describe evidence that a synthesis of native American
and introduced English ideas took place during his negotiations with
James Coffin, who acted for the English proprietors at Nantucket. This
synthesis of methods of land assignment incorporated the Indian customs
of tribute (periodic payment of something of value) and usufruct (rights to
the use of a sachem's land, generally in return for tribute) with the English
customs of rent (temporary use of land for a fee) and commons (rights to
the use of undivided land held in common by the proprietors, who pay
periodic taxes).

193

Background

The negotiations of cultural differences between Indians and English at Nantucket differ in quality from Indian/English interactions in the Massachusetts Bay region, where Indian leaders found themselves selling (permanently alienating) their lands to the English settlers. A major reason for the differences may have been that Massachusetts Bay had a rapidly increasing Puritan population after 1635, while Nantucket, with an estimated presettlement population of 3,000 Indians, was settled by a group of twenty to thirty-four English entrepreneurs and their families (Macy 1810). Focusing on establishing a wool and fishing industry, these settlers did not establish a church during the colony's first fifty years.

The island, with its mild winters, a good supply of saltmarsh and freshmarsh for winter hay, grasslands for pasture, no animal predators, and no need for extensive fencing, appeared to the early English colonists an ideal place to raise sheep, horses, and cattle. By 1660, a group of settlers from Salem, Massachusetts, and Salisbury, New Hampshire, uncomfortable with the Puritanism of Massachusetts Bay, had purchased from Thomas Mayhew the Nantucket rights that he had bought from Sir Ferdinando Gorges and the Earl of Sterling. Following the 1661 purchase from the Nantucket sachems of the land at the west end of the island and the grass on the entire island after Indian harvest, the settlers moved to the island. New York had jurisdiction over Nantucket until 1692 (Byers 1987).

Ethnohistorians agree that in Massachusetts the Indian sachemship, with its sachem, elders, and precise boundaries, was the primary sociopolitical and economic unit, supplemented with an episodic or segmentary organization sometimes assembled from cooperating sachemships (Salisbury 1982; Simmons 1986; Winslow 1841:360–63). Figure 1 shows the five main sachemships and lands at Nantucket sold to the English before 1684.

Seiknout, Pattacohonet, Attapeat, Wanachmamack, and Nickanoose were the major Nantucket sachems in 1684. The first three held sway over lands on the west end of the island. The latter two controlled lands on the east end. After marrying the daughter of Nickanoose, Spotso, who shared land with Attapeat, moved to land on the eastern end of the island given him by Wanachmamack.

Wanachmamack may have had some claim to preeminence (the En-

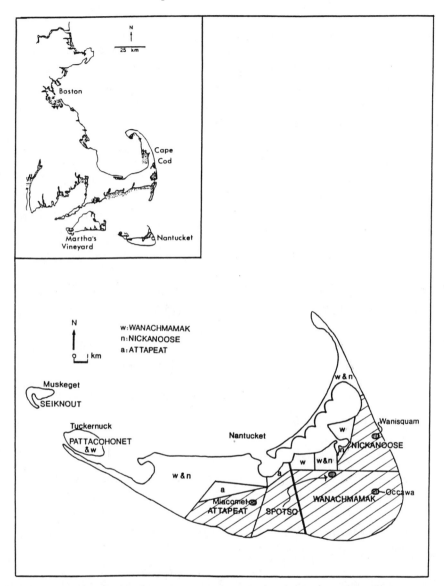

FIGURE 1: Coast of Massachusetts (see insert) and map of Nantucket Island in late seventeenth century, based on deeds, wills, and memoirs. Shows territories and villages of major sachemships, and lands sold by Pattacohonet, Wanachmamack, Nickanoose, and Attapeat to the English (indicated by "w," "n," and "a") by 1684. Heavy black line marks boundary between eastern and western sachemships. Village locations based on approximate locations of documented eighteenth-century Christian Indian meeting houses (not confirmed archaeologically). After marrying Nickanoose's daughter, Spotso lived on land given him by Wanachmamack (Little 1981b, 1990b, Dukes County Deeds [1]:6).

glish called him the chief head sachem of Nantucket), but a number of Indians protested his sales of lands on the west end, which was presumably outside of his territory. The Nantucket sachems deferred to a "head sachem at Plymouth" (presumably Massasoit) for external issues such as the murder of an English sailor and the business of rendering stranded whales (Little and Andrews 1982; Little 1976).

Daniel Spotso

Daniel Spotso was a son of the western sachem Spotso and of Askammapoo, a daughter of the east end sachem Nickanoose. This marriage probably provided the basis for the Nantucket legend of a union that established peace between people living on eastern and western ends of the island (Freeman 1846 [1807]). Because there are almost no secondary sources for the history of the Spotso family, I shall of necessity emphasize the primary sources, deeds, wills, and plans in the Nantucket County Records. Figure 2 gives additional documentary evidence for the existence and location of Spotso's meeting house and dwelling.

Daniel Spotso's name first appears in a 1687 deed in which he was assigned power of attorney to represent his father in New York, in the sale of twenty acres at Shimmo to Stephen Hussey:

> NY 29 June 1687. Daniel Spotso as attorney to his father Spotso the Indian Sachem of Nantucket came before me & pursuant to sd letter of attorney from his sd father did deliver this above Instrument as his fathers act and deed to the use therein exprest—N. Bayard mayor— Recorded in the Secretaries Office of the Province of New York, W Winton, Secy. (Nantucket County Deeds [3]:110)

Daniel was probably a young man when he first appeared in the county records. His accession to his father's position shortly after his return from New York suggests that the elder Spotso was either aged or infirm at the time (see Figure 3). Daniel's father's disappearance from the county records indicates that he may have died sometime around 1688 or 1689. Daniel's maternal grandfather, the sachem Nickanoose, had died in about 1682. Daniel's uncle, Wawinet, served as Nickanoose's successor until his own death sometime between 1687 and 1690.

Daniel's mother, Askammapoo, possessed rights to her own land (see

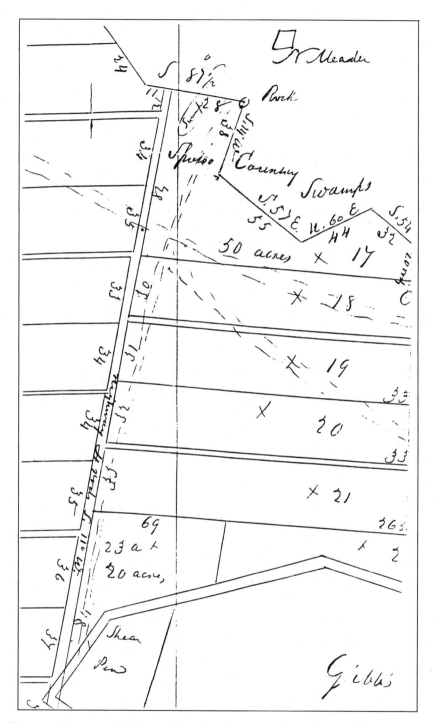

FIGURE 2: Portion of 1821 map (Nantucket Proprietors Book of Plans [1]:39) showing "Spotso Country" in the vicinity of Spotso's meeting house, north of Gibb's Pond. Vertical line through center is part of a north arrow, with north toward the top; scale is not provided.

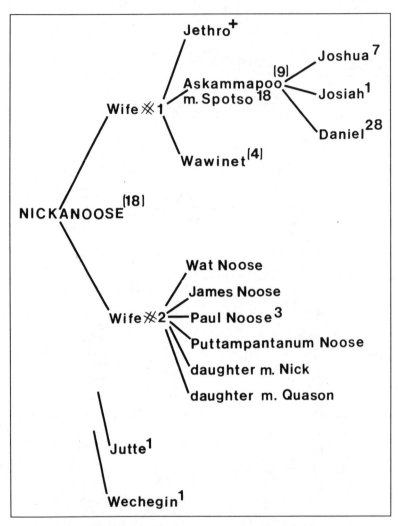

FIGURE 3: Genealogical chart of the family of Sachem Nickanoose and his heirs and grantees, showing (from left to right) Nickanoose, his relatives (possibly brothers), children, and certain grandchildren (Little 1976, 1981a, 1990b). The superscripts after names indicate the number of horse commons owned. Brackets indicate assumptions. The plus sign after Jethro signifies his rental of four horse commons from Wanachmamack.

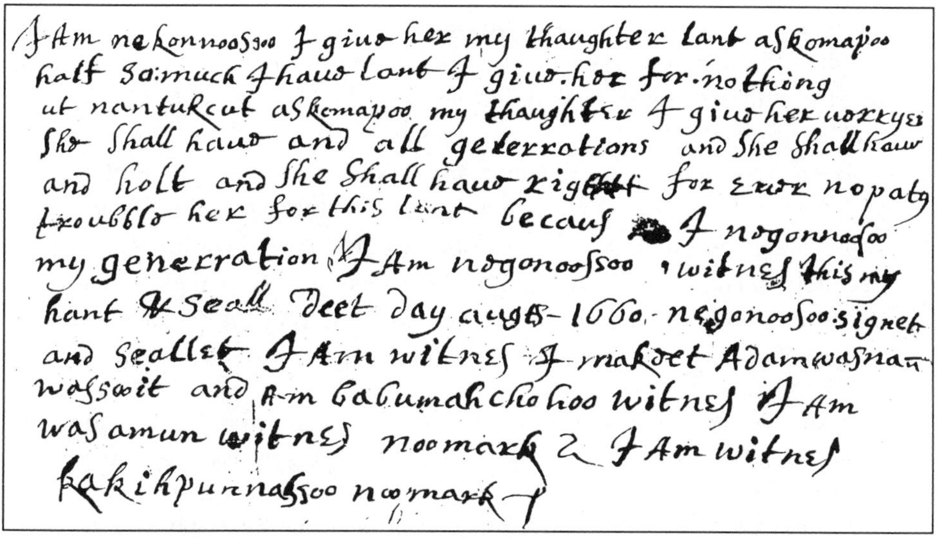

FIGURE 4: Facsimile of manuscript by which Nickanoose in 1660 gave half of his land to his daughter, Askomapoo, witnessed by Adam, Wasamun, and Kakihpunnassoo and made by Adam. From the Nantucket Historical Association Manuscript Collection No. 126, Folder 1. Reproduced with permission of the Nantucket Historical Association.

Figure 4). Later in life, she inherited Wawinet's lands and a dower right from Spotso (Nantucket County Deeds [2]:40; Dukes County Deeds [1]:355; [2]:209, 211). She died sometime around 1708.

Daniel Spotso was noted as sachem of his father's lands in 1691 and of Nickanoose's territory in 1702. He conveyed title to nine very large parcels of land in both sachemships to the English settlers between 1690 and 1726. He also transferred rights to twenty eight commons to both Indians and colonists during these same years. These transactions resulted in the loss of all of Spotso's and most of Nickanoose's lands to English purchasers. Because of this, it is easy to view Daniel as a profiteer who squandered the lands of his ancestors. But his story is worth pursuing further for what it tells us about local responses to the ongoing introduction of new cultural, political, and economic forms in Nantucket.

Land Transfers and Land Use Assignments

Unlike most Indians elsewhere, some of Nantucket's native people could read and write by the middle decades of the seventeenth-century. Most had learned these skills while studying under missionaries such as Thomas Mayhew, Jr., and Peter Folger on nearby Martha's Vineyard. Extant specimens of their writing show that they wrote in the Massachusett language and in a phonetic Massachusett version of English.

Deeds represent the largest surviving body of these writings. Both the structure of the language of these documents and the absence of English witnesses suggest that many were written without the help or interference of colonists. Here is the transcription of the deed (Fig. 4) from Nickanoose to his daughter Askammapoo. This deed is the earliest in date and least English in form and content of these Indian documents written in English:

> I Am nekonnoossoo I give her my thaughter Lant askomapoo half So:much I have Lant I give. her for. nothing ut nantukcut askomapoo my thaughter I give her vorryer [forever?] She Shall have and all geterrations [generations] and She Shall have and holt and She Shall have rightt for ever nopaty troubble her for this Lant becaus I negonnoosoo my generration. I Am negonoossoo . witnes this my hant & seall deet day augts-1660 - negonoosoo. signet and seallet I Am witnes - I make it Adam wasnan wassooit and Am babumahchohoo witness I Am wasamun witnes noomark I Am witnes kakihpunnassoo noomark.

Recent research (Little 1976, 1980, 1981a, 1990b) shows that at least 223 deeds documenting transactions involving Indians during the seventeenth and eighteenth centuries are on file at the Nantucket Registry of Deeds. Approximately twenty-five were authored by Indian people. The rest evidently were written by Englishmen for Indians. This documentation provides a rare glimpse into life in an Indian community during years of transformation.

Nantucket Indian deeds disclose the pattern of native land use and alienation; analysis of these patterns shows that both Indians and Europeans, struggling to arrive at some form of accommodation with one another, employed complex and innovative strategies to bridge the cultural gaps that separated their peoples. Nowhere is this creative adaptation more evident than in the record of horse common deeds.

English proprietors purchased all land on the west end of the island in 1661. This deed also transferred rights to all grasslands on Nantucket. These grasslands were essential for grazing sheep, horses, and cattle. The proprietors allotted twenty-two-acre house lots to each of the twenty shareowners contributing to these purchases. They held most of their remaining lands as common pastures for their animals.

Increasing numbers of animals owned by growing numbers of settlers soon began to overgraze the common lands. Alarmed by the rapid deterioration of their grasslands, the twenty-seven shareholders holding rights to common lands in 1669 limited the grazing rights of each proprietor to no more than forty sheep, three cows, and one horse. Animals in excess of these limits were impounded and their owners fined.

When the Indians, with a population larger than that of the English, found themselves prevented from keeping horses on their own lands because they had sold all of their grass, they let the English know in no uncertain terms that this would not do. In an innovative move, the sachem Nickanoose had a deed written in 1675 by an Indian named Tehas. This deed gave Nickanoose's brother Judah the right to keep six cattle in return for "penys all the year in victualls and cloths" (Nantucket County Deeds [3]:41); Nickanoose's son, Wawinet, renewed the deed in 1687.

This gift to a brother, witnessed by Indians and referring to tribute, lay within the sachem's traditional authority. The English, however, saw it as a loss of control of the commons. After thirteen years of negotiations, the four major sachems, Jeptha, Musaquat, Spotso, and Nickanoose, again gave all their grass to proprietary representatives James Coffin, John Swain, and William Worth. In return, the proprietors gave the sachems a total of eighty-seven horse commons. Each horse commons represented a right to herbage or pasturage for one horse on the Nantucket commons (see Figure 5). English and Indian cooperative control of the use of a limited resource, hay and pasture grass, had averted a "Tragedy of the Commons" (Hardin 1968). They did not do so well with timber; by 1712, even "wigwam poles" and firewood had to be imported (Starbuck 1683–1744:62; Nantucket County Deeds [1]:110; see Cronon 1983).

Sachem Daniel Spotso

Deeds record sachem Daniel Spotso's genealogy (Fig. 3). Documents at the Registry of Deeds at Nantucket also show that a sachem received tribute from his people, ruled with the advice of his chief men, and endeavored to manage his town's affairs by means of love and redistribution of valuables. A new sachem traditionally renewed or confirmed land assignments upon his accession. The following excerpts from a single document illustrate traditional land assignment practices of love, tribute, and deed renewal:

FIGURE 5: A view of Siasconset, a fishing village on Nantucket, 1791, from the Nantucket Historical Association Collection (F2450). Note emphasis on horses as well as boats. Reproduced with permission of the Nantucket Historical Association.

I Nickanoos you waquakonooit have land in my land . . . [100 acres] . . . because I necanoose, you waquakonooit, are greattly akin to me, and I love him and also he loves me, and hath, formerly, given me, many times five shillings. [1670]

I Wawenut doo aprove of what my Father Necanoose hath done to Waquakonooit about his land. . . . [ca. 1682–90]

[1702] These presents are wittnesses that I Daniell Spottso now Sachem one Nantucket, do declare that . . . I . . . am freely willing that ye sd Waquakonaway his heirs and successors shall peaceably poses and injoy the above said hundred ackers of Land granted by my ancestors to have and to hold for ever, as wittnes my hand and seall, the day and year above- Nen Daeil Spasoo O. (Nantucket County Deeds [3]:39)

The increasingly English style in the wording of the deeds reflects the growing familiarity of Indian scribes with English literary and legal conventions.

Daniel Spotso's Mother

The manuscript by Adam in 1660 (Fig. 4) is an unregistered land transfer in which Nickanoose, who had at least six sons and three daughters, gave one half of his land to one daughter, Askammapoo, who was Daniel Spotso's mother. Although a 1750 document mentioning a governing squaw sachem at Miacomet ("sachemess" in Nantucket Proprietors Records [1]:74) shows that the office of sachem was not exclusively a masculine domain, the existence of matrilineal kinship, documented elsewhere in southern New England (Simmons and Aubin 1975), has not yet been demonstrated on Nantucket. Extant documents do disclose the fact that women possessed land rights in Nantucket native society. Focusing on the fine print of deeds given by her son Daniel or brother Wawinet while acting as sachems, we find that Askammapoo ("Spotso's Squaw") witnessed a land sale by Wawinet (Nantucket County Deeds [3]:77). Another Nantucket deed signed by Daniel Spotso states that he made the sale "with the approval of my mother" (3:51).

A document written sometime between 1690 and 1702 noted that "squaw-sachem Askammapoo" gave her son Daniel Spotso the power of attorney to represent her in a court action (Bragdon 1981:45). The accumulation of these tiny details begins to define the powers of a heretofore unknown Native American woman at Nantucket.

In 1624, Plymouth colonist Edward Winslow (1841) noted the high rank of a sachem's first wife compared to that of subsequent wives, and the existence of two ranks among the Indians. A similar authority framework on Nantucket is indicated by Zaccheus Macy's story of a son of Nickanoose named Jethro (Macy 1835:262–71). Jethro had left the island for Nauset in anger after his father took a second wife of low rank. This fact probably explains why the six children of Nickanoose's second wife received only three horse commons (see Fig. 3).

Documents like these also reveal the existence of status differences in Nantucket Indian society. Only members of high ranking or well-connected Indian families used deeds and wills. Less influential people did not ordinarily own land or horse commons. Further corroboration of these differences can be discerned in the lists of those who died in the epidemic of 1763–64; most of the Indian family names on this list do not appear on deeds and wills (Little 1990a).

Sachem Daniel Spotso as a Deed Merchant

The ways that sachems handled horse commons (Little 1990b) exhibit individuality in response to English pressures; i.e., they were not all passive participants in sociocultural change. Wanachmamack's followers, at a traditional meeting of the great men of his town and by deeds, assigned their twenty-four or twenty-five horse commons to senior men and sons, as well as to the English in return for cash. Attapeat's heirs exchanged most of their sixteen to nineteen horse commons one at a time to the English for cash or credit. Spotso's eighteen and Nickanoose's seventeen to eighteen horse commons have an incomplete documentary history, but by 1691 Daniel Spotso and his brothers had started to sell what would amount to nearly a double ration of horse commons. I propose that Askammapoo's sons, Daniel, Joshua, and Josiah Spotso, inherited at least nine of their grandfather Nickanoose's horse commons, as well as their father Spotso's eighteen (see Fig. 3). Over the years, Daniel Spotso sold to English or Indian men ten horse commons for "a valuable consideration." Another eighteen were sold for a total of fifty-eight pounds, four shillings.

English terms such as "valuable consideration," "bargain for," "sell," "alienate," "ratify and confirm," and "binding me, my heirs and assigns forever" distinguish permanent deeds of sale from renewable usufruct in return for periodic gifts (tribute). But the Indian renewal or confirmation deeds suggest that the word "forever" may have meant "for my lifetime" to an Indian sachem, with the original payment or gift being only the first installment. Indications of misunderstanding show in 1708, with Daniel Spotso's renewal deeds to John Worth and Richard Gardner for three horse commons that he had sold in 1691–92 without having specified the "heirs and assigns forever." In negotiating these different meanings of forever, a number of English and Indians tried renting land or horse commons, a process that resembles the Indian pattern of land and land use assignment.

And then, among the horse commons deeds from Daniel Spotso to James Coffin, one of 1716 illuminates a rare Indian-English interaction in which leaders of each culture tried to accommodate the other's traditional cultural patterns. Daniel Spotso signed a deed in which he both sold to James Coffin for the proprietors a large piece of Nickanoose's land and confirmed the 1682 sale of all the herbage on the sachemship of Nickanoose along with a previous sale of Sesapana Will's land to the English. In return, he received ten pounds, two horse commons, and confirmation of eight horse commons previously granted by the English. In addition, Spotso promised to reconfirm all these matters to Coffin if required. Here are extracts:

> Know all men by these presents that I Daniel Spotso of the Island of Nantucket in the province of the Massachusetts Bay in New England, Indian Sachem, for and in Consideration of the Sum of Ten pounds Currant money or bills of Credit of this province and the Confirmation of the liberty formerly granted me by the English of Commonage for Eight Horses and the additional Liberty of two more at this time to me paid by James Coffin Esqr of sd Island . . . I the sd Daniel Spotso Have given granted bargained sold conveyed and confirmed . . . unto the sd James Coffin on the behalf of the Inhabitants freeholders on the sd Island of Nantucket these several Tracts of Land and herbage on the island . . . one tract of land bounded on a line to Sesapana Will's old cellar to . . . John Swain's gate by the creek . . . and also all the herbage being arising or growing yearly and Every year Successively from the time of Indian harvest untill the first day of May on all the land which was formerly the Territory or Sachemship of Nickanoose Deceased and also my free Consent and full Confirmation of a sale of a tract of land made by Sesapana Will to Eleazer Folger Jun [1711] . . . the twenty ninth day of february . . . 1715/16.
>
> I Daniel Spotso do further Covenant promise and agree to and with the within mentioned James Coffin that I the Sd Daniell Spotso will at any time within Ten years next insuing the date of the within written deed make such other or further assurance and Confirmation of all matters and things Contained in the within written deed unto the said James Coffin or to the Inhabitants of Sd Island of Nantucket if by them or him thereto Required as he or they may think necessary to be done . . . Daniell Spaso O. (Nantucket County Deeds [3]:91)

This deed between the English proprietors and Daniel Spotso is remarkable because land assignment renewal (confirmation and tribute) have not been reported previously for English purchases from Indians. From these negotiations we can understand that Indian expectations of deed renewals looked to the English like ongoing demands for payment for previous sales, and perhaps led to the derogatory term "Indian giver," which is still in dictionaries. Coffin and Spotso turned these ideas around and introduced confirmation and a gift of two horse commons into the written English deed.

Most of Daniel Spotso's horse commons sales to Indians took place after 1716 and included Israel Jafets (1690), John Aaron (1717), Jonathon Micah (1718), Sam Humphrey (1720), and Micah Phillips (1721) (Nantucket County Deeds [2]:41; [3]:107, 128, 147, 412).

Throughout Spotso's sachemship, he sold most of his land to the English proprietors. We should not misjudge the Nantucket sachems for having sold their outlying ancestral lands, which had little economic value with the onset of North Atlantic whaling and a seaport economy. At that time, a number of Indian whalemen and others appear to have been building framed houses on the commons, close to the busy whaling town of Nantucket. Possibly they no longer paid tribute to their sachems.

We can follow Daniel Spotso and his family through three subsequent generations in county records. By 1741 Barney Spotso, now sachem, sold his rights in lands that had belonged to his father, Daniel, who must have been deceased. In 1748 Josiah Spotso deeded twenty acres and a house, barn, cellar, shop, horse, and cattle to his cousin Barney Spotso. Jonathan Spotso, his wife and two children, Barney Spotso's widow, Josiah Spotso, Easter Spotso, Hannah Spotso, and a boy Spotso all died in the sickness of 1763–64. And finally, in 1793, Barney Spotso, a whaleman (called "whalefisherman" in deeds), sold land to Abishai Folger that had belonged to his grandfather, Barney Spotso, and his ancestors (Little 1990a; Nantucket County Deeds [4]:105, [5]:17, 147).

Nickanoose, while striving to retain most of his lands and traditional land use rights, issued the first herbage use deed in 1675. This deed was written in English and reflected English usage and management of common lands, but the internal evidence shows that it was written by an Indian independently of English supervision and can be understood as including renewable usufruct and tribute. Nickanoose's grandson, Daniel Spotso, an active land merchant, did not retain most of his lands, but carried on and won the struggle over usufruct and tribute. He succeeded in talking James Coffin into something like a traditional Indian renewal of deeds accompanied by gifts. A son of Tristram Coffin, James Coffin handled negotiations with the Indian sachems from 1682 to 1716 and deserves recognition for a flexible response to the Indian leaders.

Conclusions

The issuing of horse commons deeds by the English to the Indians was an innovative strategy to meet the demands of the numerically superior Indians for the right to own horses while maintaining control of the commons. Once the sachems had rights to the English commons, both societies cooperatively as well as independently created a complex redistribution system. Horse commons were issued, given, sold, purchased, and rented by both the English and the Indians within and between their communities. From the absence of deeds and the presence of historic houses, I suspect that, in a transfer of Indian tradition, both societies came to use possession of a horse common as a right to build a house on the island (Little 1990a).

Through deeds of the seventeenth and early eighteenth centuries, we have been able to obtain a rare glimpse of Nantucket Indian politics, lineages, assignment of land use and its renewal, the strong role of women in connection with land, and the role of one Indian sachem, Daniel Spotso, in connection with land and land use sales. Like folktales or archaeological materials, this assemblage of public documents, many authored by Indians, provides a new and exciting dimension of contact with southeastern Massachusetts Indians of 300 years ago, heretofore viewed chiefly through culturally or politically biased tradition. Indeed, such data as these are the lure of ethnohistoric studies.

Notes

I should like to thank Sandra M. Chadwick, Nantucket County Registrar of Deeds; Dr. Louise Hussey, former Research Librarian; and Jacqueline Haring, former Curator of Research Materials, both at the Nantucket Historical Association Research Center; and Dr. Dena F. Dincauze, University of Massachusetts at Amherst, for their help and encouragement.

CHAPTER TEN

≈

Theyanoguin

Dean R. Snow

Introduction

THEYANOGUIN WAS probably born between 1675 and 1680 near Westfield, Massachusetts (Stone 1901:28). His father was Mohegan and his mother Mohawk, a circumstance that made him entirely Mohawk in the eyes of the matrilineal Iroquois. His adult Mohawk name was Theyanoguin. He was later also known as Sharenhowaneh (spelled variously as Soienga-rahta, etc.), the traditional title name of the fourth League sachem of the Mohawks (E. Tooker 1978:424). This office was one of three held by the Mohawk Wolf clan. The Turtle and Bear clans also held three each, although the Turtle clan position named for Ayonhwathah (Hiawatha) was always left vacant in honor of its first occupant. Fifty such names made up the roster of sachems of the League of the Iroquois, which at the time was comprised of the Mohawk, Oneida, Onondaga, Cayuga, and Seneca nations. Each sachemship was held as a name by a particular clan segment (matrilineage), and the matrons of that unit were charged with the duty of nominating a suitable man to assume the position and name upon the death of its previous holder (E. Tooker 1978).

Theyanoguin was born just after the close of King Philip's War, which put an end to the independence of the Indian nations of southern New England. Most of the southern New England Algonquians had been hostile to the Mohawks and other Iroquois. This was largely because the Mohawks continued to trade with the Mohegans, and the Mohegans were pariahs among the other New England Indians. The special relationship between the Mohawks and the Mohegans probably led to the marriage of Theyanoguin's parents.

He had at least two brothers. These were Cenelitonoro, who was known to the British as John, and Abraham, later called Old Abraham (Lydekker 1938:196–97). Both were apparently younger than Theyanoguin. They-anoguin became known to the British as Hendrick, and later as King Hendrick. The French later called him Tete Blanche for his white hair. He has sometimes also been referred to as Henry or Henry Peters (JP [1]:405, [8]:19, 24; Kelsay 1984:40).

Move to the Mohawk

Theyanoguin moved to the Mohawk Valley at a young age and took his place with the Wolf clan. Around 1690 he was persuaded to convert to Christianity by the Dutch pastor Godfrey Dellius (M. Hamilton 1974:622). He later became a preacher. He visited Catholic Mohawks in Canada in 1697, but as a Protestant he was not tempted to stay. He also persuaded other Mohawk chiefs not to settle there (NYCD [4]:281). He was by this time about six feet tall, and regarded by others as handsome and well-proportioned (Bolus 1973:5).

In 1698 Theyanoguin and another Christian Mohawk accused Peter Schuyler, Godfrey Dellius, and three others of fraudulently obtaining their signatures on a deed of land. The deed was subsequently invalidated and Dellius was suspended from his religious duties (M. Hamilton 1974:622).

Various Iroquois leaders signed a treaty with New France on behalf of the Six Nations in 1701. The treaty stipulated that the Iroquois would remain neutral in any future conflict between France and England. How-ever, Queen Anne's War (also called the War of the Spanish Succession in Europe) broke out almost immediately, and the Iroquois found themselves under heavy pressure to support the British. The British attempted to counter the French treaty by getting a deed to the American interior from the Iroquois. Despite his youth, Theyanoguin was one of the signatories to a deed of eight hundred square miles of Iroquois hunting grounds to William III in 1701. The transcribed name is spelled "Teoniahigarawe," but it appears to identify Theyanoguin through his Hendrick alias (Lydek-ker 1938:11, 26, 190–94; NYCD [4]:908–11). The sale came as a result of the efforts of Robert Livingston, then Secretary for Indian Affairs in Albany. Livingston argued that the Crown should acquire Iroquois lands and then reinstate the Indians as tenants. It was an attempt to subjugate the Indians that continues to be resisted by modern Iroquois.

Theyanoguin was persuaded to recruit warriors to join Francis Nicholson's planned attack on Canada in 1709. Nicholson, who had served a lieutenant governor of New York, was by now committed to the idea of throwing the French out of Canada. The expedition was aborted, but Theyanoguin's participation put him solidly on the side of the British interest (M. Hamilton 1974:622).

First Trip to England

Peter Schuyler and Francis Nicholson took Theyanoguin, his brother Cenelitonoro (John), Sagayonguaroughton (Brant, the grandfather of Joseph Brant), and a Mahican man to London to meet Queen Anne in 1710. Captain Abraham Schuyler was brought along as interpreter; it appears that none of the Indians spoke English. Schuyler and Nicholson's purpose for the trip was to gain support for another assault on New France, and they wished to emphasize the importance of their Indian allies. Theyanoguin's agenda was to appeal to the Queen for aid in fighting the French and for Anglican missionaries. All were treated to an expensive dinner at the Hudson's Bay Company in London on May 3. The British thought it odd that the Indians preferred to squat on their haunches rather than to sit on chairs or benches; for their parts, the Indians found it hard to believe that able-bodied Englishmen would allow themselves to be carried around town in sedan chairs (Bolus 1973:4–7).

Theyanoguin and the others addressed the Queen at length on April 19, stressing their loyalty to England and their rejection of French influence. The Queen responded by passing their request for missionaries on to the Society for the Propagation of the Gospel. Theyanoguin and the others later signed a letter to the Society for the Propagation of the Gospel requesting religious assistance (Bolus 1973:7). The Society presented all four chiefs with quarto-sized Bibles bound in Turkish red leather (Lydekker 1938:26–31).

The Indians stayed in London long enough to become celebrities. Crowds followed them, and songs were written about them. Enterprising publishers made quick money selling pamphlets that reported all kinds of invented nonsense about the Indians and America (Garratt and Robinson 1985). They went to bear fights, cock fights, wrestling matches, the theater (Macbeth), the opera, and a performance of Punch and Judy. They reviewed the Life Guards and toured the lunatic displays at Bethlehem (bedlam) Hospital. They were lionized at all of these events, but no one thought to make a careful record of their reactions, which had to have reflected a strong dose of culture shock. They took the royal barge to Greenwich and back, and were present at services in the barely finished Cathedral of St. Paul. Someone did (or pretended to) record their views on the latter, which focused on the immense size of the building and the lack of devotion of those in it. Many in the congregation apparently slept through the service (Bolus 1973:8). No proper Iroquois would have insulted an orator in this manner.

Queen Anne ordered the construction of a fort at the mouth of the Schoharie Creek, along with a chapel and a house for two missionaries. She also arranged for the Mohawks to receive a six-piece silver communion set bearing the inscription "The Gift of Her Majesty Anne, by the Grace of God, of Great Britain, France and Ireland and of her Plantations in North America, Queen, to her Indian Chappel of the Mohawks." There were other gifts as well, including Bibles, prayer books, and related items (Lydekker 1938:31). The communion set was later divided between Mohawks who fled to Niagara and the Bay of Quinte respectively during the American Revolution. A matching set, originally intended for the Onondagas, remains at St. Peter's Episcopal Church in Albany.

All four sat for portraits by John Verelst (fl. 1648–1734), a leading artist of the day. Theyanoguin's portrait bears the caption "Tee Yee Neen Ho Ga Row, Emperor of the Six Nations 1710" in the lower left corner. The portrait is now in the Public Archives of Canada.[1] In it Theyanoguin is wearing European clothing, including a red cloak that was given to him in London. His waistcoat and breeches were black, for the court was in mourning over the death of the Queen's consort, Prince George (Bolus 1973:5). The exception was a belt or burden strap decorated with dyed moose hair or porcupine quills in red, black, and white. He is shown holding a wampum belt and with a wolf behind him to indicate his clan. Curiously, both the three tattooed lines and the long scar that appear on his face in later portraits are absent in this earlier portrait. All of the portraits were later reproduced by a Huguenot engraver named John Simon, and

the engravings sold very well. There were in addition various other unauthorized (and inaccurate) prints sold around London at the time (R.
Bond 1952:66–67).

The four Indians were painted again just before they left London for
Hampton Court, Windsor Castle, and Portsmouth. This time they were
depicted in miniature portraits on ivory by Bernard Lens, Jr. All four were
shown with down-feather ear decorations, white shirts, and black waist-
coats. The elder Lens subsequently printed mezzotint reproductions of the
ivory miniatures.

They sailed home on the *Dragon*, reaching Boston on July 15, 1710.
They had gifts with them—a large supply of the kinds of goods usually purchased by the Indians in Albany. There were kettles, lead bars,
knives, mirrors, scissors, razors, combs, necklaces, mouth harps (a gross),
gunpowder, vermillion, clothing, yard goods, and a magic lantern (Bolus
1973:10; R. Bond 1952:68).

Fort Hunter and the Palatines

Theyanoguin might have already been a League sachem in 1710, although while in London he did not go by the sachem name he would
sometimes later use. If not already a sachem, he became one soon after his
return from London. His request for missionaries was successful. The
Queen funded missionaries and established a chapel at Fort Hunter in
1711. The chapel was a stone building, twenty-four feet on a side (Lydekker 1938:33), for which the society for the Propagation of the Gospel
supplied a missionary. The fort was built nearby at the same time. They
stood together on the east side of Schoharie Creek, at its junction with the
Mohawk River. The modern village of Fort Hunter still stands at the same
place.

Queen Anne also attempted to assist Palatine German refugees by
finding them homes around Livingston Manor in the Hudson Valley. They
lived there for two years, during which time they were supposed to repay
her kindness by producing pine tar for the navy. This arrangement did not
work well, and by 1710 the Palatines were agitating for farmland in
the Schoharie Valley. Theyanoguin offered them land through Governor
Hunter upon his return from London, although the Palatines had already
begun to stir. With John Weiser's aid, the Palatines finally moved to the

Schoharie in the fall of 1712. By this time Fort Hunter was well under construction.

A story persists that the German refugees were seen camped outside London on Blackheath near Greenwich Park by the four Indian chiefs who visited the Queen in 1710 (P.A.W. Wallace 1945:13). Hendrick is supposed to have been so moved by their plight that he offered to give them Mohawk land on the spot. However, the Palatines had left England for America three months before he and the other chiefs arrived, so things could not have happened that way (R. Bond 1952:11).

The Tuscaroras also began moving north around this time. They took up residence with the Oneidas and would eventually be brought into the League of the Iroquois as a sixth nation. However, they were never given any League sachemships.

Theyanoguin, Taragiorus, and three other sachems went to Albany in November 1712 to meet with the Reverend William Andrews, the new missionary sent out by the Society (DHNY [3]:902). Theyanoguin made a long speech thanking the Queen and the Archbishop of Canterbury for sending Andrews. Young Conrad Weiser, son of the already famous John Weiser, returned with them to the valley a few days later, and there he began learning Mohawk in the house of a Mohawk chief named Quaynant (P.A.W. Wallace 1945:17). Theyanoguin served as a lay preacher and took up residence near the chapel. The arrangement was not ideal, for Andrews's translator was Dutch and did not understand English. Consequently, Thomas Barclay, who was in charge of religious affairs in Albany, sent John Oliver along to facilitate translation from English through Dutch to Mohawk (Lydekker 1938:34; P.A.W. Wallace 1945:326).

Middle Years

Theyanoguin was deposed in the winter of 1712–13, revealing that the matrons could recall as well as nominate League sachems (P.A.W. Wallace 1945:22). This was apparently because he decided that welcoming Andrews as a missionary had been a mistake. Theyanoguin objected to tithing ten percent of all income to the new chapel, but he was in a minority and the matrons turned him out (Lydekker 1938:35; NYCD [5]:358). This incident might have caused Theyanoguin to move approximately twenty-nine miles westward up the Mohawk, from the Lower

Castle to the Upper Castle at Canajoharie, where he later became one of the chiefs. In any case, he was restored to his position as League sachem by 1720, for he reappears as a sachem in the colonial documents (Benton 1856:24; NYCD [5]:569).

Andrews grew weary of his duties after a few years. He resigned his post at Fort Hunter in June 1719 and went to Virginia, leaving the chapel and its contents in the charge of the fort commandant (Lydekker 1938:51). The mission to the Iroquois was thus suspended for eight years. Discipline lapsed after this, and Theyanoguin complained to the authorities in Albany that soldiers at the fort were selling liquor to the Indians (NYCD [5]:569).

Theyanoguin led a peacemaking expedition to Massachusetts and Maine in 1722 (A. Hamilton 1948:112). The Abenakis were at odds with the New Englanders, and Theyanoguin thought that it would serve the interests of everyone if the Mohawks (and thus the Iroquois) could extend their dominance over the Abenakis. However, Massachusetts officials regarded his travels as a recruitment effort, and kept the Mohawks from making direct contact with the Abenakis. Theyanoguin and most of his party were kept at Falmouth while another chief, Tagnaynaut, and an English officer searched the woods for an Abenaki headman to bring in for talks. Meanwhile, the New Englanders spent two weeks reciting Abenaki offenses, while Theyanoguin recited the benefits of condolence, peace, and participation in the great Covenant Chain (MDH [23]:119; Richter 1992:375). This was the metaphorical chain of friendship forged by the Iroquois and Governor Andros at a 1677 meeting in Albany (Jennings 1984:8–9). The arrangement had made the Iroquois first among Indian nations and cemented their friendship with the British. On this occasion, however, the New Englanders rebuffed Mohawk politics.

After deciding that the Mohawks had become more civilized by contact with colonial neighbors, the Society for the Propagation of the Gospel reopened its mission in 1727 (Lydekker 1938:52). Thomas Barclay, who had been in charge in Albany, had become deranged over the years, so the Society appointed John Miln to fill the positions of both Barclay and Andrews. Miln lasted four years before his health failed and he had to return to England. He was replaced by Henry Barclay, son of Thomas. The younger Barclay was very active, extending his preaching to the Upper Castle at Canajoharie so that both Mohawk communities were now being served. Barclay built a new stone church at Fort Hunter in 1741 and opened schools in both Mohawk villages the following year (Lydekker 1938:53–54).

Second Trip to England

Theyanoguin made a second trip to England around 1740 (M. Hamilton 1974:623). On that occasion King George II presented him with a suit of clothes in the style that was popular at the time. It included a green coat with gold lace and a cocked hat (Lydekker 1938:26; Stone 1901:34). Theyanoguin sat for a portrait in this costume, and engravings were later made from the portrait (Schoolcraft 1847:415–16). Various engraved versions have since been published many times. All show Theyanoguin holding a stylized tomahawk in his right hand and bearing a pronounced scar on his left cheek. An apparently earlier portrait shows the same scar (Lydekker 1938:26), but in this case Theyanoguin is wearing Indian attire, and his head is shaved except for a small scalp lock. Both portraits show small, stylized tomahawks as well as the distinctive set of three long, tattooed lines across Theyanoguin's face and forehead.

Many years later, Julia Grant visited Theyanoguin's son, Sahonwadie, who wore his father's green coat for the occasion. Grant later confused Sahonwadie (Paulus) with his father, thinking she had seen Hendrick himself (Lydekker 1938:81). This was clearly a mistake, for Grant was born the year Theyanoguin was killed.

Theyanoguin apparently wore the same costume on a visit to Boston in 1744. The War of the Austrian Succession had spread to America that same year, where it was known as King George's War. The Iroquois were nominally neutral, but many Mohawks and some other Iroquois were eager to side with the British. Around the middle of January 1745, some Mohawks coming home from Schenectady in the middle of the night spread the alarm that whites were coming to kill them all. Many Mohawks fled into the woods. Barclay convinced the people in the Lower Castle that the rumor was groundless, but the Upper Castle Mohawks were not mollified. They threatened the settlers around them and sent the alarm on to the rest of the Six Nations. Theyanoguin later blamed French agents for having caused the commotion, but without much evidence (Lydekker

1938:56–58; P.A.W. Wallace 1945:219). The incident was probably con-
cocted by Theyanoguin as a means to force the British to face up to the
growing influence of the French among the Mohawks (Flexner 1979:48–
49).

Conrad Weiser, by now a well-known frontier diplomat and rival of
William Johnson, visited Theyanoguin, Abraham, and Arughiadekaa, the
chiefs of Canajoharie, in July 1745 (P.A.W. Wallace 1945:226). By this
time Theyanoguin was living in a house there on a "handsome elevation,
commanding a considerable prospect of the neighboring country" (Stone
1901:28). New York's governor George Clinton called a hastily arranged
conference in Albany in October of the same year, after hearing a rumor
that the Six Nations had struck a deal with the French. The Six Nations
raked out their fire, leaving behind pressing business concerning both the
Catawbas and the Shawnees, and came to Albany. The conference turned
out to be a mess of bad temper and mutual accusations. Weiser knew the
value of keeping the Iroquois neutral, but at this conference he was only an
interpreter. Clinton chided the Iroquois for the recent alarm and Theyanoguin replied in kind. Eventually Weiser took up the governor's wampum
belt and told Theyanoguin to hold his tongue. Clinton wanted war with the
French, and the young Mohawks had to be restrained from going along
with this by their chiefs. The conference achieved nothing. Clinton's reputation suffered, and the Indians went home disgusted (P.A.W. Wallace
1945:229–31).

Theyanoguin went to Montreal with a delegation of Mohawks in the
fall of 1746. There they accepted gifts of good will from the French
governor. Nevertheless, on their way home they attacked some French
carpenters at Isle La Motte, near the north end of Lake Champlain, an act
that made Theyanoguin a marked man amongst the French. The French
sent out a party to kidnap Theyanoguin in the spring of 1747. They were
unable to find him because he was himself with a large war party, raiding
up and down the St. Lawrence. The French eventually found and broke up
the Iroquois force, but Theyanoguin and several comrades made it back
safely to Mohawk country (Flexner 1979:66–68).

The Indian Commissioners of Albany resigned in 1746, and Governor
Clinton appointed William Johnson Colonel of the Six Nations, later
Commissary of New York Indian Affairs. Johnson's expense account for
1746–47 contains several entries for presents to Theyanoguin and costs
associated with various services performed for him (JP [9]:15–31).

Association with William Johnson

It was probably at about this time that Theyanoguin moved his residence downstream from Canajoharie, across the Mohawk River to a location on the north bank. According to Schoolcraft (1847:416), this later home was "a little below the residence of Major Jellis Fonda, near a place then and now call the Nose." This would have been at or very near the modern hamlet of Yosts.

From his new home closer to Fort Hunter, Theyanoguin became a close friend and confidant of William Johnson. The two visited each other frequently, for Theyanoguin was Johnson's principal link to the Mohawk leadership in these years before the emergence of Joseph Brant.

The Iroquois put great stock in dreams, which they consider to be expressions of suppressed desire. There is a now-famous story that Johnson appeared one day in a new scarlet uniform. A while later Theyanoguin told Johnson that he had dreamed that Johnson had given him the uniform. Johnson knew Iroquis culture, and he knew that he had little choice but to hand it over as a gift. But with the gift Johnson reported a dream of his own. He had dreamed that his friend Theyanoguin had given him five hundred acres of good Mohawk land. Theyanoguin had no choice but to comply, but he added, "I will never dream with you again" (Benton 1856:23–24; J. Hubbard 1886:41–42). The story is probably apocryphal, for it was told many times about other men. A variant of the story attributes the same roles to Conrad Weiser and Shickellamy (P.A.W. Wallace 1945:151).

Theyanoguin was ill in March of 1747, but Johnson was anticipating sending him out with other Mohawk warriors to raid the French and relieve the strategic Fort Ontario, which was located at the mouth of the Oswego River on the southwestern shore of Lake Ontario (JP [1]:81). The Mohawks obliged, and by late April they already had prisoners and scalps to show for their efforts. Theyanoguin, like most other Iroquois chiefs, received an invitation to treat with the French early in 1748. Johnson was very agitated by this effort to split the Iroquois from the British, and begged his superiors anew for resources to hold on to his allies. The French invitation had come from a priest at Cataraqui (now Kingston, Ontario), probably the Sulpician Abbé François Picquet (JP [1]:50).

Theyanoguin addressed William Johnson at a meeting with him and the chiefs of the two Mohawk castles, which took place at Johnson's new mansion, Fort Johnson, on February 2, 1750 (Flexner 1979:104–5; NYCD [6]:548–49). (Johnson had built the stone mansion just west of modern Amsterdam only the previous year, and it was initially called Mount Johnson.) Theyanoguin explained that the sachems of the Six Nations had met with western Indians in Philadelphia, and that the westerners had brought a gift of two bushels of wampum to show their good will. This was to be divided amongst the six Iroquois nations, including the Tuscaroras, who had no League chiefs. Theyanoguin also explained that the French had tried but failed to attach the Iroquois to their interest. Having failed, they had apparently threatened to attack and destroy the Iroquois in the spring; at least this is what Johnson was told. Such stories were often exaggerated in order to keep British supplies coming.

By May 1750, the British were at peace with the French again, but the French busied themselves with trying to convert the Ohio River Iroquois (the Mingos) to their interest. Johnson perceived that if that happened, the Six Nations would have to go over to the French cause as well. Johnson begged Clinton to come to Albany to brighten the Covenant Chain with the Iroquois. Johnson held out the possibility that Theyanoguin and Seth, another Mohawk leader, could get the Six Nations to agree to peace with the Catawbas if Clinton could bring along a small Catawba delegation (JP [1]:278). The Catawbas were southern enemies of the Tuscaroras, and the Six Nations had been raiding Catawba villages for years, disrupting British efforts to keep peace within their colonies.

By August of 1750, Theyanoguin and other chiefs were claiming to Johnson that they feared that the French and the British were about to join in suppressing the Iroquois. This was probably a ploy to blunt British complaints about French gifts and overtures to the Iroquois (JP [9]:62–66). Johnson mollified them, blaming the French for stirring up trouble. He later reported the whole episode to Clinton in breathless detail. Theyanoguin refused initially to shake hands with Johnson at this meeting. The problem was that Canadian Indians were always coming to Albany to trade, and it appeared to Theyanoguin that the Iroquois were being bypassed (JP [9]:153).

Arent Stevens, an agent for William Johnson, negotiated with Theyanoguin for the sale of land to Johnson in May 1751 (JP [1]:330–31). The land Johnson wanted was to the west, and he was unsure as to its ownership. Theyanoguin assured Stevens that the land belonged to the Upper Castle Mohawks and not to the Oneidas. Theyanoguin, eight other Mohawk chiefs, and one Oneida chief conveyed a vast tract south of the Mohawk River and west of the Schoharie to Johnson (JP [13]:15).

Clinton staged a council to treat with the Iroquois in Albany in July 1751. Theyanoguin was there with Nichus, Abraham, and other chiefs, and he spoke for the Indians. Theyanoguin was distressed that Johnson had resigned as agent to the Indians. Theyanoguin gave Clinton a wampum belt "in order to raise up the fallen Tree," a reference to Johnson that made use of an Iroquois metaphor for the replacement of a deceased sachem (JP [1]:340). Clinton claimed that he could not change Johnson's mind, so Theyanoguin offered to give it a try. At about this time, Johnson arrived in Albany and gave his reasons for resigning. He said that he could not continue because he received insufficient resources and had used up much of his own fortune in the government's interest. Clinton promised to get compensation from the Crown, but Johnson still refused to resume his post formally, for he knew that this would require a new round of gift-giving to the Iroquois.

Theyanoguin also complained about Catholic Mohawks from Canada, who were in town to sell furs. He groused that he and his friends would not get such a friendly reception in Montreal, and that he could not open his heart to Clinton in the presence of the French Indians. Weiser, who knew that the Catholic Mohawks were generally welcome at Fort Hunter and Canajoharie, thought that this was just a ploy (P.A.W. Wallace 1945:326). When the meeting was over, Weiser sent his son Sammy to live with the Mohawks in order to learn the language, as he had done himself nearly forty years earlier.

In 1751 Theyanoguin travelled to Stockbridge, Massachusetts, at the invitation of Jonathan Edwards. The purpose of this trip was consultation about a project to educate members of the Mohawk nation (W. Smith 1960:532).

By the middle of the century, many Iroquois were living away from their traditional home communities, some as far away as Ohio. Pro-French Mohawks had long since moved north to live near Montreal. Disaffected people from this community, Caughnawaga, moved upstream to found a new village at Akwesasne (St. Regis) in 1747. Between them, near modern Ogdensburg, Pro-French Onondagas founded the community of Oswegatchie with the assistance of Abbé François Picquet. By 1753 so many Onondagas had moved there that Theyanoguin observed that the fire at Onondaga had nearly expired (NYCD [6]:810).

Albany Plan of Union

Theyanoguin was present at the 1754 conference in Albany in which Benjamin Franklin proposed his famous Albany Plan of Union. Much of the conference was given over to mollifying the Iroquois. Land sharks were pestering the Mohawks, and Clinton's arrogance was not helpful. The conference occasioned what Schoolcraft (1847:416) referred to as "Hendrick's greatest speech" on June 19. In his opening speech three days earlier, New York Lieutenant Governor James de Lancey had said,

> We came to strengthen and brighten the chain of friendship, and [handing Theyanoguin the chain belt] this chain hath remained firm and unbroken from the beginning. . . . The French are endeavoring to possess themselves of the whole country, although they may have made the most express treaties with the British to the contrary. . . . Therefore open your hearts to us, and deal with us as brethren. (Stone 1901:29)

Theyanoguin was introduced by his brother Abraham, and he held up the chain belt as he spoke;

> Brethren: As to the accounts you have heard of our living dispersed from each other 'tis very true. We have several times endeavored to draw off these, our brethren, who were settled at Oswegatchie but in vain, for the Governor of Canada is like a wicked, deluding spirit. However, as you desire, we shall persist in our endeavors. You have asked us the reason of our living in this dispersed manner. The reason is your neglecting us for three years past.

As Theyanoguin spoke he threw a stick over his shoulder and said;

> You have thus thrown us behind your backs, and disregarded us, whereas the French are a subtle and vigilant people, ever using their utmost endeavors to seduce and bring our People over to them. This is the ancient place of treaty where the fire of friendship always used to burn; and 'tis near three years since we have been called to any treaty here. . . . Tis true these Commissioners are here, but they have never invited us to smoke with them. But the Indians of Canada come frequently and smoke here, which is for the sake of their beaver. But we hate them. We have not as yet confirmed the peace with them. . . . Tis your fault, Brethren, that

we are not strengthened by conquest; for we would have gone and taken Crown Point, but you hindered us. We had concluded to go and take it, but we were told that it was too late and that the ice would not bear us. Instead of this, you burnt your own fort at Saratoga, and ran away from it, which was a shame and a scandal on you. . . . Look about your country and see; you have no fortifications about you; no, not even to this city. Look at the French; they are men; they are fortifying everywhere. But, we are ashamed to say it, you are all like women, bare and open, without any fortifications. (Stone 1901:29–30)

Weiser saved the day by advising both sides, smoothing ruffled feathers, and rebutting Theyanoguin's attacks on Virginia and Pennsylvania. The incident reveals the ways in which the Iroquois still played the British and French off each other. It also reveals a fundamental premise of Iroquois diplomacy. No treaty settled anything once and for all. The Iroquois regarded friendship as a condition that needed constant nurturing and renewal. In the absence of new treaties, the Iroquois believed that things would soon devolve into their natural state of war.

Pennsylvania wanted to buy lands west of the Allegheny Mountains, and most of the Indians were inclined to sell. Theyanoguin objected, but the commissioners replied that the Mohawks had no say in the matter because it was the Oneidas and Cayugas who had taken the land from the Susquehannocks. Weiser shrewdly gave this message to Theyanoguin to take to the other chiefs, which simultaneously honored him and put him in his place (P.A.W. Wallace 1945:358–59).

Theyanoguin's speech to the other chiefs was pathetic. Pennsylvania was generous to the Indians, he said, and he advised them to take the frowns off the brows of their brothers by agreeing to the sale. Weiser was called in and vague boundaries were set. Theyanoguin told them to draw up a deed, and testily advised them to "be not long about it" (P.A.W. Wallace 1945:359). The deed was signed by Hendrick, Abraham, Brant, John Shickellamy, Tagashata, and others of the Six Nations. The Indians agreed to sell the land for two payments of four hundred pounds sterling each, but four years later they got most of the land back.

Theyanoguin's speech made a profound impact on the British public when it was published in *Gentleman's Magazine* in June 1755. His words were matched by glowing descriptions of him that were circulating by that time. Timothy Dwight said that "his figure and countenance were singularly impressive and commanding; that his eloquence was of the same superior order; that he appeared as if born to control other men, and possessed an air of majesty unrivaled within his knowledge" (W. Smith 1960:533).

As the conference broke up, John Lydius (another land agent) got Theyanoguin and fifteen other chiefs drunk at his house and tricked some of them into signing the now-infamous Wyoming Deed (JP[1]:405, [3]:715, [9]:142–45; Nammack 1969:43). Theyanoguin and many other leading men refused to sign. Lydius later rode to the Mohawk castles, intending to get more signatures. He had made the fraudulent deal on behalf of Connecticut, which was looking for western lands. In the end it caused serious fighting between the colonies, and was later regarded as one of the key events that precipitated the Wyoming Massacre of 1778 (P.A.W. Wallace 1945:361–63).

Massachusetts governor and military commander-in-chief William Shirley responded to Johnson in December 1754. He was particularly eager to reassure Theyanoguin and the Mohawks that their lands were guaranteed to them (JP [1]:427). The support was important for countering the claims of Philip Livingston and others, who were still attempting to acquire Mohawk land by fraudulent means.

Theyanoguin went to Philadelphia in December 1754 at the urging of Robert Morris, a Philadelphia businessman who would later become a key figure in the financial affairs of the American Revolution (JP [1]:433; [9]:142–45). Theyanoguin and others stopped by Fort Johnson on their way (JP [9]:148) to deal with problems resulting from shady land purchases by various people from Connecticut (JP [1]:441). Unlike the middle colonies, Connecticut was blocked from westward expansion, and attempts by Connecticut land speculators to establish themselves in western Pennsylvania or New York caused problems from this time until the nineteenth century.

Theyanoguin arrived in Philadelphia on January 7, two weeks after Christmas, delivering letters from Johnson to Robert Morris and Richard Peters (JP [9]:153). He was accorded an enthusiastic public welcome and escorted to the State House, where he was entertained elegantly. There the governor of Pennsylvania gave Theyanoguin a belt with a string of wampum attached as a token of Pennsylvania's desire to see the Connecticut deed broken. The string was to request Johnson to convene the League Chiefs at Fort Johnson to consider how best to do this (JP [9]:156). The logic of the Indian position in this was laid out by Richard Peters (JP [9]:158).

The conference lasted several days and included some Cherokees, who were passing through on their way home from captivity in Canada. Theyanoguin complimented the governor on his treatment of the Cherokees and complained about the contrasting deceit of New York. New York aristocrat Philip Livingston had wangled a fraudulent deed to Mohawk lands in the valley, and Governor George Clinton had left for England in disgrace. Theyanoguin also argued for getting rid of the fraudulent Wyoming deed by convening a conference of Pennsylvania and the Six Nations in which the Iroquois would convey all lands within the Pennsylvania royal grant to the proprietaries (P.A.W. Wallace 1945:376).

Theyanoguin left Philadelphia after January 23, 1755, and arrived in Albany on February 10 (JP [9]:159, 161). He was back in Canajoharie by May 1755 (JP [1]:489). Curiously, he had been called upon to solve a problem that he may well have been involved in creating in the first place.

The Battle of Lake George

In June 1755 Theyanoguin and his brother Abraham came to Johnson's house with their families, and Johnson paid them both for helping him translate a speech to the Six Nations (JP [2]:573). The French appeared ready to advance on Albany by August 1755. Theyanoguin and another Mohawk chief, Taragiorus, led over two hundred Mohawks up the Hudson to Fort Edward to assist the British. Fort Edward still lies on the upper Hudson River, at the southern end of a portage connecting the Hudson with Fort William Henry, on the southern tip of Lake George. Unfortunately, the French had many Caughnawaga Mohawks on their side, and Theyanoguin thus faced the unpleasant possibility of fighting kin (Claus 1904; JP [1]:883). Theyanoguin spoke formally to Johnson at Lake George on the morning of September 4, 1755. The New York Mohawks were concerned about the possibility of engaging Catholic Mohawks from Caughnawaga, and they were looking for a way to meet with them in the forest. The New York Mohawks arranged a meeting in no-man's land, providing their own men as pickets for the British so that they would not be mistaken for the enemy when they returned (JP [2]:383).

Johnson used Indian scouts at Lake George, and Theyanoguin served as translator (JP [2]:16, 380), his English apparently now being up to the task. At one point Theyanoguin expressed alarm at the negligence of British sentries. He went on to urge Johnson to take the advice of the

Iroquois when fighting in the wilderness, pointing out that both Fort Edward and Fort William Henry were exposed and could easily be out-flanked (382).

Johnson nevertheless made the error of sending out two detachments of five hundred men to try to take the French from the rear. Theyanoguin was alone in disagreeing with the plan, saying, "If they are to fight they are too few; if they are to be killed they are too many." As to the idea of sending the men in three parties, Theyanoguin is supposed to have taken three sticks from the ground and said to Johnson, "Put these together and you cannot break them; take them one by one, and you will do it easily" (Stone 1901:31).

The quote is oddly similar to one attributed to Theyanoguin by Parker: "Five arrows shall be bound together very strongly and each arrow shall represent one nation. As the five arrows are strongly bound, this shall symbolize the union of the nations" (Parker 1916:11). Both stories may well be apocryphal. The bundle-of-sticks symbol comes out of European political tradition, but it is still often attributed to American Indians, testimony to the complexity of cultural interaction in America over the last four centuries (E. Tooker 1993).

Instead of taking the French by surprise, the British and Mohawks marched into a French trap south of Lake George. One of the French-allied Mohawks was later said to have deliberately fired his musket early in order to warn the British-allied Mohawks of the trap (Stone 1901:32). Theyanoguin led the Mohawks on Johnson's charger. When the ambush was sprung, the horse was shot out from under him, and the old chief was bayoneted before he could get up from the ground (NYCD [6]:1008). The British fell back. Johnson was wounded and there were many losses, but they rallied and defeated the French after retreating to strong positions nearer the lake.

According to a later account, "His son [Sahonwadie] on being told that his father was killed, gave the usual groan, and suddenly putting his hand on his left breast, swore that his father was still alive in that place, and stood there in his son. It was with the utmost difficulty Gen. Johnson pre-vented the fury of their resentment taking place on the body of the French General, Dieskau, whom they would have sacrificed without ceremony, but for the interference of Gen. Johnson" (Schoolcraft 1847:420–21).

Theyanoguin and Taragiorus were both killed in the battle of Septem-ber 8, along with Colonel Williams and several other British officers. The

Mohawks had stood their ground and lost both of their war chiefs as well as thirty other men. The next day Theyanoguin's body had still not been found, but Johnson was sure that he had been killed. Johnson reported that he had lost many men, some of them "Indian Officers, and, the Indians Say, near 40 of their People, who fought like Lyons, were all Slain. Old Hendrick, the great Mohawk Sachim, we fear is kill'd" (JP [9]:231).

Epilogue

Gifts came in for Theyanoguin's family and friends in the weeks following his death (JP [9]:278, 294). In addition to his son Sahonwadie (Paulus), he had a daughter who had married an Oneida sachem. There might have been others as well.

League chiefs from Oneida and Tuscarora came to Canajoharie in February to condole the deaths of Theyanoguin and Taragiorus (JP [9]:349–50). A new chief was raised up to replace Taragiorus at the condolence, but the Mohawks held off from replacing Theyanoguin (391). As late as 1758, Stockbridge Indians gave Johnson a French scalp to "replace" Theyanoguin. Three others were given for Old Nichus, the son of Nichus, and for Eusenia, who had been the wife of Taragiorus (JP [13]:113).

Livingston's efforts to acquire Mohawk land in 1754 came back to haunt the Indians after Theyanoguin's death. In 1761, George Klock settled in the valley, taking land in the supposed Livingston patent that he claimed was now his. The Livingston family had long since given up the claim, and tenants on the patent were paying rent to the Mohawks. Klock was having none of that, however. He intimidated the tenants and plied young Mohawks with liquor. Johnson detested Klock and made every effort to remove him (JP [10]:336–39). The discredited Lydius purchase of 1754 resurfaced again in 1762 when the claim was pressed in London (484).

A portrait of Theyanoguin once hung in the New York State Capitol. It was unfortunately destroyed in the 1911 fire that also consumed many priceless objects in the collection of the New York State Museum. The Theyanoguin portrait and others of Joseph Brant and John Brant had been included in the New York exhibit at the 1907 Jamestown Exposition. Two photographs of the exhibit are the only surviving visual records of the portraits.

The lost Theyanoguin portrait was apparently a colored engraving that had once belonged to William Johnson. Confiscated with other property of John Johnson and auctioned during the American Revolution, it was later acquired by Jeptha Simms, and went with the rest of the Simms collection to the New York State Museum.

Theyanoguin might be viewed as having been a culture broker, but it must be understood that he did not live in the cultural purgatory to which culture brokers are usually assigned. It cannot be easily claimed that he lived between two cultures, for he was clearly and permanently Mohawk. Like many modern brokers, he was working for the interests of one of several parties in eighteenth-century politics, not brokering between them as a mediator. Theyanoguin was a great ally in the eyes of the British, but he never lost sight of his primary loyalties, which were to the Mohawks, or of his secondary ones to the Iroquois as a whole. His old friend William Johnson understood this. It was perhaps fortunate for both that neither lived to see their world turned upside down by the American Revolution.

Notes

I thank George Hamell and Harald Prins for helping me to track down crucial but elusive sources, and Robert Grumet for editorial suggestions that improved the manuscript.

1. It is catalogued under Accession Number C–92420.

CHAPTER ELEVEN

∾

Shickellamy,
"A Person of Consequence"

James H. Merrell

Introduction

SHICKELLAMY, AN Oneida who lived along the Susquehanna River from the late 1720s until the late 1740s, has never lacked for admirers.[1] "[O]ur good friend," proclaimed Pennsylvania's proprietor, Thomas Penn (quoted in Aquila 1983:180). "[A] trusty, good man, and a great lover of the English," proclaimed the colony's governor, James Hamilton (quoted in Sipe 1927:164). "[T]rue and Honest," wrote Conrad Weiser, the colony's ambassador to the Six Nations Iroquois (PA 1st Series [1]:758). "[T]ruly an excellent and good man," announced the Moravian leader Count Nikolaus Ludwig von Zinzendorf grandly, "possessed of many noble qualities of mind, that would do honor to many white men, laying claims to refinement and intelligence." "He was," Zinzendorf concluded, "possessed of great dignity, sobriety and prudence" (Sipe 1927:164). Iroquois spokesmen, while less effusive, nonetheless called Shickellamy "very honest" and one of the "good Men" (MPCP [3]:446).

Since Shickellamy's death in December 1748, the encomiums have become more extravagant. "[T]he most picturesque and historic Indian character who ever lived in Pennsylvania," one historian argued (Sipe 1927:162). "[A] just, generous, far-sighted statesman and gentleman," wrote another (P.A.W. Wallace 1945:40). A modern biographer considered him "Pennsylvania's most influential Indian statesman" (Carter

227

1931:52). "In the exercise of tactful government, in the skill of transforming hostility into obedience, and in the art of subtle negotiation," proclaimed still another, "Shikellimy was the greatest representative of the Iroquois Confederacy." Not only that, this student of the Pennsylvania frontier went on, but Shickellamy was "one of the greatest Indians, who ever lived" (Brewster 1954:9–10).

What is remarkable about all of these songs of praise—especially those sung by historians—is that they are based on very little information. Beneath the hyperbole lie many unanswered questions. What, for example, was this Indian's name? At different times he was called Ungquaterughiathe, Takashwangaroras, and Swateney—which may be a corruption of Onkhiswathetani, "he causes it to be light for us" or "our Enlightener"[2]—and it is not even clear if the most common appellation, Shickellamy, is Delaware or an Anglicized form of an Oneida name.[3] Equally obscure is this Indian's life before he showed up in Philadelphia one June day in 1728. While all sources concur that he was adopted by the Oneidas and was always identified as an Oneida (though they differ on his clan),[4] there is considerable disagreement about his origins. Was he a Frenchman by birth? A Cayuga? Of Cayuga-French heritage? A Susquehannock?[5]

No less a source of dispute is exactly what Shickellamy was doing on the Pennsylvania-Iroquois frontier. Everyone agrees that the Six Nations Iroquois—Mohawks, Oneidas, Tuscaroras, Cayugas, Onondagas, and Senecas—had sent him to the junction of the North and West Branches of the Susquehanna River to play some formal role in the life of that region, but what his authority was and how far it extended are unknown. He was, depending on whom one reads, an Iroquois "deputy" or an "ombudsman," a "viceroy" or a "vice-regent," an "over-lord" or an "overseer," an "ambassador" or a "first magistrate."[6] And his task was "to preside over the Shawanese," as the Pennsylvania council thought, or perhaps, as one colonist put it, to be a "watch over" all of "our Indians."[7] Or maybe he was there, more generally, "to attend to the affairs and interests of the Six Nations . . . in Pennsylvania" (Carter 1931:28–29).

The bewildering array of titles and responsibilities assigned to Shickellamy illustrates just how uncertain people then and since have been about his position on the Iroquois frontier. It does nothing to help solve the many mysteries shrouding this Oneida's life that he remained in the background at the grand treaty councils that brought hundreds of Indians and Euro-

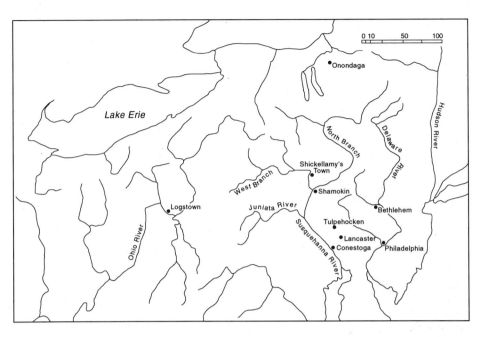

peans together during these years, occasions when, had he taken center stage, he might have caught the eye of some colonist who would have more fully described him for posterity. A Maryland observer at the Lancaster Treaty in 1744, for example, wrote colorful sketches of several Iroquois leaders, but scarcely mentioned Shickellamy (Marshe 1884).

Shickellamy was, then, an elusive figure on the early American stage. But he was no less important for that. This Oneida merits another, closer look, not because he won the favor of a proprietor, not because he impressed the likes of Count Zinzendorf, not because he was "the greatest" Iroquois or "the greatest" Indian (however one might define greatness), but because he was among a handful of people managing contacts between the Six Nations and their southern neighbors—colonial *and* Indian—at a turning point in the history of those contacts. Standing astride the principal highway connecting Pennsylvania and Iroquoia, he helped to arrange an alliance between Philadelphia and the Iroquois capital at Onondaga, and he lived to see that alliance challenged by the colony's new relationship with tribes in the Ohio Country.

Shickellamy's significance goes well beyond a chronicle of his accomplishments or a catalogue of his disappointments, however. As a go-between, he was vital to carrying on the conversations between cultures, conversations that are central to the colonial experience.[8] It was Shickellamy and others like him who knew how to cross the cultural divide, whom to approach on the far side, what to say, and how to say it. Despite the essential role these people played, they have received too little attention, both in their day and in our own. Thus a search for Shickellamy, the "Enlightener," can enlighten us not only about one Indian man's life, but also more generally can "cause it to be light for us" in the shadowy realm of the go-betweens.

The Road to Philadelphia

In the late 1720s, the time was ripe for the Iroquois and Pennsylvania to forge closer ties. The Six Nations, by then bound to European colonists through a system of trade and diplomacy, were seeking other connections to that colonial world in order to offset their dependence upon French Canada and New York. It was natural to look southward, for the Iroquois had a long history with the lands and peoples in that direction. To the south lay the paths that took men in search of glory to battle against faraway foes like Catawbas and Cherokees; to the south, at Conestoga and elsewhere on the lower Susquehanna River, lived remnants of displaced and destroyed peoples—Susquehannocks whose homeland it was, Delawares from the east, Shawnees from the south and west, Conoys and Nanticokes from Maryland, Tutelos from Virginia—peoples who had suffered from Iroquois or colonial raids, European diseases, and provincial settlers. Among these refugee groups lived Senecas, Oneidas, and other emigrants from Iroquoia, further binding natives at the Susquehanna's headwaters to those near its mouth.

To the south, too, were Pennsylvania colonists, who had reasons of their own to welcome closer ties with Iroquoia. These people, bent on economic and geographical expansion, were eager to fashion their sporadic contacts with the Six Nations into something more enduring and more profitable.[9] No less important in these years was that Pennsylvanians were scared, and they looked to the Iroquois for help. The famous "long peace" that William Penn's colonists enjoyed in their relations with native peoples from the early 1680s to the mid-1750s makes it easy to forget how fragile that peace was, how fearful Pennsylvanians sometimes were that another Opechancanough or Metacom was about to arrive on their doorstep, bringing death and destruction in his train. The late 1720s was one of those anxious eras, a time when "thereis som Miscif hacin by the Indians" was a common refrain (PA 1st Series [1]:227). Rumors reaching Philadelphia spoke ominously of a vast Indian conspiracy against the English, a plot hatched in remote lands by remote peoples but including, it was said, natives near as well as far (MPCP [3]:295–98; PA 1st Series [1]:210–11).

Incidents on the frontier gave frightening shape to these vague forebodings. In the summer of 1727 a delegation of Cayugas, after an unhappy meeting with provincial authorities in Philadelphia, tangled with settlers on the way home.[10] A year later came news that another delegation of Iroquois was bypassing the province altogether en route to Maryland (229–32). Meanwhile, unnamed Indians had killed a Pennsylvania trader along the Susquehanna, and later another barely missed being hung by Shawnees on that river's West Branch (MPCP [3]:285–87, 330–31; PA 1st Series [1]:227). Still other Shawnees had gotten into scrapes with Conestoga Indians (who swore revenge) and with colonists (who took a peculiar form of revenge, murdering some Delawares) (PA 1st Series [1]:213, 216, 218–20; MPCP [3]:302–4, 309). Peering in their mind's eye past the farther reaches of "the inhabited parts" of the province, men in Philadelphia often spoke with a shudder of the strange lands and alien peoples out there. "[T]he Woods," said one official in July 1727, "are so thick and dark" (MPCP [3]:275). Those woods seemed especially dark in the late 1720s.

Enter Shickellamy, "our Enlightener," to bring light to the darkness for both colonists and Indians. By 1728 he lived with his family—a Cayuga wife, five sons, and two daughters—at a place on the West Branch that came to be called "Shickellamy's Town." From there he and his family followed the patterns of existence common to other Susquehanna Indians: farming near the river, hunting deer in the uplands, trading with colonists, going off to war against Catawbas. What his formal position was will never be known with certainty. Perhaps the best way to put it is that those among the Six Nations most keen on looking southward for new opportunities and new adventures sent him down the Susquehanna to look after things (Richter 1992:273–76). Initially his principal responsibility may indeed have been to keep an eye on the Shawnees, foreigners in those parts who were, it seemed, causing more than their share of trouble at the moment. But it is also likely that Shickellamy's duties included serving as a liaison with Pennsylvania and with the Delawares, as well as more generally to look out for Iroquois interests on the Six Nations' troubled southern frontier.[11] He was, as one colonist put it, "a person of Consequence" (MPCP [4]:653).

Though nothing is known about the process of selecting such a pivotal figure, it is clear that in many ways Shickellamy was, from the Iroquois point of view, a wise choice. Not only was he apparently a man of some prestige, he was also an Oneida, "which nation," Conrad Weiser later wrote, "pretents to have the greatest right to the land upon Susquehana."[12] Moreover, perhaps by birth and certainly by marriage, Shickellamy was also connected to the Cayugas, another Iroquois people with interests to the south. These qualifications, along with the "Kingly robes" that he donned for special occasions and the ceremonial wampum belts and strings that were his credentials, combined to give him authority in Indian eyes (Shamokin Journal, in Carter 1937:67; Snyderman 1954:491).

It is less certain what Pennsylvanians saw in him, for according to colonial lights, Shickellamy was ill-equipped to be a go-between. Unlike Indians, colonists chose intermediaries more for their cultural and linguistic knowledge than for their social and political prestige; a lowly fur trader was far more likely to serve as a messenger or ambassador than was a governor or councillor. But now here stood Shickellamy, probably baptized by Catholics as an infant but otherwise—as far as we can tell—little acquainted with colonial ways. The new arrival overcame any doubts soon enough, however. Part of his success was due to his temperament. "[I]t is not his Custom," he once assured colonists, "to bear any Man Ill will," and if he did not always live up to this boast, he kept his equanimity often enough to impress colonists.[13] It helped that, unlike other Indian leaders, he apparently was not prone to indulge in alcoholic binges, those native drinking bouts that frustrated and frightened colonists. It helped, too, that Shickellamy early befriended important Pennsylvania men involved in Indian affairs, such as the proprietary secretary and merchant James Logan—who by 1730 trusted the Oneida enough to propose storing trade goods with him—and Conrad Weiser, a man well-versed in things Iroquois (Logan to Edward Shippen, [1730?], Logan Papers [HSP], vol. 1, folder 101; MPCP [3]:425).

In 1728, of course, colonists shaking hands with Shickellamy in the provincial capital knew only that this Indian was a prominent Iroquois with important (albeit vague) responsibilities on the frontier. In that atmosphere of fear and uncertainty, this was more than enough. After meeting Shickellamy for the second time, the Pennsylvania Council remarked hopefully that his "Services had been and may yet further be of great advantage to this government" (MPCP [3]:337). Over the next two decades the Council's prediction was more than borne out: Shickellamy crisscrossed the frontier in an effort "to clear," as an Iroquois speaker in Philadelphia once said, "the Road from this Town to the Six Nations" (451). From Shickellamy's Town—and after 1737 from his new base at Shamokin, a village of Iroquois, Delawares, and Tutelos at the forks of the Susquehanna—he made at least seven trips to Onondaga, and twice that many to Philadelphia. Added to these arduous journeys—some in the dead of winter, when snow blocked the path and starvation loomed; others amid the heat and insects of summer—were countless shorter trips along the Susquehanna to an Indian town or a trader's post, and still others over the "Endless Mountains" to confer with Weiser at his home in Tulpehocken.

Many of these journeys were for "preparatory Conferences," the round of talks that Indians insisted upon as a prelude to the great treaty councils.[14] Before those grand gatherings could take place, relations between groups had to be established on a friendly footing, with tokens of good will exchanged, all obstructions in the path between peoples removed, and a clear agenda set.

There was much to discuss during these years. The wars with southern Indians dragged on. Could peace be made? Some Shawnees, having migrated to the Ohio Country, were flirting with the French. Could they be lured back across the mountains? Indians remaining behind in Pennsylvania were politically fragmented, confusing to deal with, and—especially Delawares—stubborn about surrendering their lands. Was it possible to simplify matters, to deal less with Conoys and Conestogas, Delawares and Shawnees, and more with the capital of Onondaga—and, with Onondaga, to manage all of the others? Both the Iroquois and Pennsylvanians wanted coherence and Iroquois hegemony in the region, and both wanted trade. Moreover, for the Iroquois, pleasing Penn's province had the added advantage of helping to secure their claim to lands from the lower Susquehanna River all the way into Virginia.

With so much to talk about, no wonder Shickellamy was so often on the road, "in his Bosom" a message, in his pack the wampum strings containing the precious words, along with gifts of deerskins from Onondaga to Philadelphia or of matchcoats trimmed in silver, headed the other way (MPCP [4]:447, 573; MPCP [3]:506, 508). Traveling with his sons or with other Indians, sometimes guiding colonists to Iroquoia, he was bent on fulfilling the Six Nations' wish, voiced at Philadelphia in 1732, "that there may be more frequent Opportunities of conferring and discoursing with their [Pennsylvania] Brethren," conferences and discourses "managed" largely by Shickellamy (440).

How Shickellamy went about setting up these treaties is hard to recover, because so much of his work consisted of "private Discourse" that took place either literally "a little way distant from the Town" or figuratively "in the Bushes."[15] No doubt when among the Indians he shared what he was learning of the colonial world, but those talks, deliberately held out of earshot of foreigners, have been lost forever. What snatches of conversation from these "preparatory Conferences" do survive include colonists, and show Shickellamy teaching them Iroquois ways.[16] "[L]ye still, *John*," he cautioned the novice John Bartram on their first night in an Onondaga longhouse when an Iroquois False Face honored the new arrivals with a boisterous visit (Bartram 1751:43). Even Weiser, who had lived among the Mohawks, needed coaching. When an Iroquois entourage·approached the province in 1736, Shickellamy instructed Weiser to tell the colonial provisioners not to cook for these guests; the Indians "must have the victuals raw," he advised, "and let their wimens Boil it" (Weiser to Logan, 16 Sept. 1736, Logan Papers [HSP], vol. 10, folder 62). And when, seven years later, Weiser asked him why another delegation had not yet come south to meet with colonists, a surprised Shickellamy "ask'd," Weiser wrote, "whether I could not Guess at it. I told him No. Then he said how should [they] come down with a Hatchet Struck in their Head." Virginians had recently attacked a party of Iroquois, Shickellamy explained, and "the Governor of Virginia must wash off the Blood first, and take the Hatchet out of their Head and Dress the Wound (according to Custom he that Struck first must do it), and the Council of the six Nations will speak to him and be reconciled to him" (MPCP [4]:650).

Laying the groundwork for treaties with colonists was only part of what occupied Shickellamy's time. He was also, for example, busy sending and receiving news across the cultural divide, an exchange of information so important that it was part of treaty agreements. "[I]t was agreed" at our last council, Shickellamy reminded Pennsylvania officials in 1740, "that in case any Thing of Moment happened to either of Us, we should communicate it to the Others."[17] For his part Shickellamy promised "that himself and the Indians about Shamokin [would] keep their Ears open to" news in

Indian Country.[18] Some of this swapping of information took place in the Pennsylvania Council chamber; more often, however, the venue was Weiser's house in Tulpehocken, Shickellamy's lodge at Shamokin, or somewhere in between. In these places Shickellamy and his colonial counterpart Weiser met time and again, shared a meal or a smoke, and "Sat down to discourse." "[H]e asked me," Weiser wrote after one typical chat with Shickellamy, "what news accured among the white people." After telling his side of the story, Weiser then "asked what news accured among the Indians."[19]

A vital part of these talks was sifting "news" from rumors and squelching the rumors. Sometimes a scornful laugh was enough to put fears to rest. "[A]t the Story of the Snow Shoes he laughs," Weiser reported in 1746 after visiting Shickellamy with word that enemy Indians were stockpiling snowshoes for a winter attack on the English colonies (MPCP [5]:2; Weiser to [Peters?], 24 Jan. 1745/6, Du Simitiere Papers, 966.F.24). Other stories required more careful investigation. Did someone hear that a party of Conoys had returned from a raid on southern Indians with two Virginia scalps? Shickellamy visited their town, heard their version of the story, inspected the scalps, and assured Pennsylvania officials that the story was false.[20] Had several messages reached Shickellamy of a vast colonial conspiracy against the Indians, including one warning that "the Proprietor of Pennsylvania, . . . whom they accounted their good friend, would have a chief hand in their Destruction"? Back went Shickellamy to Philadelphia to get reassurances from provincial authorities (MPCP [3]:500–1).

Occasionally, of course, the talk flying from town to town turned out to be true, and then Shickellamy had to act. Shawnees on the Susquehanna—angered by the news that Virginians had fired on Iroquois warriors and convinced "that the white People are all of one Colour and as one Body"—had indeed ransacked a Pennsylvania trader's storehouse. In this case Shickellamy joined Weiser to host a council of Iroquois, Shawnees, and Delawares at Shamokin to "Concert Measures," sent one of his sons to retrieve the goods, and headed north to Onondaga with words of peace (MPCP [4]:633, 636, 630–46).

Shickellamy, who went to such lengths to deal with Indian troubles that arose on the borderlands, took complaints about unruly colonists to provincial authorities and expected them to be just as diligent. A Pennsylvania trader was building a house and clearing fields "on Lands which they [the Six Nations] have always desired to be kept free from any Persons settling

on" (MPCP [3]:504). Another problem was the bringing of rum into Indian villages, with terrible consequences. Still other complaints concerned
the stealing of Indians' peltries, horses, and guns (MPCP [3]:501–4,
[5]:87–88; PA 1st Series [1]:758–59). Shickellamy, after bringing these
crimes to the colonists' attention, went on to warn that "some Mischiefs
may happen" "[i]f these [Pennsylvania] Counsel don't find a remedy"
(MPCP [3]:504).

The Armstrong-Mushemeelin Affair

All of these measures enabled Shickellamy to stamp out sparks of contention before they flared up into a conflagration that might engulf the
frontier. But because he so rarely emerged from the bushes into the
clearing, it is easier to chart the range of tasks he performed than it is to
recover their complexity, to appreciate the skill they required. On occasion,
however, Shickellamy did step from the shadows long enough to leave a
vivid imprint on the surviving records. The most illuminating of those
occasions, the clearest of those imprints, came in the spring of 1744.

Early one morning a Tutelo living in Shamokin hurried over to Shickellamy's house with some bad news that he had learned from a drunken
Delaware the night before: three Shamokin Delawares had killed the
Pennsylvania trader John Armstrong and two of his servants. Shickellamy
must have realized at once the potential for disaster here; relations among
peoples in his part of the world were particularly delicate that spring. From
across the sea came rumors of another war between England and France.
In the Ohio, Shawnees were said to be abandoning the English and
inviting other unhappy Indians still living in Pennsylvania to follow them
across the mountains and into the arms of the French. The Six Nations,
who might have been able to exert some influence with disaffected natives
and at least would serve as a buffer against French Canada, were myste-
riously, ominously quiet about the upcoming conference at Lancaster with
Pennsylvania, Maryland, and Virginia. Then, while people worried about
the French and wondered about the silence from Iroquoia, came news of
Armstrong's killing.[21]

Shickellamy, knowing the perils of delay or failure, set to work. He
"went Imediately to Olumapies [Sassoonan] the delaware Chief and told
him, and pressed upon him to make Imediatly inquiry and find out the

murderers." Next he sat in on the Delaware council, which agreed to send four Delawares to Weiser with a letter asking for his help and to enlist the aid of a conjurer "to find out the Murderer." The following day he listened to the report of the Delawares who, acting on the advice of "the seer," had questioned two young Delaware men about the killings. One, whom the English called John, said nothing; but the other, "Billy," "told the whole Story very freely" and implicated an older Delaware named Mushemeelin. Shortly thereafter Shickellamy met again with the Delawares and several Pennsylvania traders—including John Armstrong's brother, Alexander—who came "To Consult . . . what they should do Concerning the Affaire."

So far everything was going about as well as Shickellamy could hope; the Delawares, with only a little prodding on his part, were moving in the direction of restoring peace. But then came a crisis: though "it was agreed"—the passive voice here makes it unclear who was agreeing, but we can suspect that Shickellamy had a hand in it—"to Secure the Murderers, and deliver them up to the White People," not everyone was happy with the arrangement. Mushemeelin was a noted conjurer, John the son of a prominent man; few Delawares wanted to risk reprisal by handing them over to colonists. Moreover, the accounts of the killings differed dramatically: Billy claimed that he and John had been terrified bystanders as Mushemeelin slaughtered all three colonists; Mushemeelin asserted that while he had indeed killed two of the traders in self-defense, John had murdered the third, and indeed the two young men had planned the whole thing. Faced with this impasse, "a great noise arose among the delaware Indians," and they were "in great Confusion among themselves" about what to do. "[T]he old people," Shickellamy learned, "wer inclined to make Every thing Easy [that is, surrender the suspects,] but they had no Command at all over their yong men [*sic*]." Some Delawares, fearing for their lives, fled into the woods; others got drunk; Sassoonan, "in danger of being killed, fled to Shick Calamy and begged his Protection."

Shickellamy enlisted the aid of his children to break the impasse. "Pressed by Shick Calamy's Sons," who talked darkly of colonial (and perhaps also Iroquois) reprisals, at last a handful of Delawares tied up John and Mushemeelin and, with two of the Oneida's sons, piled the prisoners into canoes for the trip downriver. Halfway to jail, however, John goaded Mushemeelin into a rage, during which the older man boasted that he had indeed killed all three. Though Mushemeelin was quick to recant, the two brothers were quicker still: they set John free, handed Mushemeelin over to the colonists, and hurried back to Shamokin.

Such a move might have pacified the Delawares; it angered not only Mushemeelin but also colonists. From Armstrong's brother came letters to Shickellamy and Sassoonan insisting that "you . . . send us all the murderers" and warning that "we do not want to fall out or quarrel with you without you make us do it." From the Pennsylvania governor came a "demand [for] those that had been concerned with Mussemeelin" in the killings. Meeting with Weiser at Shamokin in early May, Shickellamy worked to get around the ultimatums. He insisted that John was innocent, and told, "from the beginning to the end," what he "declared to be the Truth of the Story," a "Truth" that implicated Mushemeelin and Mushemeelin alone. "We desire, therefore," he had Weiser tell the governor, "our Brother the Governor will not insist to have either of the two Young Men in Prison or Condemned to Dye. . . . We will give you faithfully all the particulars," he went on, "and at the ensueing Treaty entirely satisfie you."

Having staved off immediate calamity from the Delawares in his midst and the colonists to the south, Shickellamy next turned his attention to the north and the Iroquois delegation now en route to Lancaster. If that treaty was to go forward, they, too, must get his version of recent events. Thus the Oneida "Sent a Message to me[e]t the deputies of the Six nation in their way to pensilvania," Weiser reported, "to let them Know that if they should happen to hear of this noise not to be discouraged to Come, but to Come along, and take no Notice of the Storrys that would be industrously Spread among the Indians by the delawares about this affair." The message, and the conversations with the delegation that ensued at Shamokin, worked to muffle the "noise" and to make the Armstrong affair a sidelight to the main events at Lancaster that June. A suitable compromise had been arranged: the Delawares would bring John and Billy to Philadelphia for questioning, "but not as prisoners."

In August the scene shifted to Philadelphia for the last act of the drama. A prominent Delaware spoke to the governor and council, but it was Shickellamy who, at the right time, "caused the two Young Men to stand up, and pointing to them said, they were the two." It was Shickellamy, too, who made sure that Mushemeelin stayed in his cell, warning the governor that this man had said "he would make his Escape this Night; he is Master of the Black Art and a Conjurer," Shickellamy warned, "therefore take care of him." And finally, when the two Delawares had been questioned and cleared, when Mushemeelin had been put in irons to await the gallows, it was Shickellamy who stood to deliver to Pennsylvania the customary words and wampum to remove and bury the hatchet, "Clear the Air that was rendred foul and Corrupted," and "take the Overflow of Gall out of your Entrails."

Measures and Methods

Whether or not justice was done to Mushemeelin, the Armstrong business, in luring Shickellamy out of the shadows, offers a rare opportunity to watch him at work. Things did not always go so smoothly, however. One year, charged with a message from Philadelphia to Onondaga, Shickellamy, halfway there, handed over the wampum to another Indian who then, "Some whate Neglect full," went hunting instead (Weiser to Col. Gale, [1743], Richard Peters Papers [2]:5). On another occasion Shickellamy made it all the way to Onondaga himself, but took so long on the return trip that impatient officials in Philadelphia sent someone to fetch him (MPCP [3]:506). These were not the only times Shickellamy frustrated or disappointed colonists. He and Conrad Weiser squabbled at least twice over what route to take, and at Lancaster in 1744 he stunned everyone by refusing—until other Iroquois and Weiser had a private chat with him—to agree to the very treaty he had done so much to arrange.[22]

Nor was Shickellamy always as successful as he was in the Mushemeelin-Armstrong affair. The frontier was a messy and chaotic place, rife with mistrust and misunderstanding; neither he nor anyone else could remove every stump, every root, every bush that littered the road between Iroquoia and Pennsylvania. He never managed to retrieve the Shawnees who had left the Susquehanna for the Ohio Country, and his efforts to make peace between the Iroquois and the Catawbas were not to bear fruit in his lifetime (Merrell 1987:115–33).

Shickellamy could not achieve all of his aims, in part because he lacked sufficient authority. Despite one historian's claim that "his word was law in all the hinterland of Pennsylvania" (P.A.W. Wallace 1945:40), Shickellamy was not, in fact, a powerful man. His handling of the Mushemeelin-Armstrong affair, deft as it was, only revealed his inability to compel the Delawares to do his bidding. At no point—not when he first heard the alarming news, not at the Delaware council, not even when Mushemeelin and John were trussed up, ready to be hauled off to jail—could the Oneida take matters into his own hands. This was a Delaware affair: he could sit in on councils; he could cajole, negotiate, and manipulate; he could not issue commands. In fact, Shickellamy was not even master of his own house. One February day in 1748, a colonist reported that the Shamokin "Indians ware most all Drunk Except Shekelleme and his Eldest Sone, [and] he being tier'd [sic] with the n[o]ise he must Continually hear in his owne House, came to us . . . , was Displeas'd tho knew not how to prevent the greatest Disorder thay oft made," the colonist repeated, as if scarcely able to believe it, "in his owne House."[23]

But if Shickellamy could not command frontier folk—native or colonial—the aftermath of the Armstrong killing shows that he did have resources at his disposal. Not least of these were his own skills, which included patience, persuasion, and a shrewd sense of the possible. He was also a master of indirection. When in 1731 James Logan heard that Ohio Shawnees were flying a French flag in their village, in a panic he sent word to Weiser that Shickellamy and another Indian messenger, whom Pennsylvania had just dispatched to Iroquoia, should "mention" this troubling news, too, "after they have delivered their first message, *but,*" the anxious Logan cautioned Weiser, "not as a part of their message, or as if they were sent back [to Onondaga] about it, but only occasionally as a piece of news" (Logan to Weiser, 15 Dec. 1731, Logan Papers [HSP], vol. 2, folder 14 [emphasis added]). Logan need not have worried; Shickellamy was adept at disguising his purposes. When he went off, two years later, to look into those suspicious scalps taken by Conoys, he started plotting his approach before he had even left Philadelphia. "[H]e believed," he said, "it would be most proper for him first to go to his own home and taken [sic] some people from thence with him; that if he should go from Philadelphia directly amongst these Indians, he might probably find them more reserved" (MPCP [3]:503).

Added to his knack for dealing with people was Shickellamy's skill in handling the tools of the go-between's trade. Like all Indians, he knew that every conversation required the wampum containing the spoken words as well as a pipe of tobacco to smoke in order to promote "good thoughts" (Fenton 1985:25). But even though he never learned to read or write, he added to his repertoire the paper and ink of the colonists. The letter to Weiser regarding Armstrong's death was only one of many Shickellamy mailed. As early as 1733 he and Sassoonan were sending a letter of complaint to a trader, and the following year he and a Seneca named Hetaquantagechty, trying to stanch the flow of liquor into Susquehanna River villages, asked for a copy of the Pennsylvania law "which gives Power to any Persons to Seize and Secure Rum found in any Indian Towns or Settlements."[24] Shickellamy even added to his credentials "a Letter of Recomendation Rote and given him by the Goavener" and a copy of Pennsylvania's 1742 treaty with the Iroquois, documents that he kept for years, pulling them out from time to time in order to listen, "much pleas.d," as a colonist read them aloud (Shamokin Diary, 28 Feb. 1748, MA 6/121/4/1).

Among Shickellamy's many tricks of the trade was his willingness to work with others to achieve his ends. James Logan and Conrad Weiser are only the most famous of his collaborators. Less well-known but perhaps no less important were three of Shickellamy's sons—Tachnechdorus (John Shickellamy), Soyechtowa (James Logan), and Sagoechyata (John Petty) (PA 1st Series [4]:91)—and Hetaquantagechty, who during the 1730s often visited colonial officials with Shickellamy and spoke for the two of them.[25] Never was Shickellamy's reliance on other minds, other ears, other tongues clearer than when he spoke with a German visitor in 1748. Another colonist translated the speech from German into Mahican for Soyechtowa's Mahican wife, "she then into Shawanese to her husband, and he into Oneida for his father"; in Shickellamy's reply the current of words was reversed, traveling from Oneida through Shawnee and Mahican to German again (Jordan 1905:174–75). As translators and advisers, as traveling companions and extra pairs of eyes and ears, all of these people extended Shickellamy's reach and strengthened his grasp of languages, customs, and peoples, both colonial and Indian.

Tireless and temperate, shrewd and subtle, armed with paper as well as wampum and acquainted with important people throughout the region, Shickellamy was instrumental in forging the axis of interest that ran from Onondaga to Philadelphia, an axis that, as James Logan had predicted, helped "to Strengthen both themselves and us" (quoted in Jennings 1984:312). From this connection the Six Nations got the outlet for their traders and their diplomats that served as a counterweight to Canada and New York, extracted from Pennsylvania payment for Susquehanna lands, enlisted that colony's aid in asserting an Iroquois "right of conquest" to territory still farther south in Maryland and Virginia, and won acceptance of Iroquois claims to supervision of the Susquehanna River peoples. For its part, Pennsylvania now had not only a new source of pelts but also a simpler, more efficient (and more ruthless) means of dealing with the congeries of native peoples on its frontiers. Together the Iroquois and the Pennsylvanians cheated and ousted the Delawares; together they faced the French; together they fretted about the Shawnees; together they handled the frictions of the frontier, pulling hatchets from heads and burying those weapons out of sight.

It is easier to measure what Pennsylvania and the Iroquois reaped from Shickellamy's labor than to gauge what he got out of all that travel and talk. We know that Pennsylvania supplemented praise and gratitude with material rewards. Bushels of wheat and pieces of eight, a gun and a shirt, a saddle and a hand vice, a log house and that "Letter of Recomendation"— the province bestowed all of these upon Shickellamy.[26] Nor did colonial solicitude stop there. When someone in Shickellamy's family died, a gift and words of condolence arrived from Philadelphia. When he or his kin fell ill, the province dispatched Weiser with medicine and instructions from a physician on the proper dosage.[27]

Whether all of this attention added up to prestige in Indian Country is less clear. Having merchandise to display or distribute could be a mark of one's favored status and a source of authority; but it could also brand one as a pawn of those bent on dulling Indian minds with liquor and stealing Indian lands with paper. What we do know is that Shickellamy was at the center of life in the region. His house, more public assembly hall and inn than dwelling, was a popular resort for Indian hunters and ambassadors as well as colonial traders and missionaries. To his door came Shawnees and Germans, Englishmen and Mahicans, Scots-Irish and Iroquois, sometimes in such numbers that even the 49½- by 17½-foot shingled house that a colonial crew had built for him in September 1744 could not hold them all.[28] We may wonder whether Shickellamy, faced with housing and feeding so many, always considered such popularity a blessing; but he would have had no doubt that the hordes of visitors testified to his stature as "a person of Consequence" in the region.

The Moravians

In the fall of 1742, a different sort of visitor arrived at Shickellamy's house: Moravian missionaries. For the last six years of the Oneida's life, these people would play a central role, first as an additional link in the chain of friendship with Philadelphia, then as a competing claimant for his loyalty.[29] Shickellamy had met these pious folk before—if not at the great 1742 treaty in Philadelphia that July, then in August on the way home, when Count Zinzendorf met the Iroquois delegation at Conrad Weiser's. At that meeting, Zinzendorf got the Indians' permission to scout a possible mission site in the Susquehanna Valley; his first stop was Shamokin, and—although on this tour the reichscount would offend almost everyone with his impatience, his ignorance, and his arrogance—Shickellamy greeted him warmly (Reichel 1870 [1]:65–66, 85–92, 102–8).

It was another three years before Moravians would set up a mission station in Shamokin, however. By then Shickellamy had had an opportunity to observe these people at closer range. During the summer of 1745 he and his son Soyechtowa (James Logan) traveled to Onondaga with Weiser and two Moravians, David Zeisberger and Augustus Spangenberg, men cut from different cloth than their imperious leader. Spangenberg and Zeisberger were humbler folk, not given to complaining; indeed, they were so easy to get along with that Soyechtowa later observed that he had never "traveled with such a good man as Spangenberg before" (P.A.W. Wallace 1945:220).

Soon after Shickellamy's return home from that Onondaga journey, he had a chance to watch Moravians at work in Shamokin—the first missionaries arrived there in September—and he was impressed with what he saw.[30] These people were different from most colonists he had met. Unlike fur traders, they neither brought nor drank liquor and, far from picking fights with Indians, they actually submitted meekly to the taunts, threats, even assaults of drunken natives.[31] Unlike other missionaries, they did not try to corral Indians into a congregation to hear a sermon, preferring instead to lead exemplary lives, earn the natives' trust through regular visits, and broach the subject of salvation only when the time seemed right.[32] Unlike any colonial or Indian man, they helped natives harvest crops. And they never complained about the size of their portions at dinner or the comfort of their beds at night (Shamokin Diary, 17 Oct. 1745, MA 28/217/12B/1). When in early November the Moravians approached Shickellamy about living with him, he "reply'd," the missionaries happily reported: "If a Trader or any other white Man desired to live with him he wo.d not permitt it. But he gave us Leave because he knew something of us, and that we liv'd with him for the good of the Indians" (3 Nov. 1745, MA 28/217/12B/1).

Shickellamy had still other reasons to welcome these people. Whatever one thought of Zinzendorf, his boast in 1742 "that already in early child-hood I had been favored with an intimate acquaintance with God," cou-pled with the healing powers of the missionaries that Shickellamy himself had seen, suggested that these people had access to potent medicines and spirits, access that Shickellamy may have thought Shamokin inhabitants could tap (Reichel 1870 [1]:87; Jordan 1878–79:429, 460–61; 1905:172–73). The newcomers also were free with gifts to him of shirts, blankets, and knives,[33] and no less generous about inviting his family to share meals with them or feeding his children and grandchildren when they were sick.[34] Last but by no means least, the Moravians agreed to erect a blacksmith shop near Shickellamy's house, something the Shamokin peoples had been requesting since 1735 (MPCP [3]:579). The smith's arrival in Au-gust 1747 increased the town's importance—and Shickellamy's (Jordan 1905:173; Carter 1937:67–68).

Moravians were generous in part because from the first their Shamokin strategy was to win Shickellamy's favor. At Zinzendorf's meeting with the Iroquois at Weiser's that August day in 1742, he "took occasion to study" the assembled Indians. "One of them in particular arrested my attention," he wrote. "I was irresistibly drawn toward him, and I longed to tell him of the Saviour" (Reichel 1870[1]:87). This was Shickellamy, and for the rest of the Oneida's life he was the cornerstone of Moravian mission policy in the region. When Bishop John Christopher Frederick Cam-merhoff visited Shamokin to inspect the mission, he reminded his people there to "Strive to secure the good-will of Shikellmy and his family" (Jordan 1905:178).

In response to these overtures, Shickellamy gradually established close ties to the people from Bethlehem. Saying that the Moravians' names "were too difficult . . . to pronounce," one reported, he "saw fit to give us Magua [Mohawk, or Iroquois] names."[35] When the Moravians set up their mission, Shickellamy not only housed them but also, after they had built their own quarters, brought them gifts of food.[36] He offered horses to haul logs to the Moravians' building site, helped them erect the dwelling, gave them a field to plant, assisted them in getting blacksmith tools upriver, and kept an eye on the smith's shop when they were away.[37] He even taught them Oneida—"contrary," as Cammerhoff noted with pride, "to their reluctance and prejudice to teach whites their language."[38]

Shickellamy also worked to head off trouble from natives less enamored than he with these foreigners. When intoxicated Indians invaded the

Moravians' house, Shickellamy helped the missionaries round them up and escort them out again (Shamokin Diary, 14 May 1748, MA 6/121/4/2). When a Delaware refused to pay the smith for repairing a musket, Shickellamy, "Displeas'd," advised the Moravians to keep "the Gun by Fors till he paid"; failing that, he apparently pulled the Indian aside and convinced him to pay what he owed (12 Feb. 1748, MA 6/121/4/1). When an elderly Shawnee named Neshanockeow proclaimed his hatred of missionaries, announcing—once to the Moravians, once to Shickellamy—that these people "are like the Pidgeons, when you come to a Place, 1 or 2 don't come alone, but imediatly a whole Company fly thither . . . , Shickeleme was quite still and did not answer him a Word." The visitor, sensing the chill, promptly left.[39] Finally, to further his relationship with these newcomers, Shickellamy rode to Bethlehem to learn more about the Moravian people and their faith.[40]

Rivals and Enemies

Another, less obvious reason that Shickellamy may have let the Moravians into his house and his life is that he was, amid all of the traffic through his doorway, an oddly isolated figure. Whether or not his dwelling was in fact set up on posts to raise it above the rest (Loskiel 1794[2]:119), there is a sense in which he was indeed increasingly removed from those who inhabited or passed through Shamokin—so removed, indeed, that he could get no one to help him build a fence (Shamokin Diary, 1 May 1748, MA 6/121/4/2); so removed that Shickellamy urged one visitor to Shamokin to live there so that the two men could converse from time to time, as if otherwise the Oneida would have no one to talk to (13 Oct. 1747, MA 6/121/3/3).

One potent source of his isolation was his aversion to liquor. Shickellamy was no teetotaller—at treaties he apparently drank the standard toasts like everyone else—but he saw what havoc alcohol wreaked and wanted no part of the drunken sprees, some of them lasting for several days, that were so prominent a feature of the Shamokin social calendar. Quite the contrary: convinced that alcohol "is from the devil," he tried to shut down the flow of rum, which endeared him neither to colonial traders nor to his native neighbors.[41]

Shickellamy was also set off by long-running feuds with some of those traders and neighbors. Though he named one of his sons after a colonial fur trader and had cordial relations with others, the Oneida despised most Pennsylvania traders for their eagerness to channel rivers of rum into his village and their habit of robbing, beating, and otherwise abusing Indians.[42] One of those traders, Peter Chartier—the son of a Frenchman and a Shawnee woman—particularly drew Shickellamy's ire. Not only was Chartier the most flagrant of those defying Pennsylvania laws against shipping liquor to the Indians, but—even worse—he scoffed at the Iroquois delegation that the Oneida had brought to Philadelphia in 1732. "[T]hose Indians," Chartier told an outraged Shickellamy, "are a parcel of idle, cheating fellows, that came without any Authority from their People; that they were not Chiefs, but loose fellows picked up from all parts; that the present given them [by Pennsylvania] was in Effect no other than robbing the Government of so much money. . . . This," concluded Shickellamy, "he must resent" as a lie and a challenge to his claims of influence in Iroquoia (MPCP [3]:501). When, more than a decade later, Chartier led some Shawnees over to the French, Shickellamy was not surprised. That "very wicked and prowd" man, he told Pennsylvania officials, was "a great Cowart."[43]

Shickellamy's contempt for his neighbors, the Shamokin Delawares, was if anything even deeper. Determined to inflate his own authority, the Oneida go-between generally belittled them. They cheat the blacksmith, he declared, and they drink too much. Their leader, Sassoonan, was the worst of the lot. He is "an inebriate," the Oneida claimed, "and had nothing to say at Shamokin."[44] Confident of the Delaware headman's weakness, in 1747 Shickellamy, working with Logan and Weiser, tried to ruin him. In May he forbade Delawares from joining talks with Moravians about the smithy, and the following month he joined Weiser in telling Philadelphia officials that Sassoonan, "still alive but not able to stir," had "lost his Senses and is uncapable of doing anything." Since the headman had, Shickellamy and Weiser lied, "no Successor of his Relations," Pennsylvanians should simply appoint someone "and set him up by their Authority." That chosen successor, Lappapitton, fearing for his life, refused to go along. But even if he could not plant a suitable puppet in the Delawares' midst, Shickellamy did manage to prevent Pisquitomen, Sassoonan's heir—and an opponent of most of what Shickellamy, Logan, and Weiser had wrought in the past fifteen years—from becoming a headman when Sassoonan died in an epidemic in September 1747.[45]

The Road to Bethlehem

Shickellamy fell ill in that same epidemic, which already by the end of August had left Shamokin littered with the sick and the dead (Letter from Shamokin, 25 Aug. 1747, MA 6/121/8/6). Had he perished with Sassoonan, his life and career would have had a very different cast. By that fall of 1747, Shickellamy had carried on conversations that strengthened not just the Six Nations, not just Pennsylvania, but also Shickellamy himself and his large family. He had outmaneuvered the Shamokin Delawares, who with Sassoonan's death were leaderless. He had won the trust of colonial officials and befriended Moravian missionaries. The coveted blacksmith shop that marked this friendship confirmed Shamokin as the most important town in the region, and Shickellamy as its most prominent citizen. Moreover, he had done all this without losing his attachment to Indian culture or his contempt for the ways of colonists. His dislike of colonial life, usually muted, was nonetheless genuine. He once told Weiser a pointed story about how Iroquois warriors watched New Yorkers trying to fight the French, and how then the Indians "said to [the] Albany people: Brethren, stand still and look at us, and learn how to fight" (PA 1st Series [1]:757). And he was probably one of those who, "among themselves" or "in familiarity with" Weiser, would "under value, or Rather make Nothing of our [English] Valour" (761). On occasion he could be more critical, and more blunt. "We are Indians," he was said to have replied when a Presbyterian missionary showed up in the spring of 1745 and invited him to convert, "and don't wish to be transformed into white men. The English are our Brethren, but we never promised to become what they are. As little as we desire the preacher to become Indian, so little ought he to desire the Indians to become preachers" (Jordan 1878–79:428).

A man who helped vanquish the Delawares, a man who secured Iroquois hegemony in the region, a man who kept colonists at arm's length even as he made the most of their good will—Shickellamy's obituary, had it been written in the fall of 1747, would have had about it an air of accomplishment, of high achievement in Iroquois terms. But Shickellamy did not die that fall. And during the next fifteen months his life would undergo profound changes.

The first and most devastating change was "the feaver" that afflicted

Shickellamy's family throughout the autumn. Weiser arrived in Shamokin on October 9 to find "Shikalamy in such a miserable Condition as ever my Eyes beheld; he was hardly able to stretch forth his Hand to bid me welcome." His wife was just as sick; four of his children and two or three grandchildren were little better; a son-in-law, a daughter-in-law, and one grandchild had succumbed a few days before. After a dose or two of Weiser's medicine, Shickellamy was strong enough to hobble about with the help of a stick. But while Weiser left the village on October 12, the fever did not. By winter more than eleven members of the family were dead, including Shickellamy's wife, five of Tachnechdorus's children, and three of Soyechtowa's.[46]

More ominous still, one of those dead grandchildren, the four-year-old daughter of Soyechtowa and his Mahican wife, had not succumbed to the fever; she had been bewitched by a Delaware. "The sorcerer, the sorcerer has stolen my child from me," the mother "sang and cried."[47] After building a coffin, painting the corpse, and surrounding it with goods for the next world—moccasins as well as a needle, thread, and leather to make new ones; "flint, steel, and tinder" for building a fire; a kettle to hang above it; and bear meat and corn to cook in the pot—at last the family buried the child, all the while broadcasting to the whole town their accusation. "Wake up, my child, arise and eat," the Mahican woman "wept and sang," sitting beside the grave; "for five days ye have tasted no food—this my child was killed by the sorcerer!" (Jordan 1905:173–74).

Death had been no stranger to Shickellamy before that terrible autumn—he had lost two sons in the Catawba wars, and Virginians had killed a cousin[48]—but this episode was different. Not only was a Delaware conjurer at work to gain revenge on Shickellamy for his attempted coup, but before winter the mourned outnumbered the mourners, irreparably tearing the fabric of the family. To make matters worse, hunger accompanied disease, because with so many sick or dead and so many others in mourning the ordinary round of subsistence ground to a halt. Horses got into the corn. Clothing went to "Indian Doctors" in the vain hope that they could find a cure for Shickellamy's kin. Cajadies, his daughter's husband, who had been "recon'd the best Hunter among all the Indians," was dead, and those still alive had their hunting curtailed by sickness and mourning.[49]

"I cannot see how the poor old Man can live," Weiser wrote to Philadelphia. Reminding his superiors that Shickellamy "has been a true Servant to the Government and may perhaps still be, if he lives to do well again," the colonial go-between asked the provincial council to send help (MPCP [5]:138). When Shickellamy arrived at Weiser's in late November to pick up the food and clothing, he met his next crisis.[50] With Weiser were ten Indians from the Ohio Country, on their way home from Philadelphia. At the provincial capital, in the first official contact between Pennsylvania and the Delawares, Iroquois, Shawnees, and other peoples of the Ohio, they had told the provincial council of their war with the French and asked for English assistance (Aquila 1983:193–99; McConnell 1992: ch.4). When, at Weiser's, "the Ohio Indians repeated to Shikalamy what had pass'd at Philadelphia," the Oneida pronounced himself "mightily pleas'd."[51] In fact, he must have been appalled. Here was Weiser, his old companion, talking with other Iroquois; here was another Oneida, Scarouyady, who aspired to become the Shickellamy of the Ohio peoples; and here was news that Pennsylvania was encouraging this new relationship by planning to send Weiser west the following spring with gifts and words of friendship. The axis of common interest and common enterprise that Shickellamy had fashioned, running from Onondaga to Philadelphia by way of his house at Shamokin, was now in danger of being realigned.[52]

By spring Shickellamy had recovered enough from the surprise (and the fever) to launch a campaign aimed at putting a stop to these negotiations. When Weiser, in late March, "wanted to consult with him about the Journey to Ohio," the Oneida gave him plenty of advice. "[T]he Journey to Ohio wou'd," he insisted, "avail but little." He had learned from "several free Conversations" with an Indian in that November delegation who had wintered on the Susquehanna that in fact the Ohio peoples had not declared war on the French. Moreover, they would not do so until Onondaga did, for, Shickellamy had this native say, the Ohio Indians "were altogether subject to the Six Nations." Besides, he went on, Weiser must not leave Pennsylvania now; word had just come to Shamokin that the council at Onondaga was sending, "early this Spring," a delegation to Philadelphia "to treat about some Business of Consequence."[53]

These words bought the Oneida several months, time enough to send his son Tachnechdorus to Onondaga with the news of Pennsylvania's western enterprise. By July, when Tachnechdorus returned (alone), time was running out. Shickellamy invited Weiser to Shamokin "to be Informed of what passes among the 6 Nations," but by then it was too late; Weiser was about to head west. On July 20 the Ohio Indians forced the issue, arriving more than fifty strong in Lancaster for a treaty (PA 1st Series [2]:8–12; MPCP [5]:300, 307–19, 327). By the end of August, Weiser was at Logstown on the Ohio River to raise the Union Jack, join Indians in a toast to the king's health, and establish a relationship with Pennsylvania's newest friends (P.A.W. Wallace 1945: ch.32).

The current of events was now running strong against Shickellamy. "He is not alltogether pleased with my Journey to Ohio," reported Weiser that July in something of an understatement, "nor is he much liked by the Indians on that place" (PA 1st Series [2]:8). Ironically, in a sense the Oneida was a victim of his own success. His help in weakening the hold of Delawares in Pennsylvania—help that drove many of them west of the mountains—created a new alignment of people with little use and less love for Onondaga, or for Shickellamy.

By the early fall of 1748, then, Shickellamy's world looked very different than it had only a year earlier. His children had survived the epidemic, but their mother—and many of their children—had not.[54] Now Conrad Weiser, the man with whom he had worked closely for almost twenty years, was raising the glass with other "viceroys" and declining invitations to hear the latest news from Onondaga.

In this avalanche of unhappy events, while Shickellamy watched his family be destroyed and his work unravel, one thing endured: the missionaries' generosity and devotion. Indeed, during these months the Moravians even stepped up their campaign to win Shickellamy over. In January 1748 Bishop Cammerhoff, braving treacherous paths in the dead of winter, visited Shamokin to resolve problems with the blacksmith's business, give Shickellamy presents, and draw up a set of rules for the missionaries to follow (Jordan 1905:160–79). In June those missionaries, honoring Shickellamy's repeated requests, set to work fencing his fields.[55] And that October came another prominent visitor, Bishop John de Watteville, with a gift from the Moravians' leader and the promise of salvation from the Moravians' god. A month later Shickellamy, setting aside his fear that "it is too cold for him to travel,"[56] followed the bishop back to Bethlehem. There he received daily instruction in the faith, and finally embraced the Moravian way. He was not baptized—his earlier Catholic baptism precluded that—but "in token of his entry into the Christian communion, he was persuaded to throw away the 'manitou' he wore around his neck as a charm to keep off sickness."[57]

Why did the man choose the path that led to Bethlehem and to Christ?

No one can measure grief or assess its effect on another's life; to do so with an Oneida dead almost 250 years would be as presumptuous as it would be preposterous. Nor can we plumb the depths of Shickellamy's heart in order to test his sincerity. What can be said is that the personal and political ground he stood upon had, over the past year, shifted beneath his feet. Almost the only constant, besides the rhythm of the seasons and the Susquehanna flowing past his door, was the Moravians' attention and affection. It may have helped the missionaries' cause that Weiser, having had a falling out with Zinzendorf's flock, now hated them as much as they hated him, and that Shickellamy knew this.[58] Whether the chance to slight Weiser made the prospect of conversion even more attractive is unknown, of course. But at Bethlehem that fall, the Moravians did nothing to hide their dislike of Weiser, even telling Shickellamy that the man had, from the first, opposed their labors at Shamokin. Shickellamy knew that, they said, "for Conr. Weiser followed the evil Spirit" (quoted in P.A.W. Wallace 1945:255).

In late November, with a new faith and without that amulet to ward off sickness, Shickellamy left Bethlehem for Shamokin. He fell ill on the road, and barely made it home before dying in early December. The Moravians with him near the end reported that he died with "a bright smile illumining his countenance."[59] They did not say whether behind the smile he was wondering whether his failure to recover from this, the last of his many bouts with illness, had anything to do with his decision to discard that charm in Bethlehem.

Between Two Fires

In Shickellamy's last hours, "old as well as young wept about their old father," and occasionally "a pitiful cry" could be heard (Shamokin Diary, 6 Dec. 1748, MA 6/121/4/3). The entire town—including the missionaries—attended the burial three days later. Into the coffin that the Moravians had built for the occasion went items he could use in the next life. In that other world Shickellamy would be what he had been in this: an Iroquois man of the late colonial era and a go-between. On his fingers would be copper rings, on his wrists copper and brass bracelets, on his leggings, small bells. He could paint his face with the vermilion in a stone cup, and fill his clay pipe with tobacco from an iron box. He ventured forth into the next life equipped with line for fish, arrowheads and a musket for game, and a scalping knife for enemies. If in his celestial travels he met a colonist, he could display the colonial medal he had brought. Perhaps the two would sit down together to smoke from the Oneida's iron peace pipe or to take a swig from his long-necked glass bottle. Perhaps, too, Shickellamy would take in hand a string of the glass, bone, and amber beads buried with him and begin yet another of the conversations that had defined the later years of his life.[60]

Those Shickellamy had left behind when he began his journey from this world to the next found that there was much to mourn. The delicate balance of interests that the Oneida had helped to establish and to maintain, the balance that had helped to banish from the Pennsylvania-Iroquois frontier the ghosts of Opechancanough and Metacom, was overturned soon after his death, and the darkness of the late 1720s began to close in on the region once again. Out in the Ohio Country, Pennsylvania's new initiatives competed with Virginia's and clashed with French ambitions, ultimately leaving both Philadelphia and Onondaga on the sidelines to watch the peoples their collaboration had driven west now defend a new homeland from British and French campaigns.[61] Closer to home, colonial settlers were moving up the Susquehanna River Valley at an alarming rate. In 1755 these two developments—the contest in the Ohio and the encroachment of Pennsylvanians—combined to foment brutal conflict on the Pennsylvania frontier that left Shamokin and the world Shickellamy had built in ashes.

In the aftermath of Shickellamy's death, colonists and Indians, unable to see what was coming, tried to carry on business as usual. The following spring, Conrad Weiser tapped Tachnechdorus, Shickellamy's eldest surviving son, to "follow the foot steps of his deceased father, . . . and to be our true Corespondent" (PA 1st Series [2]:23). But the path Shickellamy had trod was harder to follow after 1748, as Logstown eclipsed Shamokin and colonial farmers planted crops ever closer to Shickellamy's grave. Over the next few years, Tachnechdorus and his brothers—squabbling with one another, in debt to colonial traders, impoverished by the hordes of visitors to Shamokin—spent less time at "our old place" at the junction of the Susquehanna's two great branches (PA 1st Series [2]:776). When the wave of attacks by Ohio Indians swept over the region in October 1755, Shickellamy's family was caught in the middle. The Indians who had so hated Shickellamy now forced his children and their families to join them on the

North Branch, a staging ground for further raids on Pennsylvania. Any thoughts of escaping to Pennsylvania were discouraged, both by the Ohio warriors' threats of reprisal and by the fear that colonists would attack any Indian, even Shickellamy's kin, who dared cross the frontier. In the fall of 1756, a year into this long struggle, Soyechtowa (James Logan) sent a wampum string across that frontier to Conrad Weiser, with the words "that he (Shayetowah) had quite lost himself being between two Fires (meaning that War was carrying on each side of him, and he did not know what part to act)."[62] For twenty years Soyechtowa's father had made a life of going back and forth between those two fires—one at Philadelphia, the other at Onondaga—and always knew what part to act. But that part, that act, could not be sustained in a world where the gulf between peoples was widening, not narrowing.

Notes

1. I am grateful to Michael McConnell and Francis Jennings for reading an earlier draft of this essay, and to Carolyn Libretti for assistance with translation of the Moravian records.

2. Carter 1931:28. For the three names, see MPCP (3):435 and (4):80, 584.

3. Carter 1931:28 (Anglicized). Hanna 1911(1):192n; Beauchamp 1916a:603; P.A.W. Wallace 1945:39; Fenton 1987:79 (Delaware). There is also a possibility it was Shawnee. "Shickellimy is what the Shawnees call him," wrote one Moravian missionary. See MA 6/121/10/1. Another Moravian noted that Shickellamy "is known in Iroquois" as "Swatana," a "name he much prefers, instead of Shickellamy" (Travel Diary, 12 Oct. 1748, MA 30/225/2/1). If that was indeed the Oneida's preference, only the Moravians noted it, and only they (occasionally) used it. Weiser, the Iroquois, and others who knew the man consistently called him Shickellamy, and I continue that convention here.

4. Reichel 1870 (1):83n (wolf); P.A.W. Wallace 1945:40 (turtle); MA 6/121/10/1 (bear).

5. Bartram 1751:17; James Logan to William Logan, April 1748, James Logan Papers (APS), vol. 4:139 (French). Sipe 1927:122 (Cayuga). Jennings 1985:43 (Cayuga-French). Carter 1931:29 (Susquehannock). See also Beauchamp 1916a: 601–2 (Canadian Iroquois). Despite the assertions by John Bartram and James Logan that Shickellamy was French, I am with others in doubting this. While it may be true that he had been baptized, it is less clear that he was born to French parents. Many travelers on the Pennsylvania frontier in these years noticed Indians who were of French extraction—the Montour family being only the most famous example—and neither Conrad Weiser nor the Moravians nor anyone else remarked upon Shickellamy as being anything but Iroquois. In any case, this is

something of a moot point, since Shickellamy never asserted or implied any connection to the French.

6. MPCP (4):743; Hanna 1911(1):110; Carter 1931:28 (deputy). Aquila 1983: 180 (ombudsman). Reichel 1870(1):67; Carter 1931:41; Jennings 1965:193 (viceroy). Hanna 1911(1):110; Sipe 1927:123; Aquila 1983:179 (vice-regent). Hanna 1911(1):110 and 149; Sipe 1927:122 (overlord). Fenton 1985:26 (overseer); Aquila 1983:174 (ambassador). Loskiel 1794(2):119 (first magistrate).

7. MPCP (3):330. See also MPCP (3):404; PA 1st Series (1):228. James Logan to the Penns, 6 mo. [Aug.] 1731, Logan Letterbook (3):342, Logan Papers (HSP).

8. See Breen 1984:197.

9. See Aquila 1983: Ch. 6; Jennings 1966:406–24; Jennings 1984: Part 3; Jennings 1987:75–91; P.A.W. Wallace 1981: Ch. 14–16.

10. PA 1st Series (1):205–6. For a summary of the events of these years, see Jennings 1984:304–7.

11. Such a representative was not uncommon in the lands around Iroquoia. Some years earlier the Delawares had hosted another Iroquois chief, and some years later other Iroquois headed into the Ohio Country to serve in a similar capacity. For an earlier representative, see Jennings 1987:80, 82; for a later one, see McConnell 1992:75.

12. Weiser to James Logan, 2[?] Sept. 1736, Logan Papers (HSP), vol. 10, folder 59. Other prominent Iroquois in the region, such as the warrior Currundawanah, were often Oneidas.

13. MPCP (3):504. In addition, obstacles and hazards on the trail that drove other men to despair left Shickellamy unfazed. See Muhlenberg 1853:9–10, 18–19.

14. Quotation from MPCP (7):200. On the range of conference types, see Fenton 1985:27. See also Foster 1985:99–114.

15. MPCP (4):661. We know about this conversation only because Weiser was there and recorded it; undoubtedly there were many more he did not see or did not mention.

16. We may surmise that he also taught the Iroquois colonial ways, but unfortunately that curriculum has not survived in the records, for obvious reasons.

17. MPCP (4):434; see also MPCP (3):500.

18. MPCP (5):137; see also PA 1st Series (1):758.

19. Weiser to [Richard Peters?], 24 Jan. 1745/6, Du Simitiere Papers, 966.F.24. See also MPCP (4):650, (5):84, 212.

20. MPCP (3):500–3, 511–12. Philadelphia officials wondered later if Shickellamy had told the truth when he affirmed that they were Indian scalps. A year later Lt. Gov. William Gooch of Virginia again reported that Conoys had taken two colonists' scalps, a claim that seemed so similar it confused Pennsylvania authorities. It appears, however, that this was indeed a second, separate case. This time Pennsylvania sent not Shickellamy but local frontier officials to investigate; it is unclear, however, whether this reflected some mistrust of the Oneida or simple convenience (MPCP [3]:564–65, 605–7; PA 1st Series [1]:436–39).

21. The background for this incident is in P.A.W. Wallace 1945:175. Unless otherwise indicated, all citations relating to this incident can be found in MPCP (4):680–85, 698–737, 742–52; PA 1st Series (1):643–55; Conrad Weiser's Acct. of his Journey to Shamokin, May 2d 1744, Papers of the Provincial Council, Executive Correspondence, microfilm, Roll B2, No. 377.

22. Muhlenberg 1853:11–13; Bartram 1751:63 (squabble); Marshe 1884:21–22 (treaty). The editor's explanation is that Shickellamy was serving Pennsylvania's interests against Maryland's claim; Marshe thought that some colonist put him up to it to get more money from Maryland. It is also possible that Shickellamy knew that he could get more for the land, or that the treaty included the Ohio Country, too, which the Indians had not intended to relinquish (Jennings 1984:361–62).

23. Shamokin Diary, 19 Feb. 1748, MA 6/121/4/1; see also 18 Sept. 1745, MA 28/217/12B/1.

24. MPCP (3):503, 581; PA 1st Series (1):455; Logan to Shickellamy, 10 Oct. 1735, Papers of the Provincial Council, Executive Correspondence, Microfilm, Roll B2, No. 241.

25. MPCP (3):435, 511–15, 577–82; Weiser to Logan, 16 Sept. 1736, Logan Papers (HSP), vol. 10, folder 62.

26. MPCP (3):337 (gun and shirt); MPCP (3):504 (wheat); MPCP (5):223 (pieces of eight); Penn Family Papers, Indian Affairs (1):46 (saddle and hand vice); PA 1st Series (1):661 (log house). For other gifts of food, see Penn Family Papers, Indian Affairs (1):46; Correspondence of Conrad Weiser (1):11; PA 1st Series (1):758.

27. PA 1st Series (1):241; Correspondence of Conrad Weiser (1):11; MPCP (5):136–39, 152.

28. Shamokin Diary, 5 Mar. 1748, MA 6/121/4/1 (not enough room); 31 Oct. 1745, MA 28/217/12B/1 (Shawnee and Mahican); 25 Sept. 1745, MA 28/217/12B/1 (English visitor). Apparently there were other houses in town designated for visitors (Jordan 1905:177). Weiser wrote that Shickellamy had hired this crew; however, its arrival shortly after the settlement of the Armstrong-Mushemeelin affair makes one wonder if it was actually a reward for his services to the province.

29. For general treatments of Moravian missionary efforts, see Gray and Gray 1956; K. Hamilton 1951; McHugh 1966; Olmstead 1991.

30. According to Andrew Montour, Weiser advised him to tell the Moravians to stay with the Montours at first, not with Shickellamy (Shamokin Diary, 16 Sept. 1745, MA 28/217/12B/1). It is unclear why Weiser favored the Montours at this point.

31. See Shamokin Diary, 16 Sept.–3 Nov. 1745, MA 28/217/12B/1; Carter 1937:64.

32. Reichel 1870(1):65, 86; Jordan 1905:177–78; Shamokin Diary, 24 Oct. 1745, MA 28/217/12B/1.

33. Jordan 1905:177; Travel Diary, 13 Oct. 1748, MA 30/225/2/1; De Schweinitz 1870:149n.

34. Shamokin Diary, 7 and 13 Dec. 1747 (feed children and grandchildren),

MA 6/121/3/3. For sharing meals, see the Shamokin Diary, Jan.–Apr. 1748, MA 6/121/4/1.

35. Jordan 1878–79:57; Carter 1937:63; MA 6/121/10/1.

36. Jordan 1905:173; Shamokin Diary, 28 Oct., 25 Dec. 1747, MA 6/121/3/3; 29 Jan., 7 Mar. 1748, MA 6/121/4/1.

37. Carter 1937:66–68; Jordan 1905:177; Shamokin Diary, 4 May 1748, MA 6/121/4/2.

38. Jordan 1905:172, 174. See also De Schweinitz 1870:144; MA 6/121/10/10.

39. Shamokin Diary, 31 Oct. 1745, MA 28/217/12B/1. The name is in 6 Mar. 1748, MA 6/121/ 4/1, when a missionary recalled that the Shawnee "tould Shekellame . . . that we ware like Piggons if he suffer'd a paire hear to reside thay'd Draw to them whole Troopes and take from him all his Land." For Shickellamy's habit of handling such critics in this fashion, see Loskiel 1794 (2):119.

40. 25 and 26 Mar. 1748, MA 6/121/4/1; P.A.W. Wallace 1945:255, 272, 274.

41. Travel Diary, 14 Oct. 1748, MA 30/225/2/1. On his drinking habits, see Loskiel 1794(2):119.

42. For complaints about rum by other Shamokin leaders, see MPCP (3):405–6, 578; by Shickellamy, MPCP (3):501–2. While Shickellamy told Moravians in October 1748 that he *no longer* drank, implying that he had earlier joined Indians in drinking bouts, I have found no mention of that in the Moravian accounts or any other source.

43. Weiser to [Peters?], 24 Jan. 1745/6, Du Simitiere Papers, 966.F.24. Shickellamy apparently feuded with another family that had ties to the French, the Montours. Though he and the Montour family shared Shamokin in the mid-1740s, though he and Andrew Montour traveled to Onondaga together, Weiser reported after Shickellamy's death that the two families had never gotten along (Weiser to Peters, 7 Feb. 1754, Berks and Montgomery Counties, Miscellaneous Manuscripts, 1693–1869:55). The relationship between these two families merits further investigation.

44. Jordan 1905:175–76; MPCP (4):681; Carter 1937:65 (quotation).

45. MPCP (5):88. See also PA 1st Series (1):762. Moravians visiting Shamokin and Sassoonan in June 1745 noted that "[h]is sister's sons are either dead or worthless. . . . " (Jordan 1878–79:430). The best accounts of Pennsylvania and Iroquois treatment of the Delawares—and especially of the Shamokin Delawares—in these years are Jennings 1968 and 1965: esp. 193.

46. Jordan 1905:173–74; MPCP (5):136–38; Shamokin Diary, Oct.–Dec. 1747, MA 6/121/3/3, especially 21 Oct., 20 and 23 Nov.

47. Shamokin Diary, 20–21 Nov. 1747, MA 6/121/3/3. This may have been the second child of this woman's killed. See Loskiel 1794(2):102. Memories of this incident lasted for generations. See A. F. C. Wallace 1969:256.

48. PA 1st Series (1):241, 665–66; MPCP (4):641; Travel Diary, 14 Oct. 1748, MA 30/225/2/1.

49. MPCP (5):136, 138; Jordan 1905:175. Some did make a brief hunting trip (Shamokin Diary, 2, 4 Dec. 1747, MA 6/121/3/3).

50. MPCP (5):152, 162; William Logan to Weiser, 20, 21 Oct. 1747, Richard Peters Papers, 2:83–84.

51. MPCP (5):162, 166–67. The Philadelphia meeting is recorded in MPCP (5):145–50.

52. Pennsylvania officials had consulted Shickellamy on Ohio affairs earlier, in 1740 and 1744. See MPCP (4):432, 732.

53. MPCP (5):212, 222. I have used quotations from his reports to Weiser and to the council.

54. Shickellamy neither visited his wife during her final illness nor attended her funeral. Shamokin Diary, 21 Oct. 1747, MA 6/121/3/3. I have been unable to determine the significance of this absence. He was remarried to a Tutelo woman sometime before October 1748. See Travel Diary, 12, 15 Oct. 1748, MA 30/225/2/1.

55. For his requests, see Shamokin Diary, 31 Jan., 9 Mar., 24 Apr., 1, 13, 15 May 1748, MA 6/121/4/1, and 4/2. The Moravians started his fence on 9 June and finished it before the fall. Travel Diary, 13 Oct. 1748, MA 30/225/2/1.

56. De Schweinitz 1870:146–50; Travel Diary, 13–15 Oct. 1748, MA 30/225/2/1, quotation at 15 Oct.

57. P.A.W. Wallace 1945:274. See also P.A.W. Wallace 1945:255, 272. Carter (1937:71) argues that the conversion occurred at Shamokin. The Travel Diary suggests that the missionaries talked to Shickellamy about conversion, but makes no mention of his acceptance. See also Loskiel 1794(2):120; De Schweinitz 1870:149.

58. P.A.W. Wallace 1945: chs. 29, 31. See also Weiser to Peters, 21 Nov. 1748, Logan Papers (APS), vol. 4, 141.

59. De Schweinitz 1870:150; Shamokin Diary, 6 Dec. 1748, MA 6/121/4/3.

60. The contents of a grave on the site of Shamokin excavated by a local man in 1860 are listed in Carter (1931:52). It "was," Carter wrote, "thought to be the remains of Shikellamy." That the corpse was the only one of twenty-five burials excavated to have been buried in a wooden coffin would seem to confirm Carter's surmise, but no definitive conclusion as to this person's identity can be reached. See also Kent 1989:101 (for the type of medal, see Fig. 84); Shamokin Diary, 9 Dec. 1748, MA 6/121/4/3.

61. In the spring of 1749 Weiser found "the Indians . . . very uneasy about the white people's Setling beyond the Endless mountains on Joniady [the Juniata River], on Sherman's Creek and Else where; they tell me that above 30 familys are setled upon the Indians' land this spring, and dayly more goes to setle thereon" (PA 1st Series [2]:24). For the clash in the Ohio Country, see McConnell 1992; Jennings 1988; White 1991: chs. 5–6.

62. MPCP (7):282. For the later careers of Shickellamy's sons, see Weiser to Peters, 13 Oct. 1753, Richard Peters Papers (3):77; Beauchamp 1916b:194; J. T. Hamilton 1936:442, 444; K. Bailey 1947:154; Weiser to Peters, 7 Feb. 1754, Berks and Montgomery Counties, Miscellaneous Manuscripts, 1693–1869:55; P.A.W. Wallace 1945:355–56 *et passim;* MPCP (6):615–16, 649–50; (7):34, 47–54, 65, 244–45; PA 1st Series (2):259–60, 615–16, 634, 647, 776–78.

Chapter Twelve

꩜

Moses (Tunda) Tatamy, Delaware Indian Diplomat

William A. Hunter

On July 26, 1742, Count Ludwig von Zinzendorf, patron of the Moravian Church, set out from Nazareth, Pennsylvania, with his companions on the Count's first visit to the Indians. After three miles' ride, traveling northeast, they

> came to Moses Tatemy's reserve (near Stockertown, in Forks Township). Tatemy was a Delaware from New Jersey, professed Christianity, and was farming in a small way on a grant of 300 acres given him by the Proprietaries' agents, in consideration of services he had rendered as interpreter and messenger to the Indians. He received them well, was communicative, and, in course of conversation, gave an account of the mode of sacrifice practiced by his heathen brethren. (Reichel 1870:26–27)

Mentioned often and favorably in Pennsylvania records of the French and Indian War period, Moses Tatamy (originally Tunda Tatamy) was an Indian of some distinction: a private landowner, a Presbyterian, and a skilled interpreter, he assisted missionaries, colonial officials, fellow Indians, and Quaker politicians, and retained the respect and confidence of all. He is commemorated to the present day in the name of the village of

Reprinted from *A Delaware Indian Symposium*, ed. Herbert C. Kraft, Anthropological Series, vol. 4 (Harrisburg: Pennsylvania Historical and Museum Commission, 1974), by permission of publisher.

Tatamy, situated just south of the tract of land he once owned in North-hampton County, Pennsylvania.[1]

Later references provide few clues to Tatamy's early life. According to an estimate of his age in 1745, he was born in about 1695 (D. Brainerd 1822:210); and if we also accept a later estimate of Teedyuscung's age (PA, 1st ser. [2]:725), Tatamy was about ten years older than his more notorious associate and fellow tribesman. Both men were known to be from New Jersey, and Tatamy's early home is identified somewhat more precisely in the records of a 1758 conference at which he claimed an interest in lands near and east of Allentown, New Jersey (PA, 1st ser. [3]:344). (Teedyuscung had an interest in one of the same tracts.) In Pennsylvania these Delawares were commonly identified as "Jersey Indians" or, since a number of them lived for a time about the forks of the Lehigh and Delaware Rivers, as "Forks Indians." Their earliest known chief man in Pennsylvania was "King" Nutimus.

Tatamy's first appearance in Pennsylvania records seems to be in 1733, when he applied for his grant of land. The entry, under date of March 24, 1733, records that: "Tattemy an Indian has improv'd a piece of Land of about 300 Acres on the fforks of Delaware—he is known to Wm Allen & Jere: Langhorne—he desires a Grant for the said Land" (Pennsylvania Land Records, Applications 1732–33:17). Very few Indians became private landowners in provincial Pennsylvania, and of these few Tatamy appears to be the first. A warrant for the survey was issued on December 30, 1736, and a patent to "Tundy Tetamy one of our Indian Friends" was granted by the proprietaries on April 28, 1738 (Pennsylvania Land Records, Patent Book A8:405–6).

Tatamy's application was endorsed by two prominent men. Langhorne, a Quaker, was then chief justice of the province, a position he held from 1726 until his death in 1742 (Bucks 1883). Allen, a much younger man and a Presbyterian, was then an assemblyman but later also served as chief justice, from 1750 to 1774 (A. Johnson 1943[1]:208–9). Both men, Allen especially, became early landowners in the "Forks" area (Chidsey 1937: Maps).

Tatamy's acquisition of land coincided with negotiations for the so-called "Walking Purchase" of 1737; and that he himself had a minor role in these negotiations is shown by the Penn account books where, under date of May 7, 1735, in a record of "Sundrys Sent to Pennsbury for the Indian Treaty now held there," appears the item, "To Tetamy for going on

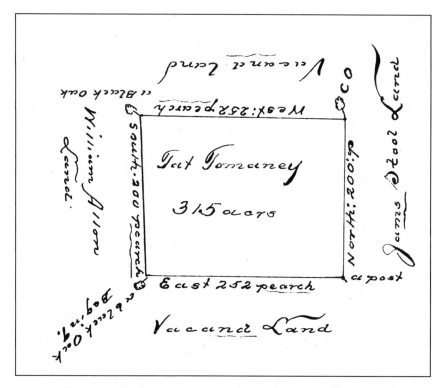

Reproduced with permission of the Pennsylvania State Archives.

a Message 20/—" (Pennsylvania Land Records, Surveyor General Journals: C[1]:69).

Technically, the Walking Purchase of 1737 was the confirmation of a sale negotiated, but not consummated, fifty years earlier; and the circumstances of the Jersey Indians' involvement in this belated confirmation seem to have been something of a puzzle to everyone concerned. These Indians not only had not been living in Pennsylvania at the time of the original negotiations; most of them had not even been *living* in 1686. Neither party, whites nor Indians, understood the basis for the other's claim to the land in question.

The Walking Purchase is far too complicated a subject to be covered in the present paper, and Tatamy did not live to hear the end of it. The purchase was to extend as far as a man could go (the deed did not say walk) in a day and a half; and there must have been little doubt, to the white negotiators at least, that it would take in the Forks lands up to the Blue Mountain. Indians complained of the unseemly haste of the walkers who measured the purchase, but there seems to have been no immediate and general outcry over the deal. The proprietaries had reserved a 6500-acre tract including the chief Indian village in the area (Chidsey 1937: Maps); and in the following year Nutimus, who had opposed the treaty, made a friendly visit to Thomas Penn at his Pennsbury home (MPCP [4]:312).

On January 2, 1742, Tatamy was granted a new patent for his land in fee simple (Pennsylvania Land Records, Patent Book A9:530–32), and in July, as has been noted, he was visited there by Count Zinzendorf. A shadow overhung the Count's peaceful picture of the place, however, for the relative quiet that had first followed the Walking Purchase was disturbed as the earlier residents of this region, Indians and white squatters alike, found themselves hemmed in by proprietary land grants. In 1740–41 protests were made—in the Indians' names but written by white settlers— including a rash threat of action by the Delawares and their Indian allies (MPCP [4]:481; [8]:255).[2] The province retaliated by calling upon the Six Nations for support; and they, taking full advantage of the opportunity, ordered the Delawares to vacate the lands they had sold and to remove to Wyoming or Shamokin (present Wilkes-Barre and Sunbury) under Iroquois supervision (MPCP [4]:575–86).

The Iroquois ultimatum was delivered at Philadelphia only a few days before Count Zinzendorf's visit with Tatamy. The Forks Indians countered by asking to be allowed, as Christians, to live among the English in "Enjoyment of the same Religion & Laws with them." Tatamy and Captain John (Teedyuscung's half-brother), who submitted the petition, were sufficiently acculturated to print their initials as signatures, and Tatamy (as Zinzendorf had noted) professed to be a Christian. When the two Indians appeared before the governor and his council on November 20, the officials were in no indulgent mood, however. They found the Indians' replies to religious questions unsatisfactory, they rejected the petition, and they permitted Tatamy and Captain John themselves to remain in the Forks only with Iroquois approval (MPCP [4]:624–25).[3]

This unsettling experience probably whetted the Indians' concern over the status of the lands they claimed, and still occupied in part, in New Jersey. By a deed dated February 21, 1743, four of the Jersey Indians gave power of attorney to their "Trusty and well beloved Friends (Tundy Tetamy and Captain John)" to search out and sell their New Jersey lands, and on January 30, 1744, two other Indians gave Tatamy similar authority. These claims were not settled until fifteen years later, however, and during the intervening time Tatamy found other occupations (PA, 1st Ser. [1]:630–31, 641–42; [3]:344).

In June 1744, the Presbyterian missionary David Brainerd, then twenty-six years old, came to preach in the Forks of Delaware, where he soon employed Tatamy as his interpreter. Tatamy, as Brainerd wrote later, was "well fitted for his work, in regard to his acquaintance with the Indian and English languages, as well as with the manners of both nations; and in regard to his desire that the Indians should conform to the manners and customs of the English, and especially to their manner of living." The interpreter and his wife were the first Indians Brainerd baptized, and the record of this event, on July 21, 1745, is the only place in his surviving writings that Brainerd identifies one of his Indians by name: "His name is MOSES FINDA FAUTAURY [*sic*]. He is about fifty years of age"; except that she too was baptized, the record says nothing of Tatamy's wife (D. Brainerd 1822:210–14). Their children were baptized five days later; Brainerd does not mention their names or number, but it is known from other sources that Tatamy had two sons, William and Nicholas, and a daughter named Jemima. In the year he spent in the Forks, Brainerd baptized twelve members of the dwindling Indian community there, and Tatamy's family provided five of these twelve (D. Brainerd 1822:245).

Until bad health ended his work near the end of 1746, Brainerd ministered to larger Indian groups near Crosswicks and Cranbury in New Jersey. Tatamy continued to serve as his interpreter, and accompanied him on four extended missionary journeys, one to Wapwallopen in October 1744; two to Shamokin (present Sunbury) in May and September 1745; and a final one, beyond Shamokin to the Great Island (near present Lock Haven) in August and September 1746. David Brainerd was succeeded in the New Jersey mission by his brother John, whom Tatamy probably accompanied on a journey to Wyoming in May 1751 (T. Brainerd 1865:231–38).[4]

In Pennsylvania, on the other hand, the Moravians took over the Indian mission field and in 1745–46 established themselves at Shamokin and Gnadenhütten (present Lehighton and Weissport, in Carbon County). Some of the Forks Indians were attracted to these missions. Teedyuscung was baptized at Gnadenhütten in 1750, but later removed to Wyoming (A. F. C. Wallace 1990:39–47). Tatamy did not join the Moravians, but his relations with them were friendly, and there are records of his sons' visits to the missions in 1752 and 1753. "Billy Dedeemi," because he could read and write, was noticed by the missionary Bernhard Grube, who tried, not very successfully, to get the young man to help him with the meaning of Delaware words.[5]

The year 1755 ushered in, for Indians and white settlers alike, a time of intense and troubled activity. It was not so much the unrest of Anglo-French hostilities as a concern about land, however, that in April of this year brought an Indian delegation from Wyoming to Philadelphia. They were headed by a Shawnee chief, Paxinosa, and the Delaware Teedyuscung; and Joseph Peepy, one of Brainerd's converts, was their interpreter (MPCP [6]:360 n). These Indians had settled at Wyoming under Iroquois supervision, and now they had heard that the Iroquois had sold this land to New Englanders who were coming to take possession.

Officially the Indians came to Philadelphia only "to brighten the chain of friendship," but they held informal discussions as well. Teedyuscung asked the Governor to inquire about "a small Pine Tract" he claimed in New Jersey (MPCP [7]:325); and Tatamy, who is not mentioned in the minutes, later recalled that when the Indians had grumbled among themselves about land difficulties, he had advised them to get a clerk who would record their agreements as the white men did. Teedyuscung's role in this episode is reminiscent of that played by his half-brother Captain John (who had died in 1747); and with his later controversial career in mind it is well to remember that Teedyuscung's concern for the Indians' lands antedated the inquiry into the Walking Purchase.

The shock of war came later in 1755, in the wake of Braddock's defeat, when French-incited Indians attacked white frontier settlers and attempted to coerce more peaceful Indians into joining them. In Tatamy's part of the country, this disturbance was climaxed by the hostile Indians' destruction of Gnadenhütten on the night of November 24, 1755 (W. Hunter 1960:168n.; Reichel 1870:197–203).

Tatamy then removed his family from the Forks into New Jersey for safety, and there gave a formal account of Indian affairs that was published in Benjamin Franklin's *Pennsylvania Gazette* (Tatamy 1755). In a later, more detailed statement, Tatamy said that

> I thought it no longer safe for me to continue on my Place in the Forks abt 3 Miles from Easton but went imediately on the other Side of the River & lived sometime wth Col Anderson . . . I left Anderson's being sent for to the Treaty at Croswicks [on January 8–9, 1756] after wch

I was settled for sometime at Maidenhead [now Lawrenceville, New Jersey] from whence I remov'd to Pennsbury. (Friends Philadelphia Yearly Meeting, D-14, Folders 65–66)

Here Tatamy was much more available, of course, as interpreter for provincial officials.

The Indian population was scattered. A small number, mostly mission Indians, sought refuge in the settled country; the rest, apprehensive of white retaliation for the attacks on the settlements, abandoned their homes on the Susquehanna and moved up the river to Tioga Point, on the present New York boundary. From here the more hostile moved to the Ohio; others, reluctant to commit themselves so fully, resettled on the Chemung and elsewhere on the borders of the Iroquois country. Teedyuscung, after a brief show of hostility, joined the latter group.

The province of Pennsylvania, too was divided by these events. The proprietary government sought to keep as many Indians as possible friendly or at least nonhostile, and took steps to defend the frontiers. The Quaker-dominated Assembly supported the pacification program, but its unwillingness to back military measures brought it severe criticism from both the governor and the frontier settlers. In self-defense a Quaker group headed by Israel Pemberton charged that the proprietors themselves had provoked the Indian hostilities by their unjust dealings: William Penn's children, who were not Quakers, had strayed, Pemberton and his followers said, from their father's path of rectitude in Indian affairs (T. Thayer 1943:97 n).

The Indians' loss of their lands would have been a cause of grief under any circumstances, and even in Pennsylvania they had at times been shabbily treated; nevertheless, the Pemberton thesis went too far, especially in ignoring the French role in inciting the Indians to hostility. And the Quaker politicans could not win an argument based on general principles; they needed a good, specific episode on which to rest their case; and after surveying the possibilities, they concluded that the 1737 Walking Purchase best suited their purpose.

At this point in the proceedings, Pemberton and his friends received the support of antiproprietary politicians such as Benjamin Franklin, who were motivated not at all by principles of pacifism and humanitarian regard for the Indians. These conflicts and the events to which they gave rise shaped Moses Tatamy's life for the next five years and involved him in work of an importance and difficulty well beyond that of the ordinary messenger and interpreter.

Shortly, some of the Indians reconsidered their hostile stand and sought to resume peaceful relations with the colonists, and in July 1756, Teedyuscung and a few companions ventured down to Easton, where to their undoubted relief they were welcomed by the authorities. This official friendliness is easily accounted for, however: Here was an opportunity to show the Indians the advantage of returning to the fold; here was a messenger who could carry peace offers to his fellow tribesmen; here, for the hard-pressed Quakers, was the very person, one of Nutimus's own followers, to accuse the proprietors of land fraud. Teedyuscung was courted on all sides—any debutante might have envied him; and when the party was over he went home to bring back more Indians for reconciliation.

Tatamy did not attend this July meeting, but he was at Easton, apparently as an interpreter, when Teedyuscung returned in November with a larger following—including some Munsee Delawares, who warily stopped at Fort Allen (the former Gnadenhütten), where despite an invitation delivered them by Tatamy they appraised the negotiations from a safe distance (MPCP [7]:318).

The mood of the treaty was edgy. Too many factions were present and too many schemes were afoot. Affability paled when the governor, at the Assembly's suggestion, asked Teedyuscung what had occasioned the Delawares' recent hostility and received in reply the Quaker-supported charge of land fraud. Tatamy was brought into the affair. On the following day, Sunday, November 14, the Quaker party obtained from him a traditional Delaware account of the Walking Purchase, of which they hoped to make use (Parrish 1877:34–35, 48; Etting Collection, Ms. 1, Folder 94). Tatamy had not thrown in his lot with Pemberton's group, however; and a few days later, when the conference was over, he discussed the proceedings with the proprietary Indian agent, Conrad Weiser.[6] Teedyuscung, he told Weiser, had departed from the speech agreed upon by the Indians; and he should have protested the Iroquois sale of the Wyoming lands, but was afraid to do so because some Iroquois were present at the treaty. Tatamy, for his part, appealed to Weiser to urge the governor to grant the Delawares "a large Tract of Land on Sasquehannah, and secure it so to their posterity that none of them could sell and nobody buy it" (MPCP [7]:431–33). Nor was Tatamy a blind follower of Teedyuscung; when a few days later, on December 2, he delivered a letter to the governor, Tatamy told him that "he believed Teedyuscung had little or no Authority among his own People, and [he] was always doubtful whether he was empowered by any other Nation" (MPCP [7]:357–58).

Indeed, the Presbyterian Tatamy, the lapsed Moravian Teedyuscung, and the contentious Quaker Pemberton constituted an odd ecumenical group. To account for their association, one needs to keep in mind the fact that each had, in his own way and for his own purposes, a deep concern over the Indians' loss of their land and a desire to secure them in the possession of some part of it.

Tatamy's caution regarding Teedyuscung was well-grounded. Both the proprietary and the Quaker parties were committed (for very different reasons) to backing Teedyuscung as their agent, however, and their favors assured him a mixed collection of Indian followers. The largely fortuitous prestige of this self-styled "king of ten nations" lasted through two more treaties at Easton, one in July and August 1757, which terminated the official state of war between Pennsylvania and the eastern Indians; and one in October 1758, at which this peace offer was extended to the Indians on the Ohio. Full accounts of these meetings are readily available; and the immediate interest lies in Moses Tatamy's part in them.

In advance of the 1757 treaty, Teedyuscung asked that Tatamy meet him at Wyoming, undoubtedly for the sake of a preliminary dealing with this problem (Friends Philadelphia Yearly Meeting, D-11, Folders 65–66; W. Bradford, ed. 1756), and in the following year the legislature had voted money to settle the Indian claims. On February 21–24, five New Jersey commissioners met at Crosswicks with some thirty Indians to define their claims (PA, 1st ser. [3]:341–46). New Jersey fortunately had no difficulty comparable to Pennsylvania's politically motivated inquiry into the Walking Purchase; unlike Pennsylvania, however, it had permitted private purchases from the Indians, and this made the ownership of individual tracts difficult to determine.

Accordingly, the Indians granted power of attorney to five of their number, Thomas Store, Moses Tatamy, Stephen Calvin, Isaac Still, and John Pumpshire, to transact their further business. All five were members of Brainerd's congregation, all but Tatamy belonged to the Cranbury community (the largest group present), and three of the five could write their names. Thomas Store used a mark that may have been intended for a letter *S;* Tatamy invariably used the printed initials MT. The five deputies, in turn, sent Tatamy and Still with a letter to Israel Pemberton, requesting his help in searching the records (Friends Philadelphia Yearly Meeting, D-11, Folders 351, 431).

These Indian deputies represented only the Delaware Indians (using this term in its narrower sense); and in northern New Jersey the Munsee (Minisink) and Wapping (or Pompton) Indians, most of whom had left the colony, had claims that the government also wished to settle. Accordingly, the governor employed Tatamy and Still to invite these Indians to a council at Burlington. The messengers left Philadelphia on June 27, but two days later met Teedyuscung on his way to that city; Still therefore turned back to accompany him, and Tatamy, with two Indian companions, traveled on to Aghsinsing (near present Painted Post, New York), where he delivered his message to the Munsee chief on July 7, returned to Philadelphia a week later, and his narrative of the journey, written from his dictation, is a valuable account, ethnologically as well as historically, of the Indians then living along the Chemung River (MPCP [8]:140; PA, 1st ser. [3]:504–8). Appropriately, Tatamy also acted as interpreter when a delegation of three Munsee, accompanied by a Seneca, came to Philadelphia and Burlington in early August to accept the invitation. The Seneca approved the arrangement but asked that the council be held at Easton, a familiar place for treaties, rather than in the "island" of New Jersey, and it was in fact held in October in conjunction with the Pennsylvania Indian treaty (MPCP [8]:149–53, 156–61).

In the meantime, Tatamy and his fellow deputies signed a treaty, on September 12, by which the Delawares sold their claims to all New Jersey lands south of the Raritan River and extending up the Delaware to the Water Gap. The 1600 pounds sterling they received in payment was used to buy them a three-thousand-acre tract in Burlington County, which they held until 1801. New Jersey's other Indian claims were settled a month later at Easton, where on October 16 representatives of the Munsee and Wapping tribes ceded their remaining lands north of the Raritan and the Delaware Water Gap (MPCP [8]:201–2, 208–11, 219–23; T. Brainerd 1865:308 n).

The Easton treaty of October 1758, which Tatamy attended as an interpreter, came at the end of Teedyuscung's greatest prestige. An Iroquois delegation formally denied his more extravagant claims to authority and land; the charge of land fraud, which he repeated, had been referred to the Crown and so removed from Pennsylvania jurisdiction; and his potential value as an intermediary with the western Indians had dwindled with the weakening French position on the Ohio.

The British victory at Pittsburgh, a month after the Easton treaty, brought Pennsylvania great benefits, especially freedom from the threat of hostile Indian attack. The way seemed open, moreover, for the province to deal directly once more with the Delawares and other Indians on the Ohio. The Quakers took a special interest in this matter, and the government was united in regarding such negotiations as a prerogative under the provincial charter and in resenting the appointment of Sir William Johnson as the Crown agent for the northern Indians. Accordingly, Israel Pemberton lent his support to the official project of establishing a Pennsylvania trading post at Pittsburgh (T. Thayer 1943:158–61, 171–76). The results were somewhat disappointing, however; the place was, as a military establishment, controlled by an officer under British command, and Johnson stationed his deputy, George Croghan, there to direct Indian affairs. Pennsylvania's plan to bring the Indians to Philadelphia for a treaty of reconciliation seemed completely frustrated.

A few months later, however, a situation developed that seemed to give Teedyuscung an opportunity to regain his waning prestige and Pennsylvania a chance to bypass Pittsburgh in transacting Indian affairs. The episode also provided the occasion for Moses Tatamy's last and most trying service to the Province. In early December 1759, Teedyuscung appeared at Philadelphia with news that an Indian council had been held at Aghsinsing, where messengers had invited tribal leaders (including Teedyuscung) to a great council to be held beyond the Ohio in April (MPCP [8]:415–23).

It appears from what later transpired that this great council was one of a series held at Sandusky between the eastern Indians (the Six Nations and their associates) and the western tribes that had been under French influence. Originally these councils may have been designed to renew relationships that had been disrupted by the French and Indian War, but they came to play a part in the preparations for Pontiac's War. They must have been intended for Indians only. Perhaps Teedyuscung did not at first understand this; perhaps he could not refrain from publishing the attention he had received. He did not object when the Governor and the Assembly proposed that the Moravian, Christian Frederick Post, accompany him and that Isaac Still go as an interpreter; he even asked that a second white man and Moses Tatamy be added to the party—the latter probably at Pemberton's suggestion. To dignify the undertaking and obtain a kind of official sanction, the governor asked the British commander, General Amherst, for a message to be read to the Indians at the great council (PA, 1st ser. [4]:48–49). The province outfitted Teedyuscung and two chiefs who were to accompany him, and the Quakers agreed, on Tatamy's request, to look after his daughter and "to get her boarded in a reputable house, where she may have the advantage of some schooling" (MPCP [8]:463–72; PA, 1st ser. [3]:707–9; Parrish 1877:117).

Misgivings about what he had undertaken may help explain why Teedyuscung set out so late on his journey. On April 22 the governor issued a passport for Post, his companion John Hays, Tatamy, and Still (PA, 1st ser. [3]:720–21); and two days later Tatamy and Still set out for Wyoming to give Teedyuscung advance notice of Post's departure. Post apparently expected to overtake them, but Tatamy seems to have felt some sense of urgency; and when Post got to Wyoming on May 10, the Indians had left without him earlier in the day and had to be called back. Then, after this premature start, Teedyuscung delayed a week repairing his garden fence. It was May 23 before they reached Aghsinsing, where they were delayed two weeks more trying to collect Indian leaders for a council. On June 1 Tatamy went on to Secaughcung (Canisteo) to invite the Unami Delawares at that place to come to a meeting, but they declined, and Seneca Indians living at that place threatened to roast Post and Hays if they continued their journey (W. Hunter 1954).

On June 7, nevertheless, the embassy went on to Secaughcung, where they stayed twelve futile days. The Seneca leader had in fact attended a western council two months before (in April) and was about to go again. The Indians of Teedyuscung's party might go on, he said, but the white men must turn back. Post therefore surrendered to Teedyuscung the responsibility of inviting the western Indians to Philadelphia; he kept General Amherst's message, however, and on June 19 he and Hays started home. Tatamy thereupon advised Teedyuscung that "he was afraid their whole affair would not turn out well." Teedyuscung replied that in that case Tatamy had better go home, too.

Tatamy, 65 years old, might easily have been excused for not continuing the long and dangerous (as well as unpromising) westward journey, but his sense of responsibility beset him. Three days on the way home, after telling Post "that the Friends trusted no body but him, & reposed their whole Confidence in him, if he shod return they wod blame him forever, seeing they expected to know the Truth by him" (so Post quoted him), Tatamy turned back to overtake Teedyuscung and the rest of the Indian delegation.

There is no reason to suppose that Teedyuscung was displeased by this turn of events. His agreement to take white men to the great council had been presumptuous, and he and Post had bickered over the leadership of the embassy; now, freed of this embarrassment and restraint, he, Teedyuscung, could make the decisions and claim the credit.

On July 10, Johnson's deputy, George Croghan, out to invite the Indians to a treaty at Pittsburgh, learned that Teedyuscung had passed that place on his westward journey (Chalmers Collection: Papers Relating to Philadelphia 1: Folder 19); and six days later Moses Tatamy and Isaac Still appeared at Pittsburgh itself to ask provisions for Teedyuscung's Indians, who were about to hold a meeting (Chalmers Collection: Papers Relating to Indians, 1750–75, Folder 9). Croghan, an Irishman, may have seen the funny side of this. There is no reason to believe that Teedyuscung ever got to the great western council at Sandusky; instead, near the end of July, he held a meeting of his own at the Salt Lick Town, a Delaware village near present Niles in eastern Ohio, where, to representatives of ten tribal groups, he delivered the Pennsylvania governor's invitation to Philadelphia. Probably some of the delegates to whom he spoke were then on their way to Croghan's treaty at Pittsburgh (Wainwright 1947:380; MPCP [8]:497).

In fact, Teedyuscung and his party also went there, arriving on August 5 for a treaty that was held from the 12th to the 18th (Wainwright 1947:383; PA, 1st ser. [3]:744–52). It opened, ironically, with the reading of General Amherst's message, carried back from Secaughcung to Philadelphia and then sent to Pittsburgh by the governor. Teedyuscung, who had no real business at the treaty and probably was aware of his own failure, behaved badly. Some western Indians had given him beaverskin blankets to be used instead of wampum in making speeches, but he sold these at the Provincial trading store (whose agent was not on good terms with either Croghan or the commanding officer) and got drunk on the proceeds (PA, 1st ser. [3]:744–52; Penn Family Manuscripts 3: Folders 91–92). The agent himself was barred from the treaty, but Tatamy translated the Indian speeches for him and afterward took to Philadelphia a letter in which the agent tried to defend himself (Friends Philadelphia Yearly Meeting D-13: Folder 515).

Israel Pemberton went up to Reading, hoping to meet Teedyuscung's party on their return to Philadelphia, but had to return home and sent another Friend, Benjamin Lightfoot, in his place. Lightfoot, arriving at Reading on September 7, found the Indians already there: "Moses Tatamy has a slight touch of the Flux," he reported (but by the next day, he added, was better); he invited Tatamy and Still to tea, and the Indians asked him to have Still's wife and Tatamy's daughter meet them in Philadelphia (Friends Philadelphia Yearly Meeting D-14: Folder 19).

Five days later, on a Saturday, Teedyuscung and his company met the governor in Philadelphia; they met with the Council in open meeting on Monday and had another private meeting on Tuesday. Tatamy was present, but at the open meeting Still was official interpreter. Only the formalities of this open meeting were recorded in the minute book, and the more vivid exchanges that must have taken place in the private sessions are left to imagination (MPCP [8]:497–501). Everyone had been caught with jam on his face. Ill-judged in planning, surreptitious and frustrated in execution, the attempt to exploit Teedyuscung's invitation had ended as a farce. Its only accomplishment, delivery of the invitation to the western Indians, bore tardy fruit in an inconclusive treaty at Lancaster in 1762.

In November Tatamy went to see Col. Andrew Johnston about his claim to a tract of land in New Jersey. Perhaps his health suffered more than had been realized. From Maidenhead he wrote on November 24 to Israel Pemberton: "I am Now at Mr Edmund Bainbridge . . . Very Sick & Expect to Die . . . I have made my Will & have made you & Mr John Bainbridge My Executors" (Friends Philadelphia Yearly Meeting D-14: Folder 55).

When Teedyuscung visited Philadelphia in the following April 1761, he was accompanied by Moses Tatamy's surviving son Nicholas who, several years later, in 1769, was granted a tract of land in "Consideration of the Services of his Father, an Interpreter and faithful Friend to this Province" (MPCP [8]:594; PA, 8th ser. [7]:6442–43).[7]

Two generations of Moses Tatamy's descendants are mentioned in later records. Little is known of his daughter, Jemima, although in February 1763, Israel Pemberton submitted a bill for a year's boarding for her. His son Nicholas, "of Easton Township," lived until 1784, when letters of administration were issued to his widow, Ann, and a son, Moses (Northampton County, Admin. File 1050, 1784). A 1789 lawsuit over Nicholas's land names Ann and two other sons, John and William (Pennsylvania Land Records, Exemplification of Recovery Role–John Brotzman v. Anne Tatamy, 1789). It would seem that by this date Moses had died or removed. The 1790 census lists "William Tatelme," of Easton, as head of a family comprising two free white males of sixteen years or older and one free white female; presumably these are William, John, and their mother (Bureau of the Census 1908:171). The 1800 census, however, lists only the "Widow Tatamy," a "free white female of 45 upwards," living alone; John and William also have gone (U.S. National Archives 1957: Roll 37, Pennsylvania Vol. 3, Northampton County, Borough of Easton). M. S. Henry, author of the 1860 *History of the Lehigh Valley,* says that "an aged gentleman of Easton, still living there, says he went to school with the two sons of [Nicholas] Tatamy, and that he had seen Tatamy's wife often, who was a white woman. The poor book of Easton of 1801 contains a record of her death and burial" (Henry 1860:50).[8]

Notes

William A. Hunter was Chief of the Division of History of the Pennsylvania Historical and Museum Commission, Harrisburg. Thanks go to Herbert C. Kraft, the editor of the volume where this article first appeared, and his students at Seton Hall University, who scanned this document for transcription in this volume.

1. On the evidence of eighteenth-century records, Tatamy's name was accented on the second syllable with a long *a;* the name of the village, however, is accented on the first syllable, with a short *a.*

2. Copies of the complaints are in the Penn Family Manuscripts, Indian Affairs, Vol. 4, p. 30, Historical Society of Pennsylvania, Philadelphia. It should be noted that in accounts of the Walking Purchase passing moral judgment often takes precedence over ascertainment of the facts.

3. The disagreement, here and later, regarding Tatamy's status as a Christian maybe explained by two circumstances. One was the fact that in early Indian-white relations the term Christian was commonly used in the sense of European; by abandoning the Indian way of life for a European one, Tatamy had become in this sense a Christian. Moreover, the fact that he had not been baptized would have been unimportant to Quakers, though Presbyterians (like Brainerd) and Moravians would have required this ceremony.

4. The Indian interpreter is not named in the source, but he lived in the Forks of Delaware; its seems unlikely that Brainerd would or could have hired anyone else at that place.

5. MA, Bernhard Adam Grube, Diarium von Meniwolagamekah, 1752: May 14, 17, June 14, Box 122, Folder 1; Martin Mack and John Jacob Schmick, Diarium von Gandanehütten, 1753: June 17, 30, Sept. 30, Dec. 22, Box 117, Folder 4.

6. Weiser calls his informant "Joseph Deedemy," but no such person is otherwise known and his true identity is not in doubt.

7. On September 20, 1760, the province had paid Moses Tatamy himself 63 £ 7s. 8d. for his services, a moderately large sum; Isaac Still received 29 £ 17s. 8d. (PA, 8th ser. [7]:5658).

8. Repeating an old error, Henry supposes that Moses Tatamy, rather than his son William, was killed in 1757; and he makes the further mistake of supposing that the woman who died in 1801 was his widow.

CHAPTER THIRTEEN

♒

Pisquetomen and Tamaqua:
Mediating Peace in the Ohio Country

Michael N. McConnell

Introduction

THE KUSKUSKIES was a settlement at war in August of 1758. As had been the case for the past three summers, the daily routines of village life were once more punctuated by the coming and going of young men, warriors bent on visiting destruction on the distant border settlements of Pennsylvania and Virginia. Free of retaliation, the four hamlets that together comprised the largest Delaware town in the Ohio Country enjoyed a measure of security that British colonists driven from their farms would have envied.

Yet, in this third year of war, the Delawares were not complacent. While some had assisted in the destruction of General Braddock's army in 1755, others wanting security from invading armies moved from the Allegheny River to the relative safety of the Kuskuskies on the headwaters of the Beaver River. And, while they had pushed back the colonial settlements as far as Lancaster and Winchester, another general, Forbes, with an even greater army, was slowly moving west, his objective the French Fort Duquesne, some fifty miles south of the Delaware town (McConnell 1992a:48–49).

The threat of a new British invasion did not intimidate Delaware warriors, however. Along with their Shawnee, Wyandot, and Ohio Iroquois allies, they had been raiding all spring, supplied from the French storehouse in their town. Their success could be measured not only in scalps drying from poles in the town center and in the booty of successful raids—

273

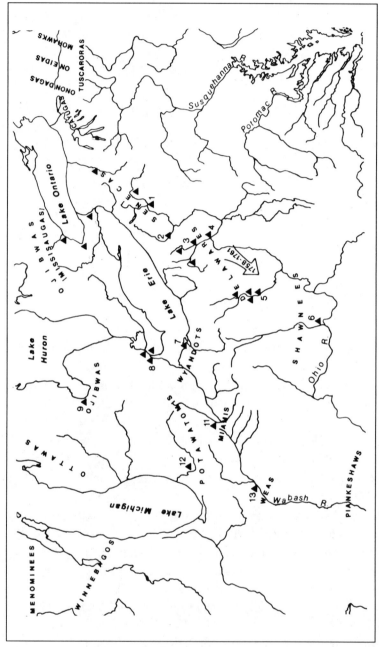

Indian towns and the trans-Appalachian frontier: 1. Conewango (Senecas), 2. Custalogas (Delawares), 3. Kuskuskies (Delawares), 4. Saucunk (Delawares), 5. Beaver's Town (Delawares [post 1760]), 5. Lower Town (Shawnees), 7. Sandusky (Wyandots), 8. Detroit (Wyandots, Ottawas, Ojibwas, Potawatomis), 9. Saginaw (Ojibwas, Ottawas), 11. Kekionga (Miami), 12. St. Joseph (Potawatomis), 13. Quiatanon (Weas). Reprinted from *The Pennsylvania Magazine of History and Biography.* Drawn by Linda Merrell.

clothing, firearms, horses, and tools—but also in the growing number of captives that added to the crowding, noise, and confusion of village life (49–50).

In the midst of departing raiders and newly arrived captives came a visitor eagerly awaited by at least a few of the leading men at the Kuskuskies. Pennsylvanian Christian Frederick Post arrived on August 13 bearing a conciliatory message from his governor—and the hope that words could begin to extinguish the fear and suffering of war. With Post was a small escort of Delawares led by Pisquetomen, the eldest of several brothers belonging to a prominent lineage and the man who guaranteed that Post safely crossed the Alleghenies. On arrival, Post was quickly ushered into the presence of Pisquetomen's brother, Tamaqua (known to the British as King Beaver), who had made this extraordinary meeting possible (Post 1904:192–93).

Together in the weeks and months ahead, Pisquetomen and Tamaqua would attempt to mediate peace between their people, their neighbors, and the British. Relying on cultural traditions, networks of kin and friends, and their own considerable skills as leaders, the brothers succeeded in ending the war in the Ohio Country and making British military successes there even more secure. The peace, as so often happened along the volatile cultural frontiers of eastern America, proved fragile and short. Nevertheless, the successes—and failures—of Pisquetomen and Tamaqua reveal much about peace, war, and negotiation across the cultural divide.

The Evolving Delaware World

The path that took Pisquetomen and Tamaqua to the Ohio Country and their meeting with Post began hundreds of miles to the east in the Delaware and Schuylkill River Valleys in what was by 1758 the most densely settled part of the colony of Pennsylvania. A century earlier, however, it had been the homeland of the Delawares, the heartland of a much larger region known to present-day Delaware elders as Lenapehoking—"land of the Lenapes," whose name roughly translates into "original people" (Kraft 1986:xi).

In 1681, strangers had arrived in Lenapehoking and began to impose their own cultural geography, calling the lands west of the Delaware River Pennsylvania, after their visionary leader. Unlike the small Dutch and Swedish outposts that had appeared earlier in the century, the arrival of

William Penn's colonists led to the rapid transformation of the land and corresponding changes in its native peoples. Already accustomed to dealing with Dutch, Swedish, and English traders with their iron, glass, and cloth, the Delawares now faced not an intrusion of peddlers but an invasion of would-be farmers and town builders. Increasingly, land was added to the list of saleable commodities as Delaware headmen traded territory for distance from the swelling population of English and Welsh Quakers and the Irish and Germans who came in their wake. By the time Tamaqua and Pisquetomen were born, near the end of the seventeenth century, the Delawares' westward movement was well underway.

Pisquetomen and Tamaqua thus grew up in a world of uncertainty. The most visible change by the beginning of the eighteenth century was the shrinking of the Delawares' land base and the corresponding consolidation of once largely autonomous villages, a process driven by a declining population faced with deadly new diseases and the rapid increase of English neighbors. By 1720 many native villagers had moved out of the Delaware and Schuylkill Valleys and were resettling at Shamokin, on the Susquehanna River (McConnell 1992b:12–13).

This swapping of land in return for distance from settlers and the rapid consolidation of villages led to the emergence of a new category of leader among the Delawares, brokers whose principal role was to negotiate with the colony on behalf of their people. Termed "kings" by the colonists, these men represented the increasing necessity for Delawares to deal with outsiders who insisted on talking with one leader rather than the many representatives of families and clans who had presided over village decision-making in the past. Over time this predisposition meant that the Penns and their agents tended to reinforce the standing of these kings, upon whom gifts and attention were lavished in return for land cessions.

At Shamokin, the king of the Delawares was Alumapees, the maternal uncle of Pisquetomen and his brothers. These men thus found themselves members of one of the most important lineages among the former Schuylkill and Delaware Valley natives, so influential that one British captive would later style theirs "the royal family" (Alden 1837:142).

Pisquetomen

Pisquetomen was closely associated with his uncle and became the older man's favorite. Exactly when Pisquetomen began to learn the give and take of frontier diplomacy and village politics is unclear. In 1759 a trader at Fort Pitt referred to him as "old Pisquitom" and the "old man," a seasoned elder whose apprenticeship may have begun not long after Alumapees emerged as the principal spokesman for the Delawares then living in the Schuylkill Valley (Jordan 1913b:433).

Pisquetomen gained his council experience at his uncle's side; in 1731 he witnessed a land transaction involving Alumapees and neighboring colonists. After the death that year of Shakataulin, the nephew originally designated by Alumapees as his successor, Pisquetomen appeared more frequently with his uncle.[1] In the process, he acquired more than a passing familiarity with English; years later, captive Hugh Gibson, who was often the object of Pisquetomen's verbal wrath, remembered that "he well understood" the language (Alden 1837:142).

By the 1740s Pisquetomen's status as Alumapees's kin and his accumulating experience made him a natural choice as an interpreter between the colony and other Delaware bands, a role that also attested to the respect he was already earning as a man of responsibility who ably performed council duties. In a larger sense, however, Pisquetomen's growing facility with English was a measure of how intercultural relations continued to evolve: Indians found it more and more advantageous or necessary to learn the language of their increasingly numerous—and powerful—colonial neighbors (Merrell 1991:129–30).

Pisquetomen learned other, harder, lessons that must have left an indelible impression: lessons of colonial repaciousness, coercion, and treachery. In 1742 he served as interpreter for Nutimus's band of Delawares from Tohickon Creek, north of Philadelphia, in what proved to be their final effort to block what has become known as the Walking Purchase. At the council the Penn's agent, James Logan, used the influence of the colony's Iroquois allies to smother Delaware objections and to order Nutimus's people off the disputed land (MPCP [4]:578; Jennings 1970:19–39, 1984:316–24).

The Walking Purchase may have only confirmed for Pisquetomen the colony's increasing tendency to substitute coercion for conciliation when dealing with Indian neighbors. For over a decade before 1742, Alumapees's own people had been facing the mounting pressures brought on by Pennsylvania's expansion and by the speculative interests of the Penns and Logan. By 1747, Alumapees, infirm and given to drink, had bartered away much of his people's land, prompting a new migration of Delawares, this time to the Ohio Country, far from greedy and intrusive British colonists.

As early as 1742 Pisquetomen was identified as both a favorite of

Alumapees and his designated successor, a fact that put the younger man on a collision course with proprietary agent James Logan and the Penn family's interests in Indian affairs (343). While the details are murky, it is clear that Logan found Pisquetomen a less than ideal successor to the pliant Alumapees. At some point early in his public life, Pisquetomen had earned Logan's displeasure; as Alumapees's health continued to fail, Logan redoubled his efforts to block Pisquetomen's succession, going so far as to promote his own candidate who declined the honor for fear of retaliation from Pisquetomen's kin (311–12).

By the time Alumapees died, in the autumn of 1747, Pisquetomen, joined by his brothers Tamaqua, Shingas, and Menatochyand [Delaware George], may already have turned west toward the Ohio Country, where a majority of his people had already settled (Jennings 1984:311–14; MPCP [4]:746–48, [5]:88; P.A.W. Wallace 1945:252–53). What thoughts Pisquetomen took with him are unrecoverable, but if actions are any indication, he may have harbored an abiding resentment toward British colonists. Years later, during the Seven Years War, he was given to violent fits of temper made worse by the effects of liquor, literally beating captives into the dirt, people who, he believed, threatened to spurn offers of adoption and good treatment by the further betrayal of running away. Even his own people learned to respect, even fear, his temper.[2]

The Ohio Country

The Ohio Country that Pisquetomen entered in the mid-1740s was itself being transformed from a haven into a cockpit of intercolonial and intercultural conflict. Delawares had traveled to and through the region since the late seventeenth century. Accumulated knowledge from these ventures made later occupation of the Ohio Country easier (Hunter 1978:31–32; Grumet 1991:186). Joined by their Shawnee neighbors from Pennsylvania, the Delawares began settling the region by 1724, establishing new towns and new relations with the Iroquois, Wyandots, Miamis, and other peoples living in the west. By 1747 Kittanning on the Allegheny River had replaced Shamokin as the center of the Delaware people. Pressures from colonial settlements ensured that the Ohio Country's Indian population would continue to grow. Alumapees's people, joined by those of other eastern Delaware kings, turned west and seized the opportunity to establish new towns in a resource-rich land far from European intruders, save for the traders who now made annual trips west to maintain contact with long-time customers (McConnell 1992b:14–20). At the same time, the lack of outside pressure seems to have eliminated a major reason for Delawares to unite under kings such as old Alumapees. Information supplied by traders and occasional official embassies reveals that the Ohio Country Delawares occupied a number of autonomous villages. Each was led by its own headman; although some of these men were related to Alumapees, all represented a cultural landscape shaped by local autonomy (25–27).

Yet there were ominous signs that colonists were beginning to turn their attention to the Ohio Country. Unable to lure wayward Delawares and Shawnees back east, Pennsylvanians remained content for the moment to trade with the Ohio towns. Virginians, however, coveted the land and their Ohio Company would, after 1748, make an earnest effort to claim and develop some two hundred thousand acres in the region. Meanwhile, the French increasingly identified the Ohio Country as the weak link in their evolving chain of forts and trading stations designed to keep British interlopers out of the middle west. By 1745 these rival spheres of ambition and empire had collided in the lower Great Lakes region, and threatened to plunge the Ohio Country and its peoples into a conflict of unknowable dimensions (McConnell 1992b:49–60, ch. 4; Jennings 1988: ch. 2; White 1991: ch. 5).

Tamaqua

It was in this fast-changing world of the Ohio Indians that Tamaqua first surfaced in the historical record. Exactly when he settled in the west is uncertain; in all likelihood he accompanied Pisquetomen in the mid-1740s. Younger by several years than his brother, Tamaqua was described in 1759 by James Kenny as a "middle aged man" of "low stature" (Jordan 1913b:429). Whatever his exact age, Tamaqua was a seasoned veteran of village politics by 1750; in that year he was described as one of the "Great Men" of the western Delawares. Moreover, upon encountering Ohio Company agent Christopher Gist at that time, Tamaqua was not shy in demanding to know "where the Indians' Land lay," now that the Delawares and their neighbors were being squeezed between British colonists from the east and the French from the north. His question would dominate Ohio Indian history for a generation (Mulkearn 1954:39).

While the younger man certainly learned much from his brother's example, Tamaqua stands in sharp contrast to Pisquetomen in several respects. Tamaqua's subsequent role as peacemaker and mediator revealed a man of "cheerful disposition" and even temperament, one prepared to accept the often tedious and trying give-and-take of the council house. Whereas Pisquetomen was at times prone to violent outbursts, no such behavior was attributed to Tamaqua, who seemed much better able to remain the "steady, quiet" man whom James Kenny met at Fort Pitt. Only once, in the aftermath of an especially frustrating embassy to Pennsylvania in 1762, did the facade crack enough to reveal his frustration and disappointment (Jordan 1913b:429). And while Pisquetomen was sometimes feared by his own people, Tamaqua encouraged respect, if not deference. Moreover, as subsequent events would reveal, Tamaqua and Pisquetomen clung to different aspects of Delaware cultural tradition, with the latter in middle age taking the warrior's path against his people's enemies, while Tamaqua consistently reflected the Delawares' role as peacemaker within the eastern Indian world, a role Tamaqua extended to include colonists as well. Yet it would be wrong to think of these brothers in terms of a stark contrast between an embittered realist and a detached idealist; each proved himself to be a calculating politician and risk-taker. Personality, experience, and cultural values remained the dominating forces in each man's life.

The Ohio Indians' World

When he met Christopher Gist, Tamaqua and his family were participants in the trade that both defined intercultural relations in the Ohio Country and was an underlying source of the rivalries turning the region into an imperial battleground. The Ohio Country trade in deerskins was merely an extension of a commerce that was generations old by 1750; as Delawares moved west, Pennsylvania traders followed, carrying with them merchandise and a web of personal and market relationships that tied both Indian hunters and colonial peddlers to a trans-Atlantic "empire of goods" (Breen 1980; Gilman 1982:passim). Like other Indian customers, Tamaqua and Pisquetomen tended to do business with a few of the many traders who came annually to the Ohio Country; indeed, it is likely that all members of their lineage frequented the same traders, accumulating debts to Thomas Mitchell, the Lowrys, and John Owen, among others. Trade, like much else within native societies, was a family affair (K. Bailey 1947:94, 100, 113, 120 [Tamaqua]; 143, 145, 157 [Tamaqua's son]; 94, 113, 120, 143, 145 [Shingas]; 94, 129 [Pisquetomen]).

Trade in the Ohio Country had never been merely an economic enterprise. As the natives regularly reminded their colonial suppliers, trade was a form of friendship, a tangible manifestation of peace and, perhaps, alliance. For colonists, however, the barter for hides and pelts often became a means toward the greater end of controlling the land and the Indians dwelling upon it. By the mid-1740s the quest for land had moved in earnest to the Ohio Valley, whose geography and growing Indian population made it a valuable prize for expanding empires. The ensuing struggle for the region was a complex affair that has too often been distorted by notions of "Indians" vs. "whites" or of a "French and Indian War" against the British. In fact, there were many contestants, whose relationships shifted as circumstance or opportunity demanded. Pennsylvania traders and the ambitious Pennsylvania imperialists behind them sought exclusive access to the region in the face of Virginia land speculators with equally grand dreams of western empire. These British rivals were watched closely by French royal officials in Quebec, anxious to keep British subjects from penetrating the Great Lakes and Mississippi Valleys, whose native inhabitants were both customers and allies. Yet French officials faced obstacles closer to home as Canadian merchants balked at supporting measures to secure an Ohio Valley that few believed worth the expense.[3]

Caught between rival Europeans, the Ohio Indians displayed little unity. The local Iroquois and Wyandots actively sought a British alliance against the French, while some Shawnees, whose relations with Canadian traders and settlers extended back into the seventeenth century, actively supported the French. The Delawares, on the other hand, remained noncommittal, though not disinterested in the aggressive manner in which French and British alike pursued their rivalry. Indeed, Tamaqua's pointed questioning of Gist revealed growing Ohio Indian anxiety for their political and cultural autonomy.

Just as mounting pressures from colonists had given rise to Delaware kings such as Alumapees, autonomous villages in the Ohio Country began to draw together under the renewed threat from expanding empires.

Whereas proprietary agents of the Penns had first demanded a successor to Alumapees, then tried to dictate the choice, now both Pennsylvania and Virginia found it expedient to simplify negotiations with the western Delawares by calling again for the natives to select one man through whom they could deal. The western Delawares responded in 1752 by recognizing another of Pisquetomen's brothers, Shingas; at the Logg's Town Treaty between the Ohio Company and the Ohio Iroquois, Shingas was presented as "king" (Anonymous 1905–6:167–68).

The Delawares' choice of Shingas reveals the continuity that prevailed even in the face of dispossession and westward migration. While Alumapees's death created a void at Shamokin, his place as spokesman and broker for his people in the west was already being filled by kinsfolk. As early as the 1730s, headmen in new Delaware towns in the Ohio Country were identifying themselves as "Alumapees," that is, as relatives of the eastern king. The appearance of his nephews in the west further assured the succession of the Schuylkill Indians' "royal family." At the same time, the selection of a western king marked the beginning of Delaware consolidation, as villages increasingly acted together in the face of outside threats and opportunities, taking the first step toward the creation of a Delaware nation west of the Alleghenies (Jennings 1965:174–98; McConnell 1992b:25–27).

While the choice of one of Alumapees's nephews made sense in light of recent Delaware history, the choice of Shingas remains a mystery. Prior to 1752 he was not well-known beyond his own people. Pisquetomen might have been the obvious choice, but earlier efforts by Logan to block his succession were still fresh in Delaware memories and may have led village headmen to seek someone who might be more acceptable to the colonists. In addition, Shingas's own character might well have been a deciding factor. He soon became a strong advocate of native autonomy in the Ohio Country and did not hesitate to turn that advocacy into military action when the need arose. By 1756 he was his people's foremost war leader and largely responsible for the aggressive campaign that turned Pennsylvania's frontier into a wasteland; such a man may have been especially appealing to Delawares who faced intrusion from both British and French during the summer of 1752. Beyond this, however, is the fact that leadership of the western Delawares continued to remain within Alumapees's lineage.

Shingas's emergence as Delaware king came at a critical moment in Ohio Indian history. In Tamaqua's words, a "high wind" was rising, threatening to destroy those in its path as intercolonial tensions reached the boiling point (MPCP [6]:156). The crude attempt by Virginians at Logg's Town to secure Indian agreement to the Ohio Company's land grant further weakened the already fragile alliance of convenience between local Iroquois and British colonists. Moreover, the French had already, in 1749, demonstrated their determination to protect the upper country by sending an armed force to the Ohio Country that openly proclaimed French ownership of the land and, by implication, control over its people. This expedition was a mere hint of things to come: in the spring of 1753 a French army entered the Ohio Country, building forts and setting the stage for a showdown with the British that Delawares and other natives dreaded. Within two more years the region had become a battlefield, while the cultural landscape itself was rapidly transformed. Many of the local Iroquois left the region for Pennsylvania, creating a power vacuum that was quickly filled by the Delawares.[4]

Ohio Indians responding to the French invasion attempted to secure British help in driving out the intruders and to restore native control over the region. Tamaqua and Pisquetomen joined Shingas in soliciting help from Pennsylvania during a meeting at Carlisle in September 1753 (Boyd 1938:123–34). The mission failed. A similar one to Virginia likewise produced little of substance; Virginian troops led by Major George Washington were soundly defeated by the French the following summer, ending Ohio Indian hopes for assistance from the colonies.

War and the Search for Peace

A new British expedition in 1755, commanded by General Edward Braddock, was at first welcomed by the Delawares. Shingas offered to help the general in return for a guarantee that the Ohio Country would remain in Indian hands once the French were driven out. Braddock's pointed reply, that "No Indian Should Inherit the Land," stunned Shingas and other natives and confirmed a lingering fear that one invader would only be replaced by another (B. Bond 1926–27:63–65). This, and the subsequent annihilation of Braddock's army near Fort Duquesne, convinced many Delawares that the time had come to strike back at what now appeared to be the greater threat: not French forts, but British settlements. By the autumn of 1755 Shingas, Pisquetomen, and numerous Delaware warriors joined other Ohio Indians in their own declaration of war against the British. There followed raids against Pennsylvania and Virginia border settlements that, for some Indians, may have served as retribution for earlier land frauds and dispossession (McConnell 1992b:120–21; P.A.W. Wallace 1945:405 [Pisquetomen's participation in raids]).

However, not all western Delawares joined the war. While Shingas led raiders against border settlements, others, including Tamaqua, stayed at home, seeking ways to end the war and still ensure their people's independence. As long as the Delawares and their Shawnee allies, supported by local French garrisons, were successful in their war, little could be done by those who searched for peace.

The Kittanning raid offered peace advocates their opportunity. In 1756, Kittanning on the Allegheny River was one of the largest Delaware towns in the Ohio Country and was the base for the raiding parties that struck settlements east of the mountains. It was thus a logical target for any retaliatory strike by Pennsylvanians. In September 1756, Colonel John Armstrong's provincial forces attacked and burned the town (W. Hunter 1956). While it did not end Delaware raids, the attack nevertheless had a sobering effect on natives who had previously enjoyed victory and immunity from reprisals. Kittanning was quickly abandoned in favor of the relative safety of the Kuskuskies towns to the west. The shift from Kittanning to the Kuskuskies proved to be symbolic as well; in the aftermath of Armstrong's raid, the Delawares began to move from war toward peace, from Shingas to Tamaqua.

Tamaqua's search for peace was in large measure driven by a desire to spare his people the ravages of war. While the Kittanning raid was not repeated, the absence of warriors placed additional burdens on those left at home. And, however few, losses in battle tore the social fabric of this kin-based society. Yet Tamaqua's efforts as a peacemaker and mediator ultimately rested on values and traditions basic to Delaware identity within the Indian world. If his brothers reached into the warrior's ethic for identity and strength, Tamaqua based his own subsequent career on two seemingly contradictory but ultimately complementary ideas: the notion of the Delawares as "women" or peacemakers within the eastern Indian world, and the notion of their role as "grandfathers," the eldest and wisest of people, a reflection of the Delawares' identity as Lenni Lenape: the original, or oldest, people.[5] Tamaqua held consistently to both concepts, using the Delawares' stature within the Indians' world to mediate an end to the fighting. Moreover, Tamaqua seems to have consciously sought the role of peacemaker: he avoided all involvement in the war and supplanted his brother, Shingas, when the latter vacated his position as king to take up arms against the British.

Tamaqua pursued peace as a means to a greater end: the continued autonomy of the Delawares and their neighbors in the Ohio Country. Finding a middle road between warring empires carried great risks and had to be done carefully. Subsequent events make it clear that Tamaqua's mediation rested on the surety that at least one European contender wished for an end to the fighting. This gave Tamaqua and his followers an opportunity to use mediation to drive the other contender from the region. This effort to play off the British and French was simply the latest variation on a strategy used widely by eastern Indian peoples during the previous century.

The details of the process by which Tamaqua convinced kinfolk and others to support negotiations with the British are lost to us. Nevertheless, documented subsequent actions suggest that Tamaqua strongly and consistently advanced his people's role as peacemaker by the force of his own example. At the same time, Tamaqua relied on equally respected kin. By 1758 Pisquetomen had joined his brother and served as his go-between with the British. Throughout the events leading to Christian Frederick Post's appearance at the Kuskuskies, contacts between Delawares and colonists carried an air of skepticism and tentativeness. In the process, Tamaqua surfaced as the spokesman—"king"—with whom the British would have to deal. Initially a number of headmen, notably Netawatwees and a Munsee leader, Custaloga, were involved in contacts with Pennsylvania. By early 1758, however, messages from the colony were being directed to the Kuskuskies—to Tamaqua (W. Hunter 1951:213–19; McConnell 1992b:126–27).

Mediating Peace

Having received noncommittal offers of peace from the Pennsylvanians, Tamaqua began some bold diplomacy of his own in the spring of 1758. He was anxious to strengthen his hand at home and was unwilling to trust intermediaries like the erratic eastern Delaware headman, Teedyuscung. Tamaqua thus sent his own representatives to the colony to investigate rumors of impending negotiations with Teedyuscung's people as well as to take the measure of colonial interest in peace (Post 1904:186–87). In late June 1758, while on a diplomatic mission to Wyoming on the upper Susquehanna River, Post encountered "Two Chiefs and several other Indians from Allegheny" who, he learned "proposed to go down to Phila-delphia" to learn British intentions (MPCP [8]:144; Jennings 1988:384–85). The two "chiefs" were Pisquetomen and an ally of Tamaqua's named Keekyuscung. They had come, so they said, to "Know the truth of affairs" (MPCP [8]:144). Thus Pisquetomen, past middle age, began the most active moment in his public life, serving both as his brother's eyes and ears and as a link between the Delaware peace faction and the British.

The truth, as Pisquetomen soon learned, was that royal officials had taken control of colonial Indian affairs and were making every effort to end the border war. By midsummer, arrangements were well under way for what proved to be the most pivotal of a series of treaties held at Easton, Pennsylvania, during which the crown offered both peace and protection of Indian lands west of the mountains. Such commitments were in the future, however. Of more immediate concern was the task of getting General John Forbes's army safely to the Ohio Country and its subsequent showdown with the French. Ohio Indian neutrality would make the gen-eral's task much easier, and Forbes urged that Post be sent west to deliver peace messages. It was this mission that brought Post to the Kuskuskies and into the presence of Tamaqua. Pisquetomen would be Post's guide and protector; as Tamaqua later recounted, the governor of Pennsylvania had put Post "into [Pisquetomen's] bosom." Tamaqua would do so again after his meeting with the emissary (Post 1904:224–25).

Post's reception at the Kuskuskies and neighboring towns through which he passed underscored the challenges that still faced Tamaqua as well as the hope that a successful meeting would add to his rising stature. At one town, Post encountered Delawares whose faces, "quite distorted with rage," reflected the anger that his arrival produced. At the Kuskus-kies, Post was also subjected to an outburst from Shamokin Daniel. This warrior accused Post of being a liar, damned the emissary, and demanded that the British and French take their war elsewhere. He accused Post of coming "only to cheat the poor Indians and take the land from them" (200, 212). The desire to be rid of all foreign meddlers, as well as the suspicion Shamokin Daniel raised, ran deep among the Delawares. Yet Post re-ceived a very different welcome from village headmen. Telling Post that "he had not slept all night, so much had he been engaged on account of my coming," Delaware George underscored the anticipation shared by those who had risked reputations and their people's security in an effort to end the war (193, 195).

Nevertheless, suspicion and tension hung over the meeting as Tamaqua, armed no doubt with information supplied by Pisquetomen (Post revealed that the two had "much conversation" on their way west), tried to bring the British to reason (190). He quickly cut to the heart of the matter by emphasizing that "the land is ours" and not British or French. He then stated that the Delawares would stand neutral only if "you will be at peace with us" on those terms (213–14). If the British agreed, Tamaqua assured them, he and his people would ensure that "all Indians from the sunrise to the sunset should join the peace" (PA 1st Series [3]:548–49). Having assumed the role of "woman," Tamaqua was prepared to act as "grandfather" and lead the younger nations to peace.

This was the message Post carried east, escorted once more by Pisquetomen. The two men arrived at Easton in the midst of what was to be the most important of the peace conferences held at that town between 1756 and 1758. The British pledge to restrict settlement west of the Alleghenies was the message Pisquetomen carried west upon his return in October.[6] Once more he was to take Post, who was now placed in his care by Provincial Secretary Richard Peters, to the Kuskuskies (Richard Peters Papers, Diary No. 15, 1758: Oct. 21). On this occasion, however, Post had a different mission: he was to act as an agent for General Forbes, collecting information while persuading the Ohio Indians to give the army undisputed passage to Fort Duquesne.

Post's dual role as ambassador and spy was not well-received by his Indian hosts, and he all but used up whatever good will he had accumulated during his earlier visit. Pisquetomen displayed his legendary anger when Post insisted on traveling to Forbes's headquarters instead of taking the direct path to the Kuskuskies. For Pisquetomen, who was openly anxious to leave Easton, any delay could weaken his brother's position at home; moreover, a detour through Indian-hating border settlements could well cost Pisquetomen and his party their lives.[7]

Pisquetomen's anger and distrust re-echoed once Post reached the Delaware towns. Recent clashes with British troops had put the Delawares on edge. The apparent contradiction between British professions of peace and their army's relentless advance on the Ohio Country did little to ease Indian fears. Pisquetomen himself pointed to the army as evidence of

British duplicity and its new road west as an avenue for settlers; other Delawares were quick to agree (Post 1904:250, 252–54).

All of this stood in stark contrast to the imposing calm of Tamaqua, who silenced angry warriors. In this he was assisted by Shingas, once the Delawares' principal war leader but now aligned with his brothers in the quest for peace (258–60). Witnessed by two Cayuga representatives of the influential Six Nations who had traveled with Pisquetomen to confirm news of the Easton Treaty, Tamaqua told Post that he would in fact carry news of the treaty and British promises to the Delawares' western neighbors. By spreading word of the treaty while urging his own warriors to remain at home, Tamaqua ensured Forbes's victory over the French in late November. Allowing the British to drive out the French, Tamaqua was gambling that the Delawares' roles as women and grandfathers, as well as British sincerity, could restore peace and the autonomy of the Ohio Indians (254, 258, 273).

The weeks and months following his second encounter with Post found Tamaqua working hard to promote peace while continuing to pursue the Indians' quest for autonomy. In early December 1758, Tamaqua met Colonel Henry Bouquet, Forbes's second in command, and took the opportunity to urge the British to take their army back east now that the French were in retreat (HBP [2]:621–26).

The following summer, Tamaqua led Delawares, Shawnees, and Wyandots to the site of Fort Duquesne to make peace formally with the British. Wyandots attending the meeting made it clear that their participation was a direct result of "a Council held over the Lakes by the Beaver King [Tamaqua]." The full impact of Tamaqua's work became clear when Ottawas, Ojibwas, Kaskaskias, and Miamis from the Great Lakes and Illinois country joined the Ohio Indians at another conference later that summer (Wainwright 1947:316–17; MPCP [8]:382–93; Jordan 1913b:421, 425, 428–29; HBP [3]:507–11). Two years later, in 1761, Tamaqua was at Detroit, now in British hands, contributing to the success of a major peace conference held between the Great Lakes Indians and British Indian Superintendent Sir William Johnson (Jordan 1913a:23–24).

Tamaqua's brand of shuttle diplomacy bore fruit for a number of reasons. Certainly impressive was Tamaqua's own dedication to peace, which must have had a profound impact upon his own people and other nations. Equally important, Tamaqua spoke to other Indian nations with the persuasive voice of a grandfather—having taken the lead in making peace,

the Delawares set an example that others could follow. Moreover, Tamaqua was also willing to go beyond words to actions in promoting peace.

On the sensitive issue of captives—many of whom were now adopted
members of Delaware families, but whom the British wanted back as a
condition of peace—Tamaqua once more took the lead. At Fort Pitt in
front of his own people, he surrendered two women, one of whom he
called his "mother," the other his "sister." In the weeks that followed this
dramatic and personally painful gesture, British officers were accepting
dozens of repatriated captives from the Ohio Indians.[8]

Yet if Tamaqua could accede to British demands in the interest of peace,
he never lost sight of his own people's interests. He surrendered his own
adoptive kin, but in return called on the British to reopen trade and extend
a generous hand to his hunters and their families. The tactic worked, as
European goods began flowing once more into Delaware towns cut off
from trade since 1754. Indeed, one colonial onlooker noted that a Delaware, during one of his frequent visits to Fort Pitt, "draws provisions
more than we do" (MPCP [8]:388–89; Wainwright 1947:350; Jordan
1913b:428–29).

Finally, this successful give and take reflects another key ingredient in
the formula for peace that Tamaqua developed: a recognition that *both*
Indians and the British required peace, if for different reasons. Natives
needed to replenish depleted stocks of goods and to normalize village life
disrupted by several years of war. British colonies desperately wanted an
end to the nightmare of border warfare, while the British army, faced with
the responsibility of supervising a vast western territory seized from the
French, also needed peace.[9] Tamaqua's strategy thus rested ultimately on
accommodating the newly arrived British in ways that would take advantage of the shared need for peace.

Unstable Accommodation

The convergence of interests that gave Tamaqua the opportunity to promote peace was inherently fragile and unstable. Even as he worked to
promote accommodation to the British, storm clouds were gathering that
would soon break over Tamaqua and the Ohio Country, washing away
much of what the Delaware king and his followers had accomplished.
Obstacles to peace appeared almost from the beginning in the form of

angry warriors and village matrons calling for revenge upon those who had made war on their people. To their voices were added those of older men—including Pisquetomen—whose historic distrust of the British was not entirely set aside in the wake of the Kuskuskies meetings. All Delawares, in fact, seemed to one observer "jealous of their lands being settled." Pisquetomen, especially, "put it close" to local traders like James Kenny "to tell what ye English . . . meant by coming here with a great army" that built newer and bigger forts rather than leaving the Ohio Country as the natives had anticipated (Jordan 1913b:423–24, 433; 1913a:12).

Tamaqua could readily confront discontent at home; overcoming the suspicions of Munsees, Shawnees, and other neighbors was more difficult, especially when outsiders like Teedyuscung and his son spread rumors that forced Tamaqua to dash off to neighboring towns such as Venango to counter their influence (Jordan 1913b:422, 425; Wainwright 1947:330–32).

Suspicion regarding British intentions surfaced in other and potentially explosive ways. During the busy summer of 1761, war belts, passed from Senecas calling for a pan-Indian rising against the invaders, appeared in the west. Though the plan was exposed at Detroit and came to nothing, it was further evidence of the challenges confronting anyone promoting peace and accommodation. Tamaqua's journey to Detroit may have been, in part, an effort to undermine support for the Senecas; both Tamaqua and Shingas, when offered the war belt, "threw it against ye Wall & would not accept it" (Jordan 1913a:24; McConnell 1992b:171–74).

British imperialists' determination to keep and exploit their conquests in the west was reflected in more than the numerous forts and the regular traffic along the military road from the Pennsylvania settlements to Fort Pitt. It also surfaced in relations among Indians, the army, and royal Indian agents. By 1762 British requests were being replaced by demands. These demands were backed by the threat of force. At the same time, traditional protocols of friendship and peace were dispensed with as local commanders, acting on orders from their superiors, curtailed gift-giving and discouraged trade in powder and lead, hatchets, knives, and anything else that might later be turned against their soldiers. Finally, the soldiers proved wholly ineffective in policing the borders and making good on the promises made at Easton. Traders ran amok in native towns, using liquor to separate hunters from their catch, while squatters from Virginia moved into the Ohio Country in numbers that alarmed both Indians and royal officials (McConnell 1992b:159–71, 176–78). Accommodation was beginning to collapse as the British increasingly insisted on behaving like conquerors rather than friends or brothers. Not only did this threaten the fragile peace in the west, but it also undermined Tamaqua's influence among his own people and, by extension, among those who looked to the Delawares for advice and guidance.

The first indication of trouble surfaced in 1762. Early that year one of James Kenny's Delaware customers told him that the "Beaver [Tamaqua] never was made a King by the Indians, but by the people of Virginia," insisting that "Neat-hot-whelme" [Netawatwees, or Newcomer] was now "king" of the western Delawares (Jordan 1913a:168, 170). At the same time, a nativist movement led by the prophet Neolin was sweeping through the Delaware towns. Neolin's identification of European— especially British—influences as morally corrupting and his call for cultural revitalization and a return to traditional values and beliefs found a receptive audience among people inclined to see the British as an increasingly dangerous threat.[10]

Both Netawatwees's emergence and Neolin's preaching were manifestations of anti-British feeling that would explode the following year in what has become known as the Western Indians' Defensive War. They were also indications of fundamental changes within western Delaware society, as individual towns continued in the direction of cooperation and a corresponding tendency toward a collective identity. Tamaqua and Shingas had been instrumental in beginning that process. By 1759 Delaware councils included not just Alumapees's people but other Delawares as well, notably those from the central Delaware Valley, one of whose headmen was Netawatwees. In addition, there were the linguistically distinct Munsees. These people had moved from their homeland in the upper Delaware Valley and were now led by Custaloga (MPCP [8]:383–92, 429– 35; PA 2nd Series [3]:745–52). By the early 1760s, the more recent Delaware arrivals began to challenge Tamaqua and his followers for a central voice in western Delaware affairs. This challenge was made stronger by Netawatwees's resistance to British claims to the Ohio Country.[11]

Finally, deaths within Tamaqua's own family further reduced his effectiveness as a mediator and peacemaker. Delaware George, a frequent visitor to Fort Pitt, died there in May 1762 (Jordan 1913a:154). Shingas's ill health and the death of his wife that same year forced him to withdraw from public affairs (158; Heckewelder 1819:268–76).

The heaviest blow, however, was the loss of Pisquetomen. The old man tried to accompany Tamaqua on one last trip to Pennsylvania in 1762, but the hot midsummer weather made it impossible for him to complete the journey. It seems likely that he, too, died that year, robbing Tamaqua and his people of decades of experience in coping with the colonial world.[12] Indeed, that experience may have hastened his death; repeated journeys over the mountains as Tamaqua's go-between must have been a punishing experience for a man already known as "old" Pisquetomen.

With Pisquetomen dead and his own people now talking of a new war against British invaders, Tamaqua, no doubt physically and emotionally exhausted, could do little else but stand by and watch the peace he had worked to build collapse into bloody ruin. Yet he did manage, in an outburst of frustration, to publicly lay blame where he thought it rightfully belonged. In the spring of 1763 he, along with other Delaware headmen, sent a message to the British at Fort Pitt condemning them and their king for destroying the peace and bringing war once again to the Ohio Country (JP [10]:685–88).

The war that followed brought little advantage to either side. British forces were unable to conquer their enemies but managed to hang on to their major forts in the west. The western Indians punished the army severely but could neither drive it away nor continue their war without the powder, lead, and gunsmiths that only trade with the British could supply.[13] Ironically, the war's only significant outcome was to re-establish the accommodation that Tamaqua had earlier espoused; neither side could subdue the other and for the next decade an uneasy peace returned to the west as the British and Indians sought ways to avoid another costly war.

While the date of Tamaqua's own death is unknown, references to him cease in the late 1760s. He may have died in 1769. His passing was one more indication of the change in leadership within Delaware society. By 1774 both Netawatwees and Custaloga had stepped aside, making room for a new generation of men who would attempt to lead their people through the increasingly treacherous currents generated by continued British-American expansion and the creation of the United States (Mc-Connell 1992b:228, 232, 238, 267). The examples of mediation and accommodation provided by Tamaqua and Pisquetomen would continue to serve as part of the foundation of the Delaware nation in the west as it continued to pursue political and cultural autonomy in a changing world.

Conclusion

As mediators, Pisquetomen and Tamaqua drew heavily on their own and their peoples' historical experiences, their own personal attributes, and the cultural values and traditions that distinguished the Delawares among native peoples in the east. It is especially important to recognize that these men represent a point on a continuum of experiences that we have come to associate with cultural brokers. Unlike the Oneida, Shickellamy, Pisquetomen, and Tamaqua did not cross the cultural divide to work within the colonies as mediators or informants for colonists; unlike the Mohawk headman, Hendrick, they could not trade on the accumulated mythology of a powerful Iroquois confederacy. And, unlike these and other go-betweens, neither Pisquetomen nor Tamaqua established firm bonds with a counterpart within the colonies; no Conrad Weiser or Sir William Johnson emerges in the dialogue between the Delawares and colonists. Rather, the Delawares of necessity dealt with a variety of outsiders—soldiers, traders, Indian agents, and missionaries—as the shifting currents of war, peace, and imperial ambition required.

Yet, like other go-betweens and mediators, Tamaqua and Pisquetomen demonstrated an ability to seize the moment, to parlay circumstances into larger opportunities to pursue goals important to themselves and their people. Indeed, this seems to be one of the attributes that runs through the histories of such people, from Squanto to Tamaqua. Finally, the experiences of Pisquetomen and Tamaqua remind us of the instability of the cultural frontiers of early America, of the inherent fragility that marked cooperation across the cultural divide, and the limits imposed on the endeavors of mediators as they attempted to bridge the gap between natives and colonists, between tribes and empires.

Notes

The author would like to thank James Merrell, Colin Calloway, and Robert Grumet for their helpful comments on earlier drafts of this essay.
   1. On Pisquetomen's early activities: Jennings 1968; Logan Papers (HSP): Logan Letterbooks 9: Aug. 11, 1731:16; MPCP (3):404–6, (4):53–56; PA 1st Series (1)344–47.

2. Alden 1837:145–46; Post 1904:236; Richard Peters Papers, Diary No. 15, 1758: Oct. 12, 21. My thanks to James Merrell for providing me with a typescript of the Peters Diary.

3. On the struggle of the Ohio Country and middle west, see McConnell 1992b: chs. 4–5; Jennings 1988: ch. 1; White 1991: ch. 5.

4. On events leading to warfare in the Ohio Country see McConnell 1992b: chs. 4–5; Jennings 1988: chs. 2–4; White 1991:196–240; Kent 1984.

5. Miller 1974:507–14; on the role of "grandfathers," see Heckewelder 1819: xli; Boyd 1938:130, 131; Browne, et al. 1883–1970 (28):300.

6. For Pisquetomen at the Easton Treaty, see Richard Peters Papers, Diary No. 15, 1758: Oct. 5, 19, and 20. For the treaty proceedings, see Boyd 1938:215–43; Jennings 1988:396–403.

7. Richard Peters Papers, Diary No. 5, 1758, Oct. 19: Pisquetomen "press'd to be dismiss'd"; Post 1904:240.

8. MPCP (8):389; HBP (3):510–511; Wainwright 1947:344–436 *passim* on returned captives.

9. This argument is developed in McConnell 1992b:145–58.

10. C. Hunter 1971:39–49; A.F.C. Wallace 1956; an analysis of the broader historical and geographic context for Neolin's movement can be found in Dowd 1992:22–40.

11. The foregoing discussion has drawn heavily on Becker 1984, 1987, 1988; Goddard 1978:223; Thurman 1974:128; W. Hunter 1978: *passim*; McConnell 1992b:181.

12. PA 1st Series (4):93; Pisquetomen was not among those Delawares listed as having attended the meeting in Lancaster. See Boyd 1938:266.

13. See McConnell (1992b:181–206) on the war in the Ohio Country. A comprehensive history of the war can be found in Peckham (1947).

CHAPTER FOURTEEN

꙳

Molly Brant: Her Domestic and Political Roles in Eighteenth-Century New York

Lois M. Feister
and Bonnie Pulis

Introduction

"HANDSOME, SENSIBLE, judicious, and political" were the words used by Thomas Jones to describe the Mohawk Indian woman Molly Brant (De Lancey 1879:374). For Jones, a Justice of the New York Colony Supreme Court who wrote a contemporaneous history of the Revolutionary War while under house arrest on Long Island, these words summarized the character and role of this important and influential woman. His account was one of many documenting Brant's role as mother, diplomat, and Mohawk matron.

Molly Brant lived an unusually active life for an eighteenth-century woman. She made choices for which she is sometimes criticized today; some have seen her as having played a large part in the loss of Iroquois land in New York State. She did not move entirely into the white man's world and leave her own culture behind; she tried to combine both worlds. In her political role, she influenced the Six Nations in decisions she thought were best both for them and for herself. In her domestic role, providing for her family was a priority. She and her children adopted a material culture that fit their status. She sent her children to English schools, but they could also read and speak Mohawk. She could act as hostess to the colonial elite and was not shy about speaking her opinion in the company of authority, white or Indian.

Some of her political power came from family connections. Her step-father Brant was a prominent Mohawk leader. Her brother, Joseph, rose to prominence during and after the Revolutionary War. She achieved further influence as consort of Sir William Johnson, the most powerful British frontier diplomat of his era. Yet Molly Brant's influence did not depend entirely upon her connections with important men. She was the product of a matrilineal society where women were respected and consulted.[1] She carried this training into Sir William's household, where she acted as one of his important contacts with the Indian groups living west of their home. Jones concluded his description of her thusly: "through her means he was always enabled to gain the most authentic intelligence, and to counteract every scheme undertaken by his enemies to set up the Indians against him" (DeLancey 1879:374).

Brant merged her abilities with the influence uniquely available to her through her connections to powerful men to become a powerful person in her own right. Before the age of forty, she was already a legendary figure; even American troops during the Revolutionary War knew about and wanted to see her. At the same time, she maintained her domestic sphere. Left to raise eight children who ranged from one to fifteen years in age when Sir William died, she was determined to see that they should keep their rightful inheritances, a task to which she devoted several years of her life.

Molly Brant has been characterized differently by writers of different time periods. It has been a long time since she was seen as "a forest child" who had experienced an "astonishing evolution" as "wigwam housekeeping has never been noted for neatness" (Pound 1930:141). As late as the 1960s, however, she was characterized during public tours at Johnson Hall as an evil concubine whose charms Johnson had found irresistible. Even in the popular media of today, she has been portrayed as a childlike woman who had to be rescued from a burning house ("Broken Chain," TNT 1993).

Prevalent in the minds of those who have studied Molly Brant's life is the question of whether a marriage bond existed between her and Sir William Johnson. In 1818, their son George petitioned against a court decision that barred his claim to land belonging to his deceased sister

because "the marriage of their said Father and Mother, although acknowledged and avowed by them, and conformable to the usages of the Nation
to which she belonged, was defective in point of legal form."[2] Yet Brant and
Johnson lived together for over fifteen years as man and wife. This was not
a clandestine relationship but a highly public one. They worked together
both in the running of a busy household and as a political force in colonial
New York. Professional historians have increasingly recognized Brant's
political power and importance to the Six Nations (Graymont 1979, Johnston 1973), to Sir William Johnson (M. Hamilton 1975 and 1976, Green
1989, E. Thomas 1989), and to the history of Canada (Johnston 1973,
Gundy 1953).

This study seeks to present a broad view of Molly Brant as a woman,
mother, and power broker and includes previously untapped primary and
unpublished sources (De Lancy 1879, Lender and Martin 1982, Elmer
1847–48, Guldenzopf 1986, Guzzardo 1975). Since Molly Brant is one of
few Native Americans who is presently interpreted to the public at a
historic site, eighteenth-century descriptions of her were sought for insights into her personality by the authors.

Johnson Hall State Historic Site is presented today as the home of both
Sir William Johnson and Molly Brant. In addition to Sir William Johnson's
life and accomplishments, Molly Brant's roles as housekeeper, hostess,
and mother, together with her influence in the management of colonial
Indian affairs, are emphasized to visitors. The house is being furnished to
reflect both of their cultures, based on descriptions such as the 1774
inventory and other primary sources. The articles in the children's room
belonged to Brant and therefore were omitted from the 1774 inventory, so
that room has been furnished with reproductions to depict how it might
have looked and includes objects from both cultures. While giving tours,
staff members discuss domestic life at Johnson Hall and Molly Brant's role
in making the Hall the unique place it was. Where else in the dozen years
just prior to the American Revolution did a baronet and a Native American
woman live as partners, raise a family, and exercise such great political
power?

An intention of recent studies in women's history is to recover the life
stories of women overshadowed by powerful white men. This overshadow-
ing did not happen to Brant during her own lifetime; it should not do so
now. Although she is honored in English Canada as one of its founders,
her story is not widely known in the United States. Whatever her politics,

Molly Brant deserves recognition for her grit and determination in the face of overwhelming odds; few women in the eighteenth century could have accomplished as much.

Canajoharie and Fort Johnson

Molly Brant was born in about 1736 to Christian Mohawk parents.[3] However, the christening records of the local church for April 13, 1735, list a child named Mary as the daughter of Margaret and Cannassware (Kelsay 1984:40). If this was Molly Brant, she had a different father than her younger brother, Joseph, who was born in 1743. Her Mohawk name was "Koňwatsi?tsiaiéňini" or Gonwatsijayenni, meaning "someone lends her a flower" (Graymont 1979:416). Molly Brant reached maturity at "the upper castle," the Indian town of Canajoharie. Canajoharie was located on the south side of the Mohawk River, thirty miles from "the lower castle," called Tionderoga and located at Fort Hunter. Both Mohawk settlements were surrounded by white farmers and traders, including William Johnson, who had emigrated from Ireland in 1738 to develop land in the Mohawk Valley on behalf of his uncle, Peter Warren. Tremendously ambitious, Johnson proceeded to acquire property and power in his own right. Part of his success was attributable to his shrewd partnership with the

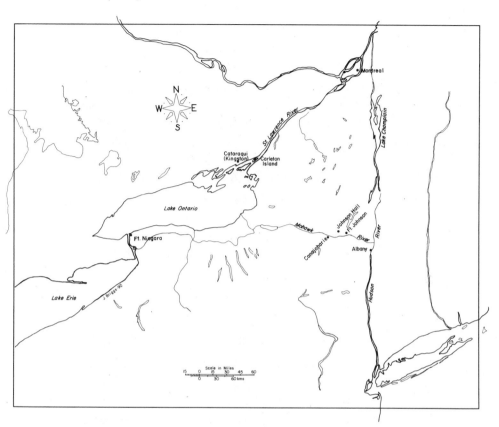

Mohawks at Tionderoga and Canajoharie. His success in enlisting the Mohawks against the French led to his appointment as Superintendent of Indian Affairs for the Northern District, a powerful position he held until his death in 1774. Johnson was made a baronet following his victory at the Battle of Lake George in 1755. In 1767, Johnson declared in a letter to the Earl of Shelburne: "I have always made use of a few approved Chiefs of the several Nations" (NYCD [7]:946). By consulting with and giving large quantities of gifts to the important sachems of both the upper and lower Mohawk castles, Johnson became a power broker in their affairs and, through them, in the affairs of others.

By 1754, Molly Brant lived in the best house in Canajoharie due to her mother's marriage to an important Mohawk sachem, Brant Canagaraduncka. The village consisted of single family cabins rather than the traditional longhouses (Cruikshank 1961:23–42; Guzzardo 1975:258–62; Kelsay 1984:52–54). Archaeological excavations at the site of this house (a house later occupied by Joseph Brant) demonstrated that it had a stone cellar, clapboard siding, a fireplace, glass windows, plaster walls, and outbuildings (Guldenzopf 1986:104–12). Molly Brant traveled to Philadelphia in 1754 with her stepfather; while they were in Albany on their way home, a military officer "fell in Love wth. Ms. Mary Brant who was then likely [good-looking]" (Wolcott 1904:8). Despite what some earlier historians have said, Brant was accustomed to European-style architecture and household goods, and she knew of the world outside her village before she joined Sir William at his home known as Fort Johnson.

Since Sir William always stayed at the Brant house at Canajoharie when he visited the upper castle (Guzzardo 1975:260; Kelsay 1984:67), he had to have known "Miss Molly" for some years. A widely believed but unsubstantiated story states that he first saw her at a militia muster when "she leaped upon" a mounted officer's horse "with the agility of a gazelle . . . and clinging to the officer, her blanket flying, and her dark tresses streaming in the wind, she flew about the parade ground swift as an arrow" (Stone 1865[1]:327–28n).

William Johnson had three children by Catherine Weissenberg, a German woman who had been a runaway indentured servant, obviously herself a woman of some spirit and determination. However, by April 1759, Johnson was ordering mourning materials, and a friend was writing, "when I left you I thought there appeared little hopes of Ms. Katys Life. I condole with you thereupon" (NYCD [2]:785). At that time Molly Brant was already a presence in the Johnson household. In September of that same year, she gave birth to her first child by Johnson, a boy named Peter Warren Johnson after Sir William's original patron. Unlike Brant, Catherine Weissenberg does not appear in Johnson's papers as having been an influence in his affairs. She is not recorded as having made purchases or having been thanked by guests for her services as hostess. Catherine was remembered by Sir William in his will as "my beloved wife," and she was the mother of his son John and two daughters, Ann and Mary. Ann later married his close aide, Daniel Claus, and Mary married his nephew, Guy Johnson. All three, in their teens and twenties in 1759, lived at Fort Johnson with Molly Brant and their father until Johnson Hall was built in 1763.

Molly Brant was in her early twenties in 1759, and Sir William was in his forties. While at Fort Johnson, she gave birth to at least two other children, Elizabeth and Magdalene. Margaret, George, Mary, Susanna, and Anne were born at Johnson Hall. Sir William once explained that

Brant's brother Joseph would be useful because of his "connection and residence" at Canajoharie (NYCD [7]:580). He must have seen Brant in the same light; he needed her for the world in which he lived. Much of his personal and professional success depended upon his ability to maintain good relations with the Iroquois, a fact that must have brought considerable tension into his daily life. Molly Brant helped him maintain these relationships. For her part, although apparently "she loved Sir William to adoration" (De Lancey 1879:374), she also recognized the access he provided to power, influence, money, and a better life for her and her future children. She moved into that world, and as Judge Jones expressed, Sir William "lived with her in all the intimacy of the most conjugal affection" (De Lancey 1879:374).

Johnson Hall

Although she was a strong influence in Indian affairs from the very beginning of her relationship with Johnson, it was at Johnson Hall that Molly Brant as housekeeper and hostess became visible. A "prudent & faithfull Housekeeper" (JP [12]:1070), she was in charge of a busy household. In the eighteenth century, a "housekeeper" was someone who supervised the female servants of the household and who was a hospitable person (OED, Compact Edition [1]:422). Johnson had many slaves, a cook, a gardener, a farm overseer, a secretary, and a bookkeeper to perform daily household tasks. Contemporary accounts show that Brant made purchases of such items as a dozen creamware cups and saucers (teaware), an iron skillet, and numerous sewing items at the local store as well as from merchants in Schenectady and elsewhere.[4] She and Sir William were hosts to many visitors, including governors, judges, English nobility and their attendants, and sometimes families (M. Hamilton 1975:35). Judge Jones described the typical day as "a kind of open house" in which the couple played host to travelers from all parts of America, Europe, and the West Indies:

> The gentlemen and ladies breakfasted in their respective rooms, and, at their option, had either tea, coffee, or chocolate, or if an old rugged veteran wanted a beef steak, a mug of ale, a glass of brandy, or some grog, he called for it, and it always was at his service . . . the bell punctually rang for dinner, and all assembled. He had besides his own family,

seldom less than ten, sometimes thirty . . . Sometimes seven, eight, or
ten, of the Indian Sachems joined the festive board. His dinners . . .
consisted, however, of the produce of his estate . . . such as venison, bear,
and fish of every kind, with wild turkeys, partridges, grouse, and quails
in abundance. No jellies, creams, ragouts, or sillibubs graced his table.
His liquors were Madeira, ale, strong beer, cider, and punch . . . The
company, or at least a part of them, seldom broke up before three in the
morning. Every one, however, Sir William included, retired when he
pleased. (De Lancey 1879:373–74)

Molly Brant was responsible for providing this hospitality. The food
served, as implied by Jones, perhaps reflected her own background and
taste. That she participated as hostess is shown by thank-you notes and
gifts from guests such as Lord Adam Gordon, who wrote after a visit in
1765, "my Love to Molly & thanks for her good Breakfast" (JP [13]:376).
Another visitor shamefacedly apologized, "sorry I did not take Leave of
Miss Molly—I begg Sir [ ] be pleased to Assure her, that it was not for want
of [ ] the Effect of Stupidity" (JP [6]:463). Witham Marsh sent compli-
ments and called her by a contraction of her Indian name, probably an
affectionate nickname, "chgiagh" (JP [11]:72).

Johnson held frequent Indian conferences at Johnson Hall. Between
1763 and 1774, when he died speaking at such an event, there were at least
twelve official conferences and numerous other meetings (JP [1]:xxv–
xxxiii). Indeed, more than once Johnson groaned, "I have . . . every Room
& Corner in my House Constantly full of Indians" (JP [4]:370; [6]:178–84;
[12]:461). Hundreds of Indians from all over the northern colonies attended these gatherings. All needed to be housed, fed, and given presents and reassurances of the British government's support and friendship.
Molly Brant's role in all of this was obvious. Years later, a traveler in
Canada reported that she "has always been a faithful and useful friend in
Indian affairs, while she resided in Johnston [sic] hall . . . When treaties or
purchases were about to be made . . . she has often persuaded the obsti-
nate chiefs into a compliance with the proposals for peace, or sale of lands"
(Ogden 1800:61). It probably pleased the Indians to see one of their own,
along with her children, living with Johnson. At the same time, Brant
increased her own power among these Indian groups as a person to be
consulted. This power she was to maintain and augment in the years
ahead, so that although not born to the position, she became one of the
Mohawk matrons.

Sir William's health was deteriorating by the end of the 1760s. Suffering from an old wound, worn out by his constant travels and the strain of a strenuous life, he was frequently ill (Burch 1990a). Brant, known in later years as a healer, no doubt cared for Johnson during these periods, adding this to her many other duties.

Archaeological excavations at Johnson Hall have demonstrated that the material culture of the household included the finest European goods available. Teawares and tablewares of porcelain, creamware, and white salt-glazed stoneware are found in abundance, along with crystal wine glasses and decanters. The 1774 inventory of the contents of the house included mahogany furniture, silver serving pieces, and oil portraits. Added to these were numerous Indian items. Hanging on a hall wall, for example, were "3 Indn. Pictures, 2 white Deer Skins & do. fox." In the formal blue parlor were "a parcell of Indn. Trinkets over the Chimney" (JP [13]:652, 655).[5] The home Sir William and Molly created contained evidence of both their cultures.

There are no known portraits of Brant, and descriptions of her personal appearance during her years at Johnson Hall are rare. Visitor Lady Susan O'Brien is reported to have remarked that Molly Brant was a "well-bred and pleasant lady" (Stone 1865[2]:244). Anne Grant, a child in Albany during this period, wrote years later that Molly Brant "possessed an uncommonly agreeable person, and good understanding" (Grant 1876:219). As Grant never met Brant, her account probably represents the opinions or observations of her elders. Brant's later claim for her losses during the American Revolution shows that she and her older daughters, at least on occasion, dressed in European clothes. Her claim listed chintz and silk for gowns, cotton and silk stockings, handkerchiefs, muslin aprons, hats, bonnets, silk gloves, and leather shoes (Guldenzopf 1986:204–5). The list also contained three side-saddles. After leaving Johnson Hall, Brant was described as "dressed after the Indian Manner, but her linen and other Cloathes the finest of their kind" (Harrison 1876:87). At an Indian conference in 1776 at German Flatts, Captain Joseph Bloomfield noted that the sachems and their wives wore clothes made of fine fabrics but that the average Iroquois did not (Lender and Martin 1982:90–91). By then, Molly Brant dressed in the fashion of influential Mohawks. In later life, she was consistently described as wearing Mohawk-style clothing made of European fabrics.

It is not known whether Molly Brant received an English education.

Some historians suggest that she received schooling (E. Thomas 1989: 141; Graymont 1979:416; Green 1989:236). While away from home, Johnson wrote her letters (JP [13]:125, 139), suggesting that she could read. Other contemporaries indicated that she could write in Mohawk. Eleazar Wheelock, for example, noted that Joseph Brant received a letter from Molly while at school, but that Wheelock had not read it because he assumed it was in Mohawk (NYCD [4]:330). In December 1778, Mohawk leader John Desorontyon wrote to Claus in Mohawk quoting a letter he had received from Molly Brant written in the same language (Gundy 1953:101).[6] The Haldimand Papers contain a letter "translated from Mary Brants letter to Col. Claus" dated Carleton Island, April 12, 1781. The "translation" no doubt was from Mohawk to English. The letter (available only in translation) is signed "Mary Brant" (Haldimand Papers, Reel A685, Ms. 21774, 180). A receipt dated October 11, 1782, is signed with the letters "wari" (Mary) and the words "Mary Brant her mark" written around the letters. Unfortunately, this too is only a transcription executed in John Johnson's hand.[7] Two Molly Brant letters in the Claus Papers, one dated 1778 and the other 1779, are in different hands. Each is in a flowery style quite unlike Claus's hand; either could be Molly's (Claus Papers, MG19 F1, 2:39, 135–36). Barbara Graymont notes that Brant's letters, "if authentically from her own hand, show that she was mistress of a fine penmanship and a proper English style. There is some evidence, however, that she was only semi-literate and that the letters were dictated to an amanuensis" (Graymont 1979:416). Coming to a different conclusion, Earle Thomas (1989:141) wrote that "the penmanship and syntax in her letters certainly would lead one to believe that she had been the recipient of some formal schooling; . . . there are enough mistakes in them to lead one to believe [she wrote them]." It is possible that some of the letters written in English were dictated to one of her daughters; ones written in Mohawk could have been written by Brant herself.

There are a few references to her children in Johnson's papers during the Johnson Hall period. Elizabeth, like her mother, purchased sewing materials at the local store (JP [13]:590, 609, 613, 615). Johnson established a school in nearby Johnstown for the children's education (JP [4]:708; [5]:403; [6]:710; [7]:169; [8]:323, 424, 488, 927, 1156). Peter went beyond the local school; after attending Wheelock's school (JP [11]:101–2) and another in Albany, he was sent to one in Schenectady (JP [5]:504; DHNY [4]:368). This was probably the same school where Brant sent her daughters after leaving Johnson Hall in 1774.[8] Molly saw little of Peter after 1772. That year he went to Montreal for more schooling, and in 1773, at the age of fourteen, he went to Philadelphia for training in merchandising. While in Philadelphia, Peter wrote and received letters from both his mother and father (JP [12]:1042–43). Correspondence with his mother included a reminder that he had asked her to send him some Indian "curiositys" to show to interested ladies and gentlemen. He asked also for a book in Mohawk, "for I am Afraid I'll lose my Indian Toungue if I dont practice it more than I do" (JP [8]:1139–40). Clearly Peter was becoming a sophisticated, urbane gentleman who took pride in his Mohawk heritage.

Molly Brant's busy domestic life at Johnson Hall came to an abrupt end with the death of Sir William Johnson in July 1774. His will left substantial bequests of land and money to her and to each individual child; her children received a total inheritance of thirty-two thousand pounds, equal to the estate Johnson left his sons-in-law (Guzzardo 1975:289). In the inventory of the contents of Johnson Hall in August 1774, Molly Brant's room was exempted; she had her own belongings. Her later claim for losses during the Revolution gives some clues as to what these were. Although that list was made following her abrupt departure from Canajoharie, many of these items probably came with her from Johnson Hall and reveal the level of material culture to which she was accustomed.

Household goods such as trunks, blankets, sheets, fine ceramics, utility ceramics, tableware, and kitchen items were listed along with cash. Following this were transportation items: one wagon, a chaise, a batteau, and saddles. Listed after an unspecified amount of corn valued at two hundred pounds were items of clothing, both Indian and European in style, items of adornment such as buckles, broaches and crosses, shoes, and a violin (probably Peter's). Molly Brant also noted that the rebels had taken all of the "Deeds of writings" in her possession (Guldenzopf 1986:204–5). Molly Brant's possessions were a combination of Mohawk and European objects.

Canajoharie and Fort Niagara

In his will, Johnson recognized his "natural" children by Brant as "her" children (JP [12]:1063–64). She came from a society based on matrilineal descent and matrilocal residence, and following these kinship practices, she took her children back to her native village of Canajoharie. There she stayed for three years. One of her daughters (probably Margaret Farley, who had moved to England in 1831) recalled years later that during their time at Canajoharie her older sisters were sent to school in Schenectady ("Testimony of a Child of Molly Brant," Hamilton Papers, Box 2, Folder 12). Peter returned from Philadelphia after his father's death and, as an accepted family member and part of a loyalist delegation, went to England with Sir John Johnson, Daniel Claus, Guy Johnson, and Joseph Brant.

Molly Brant and her family continued to be noticed by travelers coming through Canajoharie. In August 1775, Tench Tilghman, the secretary for an Indian commission appointed by Congress, stopped in Canajoharie to encourage the sachems to attend a conference at German Flatts. There he observed Molly Brant, whom he described as "fallen from her high Estate. She lived with Sir William for 20 years and was treated with as much attention as if she had been his wife . . . she was of great use to Sir William in his Treaties with those people. He knew that Women govern the Politics of savages as well as the refined part of the World" (Harrison 1876:83).

He added that Sir William left her "some money, upon which she carries on a small Trade, consisting chiefly I believe in Rum which she sells to the Indians" (Harrison 1876:83). Although Tilghman may have been repeating unfounded gossip, it is possible that Brant was selling rum to supplement her income. Although Sir William had arranged for her to inherit a total of twelve hundred pounds sterling in his will, how much of this she actually received is unknown. Whatever the amount, money was a great concern to her throughout the rest of her life.

Tilghman added further details. Noting that Molly Brant was among the Indians who met him at the conference, he wrote that "she saluted us with an air of ease and politeness" (Harrison 1876:87). What he wrote next provides a further glimpse of her as a person:

> one of the Company that had known her before told her she looked thin and asked her if she had been sick, she said sickness had not reduced her, but that it was the Remembrance of a Loss that could never be made up to her, meaning the death of Sr. William. Upon seeing Mr. Kirkland an Oneida Missionary, she taxed him with neglect in passing by her House without calling to see her. She said there was a time when she had friends enough, but remarked with sensible emotion that the unfortunate and the poor were always neglected. (Harrison 1876:87)

Perhaps Molly Brant had always acted this assertively, though Sir William's death may have changed her. For whatever reason, in an age when ease and politeness were social graces expected of sophisticated society, Molly Brant moved into the company of these authoritative white men with confidence. It is clear that the forceful missionary to the Oneidas, Samuel Kirkland, did not intimidate her. He had been her guest at Johnson Hall; she had good reason to expect some acknowledgment of her former hospitality.

Tilghman went on to add a sentence that forecast her future: "The Indians pay her great respect and I am afraid her influence will give us some trouble, for we are informed that she is working strongly to prevent the meeting at Albany, being intirely in the Interests of Guy Johnson" (Harrison 1876). Upon Sir William's death, Guy Johnson had become the Superintendent of Indian Affairs for the Northern District and, fearing capture as a loyalist, left for Canada that previous June. He was a key player in the contest between the British and Americans to enlist the assistance, or at least the neutrality, of the Iroquois. Her influence undiminished, Molly Brant also had a part to play in this contest.

Sir John Johnson fled to Canada in 1776, abandoning Johnson Hall to American troops. The commander in charge of these troops, Captain Bloomfield, visited Canajoharie twice in June. On June 9 he noted, "in this place lives Miss Molly (the noted Indian Squagh kept by Sir Wm. Johnson)

& her Eight children & who were all well provided for by the Vigorous old Baronet before his Death" (Lender and Martin 1982:61). On June 17, he called "at the house of Miss Molly & who by the generosity of her Paramour Sr. Wm. Johnson has every thing convenient around her & lives more in the English taste than any of her Tribe. She is now about 50 & has the remains of a Very likely Person" (Lender and Martin 1982:63).

Bloomfield was wrong; Brant was actually about forty years old at the time. His account confirms that she was living in a European-style house surrounded by the goods that she later listed in her loyalist claims: fine ceramics, silver, twelve black chairs, and other items. A month later, on July 14, Bloomfield "got a Pair of Elegant Leggins made in the Indian Fashion by Miss Molly & her Daughters . . . Had the Pleasure of seeing the Young Ladys, one is Very handsome, both were richly dressed agreable to the Indian-Fashion" (Lender and Martin 1982:72). Bloomfield may have ordered the leggings on his previous visit. Not everyone, evidently, could get to see Molly's daughters; another member of Bloomfield's party, Ebenezer Elmer, reported that when he stopped to visit Sir William Johnson's "squaw" on June 27 in hopes of meeting the daughters, whom he identified as "the Miss. Johnson's," he was told that "they were not up." He did see and converse with "the old squaw lady who appeared kind" (Elmer 1847–48[2]:132). This may have been either Molly Brant or her mother, Margaret.

Brant and her children were forced to leave Canajoharie after the Battle of Oriskany, fought in 1777, when Americans learned that she had sent information to the British about their troop movements (NYCD [8]:721). The bloody battle occurred in Oneida country, and Oneidas, who sided with the Americans, were burned out. Claus reported "this the rebel Oneidas . . . revenged upon Joseph's Sister and her family (living in the Upper Mohawk Town) . . . robbing them of cash, cloaths, cattle &c. and driving them from their home" (NYCD [8]:725). Molly's child later testified that they were also threatened by "persons who would remove [them] from Canajoharie to Albany." One night, men who claimed to be looking for Joseph Brant searched the house, including the sleeping rooms. "I was in one of the beds of which they drew back the Curtains, & seeing only Children in it, they declined ferther Search—& withdrew. I perfectly remember my alarm." A few nights later, after a similar experience, "my Mother then determined to leave the Country as she found her residence . . . no longer Safe. She left her House with reluctance & with a Sore heart taking her Children Seven in Number and two black men Servants & two female Servants" ("Testimony of a Child of Molly Brant," Hamilton Papers, Box 2, Folder 12).

Daniel Claus wrote that Brant and her children "fled to Onondaga the Council place of the 6 Nations, laying her grievances before that body" (NYCD [8]:725). In April 1778, Jelles Fonda, on behalf of the American Commissioners of Indian Affairs, visited Canajoharie and took affidavits documenting the plundering. He blamed the affair on former County Chairman Peter S. Dygart,. whom he said had stolen large amounts of coins, silver, gold rings, silver buckles, and broaches from Molly's house, which he then divided with an Oneida Indian. Fonda added that several silk gowns had been taken and were later seen "on the aforesaid Peter S. Dygarts Daughter" (Penrose 1981:134). The range and extent of the goods documented in this account correlates with Brant's loyalist claim.

Molly Brant abandoned much of her wealth when she was forced to leave Canajoharie. She had stayed longer than other Johnson family members, probably to protect the inheritance promised to her and her children in Sir William Johnson's will. Throughout the war, she continued to plan for her return home. On June 23, 1778, for example, she wrote that she maintained "hope the Time is very near, when we shall all return to our habitations on the Mohawk River" (Claus Papers, MG19, F1, 2:29).

While visiting Daniel Claus in 1779, Brant told him of her adventures after leaving Canajoharie. Claus reported that she said she found the Iroquois after Burgoyne's defeat "very wavering and unstable . . . that they promised her faithfully to stick up strictly to the Engagements to her late worthy Friend, and for his & her sake, espouse the Kings Cause vigorously and speadily avenge her Wrongs & Injuries, for she is in every Respect considered & esteemed by them as Sr. Wms Relict, and one word from her is more taken Notice of by the five Nations than a thousand from any white Man without Exception" (Haldimand Papers, Reel A685, Ms. 21774, 57–58).

Brant had forged new power and a new cause from her status as Sir William's widow. She was a significant political force in the lives of the Six Nations, and the British authorities recognized how useful that power could be. Because of that influence, Major John Butler successfully urged her to come to Niagara, where Indian and British forces were beginning to gather. During the winter of 1779, six councils were held there, with thousands of Indians participating (Kelsay 1984:236–37). Claus explained that "she having been their [the Iroquois] Confidant in every Matter of Importance & was consulted thereupon, and prevented many an unbecoming & extravagant proposal to the Commanding Officer at Niagara" (Haldimand Papers, Reel A685, Ms. 21774, 57–58). In an earlier draft of the letter, Claus wrote "she prevented many a mischief & much more so than in her Bror Joseph whose present Zeal & Activity occasioned rather Envy & Jealousy" (Claus Papers, MG19, F1, 2:131–33). From Niagara, Molly Brant sent a message to Claus that "the Manner She lives here is pretty expensive to her: being oblidged to keep, in a manner, open house for all those Indians that have any weight in the 6 Nations confederacy" (Penrose 1981:168). These and other stories show that Molly Brant was acting as an intermediary and a conduit for encouragement and information between the Iroquois and the British government. Meanwhile, she was living in a crowded, predominantly male environment, separated from those of her children who were in school in Montreal and from her son, Peter. After leaving the Mohawk Valley in 1775, Peter fought for the British until his death in November 1777.[9] No record has been found of his mother's reaction to the news of his death.

The strain of her family and material losses may have overwhelmed Molly Brant at this point. An account about life at Niagara published in 1831, based on the recollections of Revolutionary War veterans, indicates that she became hostile to Lieutenant Colonel Stacia (Stacey), an American captive. The account states that "She resorted to the Indian method of dreaming. She informed Col. Butler that she dreamed she had the Yankee's head, and that she and the Indians were kicking it about the fort . . . for a football . . . Col. Butler . . . then told her, decidedly, that Col. Stacia should not be given up to the Indians" (W. Campbell 1831:182).[10]

Kelsay points out that "Bolton actually did send this prisoner down to Montreal for fear of what the Indians might do to him. His action lends some credence to the story" (Kelsay 1984:686 n.2).

By June 1779, Fort Niagara became crowded with Iroquois refugees, who gathered there for protection while the men were at war. The commander suggested that Molly Brant and her family be transferred to Montreal (Haldimand Papers, Reel A682, Ms. 21764, 18). This may have been because of Brant's difficult behavior; it may also have been because he was concerned that conditions at Niagara made it impossible for her to receive the best treatment. General Frederick Haldimand, commander of the British forces in Canada, responded positively, and on July 16 Bolton wrote that "Miss Molly & Family have accepted your Excellency's Invitation and will leave this place tomorrow" (Gundy 1953:102). In August, Molly Brant visited Claus and some of her children in Montreal. Claus reported that she was unhappy because she had "to leave her old Mother & other Indn Relations & friends behind" and that she had "two grown Daughters with her whom she would willingly see appear decent which is not in her power to do" (Haldimand Papers, Reel A685, Ms. 21774, 57–58).[11] He went on to write that he was apprehensive because "her staying here would be more expensive than at Niagara, she being so near the Fountain head."

Carleton Island

Brant did not stay in Montreal; the American forces under Generals James Clinton and John Sullivan began destruction of the western Iroquois villages in 1779 in an effort to end Iroquois participation in the war. Her instant response was a desire to return to Niagara, as "her Staying away at this critical Time, may prove very injurious to her character hereafter, being at the head of a Society of six Natn Matrons" (Haldimand Papers, Reel A685, Ms. 21174, 63).[12] Knowing the Iroquois were dependent on Brant for information, Haldimand justified his decision to pay the expense of her return to Niagara in a letter to Lord George Germain, Secretary of State for the Colonies, written in September 1779. After describing Joseph Brant's importance, he reported that Molly "might be of use in encouraging the Indians to Preserve their Fidelity . . . the Care of this Woman will necessarily be attended with Some Expense to Government, but whatever may be done for her, is Due to the Memory of Sir Willm Johnson, to Her Services, and will be a handsome Mark of attention to Joseph" (Haldimand Papers, Reel A662, Ms. 21714, 42).

Molly, however, was also concerned about her family. Haldimand had suggested to Claus that she leave her children at school (Haldimand Papers, Reel A683, Ms. 21767, 29). Guy Johnson answered that he would "furnish her in the manner you are pleased to mention, but her anxiety to have her Children with her seems insurmountable, however I shall manage about it in the best manner in my power" (31). As a result, Molly accompanied a group of Mohawks to Carleton Island, leaving "her two youngest girls with me [Claus] to send to School one is 10. the other 8. year old" (Haldimand Papers, Reel A685, Ms. 21774, 279).

Carleton Island was the location of a British post opposite today's

Watertown, New York. Here she was unable to find transport to Niagara. Her letter to Claus explaining their situation may have been written by her or dictated to an amanuensis. As one of her few extant letters, it captures her own words (Claus Papers, MG19, F1, 2:135–36):

Carleton Island 5th October 1779

Sɪʀ

We arrived here the 29th. last month after Tedious and dissagreable Voyage; where we remain and by all Appearance may for the winter. I have rote to Colo. Butler and my brother Acquainting them of my Situation, desireing there advice, as I was left no Direction Concerning my self or family, Only when a Vessel Arraived, I Could get a passage to Niagara . . . I have been promised by Colo. Johnson at Montreal that I Should hear from the Gen'l. and have his directions & order to be provided at whatever place my little service should be wanted which you know I am always ready to do, should you think proper to speak to the Gen'l. on that head will be much Oblidged to you the Indians are a Good dale dissatisfied on Acc't. of the Colo's. hasty temper which I hope he will soon drop Otherwise it may be Dissadvantageous I need not tell you whatever is promised or told them Ought to be perform'd——

Those from Canada are much Dissatisfied on Account of his taking more Notice of them that are Suspected than them that are known to be Loyal, I tell this only to you that you Advise him On that head. Meantime beg leave to be remembred to all You family from Sir——

Your wellwisher

Mary Brant
My Children Join in love to theire Sisters
Colo. Danl. Claus   Montreal

The letter refers to Colonel Guy Johnson, who was becoming frustrated with his role. He may also have become frustrated with Brant, and she with him. A month later, he complained to Claus that he had heard that "Molly used to go to the Stores & take out everything she pleas'd & give to her particulars. She is certainly you know pretty large minded . . . I fear that any Expense or Attention will fall short of her Desires tho' I wish to gratify them & many other things are said that I cannot now Explain" (Hamilton Papers, Box 1, Folder 12). Knowing that the facilities at Carleton Island were inadequate, he anticipated her need for better accommodations, which he felt unable to provide. Although it had nothing to do with her, Guy was replaced by Sir John Johnson as Indian Commissioner shortly thereafter.

The British military response to the Clinton and Sullivan campaign was ineffective. Because they were homeless, hundreds of Iroquois refugees had to winter in places such as Carleton Island. Molly Brant did what she could to maintain the fidelity to the British cause among Iroquois at the latter locale. By February 23, 1780, Captain Malcolm Fraser, the senior British officer on Carleton Island, wrote that Brant had "shewen her usual Zeal for Govt. by her constant endeavours to maintain the Indians in His Majestys Interest" (Claus Papers, MG19, F1, 2:177–80). On March 21, he added that although "the Chiefs were careful to keep their people sober and satisfied . . . their uncommon good behaviour is in a great Measure to be ascribed to Miss Molly Brants Influence over them, which is far superior to that of all their Chiefs put together . . . as she checkd the demands of others both for presents & provisions" (Haldimand Papers, Reel A688, Ms. 21787, 116).

Fulfilling her political role, Brant also worked to satisfy her domestic obligations. By June 21, 1780, better quarters not yet being in place, she elected to go to Montreal to appeal directly to Haldimand. This caused considerable consternation. Fraser wrote from Carleton Island that "Joseph Brants' Sister Miss Molly left this place yesterday along with Colonel Butler much against my inclination as I have been informed she is gone to ask Your Excellency for favors & I have no Doubt but She will be unreasonable in her Demands—her family however is numerous, and not easily maintained in the decent footing on which she keeps them" (Haldimand Papers, Reel A688, Ms. 21787, 150). Claus, writing to John Johnson, reported "last Thursday arrived at my House Molly with her son George & her Attendt. Butler from Carleton Island . . . [to] get something done for her . . . to attain a certain Settlement upon her & children, three of whom now soon marriageable . . . and she expects an answer by Saturday" (Hamilton Papers, Box 1, Folder 12). Claus went on to suggest that a regular allowance of two hundred pounds a year be awarded to her. Between them, Claus and John Johnson persuaded Brant to leave the situation in their hands.

Meanwhile Fraser, in his June 1780 letter to Haldimand, was sputtering that:

she will probably wish to change her place of Residence and may want to go to Niagara where she will be a very unwelcome Guest to Col. Bolton and most of the other principal people in that quarter, and if She be not humoured in all her demands for herself and her dependents (which are numerous) she may by the violence of her temper be led to creat Mischief . . . In case Your Excellency would wish her to remain here it were good that some little box of a house were built for her as it would be more comfortable to her family than living in a Barrack Room. (Haldimand Papers, Reel A688, Ms. 21787, p. 150)

Brant evidently was justifiably unhappy over her domestic arrangements. Fraser, for his part, was afraid of losing her assistance in handling the numerous Iroquois staying on the island. Responding to her demands, Haldimand directed in July that a house be built for her. Fraser had indicated in his June 1780 letter that he had already "at my own expence made a tollerable good garden for her and I have contributed all in my power to have made her Situation as comfortable as possible—indeed she seems very well pleased with her treatment, and I have every reason to be satisfyed with her Conduct through the winter—and as I know herself and her family to be steadily attached to Government I wish them to be attended to" (Haldimand Papers, Reel A688, Ms. 21787, 150). To be built was "a House as will lodge Her and Family comfortably, chuising a favorable Situation within a few hundred Yards of the Fort" (Haldimand Papers, Reel A689, Ms. 21788, 94). Upon leaving command of the island to Major John Ross in 1781, Fraser reported that "I gave particular directions regarding Miss Molly's treatment, she had got into her new house, and seemed better satisfyed with her situation than I had ever known her before" (Haldimand Papers, Reel A688, Ms. 21787, 201). She had won.

Brant stayed at Carleton Island for the remainder of the war. She brought George, Susanna, and Mary home from school in Montreal. On July 26, 1781, Claus wrote to Haldimand regarding their progress:

The Schoolmaster tells me that the girls sufficiently read & write English, And the Boy to my knowledge has greatly improved in that respect, and is so far advanced in cyphering that with a little care and Study, he may easily require more of that Science than he will have occasion for, I have supplied him with necessary Books & Stationary, he is a promising Lad abt. 14 years old . . . There are left at School two of Brant Johnson's Daughters, whose Mother is daily expected to take them away, the eldest a fine genius & great Arithmetician. (Haldimand Papers, Reel A685, Ms. 21774, 208)

Almost exactly a year later, Claus wrote "Brant Johnsons two girls are lately gone to Niagara having finished their Learning after a 3. years stay at this place. A Boy and Girl of Mary Johnsons remain, but expect to be taken away shortly by their Mother" (279). In this note, Claus may have been calling Molly Brant by the last name of Johnson, the only time this occurred in the known documents, although the children all used the surname of Johnson. Brant Johnson was Sir William's son by a now-unknown Indian woman; Sir William's grandchildren, the daughters of Brant Johnson, were being educated in the same school as their cousins.

In a "Return of Loyalists on Carleton Island" dated November 26, 1783, Molly Brant's household was listed under the category of "Indian Department."[13] This is the first document known to record Molly Brant's age and is the basis for her accepted birth date of 1736. Her daughters were all with her; son George had apparently gone back to school. A white captive, William Lamb, was living with her. Four slaves were present, probably the same four who had escaped from Canajoharie with her in 1777. The two female slaves were originally from Johnson Hall. Jane (Jenny) was left to Brant in Johnson's will, along with one-quarter of his other slaves (JP [12]:1070); Jenny's sister, Juba, apparently was one of those. Brant, then, had managed to keep her dependents together, despite all the upsets and changes in her personal life.

All was not drudgery on Carleton Island. In February 1780, Gilbert Tice, former Johnstown innkeeper, wrote to Claus that "Miss Molley and the Children are in Good Helth—and wee Pass our time Verey Agreabel Considering all things. wee have a Ball once a week—and Sevarel other things to Pass the time" (Claus Papers, MG19, F1, 2:173, 175). This remark followed his report that she had assisted him in explaining Claus's letter fully to the Indians. This work was not forgotten.

Brant did not simply settle down on the island. In December 1780, the wife of an Army officer, Matilda Schieffelin, wrote about her meeting with Brant from Navy Hall, across the lake from Fort Niagara:

I had the honor to sup with her in Captain Butler's Tent, on a haunch of Venison. She has a sensible countenance, and much whiter than the generality of Indians, but her Father was white. She understands En-

glish, but speaks only the Mohawk. Which has something extremely soft
and musical in it when spoken by a woman. This Squaw is an expense of
three or four thousand a year to the British Government, as I am informed. She has a fine house building at Carleton Island, where several
of her daughters live with her, and a great number of dependents. She
was now in a traveling dress, a Calico Bedgown, fastened with Silver
Brooches and a worsted mantel. (L. De Forest 1941:120–23)

That Brant could speak English was established a few years later in her
travels with the wife of the governor of Upper Canada, Mrs. Elizabeth
Simcoe; here, however, she may have chosen not to do so since Butler
spoke Mohawk. It is a striking picture of her at the age of forty-four, even
though the story contains errors. Once again, she was dressed in the
Mohawk style, but her clothes were of European cloth.[14]

Hostilities between the Americans and the British formally ended with
the peace treaty of 1783. There was no mention of the Six Nations and no
attempt to protect their right to their native lands, despite the many British
promises. Brant's reaction must have been bitter. She had spent almost
eight years of her life traveling and cajoling the Iroquois to keep active on
the British side. All of her inheritance and those of her children were lost.
Many Indian leaders protested angrily, as did many of their military and
political allies (Graymont 1972:259–64). In the end, they were granted
land in Canada and given financial compensation.

Kingston

For her part, Molly Brant made one last move, to a new town at Cataraqui,
now Kingston, Ontario. Here a house was built for her by the British
government, and a pension of one hundred pounds a year was settled on
her "in consideration of the early and uniform fidelity, attachment and
zealous Services rendered to the King's Government by Miss Mary Brant
and her Family" (Haldimand Papers, Reel A685, Ms. 21775, 124).[15] A few
years later, she and her family received compensation for their losses. Guy
Johnson, John Johnson, Daniel Claus, Joseph Chew, and John Butler all
testified on behalf of Brant and the children to establish their loyalist
claims.

Receipt of this compensation provided dowries essential for any consid-

eration of marriage, though not all of Brant's daughters used their payments for this purpose; Mary remained unmarried. Her other sisters married professional or military men. None were Indians. Son George married
an Iroquois woman and became a farmer and teacher (Draper Manuscripts 13F:147, 14F:24, 27). Molly Brant continued her contacts with the
Johnson family. In June 1787, Sir John wrote to Joseph Brant that Molly,
her daughter Elizabeth Kerr, and Kerr's children were visiting (Johnston
1973:104), perhaps to receive their quarterly payments for which Sir John
was responsible.

Very active in the Anglican community in Kingston, Molly Brant was
the only woman listed in 1792 in the founding charter of the church
(Anonymous 1989).[16] That same year, traveler John C. Ogden saw her
there: "we saw an Indian woman, who sat in an honourable place among
the English. She appeared very devout during the divine service, and very
attentive to the sermon . . . When Indian embassies arrived, she was sent
for, dined at governor Simcoe's and treated with respect by himself, his
lady, and family . . . She retains the habit of her country women, and is a
Protestant" (Ogden 1800:61).

Brant continued to be active in political as well as domestic spheres. In
1793, her presence was again noted at Fort Niagara. Her travel probably
had two purposes; attendance at her daughter Susannah's marriage in
Niagara on June 5 and participation in an important political conference
with American commissioners scheduled for the same week in Sandusky,
Ohio. General Benjamin Lincoln, one of the American commissioners
attending the Sandusky conference, wrote a brief account of the Indian
women observed at a dance held in honor of the King's birthday. Lincoln
wrote:

> in the evening there was quite a splendid ball, about twenty well dressed
> and handsome ladies, and about three times that number of gentlemen
> present . . . What excited the best feelings of my heart was the ease and
> affection which which [sic] the ladies met each other, although there
> were a number present whose mothers sprang from the aborigines of the
> country. They appeared as well dressed as the company in general, and
> intermixed with them in a measure which evinced at once the dignity of
> their own minds, and the good sense of the others. These ladies pos-
> sessed great ingenuity and industry, and have great merit; for the educa-
> tion they have acquired is owing principally to their own industry, as their
> father, Sir William Johnson, was dead and the mother retained the

manners and dress of her tribe. (Hamilton Papers, Box 2, Folder 12; M. Campbell 1958:166)

While it is not clear whether Molly Brant was present at the ball, she and her daughters enjoyed an important position in their social and political world of the early 1790s.

The following year, another English observer noted Brant's presence at Niagara. Mrs. Elizabeth Simcoe, the wife of the governor of Upper Canada, was traveling from Niagara on a boat reserved for her use. Although she preferred travelling alone, she "relented in favour of [Joseph] Brant's sister who was ill and very desirous to go. She speaks English well & is a civil & very sensible old woman" (M. Innis 1965:136). Here is Brant at age fifty-eight, still strong-willed. She frequently went to the Simcoe home for dinner; at one point she was called upon to use her medicinal skills to help the governor. In April 1795, Mrs. Simcoe wrote that "there was no medical advice but that of a Horse Doctor who pretended to be an apothecary." Molly "prescribed a Root—I believe it is calamus—which really relieved his Cough in a very short time" (M. Innis 1965:155).

Molly Brant died in Kingston on April 16, 1796, when she was about sixty years old. She was buried in St. George's (now St. Paul's) churchyard, but the exact location of her burial plot is unknown. In 1986, to honor her influential role in colonial history, Canada issued a commemorative stamp; the face pictured on the stamp is an idealization of the real person about whom so many myths have evolved, even in her own lifetime. In 1989, the Anglican Church of Canada added an annual day of commemoration of Molly Brant to the church calendar, a distinct honor.

Conclusions

Brant was described variously by her contemporaries as handsome, sensible, judicious, political, faithful, prudent, pretty likely (good-looking), well-bred, pleasant, delightful, uncommonly agreeable, understanding, artful, at ease in society, capable of scolding, influential, of great use, large-minded, zealous, possessed of a violent temper, capable of mischief, civil, devout, and respected. This variety of descriptions from the eighteenth century demonstrates that Molly Brant was a woman of many dimensions. As a woman, mother, and political force, she was a legend in

Reproduced courtesy of Canada Post Corporation

her own century. For fifteen years, she was a vital link between her people and Sir William Johnson in the management of Indian affairs. For the next ten years, she acted as an intermediary and conduit between the Iroquois and the British government. At the same time, she had to provide for eight children, see to their educations, and try to regain some of the fortune they had lost. Her choice of political roles during this time is controversial; her success in her domestic role is admirable. Today she is seen by Canadians as a founder of their country. Yet in the United States, her loyalist activities have tended to overshadow her fascinating story. Unlike Pocahontas and Sacajawea, two Native American heroines familiar to the American public, Molly Brant is not yet a highly visible figure.

Notes

1. Women in Iroquois society, through their matrilineages, controlled the lands, lodges, and wealth of the families; the leading matrons chose and deposed of chiefs; they were consulted about policy, particularly when war was contemplated. These roles were well-known to eighteenth-century observers. For modern discussions, see Bonvillain 1980:47–80; Axtell 1981:150–66; Bataille and Sands 1984:18; Namias 1993; Spittal 1990.

2. Haldimand Papers, Reel C2110, R.G. 1, L3, Vol. 256 [transcribed by Paul Huey], Public Archives of Canada, Ottawa.

3. Brant's birthdate is based on her 1783 declaration that she was then forty-seven. Haldimand Papers, Reel A689, Ms. 21787, 344 [transcribed by Paul Huey], Public Archives of Canada, Ottawa.

4. Records of purchases attributed to Brant appear in Robert Adams's Day Book (in JP [13]:532–616); John Butler's Account Book (in JP [13]:506–32); and in the Campbell Papers #EP10062, New York State Library, Albany.

5. Johnson was a well-known collector of Native American artifacts (Burch 1990b). A visitor in 1776 saw Sir William's portrait surrounded by wampum and "Indian curiositys and Trappings of Indian Finery" (Lender and Martin 1982:49).

6. Gundy states incorrectly that this letter was donated to the Draper Manuscripts Collection; instead it was the one written by Desorontyon to Claus (Ms. 13F133), presently on file in microfilm at the New York State Library, Albany.

7. "Wari" is probably Molly's signature; the Iroquois language has no "m." The original is in the Haldimand Papers, Reel A684, 117, Public Archives of Canada, Ottawa.

8. "Testimony of a Child of Molly Brant, England, March 15, 1841" in the Hamilton Papers, Box 2, Folder 12, Albany Institute of History and Art.

9. Peter was present at the capture of Ethan Allen at Montreal (NYCD [8]:637). He lost his life in 1777 either at the Battle of Long Island or the Battle of Mud Island near Philadelphia (Kelsay 1984:272; JP [12]:966n; [13]:1025 n).

10. The Iroquois belief that dreams represent wishes of the soul is extensively documented (A.F.C. Wallace 1958). Unfulfilled dreams are believed to threaten the health of the dreamer.

11. See also Claus Papers, MG19, F1, 2:131–33, Public Archives of Canada. These are two different letters, each often quoted. Written on the same day, one was sent to Haldimand; one was a draft.

12. Claus added that if she did not rejoin them, the Iroquois would think she was concealing information about "impending Danger over the Confederacy."

13. Listed were Mrs. Mary Brant, age 47; Elizabeth Johnson, age 20; Magdalen Johnson, age 18; Margaret Johnson, age 16; Mary Johnson, age 12; Susannah Johnson, age 11; Nancy Johnson, age 10; William Lamb, age 13; Abraham Johnston, a Negro, age 45; Juba Fundy, a Negro woman, age 23; and Jane Fundy, a Negro woman, age 20 (Haldimand Papers, Reel A689, Ms. 21787, 344).

14. A bedgown was a loose, jacket-like piece without fastenings, which was worn by most eighteenth-century women (Robin Campbell: personal communication). Indian women by this time period had adopted the bedgown (George Hamell: personal communication). Thus, Brant's fastening such a piece of clothing with silver trade brooches (worn only by Indians) combines items chosen from two cultures.

15. The site of Brant's house in Kingston was excavated by archaeologists in 1989; the house site had been destroyed by previous development, but some artifacts and features dating to her occupation were found.

16. This leaflet is given to visitors to the church; there also is a plaque on the wall inside that lists the charter members. Brant's son George was also a founder.

CHAPTER FIFTEEN

꠸

Walking the Medicine Line:
Molly Ockett, a Pigwacket Doctor

Bunny McBride
and Harald E. L. Prins

> Remember that as you pass through life's journey, your greatest
> troubles will be found to result from ignorance.
> —Molly Ockett (ca. 1740–1816)

Introduction

MOLLY OCKETT UNDERSTOOD well that knowledge is power. Like a
hunter harvesting furs along a trap line, she gathered precious information
and carried it back and forth between her Abenaki Indian community and
the host of white settlers that poured into their vast aboriginal wooded
domains beginning in the mid-eighteenth century. As an itinerant doctor
for both natives and newcomers, Molly repeatedly crossed the line between these divergent and often antagonistic groups. Welcomed into the
homes of New England settlers, especially during their most vulnerable
times of illness and despair, she gained an unusually intimate view of their
lives.

Time and again, medicinal knowledge placed her in a position to glean
and distribute inside information about the white strangers to her Abenaki
cohorts. If there was news to be known—a conflict brewing, a demand for
Indian crafts, an odd job to be had, or a new farmer, trapper, miller, or
merchant coming to the area—surely Molly knew it. Such news was vital
to her remnant Abenaki community, which was struggling to survive in an

alien economic order dominated by outsiders who had occupied their traditional lands and threatened their established livelihoods.

To the pioneers, this large-framed, square-shouldered woman offered comforting insight into the natural healing resources secreted in the shadowy arms of an unfamiliar habitat. Her knowledge made the "howling wilderness" less threatening.[1] Her willingness to use it for their benefit no doubt tempered their fears that Indian neighbors would seek retribution for lost lands, lives, and freedoms. We might call her life's path a medicine line, an ominous, unmarked trail through the liminal zone between oppositional cultures.

During Molly's lifetime, her reputation as a healer spread far and wide. Some places where she camped were named after her, and stories about her life and deeds, handed down generation to generation, have become legendary and survive to this day. Although there is a fair bit of fabrication in many of the tales, most spring from historical fact.[2] Typically, they portray her as a generous yet indomitable character noted for effective herbal doctoring. But some reveal the highly tentative and ambiguous nature of Indian-white relations, implying that she was a "witch" endowed with magical powers to inflict harm on those who provoked her wrath.

Who in truth was this woman, remarkable enough to be among the very few native women carried through the centuries in the memory of dominant white society? She is usually referred to as "the last of the Pigwackets," a group of western Abenaki Indians named after their main village, which was originally situated some sixty miles inland from the northern Atlantic Coast, alongside the Upper Saco River near what is now Fryeburg, Maine. Occupying the area since prehistoric times, these corngrowing Indians cleared land to plant their gardens, and the word "pigwacket" seems to mean "at the cleared place."[3] In the mid-seventeenth century, some two hundred Indians resided seasonally in this palisaded farming village.[4] These inhabitants frequently intermarried and shifted residence with other Abenakis at Penacook on the Merrimack, at Amasekonti on the Sandy River, Norridgewock on the Upper Kennebec, and Narankamigouak (referred to by the English as Rocomeko, and later as Canton Point) on the Androscoggin. Their associations also included the Odanak (St. Francis) and Wawenock (Becancour) Abenakis in the St. Lawrence River Valley (Barrows 1938:3; MDH [23]:31–32, 67, 318; Prins 1988 and 1992; Ghere 1988).

Like other regional Abenakis, Pigwackets were a seminomadic people.

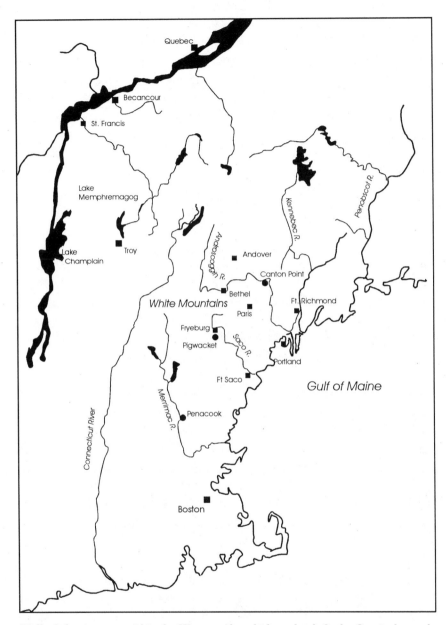

Molly Ockett's range within the Western Abenaki homeland. Scale: One inch equals seventy-five miles. Drawn by Donna Roper.

They traveled in light birchbark canoes, moving up and down rivers in pursuit of sustenance. After the fall harvest at their main village, they dispersed to widespread hunting districts where they spent the winter months. Come spring, they made their way downriver to the coast at Saco and Casco Bays to tap nature's abundant storehouses of shellfish and other foods.[5] Molly was born during one of the coastal sojourns, near the mouth of the Saco River. Legend places her birth date as early as 1685, but evidence points to her having been born between 1730 and 1744. For the sake of clarity in this sketch of her life, we mark 1740 as the year of her birth. Her name, the Indian pronunciation of Marie Agathe, indicates that she was baptized by French Catholic missionaries.[6]

Background: Pigwackets Caught in a Cycle of Colonial Conflict

Molly entered the world in a period when Abenaki people faced ongoing and violent frontier warfare and virulent epidemics (especially smallpox) introduced by Europeans. Dangerously positioned between the French Canadian colonists in the St. Lawrence Valley and hostile Protestant New Englanders on the Atlantic seaboard, the Abenakis were dragged into a destructive cycle of colonial conflict. Most sided with the French, with whom they shared Roman Catholic religious beliefs and ceremonies born of the missionary activities of French Jesuits, who had begun venturing into Abenaki country in the late 1640s. Beyond this tie, the French offered the Abenakis refuge in times of need and supplied them with weapons to stop English encroachments on their lands.[7] In the late seventeenth century, colonial conflicts turned especially gruesome when both the French and English began offering considerable bounties for "enemy" scalps. England's price on Abenaki heads soon reached fifty pounds sterling (Calloway 1990:96).

Scalp-hunting expeditions led to violent clashes between the English and the Abenaki, and with each succeeding skirmish, more Abenaki families retreated up the Androscoggin River to Catholic Indian mission villages in Canada. For some, these refuge settlements became a primary home base where they stayed between long, seasonal hunting or fishing forays. Those Abenakis who made St. Francis, east of Montreal, their new tribal headquarters became collectively known as St. Francis Abenaki (Lapham 1981:10).

However, some Abenakis stubbornly refused to abandon forever their ancestral lands. Retaining their original ethnic affiliations, they repeatedly returned to home territory after forced retreats to the St. Lawrence Valley. These families made only occasional and brief sojourns to the missions for emergency refuge, trade, or religious purposes, such as baptism, marriage, religious feast days, and burial ceremonies.

This was true of some Pigwacket families from the Upper Saco. English records make frequent note of their disappearance and reappearance. For instance, in the winter of 1703, Major Hilton and his scouting company of one hundred men marched from the coast inland. After passing several of "the Enemyes Camps," which held "betwixt Forty or Fifty Indians" each, they came to Pigwacket:

> When we came to the fort [at Pigwacket], we found about an acre of ground, taken in with timber [palisaded], set in the ground in a circular form with ports [gates], and about one hundred wigwams therein; but had been deserted about six weekes, as we judged by the opening of their barnes [storage pits] where their corn was lodged. And that they deserted it in hast, upon some alarm, because we found their corn scattered about the mouthes of their barnes. (MDH [9]:140–43)

The English, committed to "destroying" and "dislodging" the inhabitants of Pigwacket, determined to save the fort and use it as a base for Mohegan and Pequot Indian mercenaries from Connecticut (MDH [9]:173; Dudley [3]:172, 178). Yet by the start of Dummer's War (1722–25) and no doubt before, Pigwackets were back at their village site, growing corn and operating their fishing stations (Baxter 1890:370–71).

During Dummer's War, the relentless scalp hunting expeditions of English Rangers through Abenaki territories claimed the lives of dozens of Pigwacket warriors, sapped their tenacity, and succeeded in driving them from their main village once again (Baxter 1890:370–71).

The English kept well-apprised of the dramatic decline of the Abenaki population in Maine (due to death and both temporary and permanent emigration) during the late seventeenth and early eighteenth centuries. Records note that an Upper Saco River band they called the "Pigwacket tribe," able to field one hundred men in 1690 (Wendall 1866:7–9), had been reduced to a mere twenty-four warriors in 1726 (Gyles [3]:357–58). Downriver, a smaller band (the "Saco tribe") had dwindled from fifty to four men. Likewise, the neighboring "Androscoggins" had plummeted from one hundred and sixty to only ten men (Wendall 1866:7–9).

Abenakis who stayed in or returned to Maine after Dummer's War became painfully aware that further efforts to stop English encroachments would be suicidal. This was especially clear to two small Pigwacket bands inhabiting the Saco in close proximity to coastal English settlements and to lumbering activity. Anxious to remain in their homelands, these bands (headed by chieftains Weranmanhead at the Upper Saco and Saquant downriver) gave up trying to oust their unwelcome neighbors and decided upon a policy of accommodation.

This was not easy. English sawmills, in operation on the Lower Saco since 1662, were thwarting the Indians' traditional subsistence patterns— destroying the forest habitats used by game, obstructing river passage with log drives, blocking fish runs, and drawing into the region more white settlers who helped themselves to farmland, set fish nets that prevented fish from swimming upriver, and encroached on hunting and trapping territories.

In 1727, representatives of the Saco bands traveled to Biddeford to complain to trading-post agent Captain Samuel Jordan, one of very few English who could speak Abenaki. Despite Jordan's language skills, their plea went unheeded.[8]

Molly's Formative Years: From Pigwacket to Boston and Back

Molly was probably about four years old when King George's War broke out in 1744. That year, six Pigwacket warriors, fearful of bounty hunters and struggling desperately for survival, gambled on political linkage with the English, thinking it might offer more security than a long-distance French alliance. Saco River chieftains Weranmanhead and Saquant were among the warriors.[9] One of these headmen may well have been Molly's father, for it appears she was with this group, and she later claimed that her father had been a local chieftain.[10] In June, the men, along with their families (sixteen women and children, including a girl named "Marea-git"), presented themselves at the English trading post downriver, and then traveled with one Captain Cutter to Saco Falls.[11] Considerable discussion ensued about what to do with these Pigwackets. While the Indians "prefer[red] to live at Saco River" under English protection, settlers were "very averse to having any of them tarry at the Falls." Since the Pigwacket men were "loth" to "leave the women & children," authorities ultimately decided "to send all the Indians to Boston." This was their plan: "if the women & Children that belongs to [the warriors] are keept upon some Island neare Boston & Supported at the Province charge we may then have some dependance on the men as Pilates [pilots or guides] with our Scouts when they may be sent out" (MDH [23]:292–93).

In all likelihood, this group corresponds with the one noted by Captain Jordan, who in November 1744 reported from Casco Bay that he had mobilized a squad of white rangers "with whom are enlisted three Saco Indians, and their families are settled at Stroudwater [South Portland, Maine] and provided for by order of government" (Willis 1849:115–16). It appears that the families (except for one woman who died) were thereafter taken to Weymouth (MDH [23]:292) and ultimately to some coastal location in Plymouth County, Massachusetts, where they resided for about four years (Anonymous 1886a:146).

Like other "Friend Indians," these Pigwackets served in the English army during its 1745 siege of Louisbourg, the French fortress at Cape Breton, where they "prov'd themselves good soldiers" (Calloway 1990:145). It is not clear whether the men served in any subsequent military expeditions or whether the families, once removed to Massachusetts, stayed as refugees or as hostages.

In June 1749, a delegation of Abenakis came to Boston, where they met with Governor William Shirley and requested a peace conference. Shirley agreed to a meeting at Falmouth on Casco Bay the following September. Just before departing, the Abenaki spokesman inquired whether "the Pigwacket Indians . . . who are now among the English design to return to their own homes." The governor responded, "I have not spoke with them lately, I shall not Restrain them" (MDH [23]:315). Several months later, when Abenaki chieftains and English authorities gathered to negotiate the Falmouth Peace Treaty, these "Boston Pigwackets" were brought from Plymouth to Falmouth (Anonymous 1886a:146).

However, three Pigwacket girls, including Molly Ockett ("Mareagit"), did not return with the others. These girls, still in Massachusetts "by their "own Choice," according to English officials (Anonymous 1886a:146), were not brought home until the following spring. Traveling on an English sloop to Fort Richmond trading post on the Lower Kennebec, they were handed over to the Abenakis (MDH [23]:372).

Surely Molly's childhood experience among the English in Massachusetts shored up her future role as a bridge between the Abenakis and white settlers. No doubt during this time she learned English and became

acquainted with Protestantism—cultural insights that would greatly en-
hance her ability to act as a liaison between English settlers and her fellow
Catholic tribespeople, many of whom could speak some French, but almost none of whom knew English (MDH [23]:258). Because she lived
among the English during very impressionable years (from about age five
to age nine), she probably became quite used to their customs and may
even have been uneasy about leaving the Boston area.

Certainly this was the impression (albeit biased) of J. Wheelwright,
Commissary General of the Province of the Massachusetts Bay, who was in
charge of making sure Molly and the other two girls were safely delivered
to Richmond. In his report he noted that, when the girls were dropped off,
the Abenakis "carried them into the Woods, tho much against their In-
clinations" (MDH [23]:372).

Young Womanhood: Retreat and Return

Between 1750 and 1755, during Molly's early teenage years, her kin-
group appears to have had a breathing spell. They lived at least part of the
time at Narankamigouak (Canton Point), an Abenaki settlement on the
Androscoggin (Lapham 1981:78; True 1874:11–12). This former mission
village above Livermore Falls provided a rather favorable setting. It was
situated a relatively safe distance from English settlements[12] and only two
day's travel via portage from another Abenaki village, Norridgewock,
home base for the nearest Jesuit priest at the time (Dragon 1973:234–35;
Lapomarda 1977:11; Prins 1984). Nonetheless, random murders of Indians who ventured near English settlements marred the official peace
during this period, as did Abenaki retaliatory attacks (MDH [23]:327–29,
[24]:451–52; North 1870:32–33; NYCD [10]:218–19; Willis 1849:141–
44). A final Anglo-Abenaki war was brewing.

With the outbreak of the so-called French and Indian War (1755–59),
Pigwackets chose once again to avoid confronting the English, well aware
that these coastal neighbors were becoming ever more numerous and in-
timidating as a military force. Whatever their overtures may have been,
English authorities now decided upon a campaign of indiscriminate,
genocidal warfare that today would be characterized as "ethnic cleansing."

The English reissued bounty for Abenaki scalps and prisoners (MDH
[24]:31–32, 63–64; Lapham 1981:75), and sent troops on upriver seek-
and-destroy expeditions against all Abenaki individuals and camps—

regardless of their particular position toward the English (MDH [24]:38–39; Lapham 1981:75). Soon afterwards, a deadly smallpox epidemic raged through the widely dispersed Abenaki encampments in Maine (MDH [24]:71–72; Lapham 1981:78). In 1757, the English escalated the bloody pressure on any surviving Abenakis, increasing the scalp bounty to the incredibly high sum of three hundred pounds (MDH [24]:83). Given the price on their heads, literally, no Abenaki could expect quarter from an English bounty-hunting expedition ranging the Maine woods.

Overwhelmed by adversity, Molly's remnant band had no choice but to join the Abenaki exodus to Canada, finding a temporary haven at the St. Francis Mission. A few years later the French-Indian defense crumbled, reaching its denouement in 1759 with the fall of Quebec and the raid of Major Robert Rogers's Rangers on St. Francis. The Rangers burned the mission to the ground.

Some Pigwackets, including nineteen-year-old Molly, and a fair number of other Abenakis survived the raid. Tradition states that Molly managed to evade capture or worse by hiding behind a bush (True 1863). But it signalled the end of their option to serve as a valued, mobile frontier force in a highly contested middle ground between fiercely competing European colonial powers. Soon thereafter, although France did not officially surrender Canada to England until the 1763 signing of the Treaty of Paris, the French were effectively eliminated as a political force in Canada. The British Crown was free to assert its hegemony over the entire region.

Living "scattered except a few" (NYCD [7]:582), Abenaki survivors ranged widely through the vast mountainous forest domains between Lake Champlain, St. Francis, and Becancour in the St. Lawrence River Valley, and Norridgewock and the Penobscot River in Maine, keeping "a constant communication" with each other (MDH [13]:342). Without the military support of their former allies in French Canada, they had no hope of blocking the encroachments of New England settlers.

Breakdown: Dispossession of the Abenaki Nation

Seeking cheap lands for their farms, pioneering whites reached the fertile planting grounds surrounding the Pigwacket's former main village on the Upper Saco around 1762. Unhampered by opposition, they usurped these lands, founding the town of Fryeburg. Soon thereafter a number of Abenaki families, some coming from St. Francis, returned to the area (Barrows 1938:7). Forcibly resigned to English dominance yet striving to retain a measure of their traditional culture, these Abenakis and their far-flung cohorts resumed their migratory rounds of hunting and fishing, and began camping seasonally near Fryeburg and other emerging towns in their homelands for trading purposes.

Although specific traces of Molly's life disappear between Rogers's 1759 raid and 1764, she may well have been among these early homecomers. Using furs as their primary currency (supplemented by crafts, including baskets, bark pails and boxes, and beaded pouches and moccasins), the Indians purchased commodities such as "cloathing (silks) and provisions, flour, bread, corn, peas, pork, tobacco, rum, wine."[13] They sheltered themselves in bark wigwams, typically built "in the form of a cone, constructed of tall saplings, enclosing a space of about 15 feet in diameter [with the floor covered with] hemlock twigs" (Abbott n.d. [2]:56). Often they camped near a settlement for months at a time, becoming well acquainted with the white communities (Barrows 1938:7; Lapham 1981:45–46).

An English Protestant minister at Richmond on the Kennebec offered this description of visiting Abenaki at the time: "A great number of Indians frequent this neighbourhood. They . . . lead a rambling life. They support themselves entirely by hunting, are very savage in their dress and manners, have a language of their own, but universally speak French, and also profess the Romish religion, and visit Canada once or twice a year for absolution" (Bartlett 1853:83–84). They also visited Canada to have their children baptized. Mission records reveal that by 1764, Molly had married an Abenaki hunter named Piol Susup (Pierre Joseph) and had a daughter with him. That year, the child was baptized Marie Marguerite Joseph (Molly Susup) at the rebuilt mission of St. Francis.[14]

But as usual, Molly did not stay in Canada. She headed back south to familiar old haunts with her daughter. Susup may have accompanied them, but there is no record of this. Instead, in 1766, we find Molly with a fellow Pigwacket named Jean Baptiste Sabattis.[15]

Newcomers in Fryeburg and other emerging settlements in Maine purposefully ignored Abenaki title to the vast woodland domains between the Saco and Androscoggin. Remnant Abenakis like Molly and Sabattis comprised a small and harmless ethnic minority, roaming the margins of white society in small kin-groups. Some twenty-four thousand Europeans now lived in Maine, all but eclipsing this vestige native population of six hundred (MDH [3]:342; Williamson 1832[2]:373).

Molly and others in her situation faced daunting challenges in their refusal to disappear from their homelands forever. Logging gangs in search of timber to supply the ever-growing number of English sawmills on the lower Saco now reached upriver almost as far as Fryeburg (Rivard 1990:23). Despite peace agreements, English assaults on widely scattered Abenaki hunting families in Maine's woods continued.

In 1767, for instance, an Abenaki family (with whom Molly no doubt associated) was murdered "at their Wigwam near Sebago Pond, at the head of Stroudwater River," causing the band's chief to plead with the governor of Massachusetts for protection and assistance (MDH [24]:145). The physical and mental anguish of Abenakis at this time is evident in a report by an English commander at Fort Halifax on the Upper Kennebec, who noted that the Abenakis "[are] so disspirited that they will never give us further Truble. . . . but if the English wer determined to Steel their Lives by peace meals, it wou'd be best for them to Die Like Men then to be killed Lick Dogs" (MDH [24]:136–37).

Molly Ockett: "Indian Doctress"

Yet stalwart Abenakis like Molly and Sabattis managed to continue eking out a living. How should we picture them? It is likely that Sabattis dressed like other Abenaki men of his day—wearing a European shirt and coat, a red canvas breech cloth held up with a belt, scarlet leggings adorned with wampum or bugle beads and attached to the belt with ribbons, and moccasins decorated with porcupine quills. He probably wore his hair cut short over the front and sides of his head, and shoulder-length at the nape. He may have painted his face red and black for special occasions, pierced his ears with sizeable holes, and worn silver rings in them or in his nose.[16]

Molly, described by one of her contemporaries as a "pretty, genteel squaw" with "a large frame and features," wore clothing typical of Abenaki women of her day: a knee-length European dress, beaded moccasins, scarlet leggings embroidered with dyed porcupine quills, and a peaked cap decorated with beads, plus earrings and bracelets. What made her stand out among other Abenakis for settlers was her remarkably "erect" posture, her facility with the English language, her "loquacious" personality, and her extensive knowledge of herbal remedies.[17]

At some point, however hesitant they might have been about entrusting themselves to an Indian for medicinal care, farmsteaders in Fryeburg and elsewhere begun turning to Molly when ill or wounded, and her reputation as a healer began to grow. For instance, upon learning that Mrs. Evans (the wife of hunter John Evans, who had been one of Roger's Indian fighters) suffered an infected finger, Molly trekked up to Jockey Cap Ridge to gather a remedy: roots of Solomon's Seal. She pounded the roots, applied the pulpy mass to Mrs. Evans's finger, and cured the infection (Barrows 1938:11–12).

Why did Mrs. Evans and other settlers place themselves under the care of a woman whose people "awakened fear in the heart of the boldest . . . and froze the blood of the timid" (Willey 1856:48)? No doubt a paucity in health-care options and their relative ignorance about local herbal remedies lessened any reservations they might have had about entrusting themselves to Molly.

Until the late nineteenth century, rural New Englanders customarily depended upon neighborhood midwives not only for delivering babies, but also for medical care (Beck 1990:34–35). In addition, they relied upon medical itinerants—notably surgeon-dentists, cancer curers, and oculists, who traveled circuits, just like peddlers and preachers. While these transient healers represented only a small segment of the wider medical profession in New England, they were far more significant among frontier folk, who relied primarily on midwives for health care.

Traveling doctors, like midwives, tended to be self-taught or family-taught. Some made note of the fact that they used methods "acquired whilst among the Indians." Occasionally, they mixed curing with other services, such as one fellow who promoted himself as "hairdresser, dentist, profile painter," or another who advertised as "surg.-dent., musician" (Benes 1990:96, 101, 104, 111–12).

Surely Molly was as reliable as these characters—she was actually more so. While a good number of itinerant doctors were charlatans who preyed upon the vulnerabilities of rural folk struck by illness or accident,[18] Molly possessed a unique knowledge rooted in centuries of medicinal experience. The toxins and treatments in a natural environment still alien to the settlers were utterly familiar to her.

When asked to treat someone, she headed confidently for the woods to harvest the appropriate remedy, be it bloodroot, buckthorn, basswood bark, sumac berries, or any one of a great variety of herbs. She knew how to turn such raw materials into drinks, salves, or poultices (Lapham

1874:241–42). She knew that poison ivy could be cured with a coat of crushed celandine, a plant commonly known today as jewel weed (Wilkins 1977:100), dysentery with a decoction of spruce inner bark (Hutchins n.d.), and headaches with a liniment made of white birch bark, hemlock bark, bear fat, and sperm from a buck deer, boiled with wild onions, garlic, and molasses (Beck 1990:39).

Modern chemical analyses of such natural treatments utilized in the region during this era reveal efficacious enzymes and antibiotics. For instance, there is a raw form of aspirin in willow bark, penicillin in a rotten apple poultice, and allicin (an antibiotic that inhibits the growth of many bacteria and fungi) in garlic (Beck 1990:39).

The intimate understanding that Molly and other native peoples had about the natural environment—its resources and geography—had sustained them before the European invasion, aided them in their resistance efforts, and made them valuable allies to European powers competing for the region's resources and land. Now, as they found themselves cornered into accommodating to white society, these insights won them benign tolerance, perhaps even a measure of grateful respect. Familiarity with nature's medicine chest and knowledge about the best trapping grounds were among the few cards remaining in the hands of the region's first peoples. Intelligence in these areas, along with skilled craftsmanship in the construction of useful household tools (baskets, barrels, ax handles, and staves) from natural materials, were their entry tickets into the new political economy. The Abenakis may have lost possession of their lands, but they remained the possessors of unique knowledge about it throughout the eighteenth century.

Molly and Sabattis associated particularly often with the James Swan family in Fryeburg. As adjunct household members, they periodically camped near the family and provided various services in exchange for meals. In addition to doctoring and crafting birchbark containers and other useful domestic items, Molly hunted for the family. From the ducks she killed, she made a feather bed for Mrs. Swan. Sabattis also hunted for the family. In fact, he "spent most of his time in hunting and would bring home the lip of a Moose as a special delicacy to his master Swan."[19]

There is no indication that Molly married Sabattis (Lapham 1981:78), but together they had three children. Little is known of their offspring, but Sabbatis himself became one of the most noted Abenakis in the area. Said to be as proud and stubborn as Molly, this memorable character was known, among other things, for his early spring swims in the river among cakes of ice (Barrows 1938:9). He and Molly seem to have had a stormy relationship. On one occasion, his former wife came to town and laid claim on him. At his suggestion, so the story goes, the women went to battle over him, fighting "like tigers" while Sabattis sat on the woodpile, smoked his pipe, and watched. Reports vary as to whether Molly won or lost.[20] Either way, she left Sabattis soon afterwards because of his "intemperate habits and quarrelsome disposition" (Lapham 1981:78; True 1863).

Tufts on Molly: Eyewitness Account

Records from 1772 locate Molly with Chief Joachim Swassin's Abenaki band some thirty miles north of Fryeburg (Tufts 1807:69). The band camped near Bethel, then known as Sudbury Canada—a fertile stretch of Androscoggin River land granted by the Massachusetts General Court to a group of English families in 1768 and on the verge of being settled by colonists.[21] The first permanent white inhabitants arrived in 1774, and soon learned from Molly that her people had traditionally cultivated this land before they were driven away by the wars.

Molly recalled coming to the abandoned site as a child when trees, just beginning to invade the cleared fields, were shorter than she was (Lapham 1981:297, 421–23; True 1874:11–12). Beyond its agricultural benefits, this region had long been a supreme hunting ground, harboring an abundance of nearly every kind of game common to Maine (Lapham 1981:242). It is not surprising that surviving Abenakis gravitated back to this area. According to nineteenth-century historian Nathaniel T. True (1874:12), "so common were Indians during the first settlement of [Bethel] that quite a fleet of canoes on the river was a common accurance." The memoir of Henry Tufts, who traveled about traditional Abenaki territory for several years in the 1770s, offers some insight into the numbers of native peoples still abiding, at least seasonally, in the area:

[C]uriosity prompted me to visit the Indian settlements in this department in order to become more intimately acquainted with their customs and modes of life, I followed the daily practice of traveling from place to place, until I had visited the whole encampment, and from the best conjectures I could frame on the subject, found there might be about three hundred inhabitants in this quarter. The entire tribe, of which these people made part, was in number about seven hundred of both sexes, and extended their settlements, in a scattering desultory manner, from Lake Memphremagog to Lake Umbagog, covering an extent of some eighty miles. (Tufts 1807:70–71)

Tufts went on to observe, "Some Abenaki came to Bethel to have their guns and jewelry repaired, and stayed but briefly" (True 1874:13). Others, like Molly, came often and stayed so long that they became well-acquainted with settlers. Molly's connection to the town became so significant that her first daughter, Molly Susup, attended school there and played with the settler's children (Lapham 1981:78).

We have a revealing peek at Molly's life at this time, thanks to her association with Tufts, who included her in his 1807 memoir. Born in 1748 in Newmarket, New Hampshire, Tufts was indisputably a shady character, but his narrative contains rare and seemingly credible information about Abenaki life in the area between Lakes Memphremagog and Umbagog (Calloway 1991:208; Day 1974). Tufts's checkered "career" as a rogue included thieving (horses, furniture, and other men's wives and daughters), farming, soldiering (he deserted), fortune-telling, itinerant preaching, and doctoring.

He was often jailed—and just as often escaped. His life intersected with Molly's in the spring of 1772, when he followed some local advice and made a "pilgrimmage" to her Bethel camp seeking cure for his "maladies" (a serious knife wound in his side). Referring to Molly as the "Great Indian Doctress," Tufts described her as "a kind and charitable woman" who was "indefatigable in her care and attention during [his] convalescence" (Tufts 1807:69, 71). Ensconced in a birchbark wigwam, sleeping on bearskins, he received several months of care from Molly. In his words:

She was alert in her devoirs and supplied me for present consumption with a large variety of roots, herbs, barks and other materials. I did not much like even the looks of them . . . however, I took the budget with particular directions for the use of each ingredient. My kind doctress visited me daily bringing new medicinal supplies, but my palate was far from being gratified with some of her doses, in fact they but ill accorded with the gust of an Englishman. Nevertheless, having much faith in the skill of my physician, I continued to swallow with becoming submission every potion she prescribed. Her means had a timely and beneficial

effect since, from the use of them I gathered strength so rapidly that in
two months I could visit about with comfort. (Tufts 1807:70)

Tufts, who had left behind a wife in Massachusetts, remained with Molly's
band for three years and learned their language. He cohabited with Abenaki Polly Susap (niece of Chief Tomhegan), who in his estimation "re-
med(ied) the want of a female companion, while in these rude regions . . .
[and] supplied to me the place of a wife, though without the fashionable
appelation" (Tufts 1807:77–78). It was not lost on Tufts that Molly usually
had money on hand, thanks to patients who came to her or sent for her.
Seeing greater profit potential in obtaining Molly's medicinal knowledge
than in stealing her money and running, he determined to become her
apprentice, and began tagging along when she collected herbs in the forest
or went to visit patients. Although Molly appears to have shared much of
her knowledge with him, Tufts suspected she was withholding her most
powerful secrets and devised means to woo every drop of knowledge from
her:

> I was inquisitive with Molly Occut, old Philips, Sabattus and other
> professed doctors to learn the names and virtues of their medicines. In
> general they were explicit in communication, still I thought them in
> possession of secrets they cared not to reveal. Knowing them to be
> extravagantly fond of rum . . . it struck my mind [to] procure . . . that
> liquor with which to treat them occasionally [to] obtain their favor more
> effectually. (Tufts 1807:73)

It makes great sense that Molly would protect some of her knowledge; why
would she surrender all the secrets of her last remaining possession and
primary livelihood? She shared her medicinal expertise selectively and
intentionally, sometimes as a gesture of friendship. This seems to have
been the case with Martha Russell Fifield in Newry (one of Molly's regular
stopovers, five miles upriver from Bethel), to whom she "imparted much
medicinal knowledge, also how to make root beer from roots and herbs,
and various dyes" (Wilkins 1977:100).

Molly also gave information out of gratitude. This occurred when she
and several fellow tribespeople, journeying between Canada and Maine,
set up winter camp near a tiny white settlement in Troy, Vermont. It was a
difficult, near-starvation winter for the Indians, who made and traded
baskets and birchbark cups and pails to survive. It was also a tough season

for the settlers, whose children came down with dysentery. Exercising her "dignified profession," Molly cured the children. When asked to reveal her medicine, she refused. The next year, she traveled through the area again and found herself low on supplies. When a settler gave her a chunk of pork, she expressed her thanks by sharing her dysentery cure.[22]

After a three-year sojourn among the Abenakis, during which he followed Molly on her extensive rounds as an itinerant Indian doctor, Tufts left the band to practice his newly learned healing trade—in between bouts of philandering, preaching, and soldiering. He died in 1831, "in the eighty-third year of an uncommonly misspent life."[23]

Healing and Dealing: Between Fryeburg and St. Francis

Tufts's narrative touches on the fact that Molly, not unlike other Abenaki women of her time, was a good hunter and trapper (Lapham 1981:78). She sometimes went hunting with settlers—such as Benjamin Russell, who lived in Bethel and later moved to Newry.[24] Each spring she bartered her winter's catch. In addition to her own furs, it is likely that she traded those collected from fellow Abenaki, who probably remunerated her in pelts for treatment.

On occasion, she did her trading at St. Francis, when visiting the mission for confession and holy sacraments. In the spring of 1774, Molly made the 160-mile journey, probably by canoe. Upon returning to Maine, she told a marvelously droll story about her venture, later recounted by Tufts: After selling her furs for forty dollars, Molly went to the priest seeking absolution of her sins and expedition of her first husband's move through purgatory. When the old Jesuit priest (Father Charles Germain) demanded all of Molly's money to conduct her holy request, she reluctantly placed it on the table.

The priest absolved her sins and offered prayers for her husband. Molly then asked the status of her husband's soul and the holy father said that he had been safely delivered from the bonds of purgatory. Molly asked him if he was certain, and the priest assured her, absolutely—at which she snatched back her forty dollars! When the startled priest threatened to remand her husband's soul back to purgatory, Molly retorted that her husband was too clever for that: "when we used to traverse the woods together," she explained, "if he chanced to fall into a bad place, he always stuck up a stake, that he might never be caught there any more." And off she went, wrote Tufts, "leaving the poor ecclesiastic to console himself. . . . "

Tufts also described Molly's brand of no-nonsense generosity, telling a story about a destitute white man from Fryeburg who approached her for a loan to save his family from starvation. After scolding the fellow for coming to borrow from "poor Indians" who were "generally despised by white people," Molly loaned him twenty dollars, with one hitch: he was to return the following winter to hunt furs to repay her. This he did, making enough to pay her back and supply his family (Tufts 1807:64–65). This story is important because it hints at the profoundly ambivalent feelings Molly must have had toward the white community.

While it is evident that she felt a measure of sympathy toward individuals, it would hardly be surprising if she resented them collectively. In her lifetime she saw them devastate her world—kill her people, steal their land, deplete and destroy their resources. The people asking her to heal them were the nieces, nephews, and children of the very people who had won bounties scalp-hunting her aunts, uncles and parents. The descendants of those who had brought disease to her people now asked her to heal them of diseases.

Revolutionary War: Friendships and Dilemmas

However ambiguous Molly's feelings were toward the settlers who pursued their own livelihoods at the cost of her people's, she repeatedly acted as mediator and healer. Certainly this was the case during the Revolutionary War. At the start of the war, in 1776, Indians on the New England frontier generally sided with the American rebels or tried to maintain a precarious neutrality (Day 1981:53). However, some supported the British, probably in response to ongoing frustration about the effects of white settlers on native life (True 1859–61:299). Among the British allies was the Abenaki chief Tomhegan, who originally hailed from the Upper Saco area. In 1781, he and a small war party of Abenakis from St. Francis, "hideously painted and armed with guns, tomahawks, and scalping knives" (True 1859–61:51), raided a string of small white towns on the Upper Androscoggin, including Bethel—plundering several houses, killing and scalping three men, and taking another three men captive (Lapham (1981:46–51; True 1874:19–20). Then they retreated north to claim the eight-dollar bounty offered by the British for each American prisoner or scalp (True 1874:20–21).

Banking on a survival strategy of seeking alliance with close neighbors rather than retreating to faraway French friends, Molly's kin-group opted to support the local Yankee rebels. At least three Pigwackets in her circle were credited with fighting in the American Revolutionary Army and were given military titles: Sergeant Lewey, Captain Philips, and Captain Swasson, who apparently won a sword for conspicuous bravery in battle (Lapham 1981:423; True 1874:12–13).

One American officer owed his life to Molly, whose inside information saved him from Tomhegan's raid. The fortunate fellow was Colonel Clark of Boston, who had a camp in the area and came there yearly to trade for furs. When Molly, then about forty years old, learned that settlers had been killed and that Clark was to be next, she raced several miles through the woods to warn him. Clark escaped just in time, and his gratitude to Molly was profound. Again and again he pressed to reward her for her magnanimous act. Repeatedly, she refused.[26]

Although Molly and other Abenakis may actually have sympathized with Tomhegan and his warriors, whatever likemindedness they may have shared with these attackers must have been overshadowed by intense concern over the effect the raid would have on their ongoing efforts to avoid bloody confrontation with their white neighbors. Tomhegan's attack highlighted the tentative nature of Anglo-Indian relations, immediately throwing settlers into a panic. Fryeburg's citizens raised a local militia of thirty men to hunt down Tomhegan's party—tapping Molly's ex-partner Sabattis to be their scout in this (unsuccessful) expedition against his fellow tribesman and former ally (True 1874:20).

Bethel's ten families formed a small company of soldiers, built garrisons, and sent to Boston for help. In 1782, a company of twenty-seven men arrived from Massachusetts and stayed several months, until peace was declared between the Americans and British. During this time, land values in the area plummeted and several settler families moved away (True 1874:18–21).

But after this brief setback, the Revolutionary War officially ended with the 1783 Treaty of Paris. Waves of settlers soon poured into Maine. Population grew particularly in the fertile Saco, Androscoggin, and Kennebec Valleys. Massachusetts, cash-poor but land-rich, liberally allocated Abenaki land to white settlers who had helped win independence (Lapham

1981:83). In Bethel alone, forty-five soldiers received land grants (True 1874:33). By 1790, the town's population had soared to sixty families, numbering some 324 people (Bennett 1991:26).

Three years after the war, the Americans "rewarded" the Penobscot Tribe in central Maine for its support, signing a treaty that promised them modest annuities and marked off a smidgen of their aboriginal land as a reservation. In 1793, Indians at Passamaquoddy Bay acquired a similar arrangement by treaty. However, in part because their homeland was rich in agricultural potential, the Abenakis remaining in western Maine, including Molly and her kinsfolk, were left empty-handed.

Still, these survivors of a genocidal century continued to paddle their ancient waterways, winding through vast and familiar forests, stopping at regular campsites in Maine, New Hampshire, and Vermont. Most settlers treated them like trespassing tramps. They camped for weeks at a time near white communities in order to trade crafts for food, tobacco, and other goods. Beyond craftmaking, Molly continued her traditional doctoring and, for instance, when camped near Merrill Bridge in Andover in 1790, served as midwife at the birth of the first white child in that town (Lapham 1981:80).

Walking Trails and Spawning Legends

Molly returned frequently to the increasingly prosperous Bethel region, where large frame houses soon replaced log cabins. Here, Eleazer Twitchell's grist mill, built by his father in 1774, was busy grinding bountiful crops of wheat and corn. Vast new land parcels were being cleared for agriculture, and huge quantities of white pine were being launched downriver to be sold in Brunswick (Bennett 1991:38).

It is said that Molly spent much time among Bethel's Methodist settlers, whom she referred to as "drefful clever folks" (Lapham 1981:79). Apparently somewhat intrigued by their beliefs, she attended and sometimes spoke at their religious meetings. Meanwhile, she held on to confession and other threads of Catholicism (Lapham 1981:79). In all likelihood, she developed a unique spiritual middle ground, with a core of Abenaki beliefs. That she maintained personal veto power over the rules of all faiths is evidenced in the following much-told story.

Early one Monday morning, Molly brought a pail full of blueberries to the wife of Rev. Eliphaz Chapman, who had moved to Bethel in 1789 (True 1874:22–23). Noticing how fresh the berries were, Mrs. Chapman surmised that Molly had picked them on Sunday, and chastened her for breaking the Sabbath. Offended, Molly marched out of the house and didn't come back for several weeks. Upon returning, it was she who reproached Mrs. Chapman: "Choke me," she said, "I was right in picking the blueberries on Sunday, it was so pleasant and I was so happy that the Great Spirit had provided them for me" (Lapham 1981:79).

Molly's words and deeds spawned an array of legends—perhaps none told as often as her successful treatment of young Hannibal Hamlin. Traveling south toward the Paris area in foul winter weather, Molly sought shelter with several residents of Snow's Fall, only to be turned away. She cursed the place and trudged on to Paris Hill. There she was welcomed into the Hamlin household, where she healed their very sick infant, Hannibal—thereby saving the life of Abraham Lincoln's future vice president.[27]

It is noteworthy that legend places this benevolent act on the heels of a dreadful curse, implying that the white folks who traded Molly Ockett stories were as ambiguous about her as she seems to have been about them. To them, an aura of mystery surrounded this itinerant doctress, who crossed the divide between untamed forest and domesticated farmland with apparent ease.[28] Her native ties to traditional Abenaki culture, coupled with her ongoing connection to a Catholic Indian mission in Quebec, were hardly acceptable to Protestants on the New England frontier. No doubt some felt that being healed by a "savage" and "papist" was tantamount to a compromise with the devil. An excerpt from an earlier (1699) English document about Indian physicians hints at the mixed feelings Molly's white patients might have had about turning to her for help: "Indians are Incomparable Physicians; Being well-skill'd in the Nature of Herbs and Plants of that Country. But the English will not make use of them, because their Ministers have infus'd this Notion into 'em, That what they do, is by the Power of the Devil" (Ward 1699:16). Molly appears to have exploited the confusion about who she was, sometimes gaining an upper hand by playing into settlers' superstitions and fears of "otherness" and by implying that she possessed destructive magical powers. She did this by punctuating her good works with occasional curses, some of which spawned legends handed down through generations in singing rhyme:

'Tis a curious legend.
In my youth I heard it told
How Moll Ocket cursed the white man
when he stole the Indian's gold.[29]

Late in the eighteenth century, so this particular tale goes, a white settler plied his canoe under a full moon toward an Abenaki campsite on tiny Hemlock Island in the Androscoggin River—near present-day Newry, Maine, one of Molly's regular stopovers. It was autumn, and the Indians were off hunting in the Umbagog Lake region. The settler pulled his boat ashore and stole through the shadows. Later, when the small band of native people returned, they found that the cache of gold and other treasures they had buried under an old hemlock tree were gone.

Eventually Molly Ockett, when visiting a white man's home, spied an ax from that cache. Upon this discovery, she raised her hands high and called down a ghastly spell on the thief, dooming him and all of his relatives. Their homes were swept away by floods; the sap they boiled for maple sugar turned sour in the boiling pans; women in the family died young; and few children survived infancy (and those who did were mauled by wild animals, or choked in their sleep from unknown diseases). Ultimately, it is told, the culprit's family was wiped from the face of the earth (Kimball 1964; Newell 1981:16).

Only a handful of stories paint such malignant images of Molly. Most portray her as a generous and stalwart character, especially noted for her benevolent and effective herbal healing. But stories professing that she possessed magical power, good or bad, no doubt aided the efficacy of her healing work. She, like most folk-curers of the day, must have relied on good measures of faith and psychology for success (Beck 1990:36; Richards 1990:142–43, 153).

"Last of the Pigwackets": Molly's Final Years

In the 1790s, still clinging to their ancestral domains, a few remnant Abenakis ranged the woodlands of the Upper Kennebec, Androscoggin, and Connecticut Rivers. At that time, records located Molly, by then a "widely famed doctoress," as wintering with a cluster of families under Captain Susap (Joseph) on the Upper Missisquoi River in Troy, Vermont, and Potton, Quebec (Hemenway 1868–1929[3]:310–13, 315; Sumner 1860:26–27).

Just before the turn of the century, Chief Philip (whose path had often overlapped with Molly's, at least since the days of Tufts's apprenticeship) sold a tract of land in northern Coos County, New Hampshire (Hammond 1915:9, 11; cf. Calloway 1990:231; Day 1981:59). Soon thereafter, a Norridgewock Abenaki named Pierpole (Pierre Paul) and his family abandoned their small farmstead at Amasekonti at Farmington Falls on the Sandy River in Maine. Surrounded by growing numbers of unsympathetic settlers, having no Abenaki friends with whom to share their sorrows or joys, the family surrendered its long and tenacious hold on the region and departed to St. Francis (or, some say, to Passamaquoddy Bay). After Pierpole's departure, settlers referred to him as "the last of the Norridgewocks" (W. Allen 1856:32 n.).

Apparently, Sabattis remained as stubborn as ever, for he held his ground. In 1798, an itinerant Protestant preacher found the old Pigwacket camping at Caratunk, not far from Pierpole's homestead. Writing of this encounter, he noted that Sabattis was "as sensible and mild an Indian as it is to be found [and] could talk French and English" (Coffin 1798, in Collections of the Maine Historical Society [4]:379).

Molly also held firm, refusing to leave her ancestral ground. In fact, neither she nor her compatriots ever "conveyed their lands to whites north of Lewiston Falls [including Bethel]" (True 1874:12). Molly always considered herself an "original proprietor" of the town of Bethel (Lapham 1981:178). In 1799, Bethel, whose population had climbed to eighty families, got its first doctor. The arrival of Dr. Carter, who traveled on horseback to patients as far as fifty miles distant, disturbed Molly, for it cut into her business (True 1874:38–39). By the early 1800s, when she was well into her sixties, newcomers had invaded even the remote interior of northern Maine, where a handful of Abenaki hunters had taken refuge. Between 1783 and 1820, Maine's population swelled from fifty-six thousand to three hundred thousand (Bennett 1991:26). Facing stiff competition from white hunters and increasingly limited by the effects of logging, the straggling Indian families encountered ever more obstacles in their efforts to subsist.[30]

In her old age, Molly finally gave in to Colonel Clark's repeated entreaties to repay her for saving his life, accepting an invitation to stay with his family in Boston. But after a year in the city, she longed to return to her favorite haunts in the Androscoggin Valley. Seeing her distress, Clark built a wigwam for her at Rumford Falls, about fifteen miles northeast of Bethel.[31]

Despite this secure shelter, Molly continued her migratory ways, traveling long distances in all kinds of weather, setting up camp in this place and that.[32] In 1816, while camping with the Abenaki chief Metallak and his group north of Andover at Beaver Brook (between Beaver Pond and Upper Richardson Lake), she became very ill. Like Molly, Metallak had often camped near Merrill Bridge in Andover, so he brought her there, where he knew friendly settlers would help her.

The town contracted Captain Bragg to take care of her for a fee. At Molly's request that she meet death in a camp of sweet-smelling cedar, Bragg built a wigwam for her near his house. Several months later, on August 2, 1816, she died. Some say she was seventy-six at the time of her death; others say she was ten years older. Until the end, she was self-sufficient. Her possessions were auctioned, earning twenty dollars, which probably covered Bragg's caretaking costs.[33]

After Reverend John Strickland's eulogy at Molly's well-attended funeral, the Indian doctor was buried in an unmarked grave in Andover's cemetery (Lapham 1981:80). Although she lacked a gravestone, other markers emerged to commemorate Molly's life. Paradoxically, white settlers who had usurped Abenaki lands named some of the places Molly frequented after her. Signposts popped up here and there across the region, announcing Molly Ockett's Cave, Molly Ockett Mountain, Molley Ockett Trail, Moll's Rock, and Mollywocket Brooke. But what did these names signify? Certainly not entitlement. In truth, they were like grave markers for a people who lost their land and lives to colonization. Molly, with all of her insights into white society, never found the means to hold on to ancestral lands for herself and her people.

In 1867, the women of the Andover Congregational Church raised money for an engraved tombstone for Molly Ockett, memorializing her as "the last of the Peqwaukets." As part of their Fourth of July celebration, citizens of Andover gathered to dedicate the tablet. Reports of the event do not mention the presence of any Indians (True 1867).

Notes

We dedicate this essay to Seneca elder Dr. Hazel Dean-John—a linguist (Ph.D., University of New Mexico), a faithkeeper of the Wolf Clan of Allegany, and a contemporary exemplar of Molly Ockett's cross-cultural agility. We wish also to express thanks to Dr. Stan Howe of the Bethel Historical Society for reviewing an earlier draft of this essay and to Elaine Stanley of the Maine State Library.

The name "Molly Ockett" is the Indian pronunciation of her baptismal name, Marie Agathe. We have chosen to refer to her as Molly Ockett or simply as Molly, since Ockett does not represent a family surname.

1. The notion that the vast New England forest was "howling wilderness inhabited by ravenous wolves" (Indians) expresses the alienated attitude toward nature and its aboriginal inhabitants held by English settlers, in particular the Puritans, the most vocal of whom was Cotton Mather (1704).

2. Writings about Molly Ockett are legion—and often inaccurate. The principal reliable sources are the writings of nineteenth-century historian Nathaniel True (1859–61, 1863, 1867, and 1874), who wrote about her based on interviews with and correspondence from people who knew her. Although Henry Tufts was a shady character himself, his narrative about his 1772–75 association with Molly and other Abenakis (Tufts 1807) is credible and provides a rare direct look at her life. Also of trustworthy note are Anonymous (1886a), Lapham (1981), Willey (1856 and 1869), and Woodrow (1928), which profiles not only Metallak but Molly and Sabattis, and includes a chapter on Abenaki chief Tomhegan's 1781 Bethel raid—a near-transcription of Lt. Segar's first-hand account of the raid and his captivity. These, along with various other accounts of Molly's life, can be found at the Bethel Historical Society. A fair amount of this material is also available at the Maine State Library in Augusta and the Maine Historical Society in Portland.

3. Barrows 1938:3, referring to Nathaniel True's etymology. For additional evidence of corn cultivation here, see Willey 1856:47.

4. Barrows 1938:5–6. Winthrop (1853:107) refers to a 1642 English expedition traveling by canoe up the Saco, and, after ninety miles encountering the "indian town [of] Pegwagget," noting that by land it is about sixty miles from the coast.

5. For an overview of traditional Western Abenaki subsistence patterns, see, among others, Calloway 1990:3–33 and Prins 1994.

6. Assessments of Molly's place of birth, age-calculation, name, and baptism are based on information in True 1863 and Newell 1981:3.

7. For information about early missions, see Morrison 1984:80–88. For a discussion re colonials, Indians, and arms, see Prins 1995.

8. Rivard (1990:21) traces the history of mills on the Saco River. Also see MDH (10):380. According to Baxter (MDH [10]:400), in 1727, Irish settlers moved upriver from the coast, establishing themselves at Saco Falls, where "they practiced the catching of all sorts of fish with scains . . . by which means prevent the fish going up the falls [which] has been a great prejudice to the Indians, insomuch, that many of them have come to me [Captain Jordan] at Biddleford [downriver] and made their complaint [asking] that proper measures might be taken to effectually prevent the same." Jordan's facility with the Abenaki language is noted in MDH (23):66, 204, 198.

9. MDH (10):197, 400. Captain Sam was also named as one of the six Pigwacket warriors. The other three were not identified by name.

10. True (1863) noted Molly's claim that her father had been a "prominent chief" and had fought in this war.

11. MDH (23):291. The text of the Treaty with the Eastern Indians at Falmouth, 1749 (Anonymous 1886a:159) identifies Mareagit. See also Newell 1981:3 and n. 4.

12. An Abenaki palisaded village was noted at the locale in 1694. Jesuits established a mission there in 1698 (JR [65]:87, 89, and 263 n.).

13. MDH (24):118. For a description of Molly's craftmaking skills, see Lapham 1981:79 and Barrows 1938:12; for a discussion of the role of crafts in trade among Maine's various tribal groups from the seventeenth century through today, see Prins and McBride 1989.

14. Baptism records, Catholic Church of St. Francis du lac, St. Francis, Quebec, verify the baptizing of Marie Marguerite, daughter of Pierre Joseph (Piol Susup) and Marie Agathe. True 1859–61:78 notes that Molly had a daughter named Molly Susup "previous to her association with Sabattis." See also Newell 1981:4 and n. 5.

15. True 1874:17 identifies Sabattis as the Pigwacket who had lived with James Swan in Fryeburg before Swan moved to Bethel in 1779. See also Lapham 1981:75 and Drake 1857:338.

16. Castiglioni 1983:39–40—although this description is of Penobscots from Indian Island, in MDH (23):416, English officials of the period, speaking of the Abenaki, noted, "it's impossible to distinguish the Indians of one Tribe from another."

17. Based on his communication with Martha Rowe of Gilead who knew Molly, True (1863) described her as a "pretty, genteel squaw" with "large frame and features . . . [and] erect posture." He also described her as "loquacious" and noted that she wore a peaked cap and "dressed in Indian style." Details on Abenaki Indian style of the day come from Castiglioni 1983:39–40.

18. Benes 1990:101 notes newspaper warnings about "quacks."

19. True 1863. See also True 1874:17, which identifies Sabattis as the Pigwacket who lived with James Swan's family in Fryeburg. Newell 1981:17–18 summarizes Molly's craftmaking skills; see also Lapham 1981:79 and Barrows 1938:12.

20. Barrows 1938:10, says she won; Newell 1981:6, based on H. Kelsey Hobb 1883, says she lost.

21. For an overview of the founding and early settlement of Sudbury Canada, see Bennett 1991:10–17, Lapham 1981:78, and True 1874:13.

22. This story and the term "dignified profession" come from Samuel Sumner, quoted in True 1863.

23. Helfrich 1989:88, quoting nineteenth-century essayist Higgenson.

24. According to Wilkins 1977:100, "the old lien bag, flint, steel and punk [in the author's possession] was carried in the woods by Mr. Russell [her grandfather] when out hunting with . . . old Mollockett."

25. This incident is recounted in Tufts 1807:78. Father Germain's presence at St. Francis is documented in Day 1981:46.

26. Lapham 1981:79–80; Benjamin Willey quoted in Lapham 1981:46–47.

27. This story is verified on page 18 of Charles Eugene Hamlin's biography of his grandfather. Cf. Newell 1981:12–13 and "Mollockett's Curse." See Charles Eugene Hamlin, *The Life and Times of Hannibal Hamlin* (Cambridge: Riverside Press, 1899), and "Mollockett's Curse," *Lewiston Journal*, 2–6 November 1907 (copy available in Bethel scrapbook at Maine Historical Society, Portland).

28. Molly's ease in finding her way through the woods contrasted with the settlers' utter dependence on "spotted trees." See Lapham 1981:243.

29. Woodrow 1928:77–80 includes all twenty-five stanzas of this rhyme.

30. Among many sources noting nineteenth-century Abenaki subsistence struggles is a letter written about the Penobscots to the Commonwealth of Massachusetts by James Sullivan, Esq., on January 12, 1808. Sullivan (1808) noted, in part: "Their subsistence from hunting is entirely at an end, and subverted by the settlements around and between them and the wilderness towards Canada. Their support from fishing has much decreased, and will continue to decrease in proportion as the country is settled by white people."

31. Lapham 1981:80, referring to Willey.

32. For instance, Molly was "on the move" at age seventy plus, when she treated Hannibal Hamlin in South Paris, Maine, in 1810.

33. See Poor ca. 1880 and True 1863; J. Wilson (in Lapham 1981:81) notes that Metallak lived here several years; see also Woodrow 1928.

REFERENCES

Abbreviation Key

APS   American Philosophical Society, Philadelphia, Penn.

CPR   The Public Records of the Colony and Plantation of Connecticut
        (1636–1776). John Hammond Trumbull and Charles J. Hoadly,
        eds. 1850–90. 15 vols. Hartford, Conn.: Case, Lockwood, and
        Brainard.

DHNY   Documentary History of the State of New York. Edmund B. O'Cal-
        laghan, ed. 1849–51. 4 vols. New York: Weed and Parsons.

HBP   The Papers of Henry Bouquet. Sylvester K. Stevens, Donald H.
        Kent, Louis Waddell, et al., eds. 1951 to present. 5 vols. to date.
        Harrisburg: Pennsylvania Historical and Museum Commission.

HSP   Historical Society of Pennsylvania, Philadelphia.

JP   The Papers of Sir William Johnson. James Sullivan, Alexander C.
        Flick, Almon W. Lauber, and Milton W. Hamilton, eds. 1921–63.
        14 vols. Albany: University of the State of New York.

JR   The Jesuit Relations and Allied Documents: Travels and Explora-
        tions of the Jesuit Missionaries in New France, 1610–1791. Rue-
        ben Gold Thwaites, ed. 1896–1901. 73 vols. Cleveland: Burrows
        Brothers.

MA   Moravian Church Archives: Records of the Moravian Mission
        among the Indians of North America, microfilm ed. 1970. Wood-
        bridge, Conn. [cited as reel/box/folder/item].

MBR   The Records of the Governor and Company of Massachusetts Bay
        in New England. Nathaniel B. Shurtleff, ed. 1853–54. 5 vols. Bos-
        ton: William White.

MDH   The Documentary History of the State of Maine. James Phinney
        Baxter, ed. 1869–1916. 24 vols. Portland: LeFavor-Tower.

MPCP   Minutes of the Provincial Council of Pennsylvania. Samuel Haz-
        ard, ed. 1851–53. 16 vols. Philadelphia.

MPCR   The Province and Court Records of Maine. C. T. Libby, ed. 1928–
        31. 2 vols. Portland: Maine Historical Society.

349

NPNER   Records of the Colony of New Plymouth, in New England. Nathan-
         iel B. Shurtleff and David Pulsifer, eds. 1854–61. 12 vols. Boston:
         William White.

NYCD   Documents Relative to the Colonial History of the State of New
         York. Edmund B. O'Callaghan and Berthold Fernow, eds. 1853–
         87. 15 vols. Albany: Weeds and Parsons.

OED   The Compact Edition of the Oxford English Dictionary. 1985.
         Oxford: Oxford University Press.

PA   Pennsylvania Archives. Samuel Hazard, et al., eds. 1852–1949. 9
         sers., 138 vols. Philadelphia and Harrisburg.

RIC   Records of the Colony of Rhode Island and Providence Plantations
         in New England. John Russell Bartlett, ed. 1856–57. 10 vols. Provi-
         dence: A. Crawford Greene and Brother.

Manuscript Sources

Abbott, John S. C. Scrapbook. Hubbard Free Library, Hallowell, Maine.

Albany Deed Books. Office of the Secretary of State, New York State Archives,
    Albany.

Berks and Montgomery Counties, Miscellaneous Manuscripts, 1693–1869. His-
    torical Society of Pennsylvania, Philadelphia.

Campbell Family Papers. New York State Library, Albany.

Ceci, Lynn [1982]. The Motts Point Site Report: The Documentary and Archeo-
    logical Evidence. Ms. on file, New York State Office of Parks, Recreation, and
    Historic Preservation, Waterford.

Chalmers Collection. New York Public Library, New York.

Claus Papers. Public Archives of Canada, Ottawa.

Connecticut Records, Connecticut State Archives, Hartford.

Cotton, John. Diary, 1666–77. Massachusetts Historical Society, Boston.

Draper Manuscripts. State Historical Society of Wisconsin, Madison.

Dukes County Deeds. Registry of Deeds, Edgartown, Mass.

Dukes County Probate Record Books. Dukes County Court House, Edgartown,
    Mass.

Du Simitiere Papers. The Library Company of Philadelphia, Philadelphia.

Etting Collection. Historical Society of Pennsylvania, Philadelphia.

Friends Philadelphia Meeting Papers, Philadelphia.

Gravesend Town Records. New York City Archives, New York.

Haldimand Papers. Public Archives of Canada, Ottawa.

Hamilton Papers. Albany Institute of History and Art, Albany, N.Y.

Hobb, H. Kelsey [1883]. Historical Reminiscences of Mr. Samuel Wiley. Lovell
    Library, Lovell, Maine.

Jamaica Land Records. Record Group 39, M:105. Main Branch, New York Public
    Library, New York.

Logan, James. Papers (APS). American Philosophical Society, Philadelphia.

Logan, James. Papers (HSP). Historical Society of Pennsylvania, Philadelphia.

MA: Moravian Church Archives: Records of the Moravian Mission among the Indians of North America, microfilm ed. 1970. Woodbridge, Conn. [cited as reel/box/folder/item].

MacLeod, William Christie [1941]. The Indians of Brooklyn in the Days of the Dutch. Brooklyn Historical Society Archives, Brooklyn.

Massachusetts Archives, Various Series. Massachusetts State Archives, Columbia Point, Boston.

Middlesex County Court of Common Pleas, Cambridge, Mass.

Middlesex County Deeds. Cambridge, Mass.

Middlesex County Probate Records. Cambridge, Mass.

Montauk Indian Deeds. Brooklyn Historical Society Library Archives, Brooklyn.

Nantucket County Deeds. Registry of Deeds, Nantucket, Mass.

Nantucket County Probate Records. Probate Court, Nantucket, Mass.

Nantucket Historical Association Research Center. Nantucket, Mass.

Nantucket Proprietors Book of Plans. Registry of Deeds, Nantucket, Mass.

Nantucket Proprietors Records. Registry of Deeds, Nantucket, Mass.

Natick Church Records. A Record of Those Who Have Been Received into Full Communion with the Church of Natick, 1729–52. Typescript on file, Bacon Free Library, South Natick, Mass.

Natick Proprietors' Records. Microfilm, Natick Town Library, Natick, Mass.

Natick Town Records. Bacon Free Library, South Natick, Mass.

New England Company. Commissioners Minutes, 1699–1784, Ms. 7953; Correspondence, Ms. 7955. Massachusetts State Archives, Columbia Point, Boston.

New Hampshire Provincial Papers. Concord.

New Jersey Deed Books. New Jersey State Library, Trenton.

New London Records. New London, Conn.

New York Council Minutes. New York State Library, Albany.

New York Colonial Manuscripts, Endorsed Land Papers. New York State Library, Albany.

Town of North Hempstead, Court Proceedings, 1657–60. North Hempstead Town Clerk's Office, North Hempstead, N.Y.

Northampton County, Clerk of the Court Office. Easton, Penn.

Papers of the Provincial Council, Executive Correspondence. Pennsylvania Archives, Harrisburg.

Papers Relating to Indians. New York Public Library, New York.

Penn Family Papers, Indian Affairs. Historical Society of Pennsylvania, Philadelphia.

Pennsylvania Land Records. Pennsylvania Archives, Harrisburg.

Peters, Richard. Papers. Historical Society of Pennsylvania, Philadelphia.

Poor, Agnes Blake [ca. 1880]. Andover Memorials. Bethel Historical Society, Bethel, Maine.

Records of the Connecticut Particular Court. Hartford.

Rhode Island Historical Society Collections. Providence.

Rhode Island Supreme Court Records. Rhode Island Supreme Court Judicial Records Center, Pawtucket.

Starbuck, Nathaniel [1683–1744]. Account Book. Manuscripts on file in the Nantucket Historical Association Research Center, Nantucket, Mass.

Stonington Town Records. Stonington, Conn.

Sullivan, James [1808]. Letter to the Commissioner of Massachusetts, 12 July 1808. Indian File, Box 1, Maine State Library, Augusta.

U.S. National Archives. Washington, D.C.

Weiser, Conrad. Correspondence. Historical Society of Pennsylvania, Philadelphia.

York Colonial Records. Portland, Maine.

York Deeds 1887–1910. 18 vols. Portland and Bethel, Maine.

Dissertations and Conference Papers

Blok, Anton, and Andrew S. Buckser
1990   Sicilian Nicknames as Symbolic Inversions. Paper presented at the Peasant Culture and Consciousness Conference, Bellagio, Italy.

Bragdon, Kathleen Joan
1981   "Another Tongue Brought In": An Ethnohistorical Study of Native Writings in Massachusett. Unpublished Ph.D. Dissertation. Department of Anthropology, Brown University, Providence, R.I.
1987b   Social History and Native Texts. Paper presented at the Annual Meeting of the American Society for Ethnohistory.

Brenner, Elise M.
1984   Strategies for Autonomy: An Analysis of Ethnic Mobilization in Seventeenth-Century Southern New England. Unpublished Ph.D. Dissertation. Department of Anthropology, University of Massachusetts at Amherst.

Burton, William J.
1976   Hellish Fiends and Brutish Men: Amerindian-Euroamerican Interaction in Southern New England, an Interdisciplinary Analysis, 1600–1750. Unpublished Ph.D. Dissertation. Kent State University, Kent, Ohio.

Ceci, Lynn
1977   The Effect of European Contact and Trade on the Settlement Pattern of Indians in Coastal New York, 1524–1665. Unpublished Ph.D. Dissertation. Department of Anthropology, City University of New York.

Ghere, David L.
1988   Abenaki Factionalism, Emigration, and Social Continuity: Indian Society in Northern New England, 1725–65. Unpublished Ph.D. Dissertation. Department of History, University of Maine, Orono.

Grumet, Robert S.
1979   "We Are Not So Great Fools": Changes in Upper Delawaran Socio-
            Political Life, 1630–1758. Unpublished Ph.D. Dissertation. Depart-
            ment of Anthropology, Rutgers University, New Brunswick, N.J.
Guldenzopf, David B.
1986   The Colonial Transformation of Mohawk Society. Unpublished
            Ph.D. Dissertation. Department of Anthropology, State University of
            New York at Albany.
Guzzardo, John Christopher
1975   Sir William Johnson's Official Family: Patron and Clients in an
            Anglo-American Empire, 1742–77. Unpublished Ph.D. Disserta-
            tion. Department of History, Syracuse University, Syracuse, N.Y.
Handsman, Russell G.
1990   Corn and Culture, Pots and Politics: How to Listen to the Voices of
            Mohegan Women. Paper presented at the Annual Meeting of the
            Society for Historical Archaeology, Tucson, Ariz.
Hawk, William
1984   The Revitalization of the Matinnecock Indian Tribe of New York.
            Unpublished Ph.D. Dissertation. Department of Anthropology, Uni-
            versity of Wisconsin, Milwaukee.
Hoffman, Bernard G.
1955   The Historical Ethnography of the Micmac of the Sixteenth and
            Seventeenth Centuries. Unpublished Ph.D. Dissertation. Depart-
            ment of Anthropology, University of California at Berkeley.
Johnson, Eric S.
1993   Some by Flatteries and Others by Threatenings: Political Strategies
            among Native Americans of Seventeenth-Century New England.
            Unpublished Ph.D. Dissertation. Department of Anthropology, Uni-
            versity of Massachusetts at Amherst.
Mandell, Daniel
1992   Behind the Frontier: The Indian Communities of Eighteenth-
            Century Massachusetts. Unpublished Ph.D. Dissertation. Depart-
            ment of History, University of Virginia, Charlottesville.
O'Brien, Jean Maria
1990   Community Dynamics in the Indian-English Town of Natick, Mas-
            sachusetts, 1650–1790. Unpublished Ph.D. Dissertation. Depart-
            ment of Anthropology, University of Chicago.
Plane, Ann Marie
1993a   "Of the Most Royal Blood": Colonial Redefinition of Narragansett
            Systems of Governance. Paper presented to the Annual Meeting of
            the American Studies Association, Boston, Mass.
1994   Colonizing the Family: Marriage, Household, and Racial Bound-
            aries in Southeastern New England to 1730. Unpublished Ph.D.
            Dissertation. Department of History, Brandeis University.

Prins, Harald E. L.

1986   Robin Hood of Kennebec: What's in an Indian Name in Seventeenth-Century Colonial America? Paper presented at the Peoples in Contact Conference, Haffenreffer Museum of Anthropology, Brown University. Bristol, R.I.

1988   Amesokanti: Abortive Tribe Formation on the Colonial Frontier. Paper presented at the Annual Meeting of the American Society for Ethnohistory. Williamsburg, Va.

Robinson, Paul A.

1990   The Struggle within: The Indian Debate in Seventeenth-Century Narragansett Country. Unpublished Ph.D. Dissertation. Department of Anthropology, State University of New York at Binghamton.

Thomas, Peter A.

1979   In the Maelstrom of Change: The Indian Trade and Cultural Process in the Middle Connecticut River Valley, 1635–65. Unpublished Ph.D. Dissertation. Department of Anthropology, University of Massachusetts at Amherst.

Williams, Lorraine E.

1972   Fort Shantok and Fort Corchaug: A Comparative Study of the Seventeenth-Century Culture Contact in the Long Island Sound Area. Unpublished Ph.D. Dissertation. Department of Anthropology, New York University.

Published Sources

Abbott, John S. C.

1875   The History of Maine, from the Earliest Discovery of the Region by Northmen until the Present Time. Boston: B. B. Russell.

Abler, Thomas S. (editor)

1989   Chainbreaker: The Revolutionary War Memoirs of Governor Blacksnake as Told to Benjamin Williams. Lincoln: University of Nebraska Press.

Abu-Lughod, Lila

1991   Writing against Culture. *In* Recapturing Anthropology: Working in the Present. Richard G. Fox, ed. 137–62. Santa Fe, N.M.: School of American Research Press.

Alden, Timothy (editor)

1837   An Account of the Captivity of Hugh Gibson among the Delaware Indians of the Big Beaver and Muskingum from the Latter Part of July, 1756 to the Beginning of April, 1759. Collections of the Massachusetts Historical Society, 3rd ser., 6:140–53.

Ales, Marion Fisher

1979   A History of the Indians on Montauk, Long Island. *In* The History and Archaeology of the Montauk Indians. Gaynell Stone, ed. 13–124. Stony Brook, N.Y.: Suffolk County Archaeological Association.

Allen, Charles E.
1931   The History of Dresden, Maine. N.p.
Allen, Paula Gunn
1983   Sacred Hoop: Recovering the Feminine in American Indian Tradi-
              tions. Boston: Beacon Press.
Allen, William D.
1856   Sandy River Settlements. Maine Historical Society Collections, 1st
              ser., 1(4):29–40.
Anonymous
1809a   Various Accounts of the Indians: Saconet Indians. Collections of the
              Massachusetts Historical Society 10:114.
1809b   A List of Names of Indians . . . Which Live in, or Belong to Natick:
              Taken June 16, 1749. Massachusetts Historical Society Collections,
              1st ser., 10:134–36.
1886a   The Treaty with the Eastern Indians at Falmouth, 1749. Maine
              Historical Society Collections, 1st ser., 4:145–67.
1886b   A [True] Relation Concerning the Estate of New England [1634].
              New England Historical and Genealogical Register 40:66–73.
1905–6   The Treaty of Logg's Town, 1752. Virginia Magazine of History and
              Biography 13(1):148–74.
1925   Report of ye Comittee of ye Honble Comissioners for ye Indian
              Affairs and of ye Corporation of Harvard College . . . October 23,
              1729. Publications of the Colonial Society of Massachusetts 16:575–
              77.
1989   The Cathedral Church of St. George. Kingston: Diocese of Ontario.
Aquila, Richard
1983   The Iroquois Restoration: Iroquois Diplomacy on the Colonial Fron-
              tier, 1701–54. Detroit: Wayne State University Press.
Archer, Gabriel
1906   The Relation of Captaine Gosnols Voyage to the North Part of Vir-
              ginia, Begunne the Sixe and Twentieth of March, Anno 42. Eliz-
              abethae Reginae 1623. and Delivered by Gabriel Archer, a Gentle-
              man of the Said Voyage [1625]. *In* Hakluytus Posthumus or Purchas
              His Pilgrimes, by Samuel Purchas 18:302–13. Glasgow: James Mac-
              Lehose and Sons.
Ardener, Edwin
1972   Belief and the Problem of Women. *In* The Interpretation of Ritual:
              Essays in Honour of A. I. Richards. J. S. La Fontaine, ed. 135–58.
              London: Tavistock Publications.
Axtell, James L.
1981   (editor) The Indian Peoples of Eastern America: A Documentary
              History of the Sexes. New York: Oxford University Press.
1985   The Invasion within: The Contest of Cultures in Colonial North
              America. New York: Oxford University Press.

Bailey, Alfred G.
1939   The Conflict of European and Eastern Algonquian Cultures, 1504–
               1700: A Study in Canadian Civilization. Toronto: University of
               Toronto Press.
Bailey, Frederick G.
1960   Tribe, Caste, and Nation: A Study of Political Activity and Political
               Change in Highland Orissa. Manchester, England: Manchester Uni-
               versity Press.
Bailey, Kenneth P. (editor)
1947   The Ohio Company Papers, 1753–1817, Being Primarily Papers of
               the "Suffering Traders" of Pennsylvania. Arcata, Calif.: N.p.
Baker, Emerson W.
1985   The Clarke and Lake Company: The Historical Archaeology of a
               Seventeenth-Century Maine Settlement. Occasional Publications
               in Maine Archaeology 4. Augusta: Maine Historical Preservation
               Commission.
1989   "A Scratch with a Bear's Paw": Anglo-Indian Land Deeds in Early
               Maine. Ethnohistory 36(3):235–56.
Baldwin, Thomas W. (compiler)
1910   Vital Records of Natick, Massachusetts, to the Year 1850. Boston:
               New England Genealogical Society.
Barrows, John Stuart
1938   Fryeburg, Maine: An Historical Sketch. Fryeburg.
Barth, Fredrik
1969   Introduction. In Ethnic Groups and Boundaries: The Social Organi-
               zation of Cultural Difference. Fredrik Barth, ed. 9–38. Boston: Lit-
               tle, Brown.
Bartlett, William S.
1853   The Frontier Missionary: A Memoir of the Life of the Rev. Jacob
               Bailey, Missionary at Pownalborough, Maine; Cornwallis and An-
               napolis, Nova Scotia. Boston: Ide and Dutton.
Bartram, John
1751   Observations on the Inhabitants, Climate, Soil, Rivers, Productions,
               Animals, and Other Matters Worthy of Notice, Made by John Bar-
               tram, in His Travels from Pensilvania to Onondago, Oswego and the
               Lake Ontario, in Canada. . . . London.
Bataille, Gretchen M., and Karen Mullen Sands (editors)
1984   American Indian Women Telling Their Lives. Lincoln: University of
               Nebraska Press.
Baxter, James Phinney
1890   The Campaign against the Pequakets. Maine Historical Society Col-
               lections, 2nd ser., 2(1).
1893   Christopher Levett of York: The Pioneer Colonist in Casco Bay.
               Portland: Gorges Society.

Beauchamp, William M.
1916a   Shikellimy and His Son Logan. Twenty-First Annual Report of the American Scenic and Historic Preservation Society. Albany.
1916b   Moravian Journals Relating to Central New York, 1745–66. Syracuse, N.Y.: Dehler Press.
Beck, Jane C.
1990   Traditional Folk Medicine in Vermont. *In* Medicine and Healing, Annual Proceedings of the Dublin Seminar for New England Folklife. Peter Benes, ed. 34–43. Boston: Boston University Press.
Becker, Marshall Joseph
1984   Lenape Bands Prior to 1740. *In* The Lenape Indians: A Symposium. Herbert C. Kraft, ed. 19–32. South Orange, N.J.: Seton Hall University.
1987   The Forks of Delaware, Pennsylvania, During the First Half of the Eighteenth Century: The Migration of Some "Jerseys" into a Former Shared Resource Area North of Lenape Territory and Its Implications for Cultural Boundaries and Identities. Abhandlungen de Volkerkundlichen Arbeitsgemeinschaft 55. Nordhoff, West Germany.
1988   A Summary of Lenape Socio-Political Organization and Settlement Pattern at the Time of European Contact: The Evidence for Collecting Bands. Journal of Mid-Atlantic Archaeology 4:79–83.
Behar, Ruth
1990   Rage and Redemption: Reading the Life Story of a Mexican Marketing Woman. Feminist Studies 16(2):223–58.
Bell, Whitfield, Jr. (editor)
1973   A Journey from Pennsylvania to Onondaga in 1743. Barre, Mass.: N.p.
Benes, Peter
1990   Itinerant Physicians, Healers, and Surgeon-Dentists in New England and New York, 1720–1825. *In* Medicine and Healing, Annual Proceedings of the Dublin Seminar for New England Folklife. Peter Benes, ed. 95–111. Boston: Boston University Press.
Bennett, Randall H.
1991   Bethel, Maine: An Illustrated History. Bethel: Bethel Historical Society.
Benton, Nathaniel S.
1856   A History of Herkimer County, including the Upper Mohawk Valley, from the Earliest Period to the Present Time. Albany: J. Munsell.
Biglow, William
1830   History of the Town of Natick, Massachusetts, Boston: N.p.
Billington, Sandra
1984   A Social History of the Fool. New York: St. Martin's Press.
Boissevain, Jeremy
1974   Friends of Friends: Networks, Manipulators, and Coalitions. Oxford: Basil Blackwell.

Bolus, Malvina
1973   Four Kings Came to Dinner with Their Honours. The Beaver, Autumn 1973:4–11.
Bond, Beverly W. (editor)
1926–27   The Captivity of Charles Stuart, 1755–75. Mississippi Valley Historical Review 13(1):58–81.
Bond, Richard P.
1952   Queen Anne's American Kings. Oxford: Clarendon Press.
Bonfanti, Leo
1971–72   Biographies and Legends of the New England Indians. 4 vols. Wakefield, Mass.: New England Historical Series.
Bonvillain, Nancy
1980   Iroquois Women. *In* Studies on Iroquoian Culture, Nancy Bonvillain, ed. 47–58. Occasional Publications in Northeastern Anthropology 6. Rindge, N.H.: Department of Anthropology, Franklin Pierce College.
Bourdieu, Pierre
1978   Outline of a Theory of Practice. Richard Nice, trans. New York: Cambridge University Press.
Bourne, Russell
1990   The Red King's Rebellion: Racial Politics in New England, 1675–78. New York: Oxford University Press.
Bourque, Bruce J., and Ruth H. Whitehead
1985   Tarrantines and the Introduction of European Trade Goods in the Gulf of Maine. Ethnohistory 32(3):327–41.
Bouton, Nathaniel (editor)
1867–73   Documents and Records Relating to the Province of New Hampshire. 7 vols. Concord: George E. Jenks.
Boyd, Julian P. (editor)
1938   Indian Treaties Printed by Benjamin Franklin, 1736–62. Philadelphia: Historical Society of Pennsylvania.
Bradford, William
1901   Bradford's History "Of Plymouth Plantation" from the Original Manuscript, 1623–46. Boston: Wright and Potter.
1952   Of Plymouth Plantation, 1620–47. Samuel E. Morrison, ed. New York: Knopf.
1962   Of Plymouth Plantation, 1620–47. Harvey Wish, ed. New York: Capricorn Books.
Bradford, William (editor)
1756   A Treaty between the Government of New-Jersey and the Indians. Advertisement, Pennsylvania Journal and Weekly Advertiser, No. 688, 12 Feb., 3. Philadelphia.
Bradner, Leichester
1925   Ninigret's Naval Campaign against the Montauks. Rhode Island Historical Society Collections 18(1):14–19.

Bragdon, Kathleen Joan

1987a   "Emphaticall Speech and Great Action": An Analysis of Seven-
         teenth-Century Native Speech Events Described in Early Sources.
         Man in the Northeast 33:101–11.

1989   The Material Culture of the Christian Indians in New England,
         1650–1775. *In* Documentary Archaeology in the New World.
         Mary C. Beaudry, ed. New York: Cambridge University Press.

Brainerd, David

1822   Memoirs of the Rev. David Brainerd; Missionary to the Indians on
         the Borders of New-York, New-Jersey, and Pennsylvania. Serena
         Edwards Dwight, ed. New Haven: S. Converse.

Brainerd, Thomas

1865   The Life of John Brainerd, the Brother of David Brainerd, and His
         Successor as Missionary to the Indians of New Jersey. Philadelphia:
         Presbyterian Publication Committee.

Brasser, Theodore J. C.

1966   Indians of Long Island, 1600–1964. Colorado Springs: Wanblee
         Supply.

Breen, Timothy H.

1980   An Empire of Goods: The Anglicization of Colonial Americans,
         1690–1776. Journal of British Studies 25(4):467–99.

1984   Creative Adaptations: Peoples and Cultures. *In* Colonial British
         America: Essays in the New History of the Early Modern Era. Jack P.
         Greene and J. R. Pole, eds. Baltimore: Johns Hopkins University
         Press.

Brenner, Elise M.

1980   To Pray or to Be Prey, That is the Question: Strategies for Cultural
         Autonomy of Massachusetts Praying Town Indians. Ethnohistory
         27(2):135–52.

Brereton, John

1906   A Briefe and True Relation of the Discoverie of the North Part of
         Virginia . . . Made this Present Yeare 1602. *In* Early English and
         French Voyages, Chiefly from Hakluyt, 1534–1608. Henry S. Bur-
         rage, ed. 325–40. New York: Charles Scribner's Sons.

Brewster, William

1954   The Pennsylvania and New York Frontier, 1700–1763. Philadelphia:
         N.p.

Brown, Kathleen

1993   Brave New Worlds: Women's and Gender History. William and Mary
         Quarterly, 3rd ser., 50(2):311–28.

Browne, William Hand, et al. (editors)

1883–1970 Archives of Maryland. 73 vols. Baltimore: Maryland Historical So-
         ciety.

Brumble, David H., III
1988   American Indian Autobiography. Berkeley: University of California Press.

Buck, William J.
1883   Jeremiah Langhorne. Pennsylvania Magazine of History and Biography 7(1):67–87.

Burch, Wanda
1990a   Sir William Johnson and Eighteenth-Century Medicine in the New York Colony. *In* Medicine and Health, Annual Proceedings of the Dublin Seminar for New England Folklife. Peter Benes, ed. 55–65. Boston: Boston University Press.
1990b   Sir William Johnson's Cabinet of Curiosities. New York History 71(3):261–82.

Bureau of the Census, U.S.
1908   Heads of Families at the First Census of the United States Taken in the Year 1790—Pennsylvania. Washington, D.C.

Burton, William J., and Richard Lowenthal
1974   The First of the Mohegans. American Ethnologist 1(4):589–99.

Byers, Edward
1987   The Nation of Nantucket: Society and Politics in an Early American Commercial Center, 1660–1820. Boston: Northeastern University Press.

Calloway, Colin G.
1990   The Western Abenakis of Vermont, 1600–1800. Norman: University of Oklahoma Press.
1991   (editor) Dawnland Encounters: Indians and Europeans in Northern New England. Hanover, N.H.: University Press of New England.

Campbell, Marjorie Freeman
1958   Niagara, Hinge of the Golden Arc. Toronto: Ryerson Press.

Campbell, William W.
1831   Annals of Tryon County; or, the Border Wars of New-York, During the Revolution. New York: J. & J. Harper.

Campbell, Paul R., and Glenn W. LaFantasie
1978   Scattered to the Winds of Heaven—Narragansett Indians 1676–1880. Rhode Island History 37(3)67–83.

Carter, John H.
1931   Shikellamy: The Indian Vice King at Shamokin. Proceedings and Addresses of the Northumberland County Historical Society 3.
1937   The Moravians at Shamokin. Proceedings and Addresses of the Northumberland County Historical Society 9.

Case, J. Wickham (editor)
1882–84   Southold Town Records. 2 vols. Southold, N.Y.

Castiglioni, Luigi
1983   Viaggio, Travels in the United States of North America, 1785–87. Antonio Pace, trans. and ed. Syracuse: Syracuse University Press.

Caulkins, Frances M.
1874   History of Norwich, Connecticut, from its Possession by the Indians
              to the Year 1866. Hartford, Conn.: Case, Lockwood, and Brainard.
Ceci, Lynn
1980   Locational Analysis of Historic Algonquin Sites in Coastal New
              York: A Preliminary Study. *In* Proceedings of the Conference on
              Northeastern Archaeology, Research Report 10. John Moore, ed. 71–
              91. Amherst: Department of Anthropology, University of Massa-
              chusetts.
1990   Native Wampum as a Peripheral Resource in the Seventeenth-
              Century World System. *In* The Pequots in Southern New England:
              The Fall and Rise of an American Indian Nation. Laurence M.
              Hauptman and James D. Wherry, eds. 48–63. Norman: University of
              Oklahoma Press.
Champlain, Samuel de
1922–38   The Works of Samuel de Champlain [1626]. Henry P. Biggar, ed. 6
              vols. Toronto: Champlain Society.
Chapin, Howard M.
1931   Sachems of the Narragansetts. Providence: Rhode Island Historical
              Society.
Chidsey, A. D., Jr.
1937   The Penn Patents in the Forks of the Delaware. Easton, Penn.:
              Northampton County Historical and Genealogical Society.
Child, Francis J. (editor)
1858   English and Scottish Ballads. 5 vols. Boston: Little, Brown.
Church, Benjamin
1975   A Diary of King Philip's War, 1675–76. Alan Simpson and Mary
              Simpson, eds. Chester, Conn.: Pequot Press for the Little Compton
              Historical Society.
Churchill, Edwin A.
1978   The Founding of Maine, 1600–1640: A Revisionist Interpretation.
              Maine Historical Quarterly 18(1):21–54.
Claus, Daniel
1904   Daniel Claus's Narrative of his Relations with Sir William Johnson
              and Experiences in the Lake George Fight. New York: Society of
              Colonial Wars in the State of New York.
Clifton, James A. (editor)
1989   Being and Becoming Indian: Biographical Studies of North Ameri-
              can Frontiers. Chicago: Dorsey.
Cohen, Yehudi A.
1969   Social Boundary Systems. Current Anthropology 10(1):103–26.
Cook, Sherburne F.
1976   The Indian Population of New England in the Seventeenth Century.
              University of California Publications in Anthropology 12. Berkeley:
              University of California Press.

Cox, John, Jr. (editor)
1916–40   Oyster Bay Town Records. 8 vols. New York: Tobias A. Wright.
CPR
1850–90   The Public Records of the Colony and Plantation of Connecticut
               (1636–1776). John Hammond Trumbull and Charles J. Hoadly, eds.
               15 vols. Hartford, Conn.: Case, Lockwood, and Brainard.
Cronon, William
1983   Changes in the Land: Indians, Colonists, and the Ecology of New
               England. New York: Hill and Wang.
Cruikshank, Helen Gere (editor)
1961   John and William Bartram's America. Garden City, N.Y.: Doubleday.
Csordas, Thomas J.
1990   Embodiment as a Paradigm for Anthropology. Ethos 19(1):5–47.
Cushman, David
1856   Ancient Settlement of Sheepscot. Collections of the Maine Historical
               Society 4.
Day, Gordon F.
1965   The Identity of the Sokokis. Ethnohistory 12(3):237–49.
1974   Henry Tufts as a Source on the Eighteenth-Century Abenakis. Eth-
               nohistory 21(3):189–97.
1981   The Identity of the St. Francis Indians. Mercury Series, Canadian
               Ethnology Service Paper 71. Ottawa: National Museum of Man,
               National Museums of Canada.
Dayton, Cornelia Hughes
1991   Taking the Trade: Abortion and Gender Relations in an Eighteenth-
               Century New England Village. William and Mary Quarterly, 3rd ser.
               48(1):19–49.
De Forest, John W.
1851   History of the Indians of Connecticut: From the Earliest Known
               Period to 1850. Hartford: W. J. Hamersley.
De Forest, L. Effingham (editor)
1941   Hannah Lawrence Schlieffelin's Letter. New York Genealogical and
               Biographical Record 72(2):120–23.
De Laet, Johan
1909   Extracts from the "New World" [1625, 1630, 1633, and 1640]. In
               Narratives of New Netherland, 1609–64. J. Franklin Jameson, ed.
               29–60. New York: Charles Scribner's Sons.
De Lancey, Edward Floyd (editor)
1879   History of New York During the Revolutionary War, and of the
               Leading Events in the Other Colonies at that Period, by Thomas
               Jones. 2 vols. New York: New-York Historical Society.
Denton, Daniel
1670   A Brief Description of New-York: Formerly Called New-Netherlands.
               London.

Denys, Nicholas
1908   The Description and Natural History of the Coasts of North America
            (Acadia) [1672]. William F. Ganong, ed. and trans. Toronto: Cham-
            plain Society.
De Schweinitz, Edmund A.
1870   The Life and Times of David Zeisberger, the Western Pioneer and
            Apostle to the Indians. Philadelphia: J. B. Lippincott.
DHNY
1849–51   Documentary History of the State of New York. Edmund B. O'Cal-
            laghan, ed. 4 vols. New York: Weed and Parsons.
Di Leonardo, Micaela
1991   Introduction. *In* Gender at the Crossroads of Knowledge: Feminist
            Anthropology in the Postmodern Era. Micaela di Leonardo, ed. 1–
            48. Berkeley: University of California Press.
Douce, Francis
1847   A Dissertation on the Ancient English Morris Dance. *In* A Lytell
            Geste of Robin Hose, with Other Ancient & Modern Ballads and
            Songs Relating to this Celebrated Yeoman. 5 vols. J. M. Gutch, ed.
            1:329–65. London: Longman, Brown, Green, and Longmans.
Dowd, Gregory Evan
1992   A Spirited Resistance: The North American Indian Struggle for
            Unity, 1745–1815. Baltimore: Johns Hopkins University Press.
Dragon, A.
1973   L'Acadie et ses 40 Robes Noires. Montreal: N.p.
Drake, Benjamin
1841   Life of Tecumseh, and His Brother, the Prophet; with a Historical
            Sketch of the Shawanoe Indians. Cincinnati: E. Morgan.
Drake, Samuel G.
1833   Book of the Indians of North America: Comprising Details in the
            Lives of About Five Hundred Chiefs and Others. Boston: J. Drake.
1854   History of the Early Discovery of America and Landing of the Pil-
            grims. With a Biography of the North American Indians. Boston:
            Higgins and Bradley.
1857   The Book of Indians; or Biography and History of the Indians of
            North America, From its First Discovery to the Year 1841. 8th ed.
            Boston: N.p.
Dudley, Joseph
            Letter from Joseph Dudley to John Winthrop, Jr., March 6, 1704.
            Massachusetts Historical Society Collections 3:172–78.
Dunton, John
1867   Letters Written from New-England, A.D. 1686. Boston: Prince So-
            ciety.
Eckstorm, Fannie Hardy
1941   Indian Place-Names of the Penobscot Valley and the Maine Coast.

Maine Bulletin 44(4) and University of Maine Studies, 2nd ser., 55. Orono.

Edmunds, R. David
1980   (editor) American Indian Leaders: Studies in Diversity. Lincoln: University of Nebraska Press.
1984   Tecumseh and the Quest for Indian Leadership. Boston: Little, Brown.

Eliot, John
1647   The Day Breaking of the Gospel with the Indians. London. Reprint, Old South Leaflets 6(143):381–404.
1685   The Dying Speeches of Several Indians. Cambridge, Mass.: N.p.
1794   Eliot's Letters to [Robert] Boyle. Massachusetts Historical Society Collections, 1st ser. 3:182–87.

Elmer, Ebenezer
1847–48   Journal Kept during an Expedition to Canada in 1776. Proceedings of the New Jersey Historical Society 2:95–146, 150–94; 3:21–56, 90–102. Reprint, Proceedings of the New Jersey Historical Society, n.s. 1925(10):410–24.

Fenton, William N.
1985   Structure, Continuity, and Change in the Process of Iroquois Treaty Making. *In* The History and Culture of Iroquois Diplomacy: An Interdisciplinary Guide to the Treaties of the Six Nations and Their League. Francis Jennings, William N. Fenton, Mary A. Druke, and David R. Miller, eds. 3–36. Syracuse: Syracuse University Press.
1987   The False Faces of the Iroquois. Norman: University of Oklahoma Press.

Flexner, James Thomas
1979   Lord of the Mohawks: A Biography of Sir William Johnson. Rev. ed. Boston: Little, Brown.

Force, Peter (editor)
1846   Simplicities Defense Against Seven-Headed Policy . . . by Samuel Gorton [1646]. *In* Tracts and Other Papers Relating Principally to the Origin, Settlement, and Progress of the Colonies of North America, from the Discovery of the Country to the Year 1776. New York: Peter Smith.

Foster, Michael K.
1985   Another Look at the Function of Wampum in Iroquois-White Councils. *In* The History and Culture of Iroquois Diplomacy: An Interdisciplinary Guide to the Treaties of the Six Nations and Their League. Francis Jennings, William N. Fenton, Mary A. Druke, and David R. Miller, eds. 99–114. Syracuse: Syracuse University Press.

Freeman, James
1846   Notes on Nantucket. 1807 [1815]. Massachusetts Historical Society Collections. 2nd ser., 3:19–38.

Frost, Josephine C. (editor)
1914   Records of the Town of Jamaica, Long Island, New York. Brooklyn:
            Long Island Historical Society.
Gardiner, Curtis
1890   Lion Gardiner and His Descendants. St. Louis: Whipple.
Gardiner, Lion
1859   Leift Lion Gardener His Relation of the Pequot Warres. *In* Appendix
            to the History of the Wars of New England With the Eastern Indians.
            Samuel Penhallow, ed. 3–32. Cincinnati: William Dodge.
1897   Leift Lion Gardener His Relation of the Pequot Warres. *In* History
            of the Pequot War. Charles Orr, ed. 113–49. Cleveland: Helman-
            Taylor.
Garratt, John C., and Bruce Robinson
1985   The Four Indian Kings. Ottawa: Public Archives of Canada.
Geiger, Susan N. G.
1986   Women's Life Histories: Method and Content. Signs: Journal of
            Women in Culture and Society 11(2):334–51.
Gilman, Carolyn
1982   Where Two Worlds Meet: The Great Lakes Fur Trade. Museum
            Exhibit, 2nd ser. St. Paul: Minnesota Historical Society.
Ginsburg, Faye, and Rayna Rapp
1991   The Politics of Reproduction. *In* Annual Review of Anthropology,
            Vol. 20. Bernard J. Siegel, ed. 311–43. Stanford, Calif.: Stanford
            University Press.
Goddard, R. H. Ives
1978a   Eastern Algonquian Languages. *In* Handbook of North American
            Indians. Vol. 15, The Northeast, Bruce T. Trigger, ed. 70–77. Wash-
            ington, D.C.: Smithsonian Institution.
1978b   Delaware. *In* Handbook of North American Indians. Vol. 15, The
            Northeast. Bruce T. Trigger, ed. 213–39. Washington, D.C.: Smith-
            sonian Institution.
Goddard, R. H. Ives, and Kathleen J. Bragdon
1988   Native Writings in Massachusett. 2 vols. Memoirs of the American
            Philosophical Society 185. Philadelphia.
Gookin, Daniel
1806   Historical Collections of the Indians in New England [1674]. Mas-
            sachusetts Historical Society Collections 1:141–227. Boston.
1836   An Historical Account of the Doings and Sufferings of the Christian
            Indians in New England, In the Years 1675, 1676, 1677. Transac-
            tions and Collections of the American Antiquarian Society 2:432–
            517. Worcester, Mass.
Gorges, Fernando
1890   A Briefe Narration of the Originall Undertakings of the Advance-
            ment of Plantations into the Parts of America, Especially Sheweing

the Beginning, Progress, and Continuance of that of New England [1658]. Publications of the Prince Society 2. Boston.

Grant, Anne

1876   Memoirs of an American Lady with Sketches of Manners and Scenes in America as they Existed Previous to the American Revolution. Albany: J. Munsell.

Gray, Elma E., and Leslie Robb Gray

1956   Wilderness Christians: The Moravian Mission to the Delaware Indians. Ithaca, N.Y.: Cornell University Press.

Graymont, Barbara

1972   The Iroquois in the American Revolution. Syracuse: Syracuse University Press.

1979   Konwatsi?tsiaienni. Dictionary of Canadian Biography 4:416–19. Toronto: University of Toronto Press.

Green, Gretchen

1989   Molly Brant, Catharine Brant, and their Daughters: A Study in Colonial Acculturation. Ontario History 81(3):235–50.

Grumet, Robert S.

1980   Sunksquaws, Shamans, and Tradeswomen: Middle Atlantic Coastal Algonkian Women during the 17th and 18th Centuries. *In* Women and Colonization: Anthropological Perspectives. Mona Etienne and Eleanor Burke Leacock, eds. 43–62. New York: Praeger Scientific.

1981   Native American Place Names in New York City. New York: Museum of the City of New York.

1988   Taphow: The Forgotten "Sakemau and Commander in Chief of all those Indians Inhabiting Northern New Jersey." Bulletin of the Archaeological Society of New Jersey 43:23–28.

1989   The Selling of Lenapehoking. Bulletin of Archaeological Society of New Jersey 44:1–6.

1990   A New Ethnohistorical Model for North American Indian Demography. North American Archaeologist 11(1):29–41.

1991   The Minisink Settlements: Native American Identity and Society in the Munsee Heartland, 1650–1778. *In* People of Minisink: Papers from the 1989 Delaware Water Gap Symposium. David G. Orr and Douglas V. Campana, eds. 175–250. Philadelphia: Mid-Atlantic Region, National Park Service.

1992   Historic Contact: Early Relations between Indian People and Colonists in Today's Northeastern United States, 1524–1783. Philadelphia: Mid-Atlantic Region, National Park Service.

Gundy, Pearson

1953   Molly Brant—Loyalist. Ontario History 14(3):97–108.

Gutch, John M. (editor)

1847   A Lytell Geste of Robin Hose, with Other Ancient & Modern Ballads and Songs Relating to this Celebrated Yeoman. 5 vols. London: Longman, Brown, Green, and Longmans.

Gyles, John
　　　John Gyles's Statement of the Number of Indians (1726). Maine Historical Society Collections, 1st ser. 3:357–58.

Hagedorn, Nancy L.
1994　"Faithful, Knowing, and Prudent": Andrew Montour as Interpreter and Culture Broker, 1740–72. *In* Between Indian and White Worlds: The Culture Broker. Margaret Connell Szasz, ed. Norman: University of Oklahoma Press.

Hamilton, Alexander
1948　Gentleman's Progress: The Itinerarium of Dr. Alexander Hamilton, 1744. Carl Bridenbaugh, ed. Chapel Hill: University of North Carolina Press.

Hamilton, J. T. (translator)
1936　Autobiography of Bernhard Adam Grube. Transactions of the Moravian Historical Society 9. Nazareth, Penn.

Hamilton, Kenneth G.
1951　Cultural Contributions of Moravian Missions among the Indians. Pennsylvania History 18(1):1–15.

Hamilton, Milton W.
1974　Theyanoguin. Dictionary of Canadian Biography 3:622–24. Toronto and Quebec: University of Toronto Press and Les Presses de l'universite Laval.
1975　Sir William Johnson and the Indians of New York. Albany: New York State American Revolutionary War Bicentennial Commission.
1976　Sir William Johnson, Colonial American, 1715–63. Port Washington, N.Y.: Kennikat Press.

Hammond, Otis Grant (editor)
1915　The Indian Stream Republic. Collections of the New Hampshire Historical Society 11:3–128.

Hanna, Charles A.
1911　The Wilderness Trail: or, the Ventures and Adventures of the Pennsylvania Traders on the Allegheny Path with Some New Annals of the Old West, and the Records of Some Strong Men and Some Bad Ones. 2 vols. New York: G. P. Putnam's Sons.

Hardin, Garrett
1968　The Tragedy of the Commons. Science 162:1243–48.

Harrison, Alexander (editor)
1876　Memoir of Lieu. Col. Tench Tilghman. Albany: J. Munsell.

Hausfater, Glenn
1984　Infanticide: Comparative and Evolutionary Perspectives. Current Anthropology 25(3):500–503.

HBP
1951 to　The Papers of Henry Bouquet. Sylvester K. Stevens, Donald H. Kent,
present　Louis Waddell, et al., eds. 5 vols. to date. Harrisburg: Pennsylvania Historical and Museum Commission.

Heckewelder, John
1819   An Account of the History, Manners, and Customs of the Indians
             Who Once Inhabited Pennsylvania and the Neighbouring States.
             William C. Reichel, ed. Memoirs of the Historical Society of Penn-
             sylvania 12. Philadelphia.
Helfrich, G. W.
1989   An Uncommonly Misspent Life. Down East, Nov. 1989:74–77, 85,
             88.
Helm, June
1980   Female Infanticide, European Diseases, and Population Levels
             among the Mackenzie Dene. American Ethnologist 7(2):259–85.
Hemmenway, Abby (editor)
1868–1929 The Vermont Historical Gazetteer. 5 vols. Burlington.
Henry, M. S.
1860   History of the Lehigh Valley, Containing a Copious Selection of the
             Most Interesting Facts, Traditions, Biographical Sketches, Anec-
             dotes, etc. Easton, Penn.: Bixler & Corwin.
Hicks, Benjamin D. (editor)
1896–1904 Records of the Towns of North and South Hempstead. 8 vols. Ja-
             maica, N.Y.: Long Island Farmer Printer.
Hoadly, Charles J. (editor)
1857   Records of the Colony and Plantation of New Haven, 1638–49.
             Hartford, Conn.: N.p.
Hodgen, Margaret T.
1974   Anthropology, History, and Culture Change. Viking Fund Publica-
             tions in Anthropology 52. Tucson: University of Arizona Press.
Hoffer, Peter C., and N. E. H. Hull
1981   Murdering Mothers: Infanticide in England and New England. New
             York University School of Law Series in Legal History, Vol. 2. New
             York: New York University Press.
Holmes, Herbert E.
1912   The Makers of Maine. Lewiston: N.p.
Holt, J. C.
1976   The Origins and Audience of the Ballads of Robin Hood. *In* Peas-
             ants, Knights, and Heretics: Studies in Medieval English Social
             History. Rodney H. Hilton, ed. 236–57. New York: Cambridge Uni-
             versity Press.
1984   Robin Hood. New York: Cambridge University Press.
Hrdy, Sarah Blaffer
1992   The Myth of Mother Love. New York Times Book Review. 30 Aug.,
             11.
Hubbard, John M.
1886   Account of Sa-Go-Ye-Wat-Ha, or Red Jacket, and his People. Al-
             bany: J. Munsell.

Hubbard, William
1865   The History of the Indian Wars in New England from the First Settlement to the Termination of the War with King Philip, in 1677. Samuel G. Drake, ed. 2 vols. Roxbury, Mass.: W. Eliot Woodward.

Hughes, Leo
1956   A Century of English Farce. Princeton: Princeton University Press.

Humins, John H.
1987   Squanto and Massasoit: A Struggle for Power. New England Quarterly 60(1):54–70.

Hunter, Charles A.
1971   The Delaware Nativist Revival of the Mid-Eighteenth Century. Ethnohistory 18(1):39–49.

Hunter, William A.
1951   Provincial Negotiations with the Western Indians, 1755–58. Pennsylvania History 18(2):213–29.

1954   John Hays's Diary and Journal of 1760. Pennsylvania Archaeologist 24(2):62–83.

1956   Victory at Kittanning. Pennsylvania History 23(3):376–407.

1960   Forts on the Pennsylvania Frontier, 1753–58. Harrisburg: Pennsylvania Historical and Museum Commission.

1978   Documented Sub-Divisions of the Delaware Indians. Bulletin of the Archaeological Society of New Jersey 35:20–40.

Hutchins, Grace
n.d.   Green Mountain Whittlins. North Troy, Vt.: N.p.

Hutchinson, Benjamin (editor)
1880   Records of the Town of Brookhaven up to 1880. Patchogue, N.Y.: Patchogue Advance.

Innis, Harold A.
1930   The Fur Trade in Canada: An Introduction to Canadian Economic History. New Haven: Yale University Press.

Innis, Mary Quayle (editor)
1965   Mrs. Simcoe's Diary. Toronto: Macmillan.

Jacobson, Jerome
1980   Burial Ridge: Archaeology at New York City's Largest Prehistoric Cemetery. St. George, N.Y.: Staten Island Institute of Arts and Sciences.

James, Thomas
1865   Letter from the Reverend Thomas James of East Hampton to John Winthrop, Jr. Collections of the Massachusetts Historical Society, 4th ser., 7:482–83.

Jameson, J. Franklin (editor)
1909   Narratives of New Netherland, 1609–64. New York: Charles Scribner's Sons.

Jennings, Francis

1965   The Delaware Interregnum. Pennsylvania Magazine of History and Biography 89(2):174–98.

1966   The Indian Trade of the Susquehanna Valley. Proceedings of the American Philosophical Society 110(6):406–24.

1968   Incident at Tulpehocken. Pennsylvania History 35(4):335–55.

1970   The Scandalous Policy of William Penn's Sons: Deeds and Documents of the Walking Purchase. Pennsylvania History 37(1):19–39.

1975   The Invasion of America: Indians, Colonialism, and the Cant of Conquest. New York: W. W. Norton.

1984   The Ambiguous Iroquois Empire: The Covenant Chain Confederation of Indian Tribes with English Colonies from its Beginning to the Lancaster Treaty of 1744. New York: W. W. Norton.

1985   Iroquois Alliances in American History. *In* The History and Culture of Iroquois Diplomacy: An Interdisciplinary Guide to the Treaties of the Six Nations and Their League. Francis Jennings, William N. Fenton, Mary A. Druke, and David R. Miller, eds. 37–65. Syracuse: Syracuse University Press.

1987   "Pennsylvania Indians" and the Iroquois. *In* Beyond the Covenant Chain: The Iroquois and Their Neighbors in Indian North America, 1600–1800. Daniel K. Richter and James H. Merrell, eds. 75–91. Syracuse: Syracuse University Press.

1988   Empire of Fortune: Crowns, Colonies, and Tribes in the Seven Years War in America. New York: W. W. Norton.

Johnson, Allen (editor)

1943   Dictionary of American Biography. New York: Charles Scribner's Sons.

Johnson, Edward

1910   Johnson's Wonder Working Providence, 1628–51. J. Franklin Jameson, ed. New York: Charles Scribner's Sons.

Johnson, Richard R.

1977   The Search for a Usable Indian: An Aspect of the Defense of Colonial New England. Journal of American History 64(4):628–31.

Johnston, Jean

1964   Molly Brant: Mohawk Matron. Ontario History 56(2):105–24.

1973   Molly Brant. *In* Wilderness Women: Canada's Forgotten History. Jean Johnston, ed. 73–118. Toronto: Peter Martin's Associates.

Jordan, John W. (editor)

1878–79   Spangenberg's Notes of Travel to Onondaga in 1745. Pennsylvania Magazine of History and Biography 2(4):424–32; 3(1):56–64.

1905   Bishop J. C. F. Cammerhoff's Narrative of a Journey to Shamokin, Pennsylvania, in the Winter of 1748. Pennsylvania Magazine of History and Biography 29(2):160–79.

1913a   James Kenny's Journal, 1761–63. Pennsylvania Magazine of History and Biography 37(1):1–47; (2):152–201.

1913b   James Kenny's Journal to ye Westward, 1758–59. Pennsylvania Magazine of History and Biography 37(3):295–449.

Josephy, Alvin M., Jr. (editor)

1961   The Patriot Chiefs: A Chronicle of American Indian Resistance. New York: Viking.

Josselyn, John

1988   John Josselyn, Colonial Traveler: A critical edition of Two Voyages to New England. Paul J. Lindholt, ed. Hanover, N.H.: University Press of New England.

JP

1921–63   The Papers of Sir William Johnson. James Sullivan, Alexander C. Flick, Almon W. Lauber, and Milton W. Hamilton, eds. 14 vols. Albany: University of the State of New York.

JR

1896–1901   The Jesuit Relations and Allied Documents: Travels and Explorations of the Jesuit Missionaries in New France, 1610–1791. Rueben Gold Thwaites, ed. 73 vols. Cleveland: Burrows Brothers.

Kawashima, Yasuhide

1986   Puritan Justice and the Indian: White Man's Law in Massachusetts, 1630–87. Middletown, Conn.: Wesleyan University Press.

Kellaway, William

1962   The New England Company, 1649–1776: Missionary Society to the American Indians. New York: Barnes and Noble.

Kelsay, Isabel Thompson

1984   Joseph Brant, 1743–1807: Man of Two Worlds. Syracuse: Syracuse University Press.

Kent, Barry C.

1984   Susquehanna's Indians. Anthropological Series, No. 6. Harrisburg: Pennsylvania Historical and Museum Commission.

Kent, Donald H.

1984   The French Invasion of Western Pennsylvania. Harrisburg: Pennsylvania Historical and Museum Commission.

Keesing, Roger M.

1974   Theories of Culture. *In* Annual Review of Anthropology, Vol. 3. Bernard J. Siegel, ed. 73–97. Stanford, Calif.: Stanford University Press.

1985   Kwaio Women Speak: The Micropolitics of Autobiography in a Solomon Islands Society. American Anthropologist 87(1):27–39.

Kidder, Frederick

1865   Expeditions of Capt. John Lovewell. Maine Historical Society Collections 4.

Kimball, E. G.

1964   Molly Ockett's Ghost Guards Indian Treasure. Lewiston Journal, 30 July. Lewiston, Maine.

1968   Molly Ockett, and the Hamlin Prophecy that Came True. Lewiston Journal Magazine Section, 17 Aug. Lewiston, Maine.

Kraft, Herbert C.
1986   The Lenape: Archaeology, History, and Ethnography. Collections of the New Jersey Historical Society 21. Newark: New Jersey Historical Society.

Labbie, Edith
1966   Bethel Pays Tribute to a Fabled Maine Indian. Lewiston Journal, 30 July. Lewiston, Maine.

Langness, L. L.
1965   The Life History in Anthropological Science. *In* Studies in Anthropological Method. George Spindler and Louise Spindler, series eds. New York: Holt, Rinehart, and Winston.
1981   Child Abuse and Cultural Values: The Case of New Guinea. *In* Child Abuse and Neglect: Cross-Cultural Perspectives. Jill E. Korbin, ed. 13–34. Los Angeles: University of California Press.

Lapham, William B.
1981   History of the Town of Bethel. Facsimile of the 1891 edition, with a new historical essay by Stanley Russell Howe. Bethel, Maine: New England History Press and Bethel Historical Society.

Lapomarda, Vincent A.
1977   The Jesuit Heritage in New England. Worcester, Mass.: N.p.

Leach, Douglas Edward
1958   Flintlock and Tomahawk: New England in King Philip's War. New York: MacMillan.

Lechford, Thomas
1642   Plain Dealing; or News from New-England: A Short View of New-England's Present Government. London: W. E. and I. G. for N. Butter.

Leder, Lawrence H. (editor)
1956   The Livingston Indian Records, 1666–1723. Pennsylvania History 23(1):1–240.

Leger, Mary C.
1929   The Catholic Indian Missions of Maine, 1611–1820. Catholic University of America, Studies in American Church History 8. Washington, D.C.

Lender, Mark E., and James Kirby Martin (editors)
1982   Citizen Soldier, the Revolutionary War Journal of Joseph Bloomfield. Newark: New Jersey Historical Society.

Leneman, Leah, and Rosalind Mitchison
1988   Girls in Trouble: The Social and Geographical Setting of Illegitimacy in Early Modern Scotland. Journal of Social History 21(4): 483–97.

Lescarbot, Marc
1907–14   The History of New France [1618]. W. L. Grant, trans. 3 vols. Toronto: Champlain Society.

Levett, Christopher
1847   Voyage into New England, Begun in 1623, and Ended in 1624
            [1628]. Collections of the Maine Historical Society 2:73–110.

Libby, C. T. (editor)
1928–31   The Province and Court Records of Maine. 2 vols. Portland: Maine
            Historical Society.

Little, Elizabeth A.
1976   Sachem Nickanoose of Nantucket and the Grass Contest. Historic
            Nantucket 23(4):14–22; 24(1):21–30.
1980   Three Kinds of Indian Deeds at Nantucket, Massachusetts. *In* Papers
            of the Eleventh Algonquian Conference. William Cowan, ed. 61–70.
            Ottawa: Carleton University Press.
1981a   The Writings of Nantucket Indians. Nantucket Algonquian Studies
            3. Nantucket: Nantucket Historical Association.
1981b   Historic Indian Houses of Nantucket. Nantucket Algonquian Stud-
            ies 4. Nantucket: Nantucket Historical Association.
1990a   The Nantucket Indian Sickness. *In* Papers of the Twenty-First Al-
            gonquian Conference. William Cowan, ed. 181–96. Ottawa: Carle-
            ton University Press.
1990b   Indian Horse Commons at Nantucket Island, 1660–1760. Nan-
            tucket Algonquian Studies 9. Nantucket: Nantucket Historical Asso-
            ciation.

Little, Elizabeth A., and J. Clinton Andrews
1982   Drift Whales at Nantucket: The Gift of Moshup. Man in the North-
            east 23:17–38.

Loskiel, George Henry
1794   History of the Mission of the United Brethren among Indians of
            North America. Christian Ignatius La Trobe, trans. 3 Pts. London:
            Brethren's Society for the Furtherance of the Gospel.

Lydekker, John W.
1938   The Faithful Mohawks. New York: Macmillan.

MacCulloch, Susan L.
1966   A Tripartite Political System among Christian Indians in Early Mas-
            sachusetts. Kroeber Anthropological Society Papers 34:63–73.

MacFarlane, Alan
1980   Illegitimacy and Illegitimates in English History. *In* Bastardy and Its
            Comparative History: Studies in the History of Illegitimacy and Mar-
            ital Nonconformism in Britain, France, Germany, Sweden, North
            America, Jamaica, and Japan. Peter Laslett, Karla Osterveen, and
            Richard M. Smith, eds. 71–85. Cambridge: Harvard University
            Press.

Macy, Obed
1835   The History of Nantucket. Boston: Hilliard, Gray.

Macy, Zaccheus
1810   A Short Journal of the first settling of the Island of Nantucket. . . .
            1792 [1794]. Massachusetts Historical Society Collections, Vol. 3,
            155–61.

Mandell, Daniel
1991   "To Live More Like My Christian English Neighbors": Natick In-
            dians in the Eighteenth Century. William and Mary Quarterly, 3rd
            ser., 48(4):552–79.

Marcus, George E., and Michael M. J. Fischer
1986   Anthropology as Cultural Critique: An Experimental Moment in the
            Human Sciences. Chicago: University of Chicago Press.

Marshe, Witham
1884   Lancaster in 1744: Journal of the Treaty at Lancaster in 1744, with
            the Six Nations. William H. Egle, ed. Lancaster, Penn.: N.p.

Martin, Emily
1987   The Woman in the Body: A Cultural Analysis of Reproduction.
            Boston: Beacon Press.

Martin, John Frederick
1991   Profits in the Wilderness: Entrepreneurship and the Founding of
            New England Towns in the Seventeenth Century. Chapel Hill: Uni-
            versity of North Carolina Press.

Mason, John
1897   A Brief History of the Pequot War: Especially of the Memorable
            Taking of their Fort at Mistick in Connecticut in 1637. *In* History of
            the Pequot War. Charles Orr, ed. 1–46. Cleveland: Helman-Taylor.

Mather, Cotton
1702   Magnalia Christi Americana, or, the Ecclesiastical History of New-
            England; from its First Planting, in the Year 1620, unto the Year of
            Our Lord 1698. London: T. Parkhurst.
1971   Selected Letters of Cotton Mather. Kenneth Silverman, ed. Baton
            Rouge: Louisiana State University Press.

Maurault, Joseph P. A.
1866   Histoire des Abenakis, Depuis 1605 Jusque'a nos Jours. Sorel, Que-
            bec: L'Atelier Typographique de la Gazette de Sorel.

MBR
1853–54   The Records of the Governor and Company of Massachusetts Bay in
            New England. Nathaniel B. Shurtleff, ed. 5 vols. Boston: William
            White.

McBride, Kevin A.
1994   Ancient and Crazie: Pequot Lifeways in the Historic Period. *In*
            Alongkians of New England: Past and Present, Annual Proceedings
            of the Dublin Seminar. Peter Benes, ed. 63–75. Boston: Boston
            University Press.

McCartney, Martha W.
1989   Cockacoeske, Queen of Pamunkey: Diplomat and Suzeraine. *In* Powhatan's Mantle: Indians in the Colonial Southeast. Peter H. Wood, Gregory A. Waselkov, and M. Thomas Hatley, eds. 173–95. Lincoln: University of Nebraska Press.

McConnell, Michael N.
1992a   Kuskusky Towns and Early Western Pennsylvania Indian History. Pennsylvania Magazine of History and Biography 116(1):33–58.
1992b   A Country Between: The Upper Ohio Valley and Its Peoples, 1724–74. Lincoln: University of Nebraska Press.

McHugh, Thomas F.
1966   The Moravian Mission to the American Indian: Early American Peace Corps. Pennsylvania History 33(4):412–31.

MDH
1869–1916   The Documentary History of the State of Maine. James Phinney Baxter, ed. 24 vols. Portland: LeFavor-Tower.

Mendels, Pamela
1982   Indians Hopeful Elections Will Bind Factional Rift Among the Narragansetts. Providence Journal-Bulletin, 26 March, A12.

Merrell, James H.
1987   "Their Very Bones Shall Fight": The Catawba-Iroquois Wars. *In* Beyond the Covenant Chain: The Iroquois and Their Neighbors in Indian North America, 1600–1800. Daniel K. Richter and James H. Merrell, eds. 115–33. Syracuse: Syracuse University Press.
1991   "The Customes of Our Country": Indians and Colonists in Early America. *In* Strangers Within the Realm: The Cultural Margins of the First British Empire. Bernard Bailyn and Philip D. Morgan, eds. 117–56. Chapel Hill: University of North Carolina Press.

Metcalf, P. Richard
1974   Who Should Rule at Home? Native American Politics and Indian-White Relations. Journal of American History 61(3):651–65.

Miller, Jay
1974   The Delaware as Women: A Symbolic Solution. American Ethnologist 1(4):507–14.

Mintz, Sidney W.
1989   The Sensation of Moving, While Standing Still. American Ethnologist 16(4):786–96.

Mooney, James
1907   Mohegan. *In* Handbook of American Indians North of Mexico. Frederick W. Hodge, ed. Vol. 1, 926–27. 2 vols. Bureau of American Ethnology Bulletin 30. Washington, D.C.
1928   The Aboriginal Population of America North of Mexico. John R. Swanton, ed. Smithsonian Miscellaneous Collections 80 (7). Washington, D.C.

Morrison, Kenneth M.
1984   The Embattled Northeast: The Elusive Ideal of Alliance in Abenaki-
              Euramerican Relations. Berkeley: University of California Press.
Morton, Thomas
1883   The New English Canaan [1637]. C. F. Adams, Jr., ed. Boston:
              Prince Society.
Moses, L. G., and Raymond Wilson (editors)
1993   Indian Lives: Essays on Nineteenth and Twentieth Century Native
              American Leaders. Albuquerque: University of New Mexico Press.
MPCP
1851–53   Minutes of the Provincial Council of Pennsylvania. Samuel Hazard,
              ed. 16 vols. Philadelphia: N.p.
MPCR
1928–31   The Province and Court Records of Maine. C. T. Libby, ed. 2 vols.
              Portland: Maine Historical Society.
Muhlenberg, Heister H. (translator)
1853   Narrative of a Journey Made in the Year 1737, by Conrad Weiser . . .
              Collections of the Historical Society of Pennsylvania 1. Philadelphia.
Mulkearn, Lois (editor)
1954   George Mercer Papers Relating to the Ohio Company of Virginia.
              Pittsburgh: University of Pittsburgh Press.
Munsell, W. W. (editor)
1882   History of Suffolk County, New York, with Illustrations, Portraits,
              and Sketches of Prominent Families and Individuals. New York:
              W. W. Munsell.
Namias, June
1992   (editor) A Narrative of the Life of Mrs. Mary Jemison by James E.
              Seaver. Norman: University of Oklahoma Press.
1993   White Captive: Gender and Ethnicity on the American Frontier.
              Chapel Hill: University of North Carolina Press.
Nammack, Georgiana C.
1969   Fraud, Politics, and the Dispossession of the Indians: The Iroquois
              Land Frontier in the Colonial Period. Norman: University of Okla-
              homa Press.
Newell, Catherine S. C.
1981   Molly Ockett. Bethel, Maine: Bethel Historical Society.
North, James W.
1870   The History of Augusta. Augusta, Maine: N.p.
NPNER
1854–61   Records of the Colony of New Plymouth, in New England. Nathaniel
              B. Shurtleff and David Pulsifer, eds. 12 vols. Boston: William White.
NYCD
1853–87   Documents Relative to the Colonial History of the State of New York.
              Edmund B. O'Callaghan and Berthold Fernow, eds. 15 vols. Albany:
              Weeds and Parsons.

O'Callaghan, Edmund Bailey
1855   History of New Netherland. 2nd ed. 2 vols. New York: D. Appleton.
O'Connell, Barry (editor)
1992   On Our Own Ground: The Complete Writings of William Apess, a
              Pequot. Amherst: University of Massachusetts Press.
OED
1985   The Compact Edition of the Oxford English Dictionary. Oxford:
              Oxford University Press.
Ogden, John C.
1800   Tour through Upper and Lower Canada. Wilmington: Bonsal and
              Niles.
Olmstead, Earl P.
1991   Blackcoats among the Delaware: David Zeisberger on the Ohio
              Frontier. Kent, Ohio: Kent State University Press.
Orr, Charles (editor)
1897   History of the Pequot War. Cleveland: Helman-Taylor.
Ortner, Sherry B.
1984   Theory in Anthropology Since the Sixties. Comparative Studies in
              Society and History 26(1):126–66.
Ortner, Sherry B., and Harriet Whitehead
1981   Introduction: Accounting for Sexual Meanings. *In* Sexual Meanings:
              The Cultural Construction of Gender and Sexuality. Sherry B. Ort-
              ner and Harriet Whitehead, eds. 1–27. New York: Cambridge Uni-
              versity Press.
Osborne, Joseph (editor)
1887   Records of the Town of Easthampton. Sag Harbor, N.Y.: Hunt.
PA
1852–1949 Pennsylvania Archives. Samuel Hazard, et al., eds. 9 sers., 138 vols.
              Philadelphia and Harrisburg.
Paltstits, Victor Hugo (editor)
1910   Minutes of the Executive Council of the Province of New York:
              Administration of Francis Lovelace, 1668–73. 2 vols. Albany: J. B.
              Lyon.
Parker, Arthur C.
1916   The Constitution of the Five Nations. New York State Museum
              Bulletin 184:7–158.
Parkman, Francis
1851   History of the Conspiracy of Pontiac, and the War of the North
              American Tribes against the English Colonies after the Conquest of
              Canada. Boston: Little, Brown.
Parrish, Samuel
1877   Some Chapters in the History of the Friendly Association for Re-
              gaining and Preserving Peace with the Indians by Pacific Measures.
              Philadelphia: Friends Historical Association of Philadelphia.

Peckham, Howard H.
1947   Pontiac and the Indian Uprising. New York: Russell and Russell.
Pelletreau, William (editor)
1874–1910 Records of the Town of Southampton. Sag Harbor, N.Y.: Hunt.
Penrose, Maryly B.
1981   Indian Affairs Papers. Franklin Park, N.J.: Liberty Bell.
Plane, Ann Marie
1992   Childbirth Practices of Native American Women of New England
            and Canada, 1600–1800. *In* Medicine and Healing, Annual Pro-
            ceedings of the Dublin Seminar for New England Folklife. Peter
            Benes, ed. 1–12. Boston: Boston University Press.
1993b   "The Examination of Sarah Ahhaton": The Politics of Adultery in a
            Seventeenth-Century Indian Town of Massachusetts. *In* Algonkians
            of New England: Past and Present, Annual Proceedings of the Dub-
            lin Seminar for New England Folklife. Peter Benes, ed. Boston:
            Boston University Press.
Plane, Ann Marie and Gregory Button
1993   The Massachusetts Indian Enfranchisement Act: Ethnic Contest in
            Historical Context, 1849–69. Ethnohistory 40(4):587–618.
Porter, Harry C.
1979   The Inconstant Savage: England and the North American Indian,
            1500–1660. London: Duckworth.
Post, Christian Frederick
1904   Two Journals of Western Tours by Charles Frederick Post: One, to
            the Neighborhood of Fort Duquesne (July to September 1758); the
            Other, to the Ohio (October 1758 to January 1759). *In* Early Western
            Travels, 1748 to 1846. Reuben Gold Thwaites, ed. 175–291. Cleve-
            land: Arthur H. Clark.
Potter, Elisha R.
1835   Early History of the Narragansetts. Providence: Marshall Brown.
Pound, Arthur
1930   Johnson of the Mohawks. New York: Macmillan.
Prins, Harald E. L.
1984   Foul Play on the Kennebec: The Historical Background of the De-
            mise of the Abenaki Nation. The Kennebec Proprietor 1(3):4–14.
1989a   Natives and Newcomers: Mount Desert Island in the Age of Explora-
            tion. Robert Abbe Museum Bulletin 12:21–36. Bar Harbor, Maine.
1989b   Notes on Robin Hood of Kennebec. Georgetown Tide 15(4):6.
1992   Cornfields at Meductic: Ethnic and Territorial Reconfigurations in
            Colonial Acadia. Man in the Northeast 44:55–72.
1993   To the Land of the Mistigoches: American Indians Traveling to
            Europe in the Age of Exploration. American Indian Culture and
            Research Journal 17(1):175–95.
1994   The Children of Gluskap: Wabanaki Indians on the Eve of European
            Invasion. *In* American Beginnings: Exploration, Culture, and Car-

tography in the Land of Norumbega. E. A. Baker, et al., eds. Lincoln: University of Nebraska Press.

1995   Turmoil on the Wabanaki Frontier, 1524–1678. *In* Maine: The Pine Tree State from Prehistory to the Present. R. Judd, et al., eds. 97–119. Orono: University of Maine Press.

Prins, Harald E. L., and Bruce J. Bourque

1987   Norridgewock: Village Translocation on the New England-Acadian Frontier. Man in the Northeast 33:137–58.

Prins, Harald E. L., and Bunny McBride

1989   A Social History of Maine Indian Basketry. *In* Maine Basketry: Past to Present. 5–14. Deer Isle: Maine Crafts Association.

Purchas, Samuel

1905–7   Hakluytus Posthumus or Purchas, His Pilgrimes [1625]. 4 vols. Glasgow: James MacLehose and Sons.

Radin, Paul (editor)

1983   Crashing Thunder: The Autobiography of an American Indian [1926]. Arnold Krupat, ed. Lincoln: University of Nebraska Press.

Rawson, Grindal, and Samuel Danforth

1809   An Account of an Indian Visitation, A.D. 1698. Massachusetts Historical Society Collection, 1st ser., 10:129–34.

Reichel, William C. (editor)

1870   Memorials of the Moravian Church. Philadelphia: N.p.

RIC

1856–57   Records of the Colony of Rhode Island and Providence Plantations in New England. John Russell Bartlett, ed. 10 vols. Providence: A. Crawford Greene and Brother.

Richards, David

1990   Medicine and Healing Among the Maine Shakers, 1784–1854. *In* Medicine and Healing, Annual Proceedings of the Dublin Seminar for New England Folklife. Peter Benes, ed. 142–53. Boston: Boston University Press.

Richter, Daniel K.

1988   Cultural Brokers and Intercultural Politics: New York–Iroquois Relations, 1664–1701. Journal of American History 75(1):40–67.

1992   Ordeal of the Longhouse: The Peoples of the Iroquois League in the Era of European Colonization. Chapel Hill: University of North Carolina Press.

Richter, Daniel K., and James H. Merrell (editors)

1987   Beyond the Covenant Chain: The Iroquois and Their Neighbors in Indian North America, 1600–1800. Syracuse: Syracuse University Press.

Ritchie, James, and Jane Ritchie

1981   Child Rearing and Child Abuse: The Polynesian Context. *In* Child Abuse and Neglect: Cross-Cultural Perspectives. Jill E. Korbin, ed. 186–204. Los Angeles: University of California Press.

Rivard, Paul
1990   Maine Sawmills, a History. Augusta: Maine State Museum.
Rollins, Hyder E. (editor)
1923   Cavalier and Puritan: Ballads and Broadsides Illustrating the Period of the Great Rebellion, 1640–60. New York: N.p.
Ronda, James P.
1981   Generations of Faith: The Christian Indians of Martha's Vineyard. William and Mary Quarterly, 3rd ser., 38(3):369–94.
Ronda, Jeanne, and James P. Ronda
1979   "As They Were Faithful": Chief Hendrick Apamaut and the Struggle for Stockbridge Survival, 1757–1830. American Indian Culture and Research Journal 3(3):43–55.
Rowlandson, Mary
1913   Narrative of Captivity of Mrs. Mary Rowlandson [1676]. *In* Narratives of the Indian Wars, 1675–1699. Charles H. Lincoln, ed. 107–67. New York: Charles Scribner's Sons.
Ruttenber, Edward M.
1906   Indian Geographical Names of the Valley of the Hudson's River. New York State Historical Association 6.
Sahlins, Marshall D.
1962   Poor Man, Rich Man, Big-Man, Chief: Political Types in Melanesia and Polynesia. Comparative Studies in Society and History 5:285–303.
1981   Historical Metaphors and Mythical Realities: Structure in the Early History of the Sandwich Islands Kingdom. Association for Social Anthropology in Oceania 1. Ann Arbor: University of Michigan Press.
Sainsbury, John
1971   Miantonomo's Death and New England Politics, 1630–1645. Rhode Island History 30(4):111–23.
Sainsbury, William N. (editor)
1860–1912   Calendar of State Papers, Colonial America and the West Indies, 1574–1702. 20 vols. London: Public Record Office.
Salisbury, Neal
1974   Red Puritans: The "Praying Indians" of Massachusetts Bay and John Eliot. William and Mary Quarterly, 3rd ser., 31(1):27–54.
1981   Squanto: Last of the Patuxets. *In* Struggle and Survival in Colonial America. David G. Sweet and Gary B. Nash, eds. 228–46. Berkeley: University of California Press.
1982   Manitou and Providence: Indians, Europeans, and the Making of New England, 1500–1643. New York: Oxford University Press.
1987   Social Relationships on a Moving Frontier: Natives and Settlers in Southern New England, 1638–75. Man in the Northeast 33:89–99.

Saltonstall, Nathaniel
1913   The Present State of New England with Respect to the Indian War. *In* Narratives of the Indian Wars, 1675–99. Charles H. Lincoln, ed. 19–99. New York: Charles Scribner's Sons.
Salwen, Bert
1962   Field Notes: IBM Site, Port Washington, L.I., N.Y. New York State Archaeological Association Bulletin 25:7–16.
1968   Muskeeta Cove 2: A Stratified Woodland Site on Long Island. American Antiquity 33(3):322–40.
1978   Indians of Southern New England and Long Island: Early Period. *In* Handbook of North American Indians. Vol. 15, The Northeast. Bruce T. Trigger, ed. 160–76. Washington, D.C.: Smithsonian Institution.
Sargent, Carolyn F.
1988   Born to Die: Witchcraft and Infanticide in Bariba Culture. Ethnology 27(1):79–95.
Scheper-Hughes, Nancy
1985   Culture, Scarcity, and Maternal Thinking: Maternal Detachment and Infant Survival in a Brazilian Shantytown. Ethos 13(4):291–317.
1992   Death Without Weeping: The Violence of Everyday Life in Brazil. Berkeley: University of California Press.
Schoolcraft, Henry Rowe
1847   Notes on the Iroquois: Or, Contributions to the Statistics, Aboriginal History, Antiquities, and General Ethnology of Western New York. Albany: Erastus H. Pease.
Sehr, Timothy J.
1977   Ninigret's Tactics of Accommodation: Indian Diplomacy in New England, 1637–75. Rhode Island History 36(2):42–53.
Sewall, John
1847   History of Bath [1833]. Collections of the Maine Historical Society, 189–228.
Sewall, Rufus K.
1859   Ancient Dominions of Maine. Bath, Maine: N.p.
Sewell, Samuel
1973   The Diary of Samuel Sewell, 1674–1729. M. Halsey Thomas, ed. 2 vols. New York: Farrar, Strauss, and Giroux.
Shapiro, Judith
1983   Anthropology and the Study of Gender. *In* A Feminist Perspective in the Academy: The Difference It Makes. Elizabeth Langland and Walter Gove, eds. 110–29. Chicago: University of Chicago Press.
Shostak, Marjorie
1981   Nisa: The Life and Words of a !Kung Woman. New York: Vintage Books.

Simmons, William S.

1983   Red Yankees: Narragansett Conversion in the Great Awakening. American Ethnologist 10(2):253–71.

1986   Spirit of the New England Tribes: Indian History and Folklore, 1620–1984. Hanover, N.H.: University Press of New England.

1989   The Narragansett. New York: Chelsea House.

Simmons, William S., and George F. Aubin

1975   Narragansett Kinship. Man in the Northeast 9:21–31.

Sipe, C. Hale

1927   The Indian Chiefs of Pennsylvania. Butler, Penn.: Ziegler Printing.

Sleight, H. D. (editor)

1926   East Hampton Trustees Journal. 7 vols. East Hampton, N.Y.: N.p.

Smith, Carlyle S.

1950   The Archaeology of Coastal New York. Anthropological Papers of the American Museum of Natural History 43:95–200.

Smith, W. E.

1960   Hendrick. Dictionary of American Biography 4:532–33. New York: Charles Scribner's Sons.

Snyderman, George S.

1954   The Functions of Wampum. Proceedings of the American Philosophical Society 98(6):469–94.

Solecki, Ralph S.

1995   The Archaeology of Fort Massapeag. Under editorial consideration. Boston: Council for New England Historical Archaeology.

Speck, Frank G.

1928   Native Tribes and Dialects of Connecticut: A Mohegan-Pequot Diary. *In* 43rd Annual Report of the Bureau of American Ethnology for the Years 1925–26. 199–297. Washington, D.C.

1940   Penobscot Man: The Life History of a Forest Tribe in Maine. Philadelphia: University of Pennsylvania Press.

Spiess, Arthur E., and Bruce D. Spiess

1987   New England Pandemic of 1616–22: Cause and Archaeological Implications. Man in the Northeast 34:71–83.

Spittal, W. G. (editor)

1990   Iroquois Women: An Anthology. Oshwekan, Ontario: Iroqrafts.

Spiro, Melford

1993   Is the Western Conception of Self "Peculiar" within the Context of World Cultures? Ethos 21(2):107–53.

Springer, James Warren

1986   American Indians and the Law of Real Property in Colonial New England. American Journal of Legal History 30(1):25–58.

Starna, William A.

1990   Pequots in the Early Seventeenth Century. *In* The Pequots in Southern New England: The Fall and Rise of an American Indian Nation.

Laurence M. Hauptman and James D. Wherry, eds. 33–47. Norman: University of Oklahoma Press.

Stiles, Ezra
1916   Extracts from Itineraries and Other Miscellanies of Ezra Stiles, D.D., LL.D., 1755–94, with a Selection from His Correspondence. Franklin B. Dexter, ed. New Haven: Yale University Press.

Stiles, Henry Reed
1867   A History of the City of Brooklyn. 3 vols. Brooklyn: N.p.

Stone, William L.
1838   Life of Joseph Brant–Thayendanegea. 2 vols. New York: A. V. Blake, G. Dearborn.
1842   Uncas and Miantonomoh: A Historical Discourse. New York: Dayton and Newman.
1865   The Life and Times of Sir William Johnson, Bart. 2 vols. Albany: J. Munsell.
1901   King Hendrick. In Constitution and By-Laws of the New York State Historical Association, with Proceedings of the Second Annual Meeting. 28–39.

Street, Charles R.
1882   Huntington. In History of Suffolk County, New York, with Illustrations, Portraits, and Sketches of Prominent Families and Individuals. W. W. Munsell, ed. 1–90. New York: W. W. Munsell.
1887–99   (editor) Huntington Town Records, including Babylon, Long Island, N.Y. 1653 . . . 1873. 3 vols. Huntington, N.Y.: N.p.

Strong, John A.
1983   The Evolution of Shinnecock Culture. In The Shinnecock Indians: A Culture History. Gaynell Stone, ed. 7–51. Stony Brook, N.Y.: Suffolk County Archaeological Association.
1992   The Thirteen Tribes of Long Island: The History of a Myth. Hudson Valley Regional Review 9(2):39–73.

Strong, Lara M., and Selcuk Karabig
1991   Quashawam: Sunksquaw of the Montauk. Long Island Historical Journal 3(2):189–204.

Sumner, Samuel
1860   History of Missisco Valley. Irasburgh, Vt.: A. A. Earle for the Orleans County Historical Society.

Szasz, Margaret Connell
1994a   (editor) Between Indian and White Worlds: The Culture Broker. Norman: University of Oklahoma Press.
1994b   Samson Occom: Mohegan as Spiritual Intermediary. In Between Indian and White Worlds: The Culture Broker. Margaret Connell Szasz, ed. Norman: University of Oklahoma Press.

Talbot, Francis X.
1935   Saint among Savages: The Life of Isaac Jogues. New York: Harper and Brothers.

Tanner, Helen Hornbeck
1979   Coocoochee: Mohawk Medicine Woman. American Culture and Research Journal 3(3):23–41.

Tapley, Mark
1889   Moll Lockett, the Last Squaw of the Androscoggin Tribe. Daily Lewiston Journal, 6 Apr. Lewiston, Maine.

Tatamy, Moses
1755   Deposition before Justice Anderson, New Jersey. Pennsylvania Gazette, No. 1406, 4 Dec., 3. Philadelphia.

Thayer, Henry O. (editor)
1892   The Sagadahock Colony, comprising the Relation of a Voyage into New England. Portland, Maine: Gorges Society.

Thayer, Theodore
1943   Israel Pemberton, King of the Quakers. Philadelphia: Historical Society of Pennsylvania.

Thomas, Earle
1989   Molly Brant. Historic Kingston 7:141–49.

Thomas, Peter A.
1985   Cultural Change on the Southern New England Frontier, 1630–65. *In* Cultures in Contact: The Impact of European Contacts on Native American Cultural Institutions, A.D. 1000–1800. William W. Fitzhugh, ed. 131–61. Washington, D.C.: Smithsonian Institution Press.

Thompson, Benjamin F.
1918   History of Long Island. 3rd ed. 3 vols. Charles J. Werner, ed. New York: N.p.

Thurman, Melburn Delano
1974   Delaware Social Organization. *In* A Delaware Indian Symposium. Herbert C. Kraft, ed. 111–34. Anthropological Series 4. Harrisburg: Pennsylvania Historical and Museum Commission.

Tooker, Elisabeth
1978   The League of the Iroquois: Its History, Politics, and Ritual. *In* Handbook of North American Indians, Vol. 15, The Northeast. Bruce T. Trigger, ed. 418–41. Washington, D.C.: Smithsonian Institution.
1993   Review of Exemplar of Liberty: Native America and the Evolution of Democracy by Donald G. Grinde, Jr., and Bruce E. Johansen. Northeast Anthropology 46:103–7.

Tooker, William Wallace
1896   John Eliot's First Indian Teacher and Interpreter: Cockenoe-De-Long Island and the Story of His Career from the Early Records. New York: Francis P. Harper.
1911   Indian Place-Names on Long Island and Islands Adjacent with Their Probable Significations. New York: G. P. Putnam's Sons for the John Jermain Memorial Library.

Travers, Milton A.
1957   The Wampanoag Indian Federation of the Algonquin Nation: Indian Neighbors of the Pilgrims. New Bedford, Mass.: Reynolds-DeWalt.

Trelease, Allen W.
1960   Indian Affairs in Colonial New York: The Seventeen Century. Ithaca: Cornell University Press.

True, Nathaniel T.
1859–61   History of Bethel. Bethel Courier, Maine: N.p.
1863   The Last of the Pequakets: Molly-Ockett. Oxford Democrat, 2 Jan. Reprint June 1978, Bethel Historical Society Newsletter 2(2).
1867   The Parallel between Barbarism and Civilization. Oxford Democrat, 12 July.
1874   Historical Address. Report of the Centennial Celebration at Bethel, 26 Aug. 10–49. Portland, Maine: B. Thurston.

Trumbull, John Hammond (editor)
1885   The Trumbull Papers. Collections of the Massachusetts Historical Society, vol. 9, 5th ser. Boston.

Tufts, Henry
1807   Narrative of the Life, Adventures, Travels, and Sufferings of Henry Tufts, Now Residing at Lemington, in the District of Maine, in Substance, as Compiled from his Own Mouth. Dover, N.H.: Samuel Bragg, Jr. Reprint 1930, The Autobiography of a Criminal: Henry Tufts. Edmund Pearson, ed. New York: Duffield.

Ulrich, Laurel Thatcher
1982   Good Wives: Image and Reality in the Lives of Women in Northern New England, 1650–1750. New York: Oxford University Press.

Underhill, John
1897   Newes from America; or, A new and experimentall discoverie of New England; containing, a true relation of their war-like proceedings these two years past, with a figure of the Indian fort or palizado. *In* History of the Pequot War. Charles Orr, ed. 47–86. Cleveland: Helman-Taylor.

Updike, John
1989   Self-Consciousness: Memoirs. New York: Ballantine Books.

Vaughan, Alden T., and Edward W. Clark (editors)
1981   Puritans among the Indians: Accounts of Captivity and Redemption, 1676–1724. Cambridge: Belknap Press of Harvard University Press.

Vestal, Stanley
1932   Sitting Bull, Champion of the Sioux: A Biography. Norman: University of Oklahoma Press.

Vincent, Philip
1897   A True Relation of the Late Battell Fought in New-England between the English and the Pequet Salvages. *In* History of the Pequot War. Charles Orr, ed. 102–6. Cleveland: Helman-Taylor.

Von Lonkhuyzen, Harold

1990   A Reappraisal of the Praying Indians: Acculturation, Conversion, and Identity at Natick, Massachusetts, 1646–1730. New England Quarterly 62(4):396–428.

Wagatsuma, Hiroshi

1981   Child Abandonment and Infanticide: A Japanese Case. *In* Child Abuse and Neglect: Cross-Cultural Perspectives. Jill E. Korbin, ed. 120–38. Los Angeles: University of California Press.

Wainwright, Nicholas B. (editor)

1947   George Croghan's Journal, April 3, 1759 to April [30], 1763. Pennsylvania Magazine of History and Biography 71(4):305–444.

Wallace, Anthony F. C.

1956   New Religions Among the Delaware Indians, 1600–1900. Southwestern Journal of Anthropology 12(1):1–21.

1958   Dreams and the Wishes of the Soul. American Anthropologist 60(2):234–48.

1969   The Death and Rebirth of the Seneca. New York: Knopf.

1990   King of the Delawares: Teedyuscung, 1700–1763 [1949]. Syracuse: Syracuse University Press.

Wallace, Paul A. W.

1945   Conrad Weiser, 1696–1760: Friend of Colonist and Mohawk. Philadelphia: University of Pennsylvania Press.

1981   Indians in Pennsylvania. 2nd ed. William A. Hunter, ed. Harrisburg: Pennsylvania Historical and Museum Commission.

Ward, Edward

1699   A Trip to New England with a Character of the Country and People, both English and Indians. London: N.p.

Ward, Harry

1961   The United Colonies of New England, 1643–90. New York: Vantage Press.

Watson, Lawrence C., and Maria-Barbara Watson-Franke

1985   Interpreting Life Histories: An Anthropological Inquiry. New Brunswick, N.J.: Rutgers University Press.

Webster, John C.

1934   Acadia at the End of the 17th Century: Letters, Journals, and Memoirs of Joseph Robineau de Villebon, Commandant in Acadia, 1690–1700, and Other Contemporary Documents. Monograph Series 1. St. John: New Brunswick Museum.

Weinstein, Laurie

1986   "We're Still Living on our Traditional Homeland": The Wampanoag Legacy in New England. *In* Strategies for Survival: American Indians in the Eastern United States. Frank W. Porter III, ed. 85–112. Contributions in Ethnic Studies 15. Westport, Conn.: Greenwood Press.

1991   Land, Politics, and Power: The Mohegan Indians in the Seventeenth and Eighteenth Centuries. Man in the Northeast 42:9–16.

1994   Samson Occom: A Charismatic Eighteenth-Century Mohegan Leader. *In* Enduring Traditions: The Native Peoples of New England. Laurie Weinstein, ed. 91–102. Westport, Conn.: Bergin and Garvey.

Wendall, Jacob

1866   An Estimate of the Inhabitants, English and Indians, in the North American Colonies, also Their Extent in Miles, 1726. New England Historical and Genealogical Register 20:7–9.

Weslager, Clinton Alfred

1971   Name-Giving among the Delaware Indians. Names 19(4):268–83.

1974   Delaware Indian Name Giving and Modern Practice. *In* A Delaware Indian Symposium. Herbert C. Kraft, ed. 135–45. Anthropological Series 4. Harrisburg: Pennsylvania Historical and Museum Commission.

Wheeler, George A. and H. W. Wheeler

1878   History of Brunswick, Topsham, and Harpswell, Maine, Including the Ancient Territory Known as Pejepscot. Boston: Alfred Mudge and Son.

White, Richard

1991   The Middle Ground: Indians, Empires, and Republics in the Great Lakes Region, 1650–1815. New York: Cambridge University Press.

Wilkins, Martha Fifield

1977   Sunday River Sketches: A New England Chronicle. Randy Bennett, ed. Rumford, Maine: Androscoggin.

Willey, Benjamin

1856   Incidents of White Mountain History. Boston: Nathaniel Noyes.

1869   History of the White Mountains. Boston: N.p.

Williams, Lorraine E., and Karen A. Flinn

1990   Trade Wampum: New Jersey to the Plains. Trenton: New Jersey State Museum.

Williams, Roger

1866   A Key into the Language of America [1643]. James H. Trumbull, ed. Publications of the Narragansett Club, 1st ser., 1:61–282. Providence.

1973   A Key into the Language of America [1643]. John J. Teunissen and Evelyn J. Hinz, eds. Detroit: Wayne State University Press.

1988   The Correspondence of Roger Williams. 2 vols. Glenn W. LaFantasie, ed. Hanover, N.H.: University Press of New England.

Williamson, William D.

1832   History of Maine: From its First Discovery, A.D. 1602, to the Separation, A.D. 1820, Inclusive. Hallowell, Maine: Glazier, Masters.

Willis, W. (editor)
1849   Journal of the Rev. Thomas Smith and the Rev. Samuel Deane, Pastors of the First Church in Portland. Portland, Maine: N.p.

Winslow, Edward
1841   Good News from New England [1624]. *In* Chronicles of the Pilgrim Fathers of the Colony of Plymouth. Alexander Young, ed. 354–67. Boston: Little, Brown.

Winthrop, John, Sr.
1853   The History of New England from 1630 to 1649. From His Original Manuscripts. James Savage, ed. 2 vols. Boston: Little, Brown.
1908   Winthrop's Journal, "History of New England" [1630–49]. James K. Hosmer, ed. 2 vols. New York: Charles Scribner's Sons.

Winthrop, John, Jr.
1929–47   Winthrop Papers . . . , 1498–1649. Allyn B. Forbes, ed. 5 vols. Boston: Massachusetts Historical Society.

Wojciechowski, Franz L.
1985   The Paugussett Tribes: An Ethnohistorical Study of the Tribal Inter-relationships of the Indians in the Lower Housatonic River Area. Nijmegen, the Netherlands: Catholic University of Nijmegen.

Wolcott, Arthur S. (editor)
1904   Daniel Claus's Narrative of His Relations with Sir William Johnson and Experiences in the Lake George Fight. New York: Society of Colonial Wars in the State of New York.

Wolf, Eric R.
1956   Aspects of Group Relations in a Complex Society: Mexico. American Anthropologist 58(4):1065–78.
1982   Europe and the People Without History. Berkeley: University of California Press.

Wood, William
1977   New England's Prospect [1634]. Alden T. Vaughan, ed. Amherst: University of Massachusetts Press.

Woodrow, Arthur D.
1928   Story of Metallak: Last of the Cooashaukes. Rumford, Maine: Rumford Publishing.

Young, Alexander (editor)
1846   Chronicles of the First Planters of the Colony of Massachusetts Bay, from 1623 to 1636. Boston: Little, Brown.

CONTRIBUTORS

LOIS M. FEISTER is scientist-archeology for the New York State Office of Parks, Recreation, and Historic Preservation, Bureau of Historic Sites. She earned an M.A. in anthropology and a B.A. with a concentration in history at the State University of New York, Albany. She has published articles in *Ethnohistory, Man in the Northeast, Journal of Field Archaeology, Historical Archaeology*, and other journals, and is coauthor of *The Hudson-Mohawk Gateway: An Illustrated History*. Feister heads a team that has done extensive archeological research at Johnson Hall State Historic Site.

ROBERT S. GRUMET is an archeologist in the Northeast Field Office, National Park Service, Philadelphia. He received a B.A. at the City College of New York in 1972 and a Ph.D. in anthropology from Rutgers University in 1979. He has taught at several colleges and universities, worked on a number of museum installations, been a fellow at the Newberry Library, and conducted archaeological and archival research in the eastern United States and on the Northwest Coast. His publications include *Native American Place Names in New York City* (New York: Museum of the City of New York, 1981), *The Lenapes* (New York: Chelsea House, 1989), and *Historic Contact: Indians and Colonists in Today's Northeastern United States in the Sixteenth through Eighteenth Centuries* (Norman: University of Oklahoma Press, 1995).

WILLIAM A. HUNTER (1908–85) was born in Kinsman, Ohio, lived in western Pennsylvania, and graduated from Allegheny College and the University of California. He joined the Pennsylvania Historical and Museum Commission in Harrisburg in 1946 and served as the Commission's chief of the Division of History from 1961 to 1976. His main area of study was the colonial period, and his writings focused primarily upon frontier and Indian history. Besides writing articles and reviews for periodicals, he contributed to the *Dictionary of Canadian Biography* and the *Handbook of North American Indians*, wrote *Forts on the Pennsylvania Frontier, 1753–*

389

58, and revised Paul A. W. Wallace's *Indians in Pennsylvania.* [Biographical sketch written by Harold L. Myers, Publications Department, Pennsylvania Historical and Museum Commission]

ERIC S. JOHNSON is adjunct assistant professor of anthropology at the University of Massachusetts, Amherst, where he earned his Ph.D. in anthropology in 1993. He has taught archaeology and anthropology at Williams College, served as a consultant to the Massachusetts Historical Commission, and been a staff archaeologist at the University of Massachusetts Archaeological Services.

ELIZABETH A. LITTLE is curator of prehistoric artifacts at the Nantucket Historical Association. A noted archaeologist and ethnohistorian, she is also editor of *Nantucket Algonquian Studies* and the *Bulletin of the Massachusetts Archaeological Society.* She codirected a survey of archaeological sites and collections at Nantucket Island for the Nantucket Historical Association and the Massachusetts Historical Commission, and was a recipient of the Twenty-Fifth Anniversary Preservation Award of the Massachusetts Historical Commission. She has authored articles on the archaeology and history of Nantucket Indians, colonial Indian whaling, and radiocarbon dating in the Northeast. She has a Ph.D. in physics from the Massachusetts Institute of Technology and an M.A. in anthropology from the University of Massachusetts, Amherst.

DANIEL MANDELL is currently visiting instructor of history at the University of Georgia. He has also taught at DePauw University. A revised version of his dissertation, "Behind the Frontier: Indian Communities in Eighteenth-Century Massachusetts," written for the Ph.D. at the University of Virginia in 1992, is scheduled for publication by the University of Nebraska Press. Some of that work was published in 1991 as " 'To Live More Like My Christian Neighbors': Natick Indians in the Eighteenth Century" in the *William and Mary Quarterly.* He is currently researching Indian communities in nineteenth-century southern New England and in 1992 held a research fellowship from Old Sturbridge Village to begin that project.

BUNNY MCBRIDE, a freelance writer, has an M.A. in anthropology from Columbia University (1980). Since 1981, she has been a visiting lecturer in anthropology at Principia College. Focusing on cultural survival and wildlife conservation issues, she has written for a wide variety of magazines and newspapers, and contributes regularly to the *Christian Science Monitor.* Her book credits include *A Penobscot in Paris: The Life of Molly Spotted Elk* (scheduled for publication by the University of Oklahoma Press in 1995), *Our Lives in Our Hands: Micmac Indian Basketmakers* (Halifax, Nova Scotia, and Gardiner, Maine: Tilbury House and Nimbus, 1990), and *The National Audubon Society Field Guide to African Wildlife* (with Peter Alden and Richard Estes, 1995). From 1981 to 1991, she did research and community development work for the Aroostook Band of Micmac Indians in northern Maine.

KEVIN A. MCBRIDE is assistant professor of anthropology at the University of Connecticut at Storrs and director of the Mashantucket Pequot Ethnohistory Project. He received a B.A. from Assumption College in 1974 and a Ph.D. in anthropology from the University of Connecticut in 1984. He is the author of numerous publications on Southern New England archaeology and ethnohistory.

MICHAEL N. MCCONNELL is associate professor of history at the University of Alabama at Birmingham. He is the author of *A Country Between: The Upper Ohio Valley and Its People, 1724–74* (Lincoln: University of Nebraska Press, 1992) and of essays on the early history of the Ohio Country. He is currently at work on a history of the British army's role in the late colonial American frontier.

JAMES H. MERRELL is Lucy Maynard Salmon Professor of History at Vassar College. Educated at Lawrence University, Oxford University, and The Johns Hopkins University, he has been a fellow at the Newberry Library and at the Institute of Early American History and Culture. He is coeditor (with Daniel K. Richter) of *Beyond the Covenant Chain: The Iroquois and Their Neighbors in Indian North America, 1600–1800* (Syracuse: Syracuse University Press, 1987), and author of *The Indians' New World: Catawbas and Their Neighbors from European Contact through the Era of Removal* (Chapel Hill: University of North Carolina Press, 1989).

ANN MARIE PLANE is assistant professor of history at the University of California at Santa Barbara. She received her M.A. in American and New England Studies from Boston University and her Ph.D. in the history of American civilization from Brandeis University. She has written a number of articles on gender, race, and ethnicity in early New England and is currently at work on a study of marriage, household, and racial boundaries in southeastern New England from 1600 to 1730.

HARALD E. L. PRINS is associate professor of anthropology at Kansas State University. Hailing from the Netherlands, he received a *Doctoral* degree at the University of Nijmegen in 1976 and a Ph.D. in anthropology from the New School for Social Research in 1988. He has previously taught at the University of Nijmegen, Colby College, and Bowdoin College. He specializes in ethnohistory, native's rights issues, and visual anthropology. Having conducted fieldwork in South America, his research since 1981 has focused mainly on the Wabanaki culture area. For a decade, he served the Aroostook Band of Micmacs in the successful quest for federal recognition and funding for a 5,000-acre land-base. In addition to consulting with several other tribes, including the Apache, he has authored over fifty articles and book chapters; coedited a book, *American Beginnings;* and coproduced the documentary *Our Lives in Our Hands.* With a book on the Mi'kmaq just out, he is working with the Kickapoo and the Plains Apache on documentary film projects.

BONNIE PULIS is interpretive programs assistant at Johnson Hall State Historic Site, Saratoga–Capital Region, New York State Office of Parks, Recreation, and Historic Preservation. She received a B.A. in visual and performing arts with a major in museum theory and practice at Russell Sage College. She works with site manager Wanda Burch on outreach programs, public tours, special events, and other interpretive programs at Johnson Hall.

PAUL A. ROBINSON is principal/state archaeologist at the Rhode Island Historical Preservation Commission and an honorary member of the Narragansett Indian Archaeological-Anthropological Committee. He received a B.A. at Hobart College in 1971 and a Ph.D. in anthropology from the State University of New York at Binghamton in 1990. Maintaining broad research interests in the full span of human occupation in northeastern North America, his particular area of interest is Native American history during the last five centuries in southern New England.

DEAN R. SNOW is a professor of anthropology at Pennsylvania State University. He received his Ph.D. from the University of Oregon in 1966 and taught for three years at the University of Maine before moving to the State University of New York, Albany, between 1969 and 1995. His research and writing have focused on Mohawk Iroquois archaeology and ethnohistory since 1981. Recent publications include *Archaeology of North American Indians* (New York: Viking, 1976), *Atlas of Ancient America*, with Michael Coe and Elizabeth Benson (New York: Facts on File, 1986), and *The Iroquois* (London: Blackwell Publishers, 1994).

JOHN A. STRONG holds a Ph.D. from Syracuse University. He is professor of history and department chair at Pennsylvania State University. He has written extensively on the Indians of Long Island. Author of "The Imposition of Colonial Jurisdiction Over the Montauk Indians of Long Island," published in 1994 in *Ethnohistory*, his forthcoming works include "Samson Occom" in Fred Hoxie, ed., *Encyclopedia of American Indian Biography* (Boston: Houghton Mifflin, 1995), and *The Indians of Long Island From Earliest Times to 1880* (Stony Brook: Long Island Studies Institute, 1995).

ANTHONY F. C. WALLACE is an anthropologist and university professor emeritus at the University of Pennsylvania (from which he received a Ph.D. in anthropology in 1950). He served as chairman of the anthropology department from 1961 to 1971. His ethnohistorical publications on Native American subjects include *King of the Delawares: Teedyuscung, 1700–1763* (Philadelphia: University of Pennsylvania Press, 1949; reprinted by Syracuse University Press, 1990); *The Death and Rebirth of the Seneca* (New York: Knopf, 1970); and *The Long, Bitter Trail: Andrew Jackson and the Indians* (New York: Hill and Wang, 1993).